THE MEMOIRS OF
GENERAL LORD ISMAY

The

MEMOIRS

of

General Lord

ISMAY

19 60

NEW YORK : THE VIKING PRESS

PUBLISHED IN 1960 BY THE VIKING PRESS, INC.
625 MADISON AVENUE, NEW YORK 22, N.Y.

LIBRARY OF CONGRESS CATALOG CARD NUMBER: 60–14086

PRINTED IN THE U.S.A. BY H. WOLFF BOOK MANUFACTURING CO., INC.

FOR DARRY

Giving thanks always for all things

—Epistle of Saint Paul to the Ephesians 5:20

CONTENTS

PART THREE: *Rolling Stone*

FRONTISPIECE

General the Lord Ismay, K. G., in Garter Robes, from
a portrait by Allan Gwynne-Jones, D.S.O., A.R.A.

MAPS AND DIAGRAMS

KNIGHTSBRIDGE 7072.

28, HYDE PARK GATE,
LONDON, S.W.7.

I am very glad that Lord Ismay's Memoirs
should now be published.   For many years he has held
positions of high importance at the centre of our
affairs, and he has an intimate and commanding
knowledge of the great events of the war.

In the first volume of my Memoirs of the
Second World War I wrote, "I had known Ismay for many
years, but now for the first time we became hand in
glove and much more," and I am glad again to record
my tribute to the signal services which Lord Ismay
has rendered to our country, and to the free world,
in peace and war.

Winston S. Churchill

April, 1960

PREFACE

When Mr. Churchill became Prime Minister on 10 May 1940, he assumed, with the King's approval, the additional appointment of Minister of Defence, and it was my incredibly good fortune to serve as his Chief of Staff in that capacity until the fall of his Administration on 26 August 1945. I had always intended to write my account of those crucial years, a background to a pen portrait of Churchill at war, but it was not until 1957 that my retirement from the public service gave me the necessary leisure for the stewardship of my own affairs. By the end of the following year I had made considerable progress, but I was advised on all sides that my story would be incomplete unless I included an account not only of the steps which led an officer of Indian Cavalry to the fountain-head of national and Imperial defence in London, but also of my experiences as Chief of Staff to the last Viceroy of India, the Earl Mountbatten of Burma, and as Secretary-General of the North Atlantic Treaty Organisation. As a result these memoirs are a good deal more egotistical, cover a much larger canvas, and have taken considerably longer to finish than I had hoped.

A great many of my personal friends have helped me with advice and encouragement, and I ask them to absolve me from the charge of ingratitude for not mentioning them by name.

THE MEMOIRS OF
GENERAL LORD ISMAY

PART ONE

APPRENTICESHIP

CHAPTER I

Subaltern in India

1902–1914

O N A July afternoon in 1902, a diminutive Carthusian of fifteen summers was practising at the cricket nets, when somebody shouted out that the results of the examination for senior scholarships had been posted up in the cloisters. He went there as fast as decency permitted — it would have been bad form to appear excited — only to find that the name 'H. L. Ismay' did not figure in the list. It was a bitter disappointment, because I had been consistently above at least four of the successful scholars for the whole of the past year; but I swallowed the lump in my throat and returned to the cricket nets feigning nonchalance. I did not realise at the time that my failure was a blessing in disguise.

When I was alone in my cubicle that night, I may or may not have shed a few tears, but I certainly did a lot of thinking. Ever since the South African War, I had had a sneaking desire to be a cavalry soldier; but my parents wanted me to go to Cambridge and try for the Civil Service. Now that I had proved such a duffer at examinations, my chances of passing were remote. If I were to fail, what could I do for a living? I would be too old to qualify for any other profession, and in those days commerce was not considered suitable employment for a gentleman.

3

The more I thought about it, the more sure I was that I wanted to have a try for the Army as soon as I was old enough. But there was plenty of time before a final decision need be made, and it was over a year before I unburdened myself to my parents. By an unfortunate coincidence, a letter from my housemaster reached them at almost the same time. 'I have never got over your boy missing a scholarship,' he wrote. 'It is one of those exasperating miscarriages of examinations which happen often enough, but rarely in a form which can be estimated so exactly.' This high assessment of my abilities might have ruined my plans, but my parents, bless them, let me have my way. My father was particularly upset at the idea of my joining the Indian Cavalry, and never tired of telling the story about the cavalry officer who was so stupid that even his brother officers noticed it. I wish that he could have lived long enough to know that it did not turn out to be so much of a dead end as he had feared.

In the summer of 1904, I passed the necessary examination without too much difficulty, and in the autumn I entered the Royal Military College, Sandhurst. The year as a gentleman cadet passed pleasantly enough. It toughened me physically, and I learned to drill like a guardsman, shoot with rifle and revolver, dig trenches, ride, signal, draw maps, do gymnastics and wear my clothes correctly. I also learned a smattering of military tactics, history and engineering. But so far as I remember, man-management and the art of command found no place in the syllabus. Sandhurst never meant nearly so much to me as Charterhouse had done. The course lasted only one year, and there were few opportunities for making new friends outside one's own term in one's own company. Many of my contemporaries were destined to be killed or crippled in the First World War and, partly for that reason, an unusually high proportion of them went to the top of the military ladder. Notable among these were Field Marshal Lord Gort, Marshal of the Royal Air Force Lord Newall, Generals Platt, Gifford, Riddell-Webster, Franklin and Heath, and Air Chief Marshal Ludlow-Hewitt.

In those days there was keen competition for the Indian Army, and it was necessary to pass out in the first thirty or so to be sure of a vacancy. I had evidently improved at examinations, as I took fourth place and was gazetted a Second Lieutenant in His Majesty's Land Forces on 5 August 1905. I was under eighteen-and-a-half years old and the smallest officer in the Army. Fortunately for myself — and my tailor — I grew six inches in the next two years.

Every officer destined for the Indian Army was required to serve a year's apprenticeship with a British unit in India, and I joined the First Battalion of the Gloucestershire Regiment as an attached officer at Ambala in the Punjab. They were very considerate and took great pains to instruct me in the way that I should go. But I was never able to forget that I was a bird of passage, and that I was in the regiment, but not of it. Their scarlet uniform had white facings: mine had blue. They wore two badges in their helmets, one fore and one aft, in commemoration of a notable feat of arms in Egypt. My helmet had a single and not very attractive emblem. On one occasion towards the end of my year's attachment, I was given the honour of being allowed to carry the Regimental Colour on a particularly long march. I received it with due deference; but it was an awkward burden, and at the end of twelve miles my thoughts were far from reverent.

When my year with the Gloucesters came to an end, there was no immediate vacancy in the Indian Cavalry Regiment which had accepted me, and I continued to be a 'displaced person' for nine more months. Six of them were spent with the 33rd Punjabis, a fine battalion which was practically annihilated at Loos in the First World War, and the remainder months with the Carabineers (6th Dragoon Guards) learning cavalry work.

It had been depressing to belong to nobody, and I was happy and hopeful when the day came for me to join what was to be my own regiment at Risalpur on the North-West Frontier. I had to travel half across India to get there, and arrived at the officers' mess, unkempt and travel-stained, just as dinner was finishing. The scene is indelibly stamped on my memory. Eight or nine of my future brother officers in our magnificent mess kit of dark blue, scarlet and gold, were seated at the table. Behind them stood the waiters in spotless white muslin, with belts of the regimental colours and the regimental crest on their turbans. The table was decorated with two or three bowls of red roses and a few pieces of superbly cleaned silver. Over the mantelpiece hung a picture of our Royal Colonel, the late Prince Albert Victor,[1] and the heads of tigers, leopards, markhor and ibex looked down from the walls. The assembled company were all strangers to me, but

[1] Elder brother of King George V. He died in 1892.

they made me feel at home from the moment I crossed the threshold. As I went happily to sleep that night, I thanked God for parents who had allowed me to choose my own way of life.

I at once set to work to learn all about my new-found heritage. The full title of the regiment was the 21st Prince Albert Victor's Own Cavalry (Daly's Horse) Frontier Force. It had been raised by Lieutenant Daly in 1849 and had had a short but crowded history. Only twice had it left the frontier; the first time to take part in suppressing the Indian Mutiny in 1857; and the second to fight in Afghanistan in 1878. The Punjab Frontier Force to which the regiment belonged consisted of five regiments of cavalry, four batteries of mounted artillery and ten battalions of infantry, and was charged with the responsibility of guarding six hundred miles of turbulent frontier. Their duties of watch and ward have been faithfully described by Rudyard Kipling in one of those pen pictures of which he was a master. 'All along the North-West Frontier of India there is spread a force of some thirty thousand foot and horse, whose duty it is quietly and unostentatiously to shepherd the tribes in front of them. They move up and down, and down and up, from one desolate little post to another; they are ready to take the field at ten minutes' notice; they are always half in and half out of a difficulty somewhere along the monotonous line; their lives are as hard as their own muscles, and the papers never say anything about them.' [1] But let it not be thought that the units of the Punjab Frontier Force — or Piffers as they were nicknamed — were merely armed police. On the contrary, all their units were highly trained for all kinds of warfare, both in and out of India, and a proportion of them were invariably included in the organised expeditions which were launched across the Frontier in order to bring to heel this or that tribe. The churches and graveyards of Mardan, Kohat, Bannu, and the rest bore witness to the forfeits which they paid so proudly and so willingly. No soldier could wish to lie in more gallant company.

When the British left India in 1947, it was felt that perhaps these memorials to our comrades might not continue to be tended with the same loving care as in the past, and many of them were brought to England, together with the Communion plate from the churches on the

[1] Kipling: *Many Inventions*, 'The Lost Legion.'

Frontier. Thanks to the kindness of the ecclesiastical authorities in London, there is now a Frontier Force chapel in St Luke's Church, Chelsea, in which we have our Book of Remembrance and other treasures; and the crypt below has been garnished as a shrine for the brasses and other memorials of our dead. Once a year a special service is held in the chapel, and is attended by an ever dwindling number of survivors, each one of us with memories of comrades, both British and Indian, who were true as steel, and of a brotherhood in arms whose glory will never fade. But I have anticipated.

The 21st Cavalry, like nearly all other Indian Cavalry regiments, was organised on what was known as the *silladar* system.[1] When it was first raised every recruit was required to bring his own horse, saddlery, sword and other equipment, and the only Government property issued to him was his musket. As a result, the horses were of every breed, size, colour and shape, and the equipment was of many different patterns. The regiment may have presented a moteley appearance, but there was never any doubt about its fighting value. After some years the system was modified in the interests of uniformity and efficiency. The recruit, instead of having to mount and equip himself, was required to pay a sum of about £50 to regimental funds. In return, he was provided, under regimental arrangements, with a horse, equipment and uniform throughout his service; and he was repaid his money in full when he was discharged. It seems odd in these days to think that there was a time when large numbers of youths were only too ready to pay a substantial sum of money for the privilege of serving in a profession which held out no hope of financial reward. But it must not be thought that all that was needed to become a member of the regiment was a bagful of silver. On the contrary, the competition for every vacancy was very keen, and the selection of candidates was carried out with the greatest care and formality. Other things being equal, preference was given to those with relations who were serving, or had served, in the regiment. No young man had any hope of being chosen unless he was related to or at least vouched for by a past or present member of the regiment.

1 The *silladar* system, as it was called, failed to stand up to the needs of the First World War, in which replacements of men, horses and equipment were required on a scale hitherto undreamed of; and it was abolished as soon as hostilities were over. The change resulted in much increased efficiency, but it was sad to see the passing of the old order.

It follows that discipline was of a very personal kind. The Colonel was regarded as the father of a family, or perhaps the patriarch of a tribe, and the average trooper preferred almost any of the orthodox punishments to being told in public that he had brought disgrace on the regiment. Youthful delinquencies such as unpunctuality, inattention, sloppiness in deportment or dress were generally brought to the notice of one of the offender's sponsors. We never knew what transpired, but the miscreant usually seemed chastened and repentant.

The 21st Cavalry, like the majority of Indian units, had a 'mixed' composition. Half were Hindus and half Moslems, but I cannot recall a single case of communal trouble, or even of communal prejudice. If, for example, we were called out in aid of civil power, the men never hesitated to act against their co-religionists with complete impartiality; it seemed as though all else was subordinated to their common devotion to the regiment and their pride in its traditions.

The story is told of a battalion whose Colours were shot to pieces in the unsuccessful assault on Bhurtpore in 1805. They were no longer usable, but when the day came for them to be destroyed with full ceremony, and replaced by new Colours, the British officers could find no trace of them. Thirty years afterwards the same battalion took part in a successful assault on the same fortress, and the mystery of the disappearance of the old Colours was cleared up. It transpired that they had been cut up by the men into a number of pieces, each of which had been carefully preserved as an amulet, and handed down from father to son. On the day that the disgrace of the defeat had been wiped out by victory, the fragments reappeared, were sewn together, and tied to the new Colours.[1]

To this tale of surpassing devotion, a personal postscript may be added. A Pathan officer, who was retiring after thirty-two years' service, came to say good-bye to me on his last day with the regiment. He looked forlorn and I tried to cheer him up by saying that the peace and quiet of his home in the delightful vale of Peshawar would be very enjoyable after the hurly-burly of soldiering. He shook his head. 'My grandfather was killed in this regiment in the mutiny,' he said. 'My father was killed in this regiment in the Afghan war. I was born in this regiment and have spent my whole life with it. I have a house in Peshawar, but my home is here.' That evening I went to the

[1] Philip Woodruff: *The Men Who Ruled India.*

railway station to see him off. All the Indian officers, Moslem and Hindu alike, were there and nearly all of them were in floods of tears.

The Indian officers were the link between the British officers and other ranks, and bore a great share of the responsibility for the tone of the regiment. Nearly all of them had done at least fifteen years' service before getting their commissions; most of them had spent their lives on the Frontier; many of them had seen a good deal of fighting. But in the days about which I write, the standard of education left a great deal to be desired, and the senior Indian officer of my squadron, Dildar Khan by name, could not even sign his name. He was a beautiful horseman, had a good eye for country, had fought in three campaigns, and did not know the meaning of the word fear. For all his illiteracy, there was no better troop leader in frontier warfare in any army in the world. He often said that he prayed that he would be with me when I had my baptism of fire; and before long his prayer was granted. We were riding down a broad valley in Mohmand country when a sudden fusillade was opened on us from the crest of the hills. I looked round to see two or three saddles empty, and Dildar Khan gazing into my eyes as though willing me to do the right thing. I was tempted to retire to a knoll which we had just passed, but remembered Dildar Khan's advice that at the beginning of a fight, before the men were warmed up, it was a good rule to go forwards rather than backwards, I led the troop at a gallop to some rising ground about three hundred yards ahead, and ordered dismounted action. The old warrior did not say a word, but looked rather like a proud father who has watched his son kick a goal in his first football match.

To anyone who was fond of horses and riding, life with a cavalry regiment on the Frontier was blissful. The day usually started with squadron or regimental training, and Drummer Boy, my recently acquired warhorse, would be brought to my door about a quarter of an hour before the parade was due to start. He was a picture to look upon with his coat of satin, and a lovely ride. But his sense of humour on those cold winter mornings was disconcerting. As soon as I was in the saddle, he used to let me know how well he was feeling and what fun it would be to put his master on the floor. Our progress towards the parade ground was unorthodox, undignified and uncomfortable.

He would start off by putting his head between his forelegs in the hope of snatching the reins out of my hand and thus obtaining more liberty. Then perhaps we would go sideways for thirty or forty yards, and when he was tired of that he would try plunging backwards. Nothing that I could say or do had any effect on his exuberance. Coaxing, cursing, and even a sharp slap were all useless, and the ridiculous pirouette would continue until the squadron came into view. Then and then only would he confide to me that his back was now nice and warm, that his saddle tickled him no longer and that it was time we settled down to serious business. For the rest of the morning he behaved impeccably and responded to the lightest touch of rein or leg. Sometimes it was a field exercise; sometimes we practised precision drill; sometimes the squadrons would manoeuvre against each other; but whatever form the training took, it was difficult to imagine how two or three hours could be spent more enjoyably, and I for one was always sorry when the parade was over.

The next function was 'Stables.' This too was instructive, and enjoyable in a different way. It was an ideal opportunity for British officers to get to know more about the men and horses for which they were responsible. As they passed down the line they could talk with each *sowar*[1] on every kind of topic. What was the news of his father or uncle or other regimental pensioner in his village? How were his crops going? His horse's coat was staring: why not see what a little boiled linseed would do? The day was to come when I knew every man in the regiment by name and the individual characteristics of practically every horse; and a great deal of this information had been acquired at 'Stables' throughout the years.

Sometimes there was a little office work to be done; sometimes we had a rifle inspection or a kit inspection or an inspection of saddlery; sometimes either a British or Indian officer gave a short lecture on a variety of topics, such as horse management or musketry. By lunch-time the day's work was over. Soldiering was not then the highly technical profession that it has become, and the afternoons were nearly always free to do whatever we wished. Most of us played polo three days a week, and schooled ponies on the other afternoons. In addition there were occasional race meetings at neighbouring stations, and rough shooting for all who wanted it. I could never help thinking, as I

[1] Trooper.

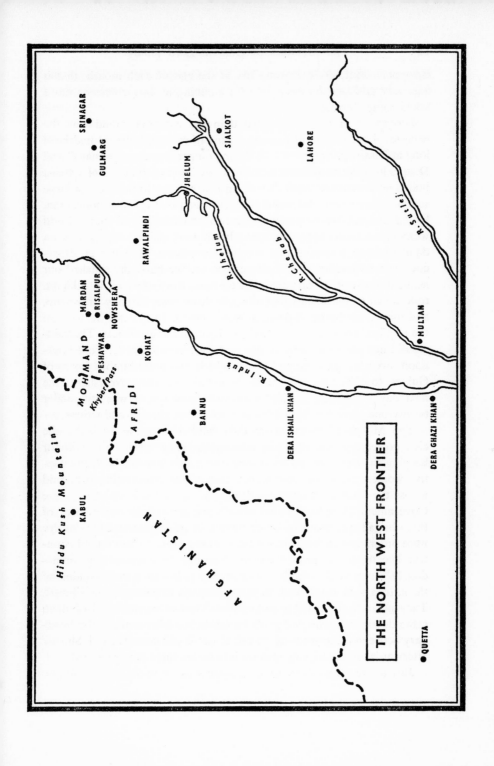

THE NORTH WEST FRONTIER

drew my admittedly meagre salary at the end of each month, that it was very odd that I should be paid anything at all for doing what I loved doing above all else.

Perhaps even more enjoyable than the common round was the occasional excitement of hunting a gang of raiders. Before I had been long at Risalpur, orders arrived during dinner one evening that C and D squadrons were to move as fast as possible to a number of specific points about twenty miles distant, in order to try to intercept a large raiding party from Mohmand country which had killed a policeman, looted and set fire to a village or two and carried off some Hindu women. I was thrilled to the core, but my enthusiasm was somewhat damped when I noticed that my brother officers were not at all excited and took it all as a matter of course. We hurriedly finished our meal, trooped off to our quarters, changed from mess kit into khaki, rode down to the lines where the squadrons were already drawn up, and moved off by the light of a kindly moon. By 4 A.M. we were in the required positions and remained there till about 10 A.M. The raiders did not put in an appearance and we returned home. That afternoon several of us drove to Mardan, the home of the famous Corps of Guides, to play polo: that night there was a dance in Nowshera: the next day I was due to ride in two steeplechases. I was still under twenty-one years old. How I blessed my ineptitude at examinations.

The Mohmand elders were duly hauled over the coals by the civil power and told that the allowances which they were paid for keeping the peace would be stopped until they handed back the captive women. But they were wholly impenitent and continued to raid across the border on an increasing scale. At last the patience of the Government of India was exhausted, and an expeditionary force of three brigades of infantry, some mountain guns and the 21st Cavalry were ordered to concentrate on the Frontier opposite Mohmand country. The tribe was now given an ultimatum that unless they immediately returned the captive women and paid the fine demanded of them, troops would move into their country and destroy their villages. They not only returned a rude answer, but a few hundred of them came down to the very edge of the foothills, which marked the boundary between us, as if to say: 'Turn us out if you can.' We did. Shortly afterwards, orders for the advance into the mountains were issued.

Just as we were about to start there was an outbreak of cholera, and I am ashamed to say that I went cold with fear when I heard the news. To die in action 'with all the world to weep or cheer' was one thing: but 'a silent, unnoticed, almost ignominious summons, scarcely less sudden and far more painful than the bullet or the sword-cut' [1] was quite another. Fortunately the outbreak was soon brought under control. The regiments which had been smitten were left behind and replaced by others; and the advance into Mohmand country started early in May.

From now onwards we were in constant action. The only way of punishing the tribesmen and making them see sense was to occupy their villages, which were perforce situated in the valley, destroy the towers or keeps which they had built for protection against their neighbours, confiscate any stores of grain that might be found and burn their standing crops. Needless to say, the most stringent orders were issued that the mosques and trees were to be left severely alone. The day's work usually followed much the same pattern. We generally broke camp at daybreak and marched on the village or villages which were next on the list for punishment. The tribes made little attempt to oppose us on the low ground and immediately made for the heights which commanded our line of advance. From there they proceeded to shoot us up with armament that ranged from the most modern rifle, which cost its weight in silver, to the home-made "jezail," which cost less than a sovereign and was dear at the price. Our first task therefore was to drive them off the heights — a laborious and some-times costly business — and occupy these ourselves. Once this was done the demolition parties could proceed to their objectives without being molested and destroy the villages at their leisure. When the destruction was complete, the column moved off either to the next village on the list, or back to camp, according to the lateness of the hour. But whichever way we turned, the tribesmen got back again on the crest of the hills almost before our men had started their retirement, and rekindled the battle. It was on these occasions that we in the Cavalry were useful in relieving the pressure, thanks to our ability to hold successive positions until the last minute, and then get away quickly. It was exciting work, and required careful timing. Nor did our troubles end when we at last reached camp, as the enemy took a delight in sniping throughout the hours of darkness. Since we

[1] Winston S. Churchill: *The River War.*

slept in shallow holes scooped in the ground, we came to little harm, but we had to pay periodic visits to the horse lines to see whether any of the animals had been hit and required attention.

As the summer wore on the sun became increasingly fierce and conditions more and more uncomfortable. In order to increase mobility, transport had been cut to the bone and beyond, and there had been no room for luxuries of any kind. An almost exclusive diet of bully beef and army biscuits had now become nauseating, and the water was so chlorinated as to be scarcely drinkable. The burning rocks had worn holes in the soles of our boots, and a good many of the horses looked like skeletons. Even the most inveterate fire-eaters were pleased when we heard that the Mohmands had sued for peace and that we were to make for home as soon as possible. Scarcely had we crossed the border into India when I collapsed with sunstroke and was carried into the hospital at Peshawar on a stretcher. When I came to my senses I found myself lying in a bed with clean sheets, and nurses clad in spotless white were flitting about the ward. At first I thought that they were angels and that I must have got to heaven, but the moans of the badly wounded subaltern in the next bed quickly brought me to earth again. When I woke up two mornings later the screens had been removed and the bed was empty.

I was discharged from hospital in time to spend my twenty-first birthday with the regiment at Risalpur and to revel in the comforts of comparative civilisation. Much that had hitherto been taken for granted was now a great treat — fresh meat, fish, fruit, vegetables, whisky, beer, and above all plenty of ice. It was a comfort too to have a roof over one's head against the midday sun, and to be able to go to sleep at night knowing that it would not be necessary to make periodic visits to the horse lines to see if the snipers had done any damage. The month in Mohmand country had been always uncomfortable, often boring, and sometimes frightening; but I wouldn't have missed it for the world. I was young enough in those days to believe everything that I read in print, and the leading article in the *Pioneer,* India's leading daily, made me feel immensely proud. 'The 21st Cavalry did remarkably fine work and amply proved their utility for trans-Frontier service . . . Hard work, they say, never kills, and it is a fact, I believe, that throughout the operations the 21st Cavalry had not a single case of sickness to report, though they were generally the first to leave and always the last to get back to camp.' When it was announced that the operations had been adjudged of sufficient importance to merit the award of a medal and clasp, my joy knew no bounds.

Alas, the day was not far distant when we had to say good-bye to the North-West Frontier. In the early years of the century, the then Commander-in-Chief in India, Lord Kitchener of Khartoum, had carried out a complete and long overdue reorganisation of the Army in India. Among other reforms, he decided that the Punjab Frontier Force should be broken up, and that its units should henceforward be liable to be stationed anywhere in India. And so it came to pass, in 1910, that the 21st Cavalry found itself transferred to Jhelum in the Punjab. It was sad to think that for the next four years there would be no more forays with border raiders. We were sure that they would not miss us as much as we would miss them. On the other hand, there were compensations. Jhelum had comfortable bungalows, well laid-out gardens, two polo grounds and a club with plenty of tennis courts. There was a larger garrison, pigsticking to be had in the neighbour-hood, and Lahore, Rawalpindi and Sialkot were all within easy reach.

Shortly after our arrival in our new station, the adjutancy of the regiment fell vacant. Godfrey Soole, who was three or four years my senior, had been earmarked for the job; but he had been killed in a rear-guard action on the Mohmand expedition, and the mantle that would have been his fell on my shoulders. My selection for this responsible appointment at an unusually early age, combined with my brief taste of active service, inspired me to take my profession more seriously. Hitherto my ambition had been limited to becoming a good regimental officer, and a first class polo player. I now began to have wider aspirations; and it was at this period in my life that Mr Winston Churchill, whom I had never met, and, as it then seemed, was unlikely ever to meet, exercised a decisive influence on my future. He had, as a junior cavalry officer, contrived to see a remarkable amount of active service. In 1895 he had been an eye-witness of the fighting in Cuba between the Spanish Army and the Cuban rebels. In 1897, when the whole of the North-West Frontier of India was ablaze, he had managed to get himself attached to the Staff of the Commander-in-Chief, and thereafter to take part in some hard fought engagements as a regimental officer. In the very next year he had succeeded in getting to the campaign in the Sudan, in spite of the opposition of the almost omnipotent Commander-in-Chief, Lord Kitchener, and had led a troop of the 21st Lancers in the charge at Omdurman. Within a matter of two years, he had seen a good deal of the South African War, sometimes wielding the sword of the soldier, sometimes the pen of the war correspondent. To cap all this, he had played in the winning team of the Inter-Regimental Polo Tournament in India, and had written several books. His mastery of the English language and the wide range of his knowledge greatly impressed me. I admit that my youthful sense of discipline was shocked by the freedom with which he criticised senior officers, and that I was amazed that anyone who had started so brilliantly should have thrown it all up and gone into Parliament. But I felt that, on the whole, I could not do better than try to emulate the example of his early years. I resolved that I must always be on the look-out for any chance of active service in any part of the globe, and that in the meantime I must do my best to educate myself, particularly in the use of the English language. I began to read voraciously, my favourites being Gibbon's *Decline and Fall of the Roman Empire,* Henderson's *Stonewall Jackson,* Kipling of all kinds, and Winston Churchill's *River War.* I got so attached to them that I read them again and again, and soon knew long passages by heart. There came a day, over thirty years later, when I thought that my memory might come in useful. Churchill and I were alone one evening in 1942, when he started a tirade against the astronomical number of vehicles that were being shipped to the Middle East. 'Will the War Office never cease adding to the interminable tail?' he asked. I thought to pour oil on troubled waters by reminding him that in the long-distant past he himself had thought up this striking metaphor: 'Victory is the beautiful bright-coloured flower: transport is the stem without which it would never have blossomed.' [1] My intervention passed unheeded.

Life in cantonments might have become monotonous if one had not spent so much of one's time on holiday. Except in the intensive training period, there was seldom any difficulty about getting away to some other station for a week or ten days in order to take part in a polo tournament, race-meeting, horse show or skill-at-arms competi-

[1] Winston S. Churchill: *The River War.*

tion. In addition we were entitled to two months' leave every year. Some would go big game shooting to the plains of Central India; some would journey deep into the mountains beyond Kashmir in search of ibex, markhor or the other great stags that lived at those heights; one or two (though this was not popular) would go 'poodle-faking' to Simla or some other social hill station. I myself almost invariably went off to Kashmir. At Srinagar I used to live in a house-boat, with my ponies tethered under the shade of great trees in the woods near-by; and after polo on Friday, three or four of us used to have our house-boats pulled out into Dhal Lake, with its flaming lotus flowers and limpid waters, and enjoy a blissful week-end. When it got too hot at Srinagar, I would migrate, ponies and all, to Gulmarg, a plateau about eight thousand feet above sea level. The climate was perfect, and the scenery breath-taking. The polo ground was of real English turf, the golf course was the best in the land, and there was a club where we could all meet to settle the affairs of the world. Most of us were very young and all of us were on holiday. It seemed almost too good to last. And it didn't. Armageddon was near at hand.

One was entitled to six months' leave to England every three years or so, but except for occasional bouts of home-sickness, I was too happy to go so far afield. In point of fact I had been seven years in India before I saw the white cliffs of Dover again, and I was glad when my holiday was over and I could get back to my friends, both British and Indian, and my ponies and dogs.

When I was on the last lap of my four years' term of duty as Adjutant, I started to think about the next step. Everyone advised me that I ought to seek a spell of extra regimental employment; but there were not many openings for subaltern officers, and this was easier said than done. I could speak Pushtu, the language of the Frontier, fluently, and was eligible for service with one or other of the many Irregular Corps which were permanently stationed on or across the North-West Frontier. But the experience would not be altogether novel, and the idea of being completely cut off from civilisation did not attract me. The only other possibility that occurred to me was to be an ADC to some civil or military potentate, but I knew of no one whom I dared approach. In the end, the question was settled — as so often happens — by accident rather than design.

Early in 1914 I chanced to run into a brother cavalry subaltern of the name of Howard [1] in the club at Jhelum. His regiment was stationed in the Central Provinces, and I asked what had brought him up north. He replied that he had joined the Somaliland Indian Contingent of the King's African Rifles about six months previously, and had been sent to India to enlist two hundred more volunteers for that unit. He added by way of explanation that a small war was brewing against the Mad Mullah of Somaliland, and that a regiment of Somalis was being raised and trained to strike the first blow. It was to be mounted partly on riding camels, and partly on ponies, and a company of the Indian Contingent was to be mounted on camels and permanently attached to it. In reply to my anxious enquiry as to whether there was any chance of a vacancy, Howard told me that the Somaliland Camel Corps were already full up, but that he thought that the Indian Contingent were still one officer short. This seemed to be just the sort of job that I wanted. There would be a good chance of seeing active service and there would probably be plenty of time to read for the Staff College without the distractions of polo and other Indian delights. It might also be possible to save a little money. I applied for the appointment the very next day, and three months later I was thrilled to receive orders to proceed to Somaliland as quickly as possible. Within a fortnight I had sold all my ponies and paid all my creditors in full. I had for some time past been living on the hire-purchase system, except that instalments to my tailor and other patient friends were not paid at prescribed intervals, but whenever I happened to have some cash to spare.

•

---

[1] C. A. L. Howard was my second-in-command in the last Somaliland expedition. Later he commanded a brigade in India.

CHAPTER II

Scallywag in Africa

1914–1920

TOWARDS the end of July I set sail from Bombay, armed with the books that I needed to study for the Staff College, and a sheaf of letters from brother officers congratulating me on my good fortune, and begging me to remember them if there was any chance of a job in Somaliland. How extraordinary it was that none of us had any inkling that all hell was just about to be let loose in Europe!

As the steamer bore me westwards, I had moments of nostalgia for all that I was leaving behind. My regiment was 'my father and my mother,' and my comrades, both British and Indian, were the salt of the earth. The frontier tribesmen had taught me a good deal about looking after my men and myself. My ponies had been the joy of my life. The polo fields and race-courses of Northern India had been my playground. I was going to miss it all terribly. Nevertheless, I consoled myself with the thought that the parting was temporary and that I was heading for a new country, new experience and new opportunities. But before we reached Aden we received news which turned my hopes to black despair. War had broken out with Germany.

It was an extremely unhappy and reluctant recruit who landed in Somaliland on 9 August 1914; but at least I was not alone in my misery. Most of my future brother officers had already arrived, and

19

nearly all of them had applied to return to their regiments, and been ordered to stay where they were. This is the point at which to explain why it was necessary for even a single soldier to be retained in a remote corner of the British Empire when we were about to engage in the biggest war in our history.

In the last half of the nineteenth century there was keen competition between the European Powers for 'a place in the sun' in Africa. In 1885 Great Britain seized the opportunity afforded by the Egyptian evacuation of their possessions in Somaliland to step in and sign treaties with most of the tribes. The new territory was henceforward known as the British Somaliland Protectorate.

In the early days no attempt was made to administer the interior, and British officialdom was confined to a Vice-Consul and a handful of assistants at the coast towns of Berbera, Bulhar and Zeyla. At first the colony was self-supporting and relatively peaceful, but this happy state of affairs was rudely changed before the turn of the century by one Mahomed bin Abdillah Hassan, who came to be known as the Mad Mullah. Authentic records of his early life are meagre, but it is certain that he was born in about 1870 and that he made several pilgrimages to Mecca. Returning to Berbera in 1895, he proceeded to denounce his countrymen for their lack of religious fervour, and their luxurious way of life: but his sermons had little or no effect on the inhabitants of the coast towns, and he moved to the home of his childhood in the south-east corner of the Protectorate. There he set about acquiring influence and collecting a following. Initially he went out of his way to co-operate with the Vice-Consul at Berbera, and to use his influence to maintain law and order. But in 1899 he evidently felt strong enough to make a bid for the power of which he had always dreamed. His letters to the Vice-Consul suddenly became more and more insolent, and he moved to Burao with a force of five thousand men. There he proclaimed that he was the 'expected Mahdi' — as Mahomed Ahmed had done in the Sudan some twenty years previously — and declared a Jehad, or holy war, against the Government. His preaching was simple: 'He who is not with me is against me.' All who were with him were dervishes (holy men), who, he said, would lay up for themselves treasures in heaven; and all who were not with him — even the most devout Moslems — were kafirs (infidels), who would be punished with eternal damnation. Our friendly tribes were

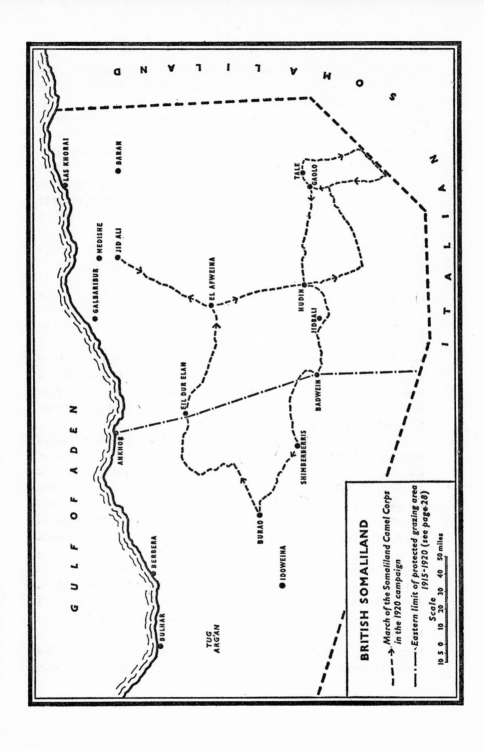

BRITISH SOMALILAND

- - - ► March of the Somaliland Camel Corps
        in the 1920 campaign

—·—·— Eastern limit of protected grazing area
        1915-1920 (see page 28)

Scale
10 5 0 10 20 30 40 50 miles

SOMALILAND

GULF OF ADEN

ITALIAN SOMALIA

LAS KHORAI

BARAN

MEDISHE

GALBARIBUR

JID ALI

EL AFWEINA

HUDIN

JIDBALI

TALE
GAOLO

BADWEIN

EIL DUR ELAN

ANKHOR

SHIMBERBERRIS

BERBERA

BURAO

IDOWEINA

BULHAR

TUG
ARGAN

thrown into a panic, and the Government had no option but to declare the Mullah a rebel, and organise a military expedition to put an end to his pretensions.

In the next four or five years there were four separate campaigns. The British forces employed were progressively more numerous, more regular and better equipped, but there was a monotonous similarity about the results. On each occasion the Mullah's following was roughly handled; on each occasion the British incurred significant losses; on each occasion the Mullah himself was harried from pillar to post. But at the end of it he was very much alive, and he never lost his robust spirit or his hard core of realism. 'I like war but you do not . . .' he wrote to His Majesty's representative, when the expedition of 1904 was being prepared. 'The country is a jungle and that is no use to you. If you want wood and stone you can get them in plenty. There are also many ant-heaps. The sun is very hot.' I can personally vouch for the truth of his every word. Nevertheless the expedition proved nearly fatal to him. It culminated in a crushing defeat at Jidbali and flight to Italian Somaliland. The British Government hoped and thought that their troubles were over, but five years later the bad penny turned up again with a considerable following. Frantic appeals for protection poured into Berbera, and an exasperated Secretary of State for the Colonies must have been tempted to exclaim: 'Who will rid me of this turbulent priest?'

The Government were in a quandary. Should they try yet another military expedition? Or should they evacuate the country? There were grave objections to both alternatives. Past expeditions had been costly in blood and treasure, and there was no reason to expect that yet another military adventure would be any more conclusive. On the other hand, evacuation would involve a breach of our obligations to the friendly tribes, a loss of prestige throughout Africa, and the possibility that some potentially hostile power would step into the vacuum and establish a naval base at Berbera.

In the end, recourse was had to a compromise. We were to abandon control of the interior of the country and to concentrate at the coastal towns; the administration of tribal affairs was to be in the hands of their own *akils* (chiefs); and the 'friendlies' were to be given arms and ammunition to enable them to protect themselves against the dervishes. The results of this melancholy policy were catastrophic.

The 'friendlies,' so far from combining against their common enemy, indulged in an orgy of inter-tribal pillaging, while the Mullah took advantage of the confusion to slaughter them indiscriminately and help himself to the arms and ammunition which were being lavished upon them. Anarchy spread throughout the land, and it was soon obvious that the policy of coastal concentration had ignominiously failed.

The Government had to think again; and again they fell back upon a compromise. It was decided that a Camel Constabulary one hundred and fifty strong should be raised at once. Its objects would be to keep open the trade routes to the coast, restore confidence among the tribes and put an end to inter-tribal warfare. It was to be a civil, not a military, force; and it was not intended to deal with the dervish problem. On that point the orders given to their first — and last — Commandant, Mr Corfield, were unequivocal. 'Should you receive news of the near presence of any considerable force, *you should carefully avoid being attacked or surrounded and should at once retire to the coast.*' [1] There may be occasions when there is something to be said for the old tag that 'he who fights and runs away will live to fight another day'; but an order to a commander of an armed force not to fight, whatever the circumstances, must be unique. Those whose business it is to issue orders should make it a rule, before doing so, to put themselves in the position of the man who has to carry them out.

By the end of 1912 the Constabulary was ready. Initially it was successful in settling quarrels between the friendly tribes and restoring order among them, and Corfield was encouraged to patrol further and further into the interior. But the days of this experiment were numbered. In August 1913 a large dervish force penetrated as far as Idoweina and looted enormous quantities of stock. Corfield moved out at once and tried to intercept them, but a dervish fighting for his loot is as fierce as a tigress fighting for her cubs, and a most bloody engagement ensued. Corfield was killed almost at once. Captain Summers[2] of the Indian Contingent, who had accompanied him, was thrice wounded, and after five hours' fighting the Constabulary were practically annihilated. The Mullah proceeded to make hay while the sun shone. Before a month had elapsed, he sent a posse of horsemen

[1] Author's italics.
[2] 26th Light Cavalry, Indian Army. Afterwards Sir Gerald Summers, Governor of British Somaliland.

to sack Burao, and a strong force of foot-men to establish a post at Shimberberris. A few months later he sent forty horsemen to fire into Berbera itself. The material damage done by this crowning insolence was negligible, but the moral effect was considerable. Something had got to be done.

The British Government now hit upon a decision which was destined to keep the Mullah within bounds for the next six years, and ultimately to encompass his destruction. The Constabulary was to be disbanded, and a military unit called the Somaliland Camel Corps was to be set up in its place. It was to have officers seconded from the British and Indian Armies, and to be five hundred strong. Two companies were to be mounted on riding camels, and one on ponies. In addition, the Somaliland Indian Contingent, which had hitherto consisted of two hundred hand-picked volunteers from the Indian Army, was to be increased to four hundred. One hundred and fifty of these were to be mounted on camels, and permanently attached to the Somaliland Camel Corps. The remaining two hundred and fifty were to be used for garrison duty. The headquarters of the new Corps was to be at Burao. Their role was to keep order in the west and prevent the further advance of the Mullah in the east. Thus the outbreak of war found a motley collection of officers, drawn from the British and Indian Armies, eating out their hearts in what had suddenly become a backwater.

Our commander was Lieutenant-Colonel Thomas Astley Cubitt, the beau ideal of a Horse Gunner — a born leader, and already a marked man in his profession. He had the stoutest and kindest of hearts, and a remarkable flow of unprintable invective. He finished the war as a very successful divisional commander in France. He was as unhappy as the rest of us at being out of the Great War, but encouraged us by the promise that he would attack the dervish position at Shimberberris the moment that he thought us battle-worthy, and would continue to harry the Mullah until he was finished and done with.

True to his word, we moved out of Burao on 17 November to a point about fifteen miles south of Shimberberris, and two days later we advanced on the three forts at the top of the escarpment. After a few miles the ascent became steep and the bush very thick, and leaving our animals under guard, we continued the march on foot. Now was the chance for the enemy's rushing tactics, but they made no attempt to molest us, and it was not until the head of the column was within half a mile of the central fort that they opened fire. The leading company deployed for attack, and the scene which ensued was reminiscent of a military tattoo. There was the typical fortress, the clatter of musketry, the defiant shouts of the defenders, and the rush of the assailants, with men occasionally falling and lying still. One almost expected to see the conventional *dénouement* — the Union Jack flying from the battlements. But it didn't work out like that. Our men charged right up to the walls, and fired through the loop-holes at point-blank range; but they could not force an entrance, and after a few minutes they withdrew. Having got their second wind, they again charged right up to the walls, but again they recoiled.

Cubitt now sent me to find out what was happening, and I joined Carton de Wiart,[1] whose name was later to become a household word, in a hollow about eighty yards from the fort. He had a bandage over his left eye, but I had no idea that he had already lost the sight of it and was in great pain. He said that the rifleman in the gallery was still a menace but that any amount of lead had been pumped into the fort and there could not be many survivors. He proposed that a couple of machine-guns should concentrate on the gallery for a full two minutes, and that the five British officers on the spot should then try to rush the door. Everyone thought this was a good idea. The five of us lined up, and two machine-guns opened fire on the gallery. Chunks of masonry at once began to fall, and it looked as though it might collapse at any moment. The seconds sped by. We kept an eye on our watches, and when the two minutes were up we raced forward in silence. Carton de Wiart, on my right, was immediately hit in the arm and the ear, but did not check in his stride. Symons,[2] on my left, was the first to reach the door, but a bullet through the head sent him reeling backwards. Lawrence,[3] on the left of the line, was hit in the arm. It was clear — so far as anything could be clear in that *mêlée* — that the gallery was still intact and that the garrison was strong enough to deal with any assault. Hornby[4] and I, who were both un-

[1] 4th Dragoon Guards and Somaliland Camel Corps. Afterwards Lieutenant General Sir Adrian Carton de Wiart, V.C.

[2] Yorkshire Light Infantry and Somaliland Camel Corps.

[3] City of London Yeomanry and Somaliland Camel Corps. Afterwards Sir Arthur Lawrence, Governor of Somaliland.

[4] 12th Royal Lancers and Somaliland Camel Corps.

wounded, retrieved Symons' body and retired to cover. Cubitt now joined the party. On hearing what had happened, he decided to break off the action and have another try as soon as he could get hold of the only gun in the whole country — an ancient muzzle-loading seven-pounder which had last seen service in 1879.

To me fell the command of the rear-guard. I thought that the dervishes were almost certain to follow us up very closely, but they did nothing of the kind, and we reached camp with scarcely a scratch between the lot of us. We had been on the go for nineteen hours on end, and the tot of whisky which Cubitt gave me when I made my report was like nectar.

The antediluvian cannon arrived three days later, and we again advanced to the attack. The gun was brought into action at about two hundred yards range, and three or four direct hits were scored. They did little damage, but the defenders were apparently unnerved by the concussion and fled incontinently. That evening I asked one of our prisoners why they had not followed up our retirement on the 19th, and he thought I was joking. He said that half of the defenders had been killed, and that most of the other half were 'full of holes,' as he described it. The idea of a pursuit had never entered their minds. On the contrary, they had suspected that our retirement was a ruse, and that we intended to return to the attack. They had therefore evacuated the fort as soon as we had gone half a mile or so. I regretted all the nervous energy which I had expended so unnecessarily during the retirement, but it taught me a valuable lesson. Ever since that day, whenever I felt frightened or discouraged I derived much comfort from the thought that mine enemy was probably in even greater difficulties, and even more unhappy.

There were still the three forts in the valley to be dealt with, and a couple of months later we again sallied forth from Burao, accompanied by a platoon of Indian Pioneers, borrowed from Aden, with supplies of gun-cotton. We found the dervishes occupying not only the forts, but also the caves with which the hill-side was honey-combed. After a brisk engagement, everything except the fort which commanded the well was in our hands. But although the gun was brought to bear at very close range, the defenders continued to resist. As a last resort, three boxes, each containing fifty pounds of gun-cotton, were placed against the wall and detonated. We had been told by the expert that the explosion would probably do no more than stun the defenders, and that we must be ready to rush them at once. But he had under-estimated. The whole building seemed to rise skywards and collapse in a tangled mass of enormous boulders, and all our efforts to dig out the defenders were in vain. I was sorry. They had fought well.

The fight at Shimberberris had done much more than wrest a few square miles from the dervish grip. It had taught us that the Somali was a far better soldier than we had been led to expect. No one had ever questioned his powers of endurance. Time and again he had shown that he could cover enormous distances on a minimum of food and water. Nor had anyone ever questioned his toughness. Once upon a time, a Somali irregular who had been given up for lost crawled into a British camp with a bullet wound in his thigh and a spear wound just missing his heart. The doctor put him on the operating table and started to probe the leg wound, only to be told by the impatient invalid that it was the spear wound which was worrying him. He complained that it hurt him when he laughed! Nor had the Somali's physical courage ever been questioned. He had shown, both on the field of battle and in hunting big game, that he could be the bravest of the brave if he felt like it. But — and it was a very big 'but' — he had earned the reputation of being so excitable as to be hopelessly unreliable. His detractors failed to take into account that in the past he had always been put into battle with little or no training, and led by officers whom he did not know. Shimberberris was the first occasion on which he had been given a fair chance, and he took it with both hands. Thereafter he went from strength to strength, and soon established a pronounced moral ascendancy over the hitherto dreaded dervish. He never ceased to be vain, volatile and sometimes exasperating; he never ceased to be excitable at the beginning of an action; he never ceased to be a scallywag. To have tried to 'regularise' him would have ruined him. But his British officers, during the last years of the Mullah's rebellion, will ever remember him as a faithful, gay and gallant soldier, who was at his best in times of scarcity and hardship.

Another lesson which we learned from the action at Shimberberris was that the dervishes, though as fanatically brave as ever, were nothing like as dangerous as of yore. They seemed to have lost their offensive spirit. Otherwise, they would surely have seized the many opportunities which they had had of attacking us in country which was ideal for their rushing tactics, instead of remaining within their defences. Their marksmanship had been deplorable, and they were evidently short of ammunition. On all counts we came to the conclusion that the Camel Corps, with a little more training, a few more British officers and a portable gun capable of breaching the Mullah's forts, could finish the business on its own. But higher authority, in view of past experience, took a less rosy view of the prospects.

Colonel Cubitt's next objective was Jid Ali, a strong fort in the north-east of the Protectorate. But just as his plans were nearing completion, orders arrived from England forbidding all offensive operations in Somaliland until further notice. The war was going badly everywhere, and it was only natural that the British Government should frown on any adventure, however insignificant, which might lead to an appeal for reinforcements. It was a blow to us all to be denied the chance of finishing off the Mullah and to be condemned to stand on the defensive in the waste places, while the rest of our world was in convulsion; and Cubitt and one or two others were allowed to escape to the war. Their departure meant that the rest of us were even more firmly anchored to Somaliland.

For the next four years our activities were limited to watch and ward. The friendly tribes were told that we would do our best to protect them provided that they did not venture to graze their stock east of the line[1] shown on the map on page 21, and our dispositions were made accordingly. The Camel Corps was held at readiness at Burao to strike in any direction at a moment's notice. Its eyes and ears were three hundred *illalos*[2] (irregulars), distributed in posts of varying size along the arc of the protected area. Their orders were that if any small dervish party penetrated the protected area, they were to deal with it themselves. But if a large dervish force put in an appearance, they were to keep in touch with its movements without getting too closely involved, and report at once to Burao. These rough

---

[1] Ankhor–Eil Dur Elan–Badwein — thence southwards to the southern border of the Protectorate, at the point where it is intersected by the 46th degree longitude — a total front of some 200 miles.
[2] Affectionately known as Tally Hos.

and ready arrangements worked satisfactorily, and on the only occasions on which the enemy attempted a big raid they were severely punished.

In addition to these 'tip-and-run' affairs, we made a practice of patrolling deep into enemy territory several times a year, in order to show the flag, give confidence to the friendly tribes, and improve our knowledge of the country and of the enemy. It became more and more obvious that dervish power was declining and that the Mullah was getting into low water. Many of his best fighting men had been killed in action; a large number of his rifles had been captured; a still larger number were no longer serviceable; and his stocks of ammunition were running dangerously low. Refusing to admit that his ill-armed, untrained, hungry following were no match for the Camel Corps, his treatment of those who returned from a foray empty-handed became more and more bestial, and desertions from his camp became more and more frequent. We were thus able to obtain and catalogue a mass of accurate information about his forts, armament, organisation and personnel. The next expedition, whenever it took place, would be far better informed than any of its forerunners.

We always hoped that, once the Great War was over, the British Government would wish to finish off the Mullah once and for all, and sure enough Major-General Sir A. R. Hoskins arrived in Somaliland shortly after the Armistice with instructions to advise how this should be done. I hoped that my intelligence reports would convince him that the Mullah was ripe for the sickle, and that only a very small addition to the local forces would be required. But Hoskins, who had served in previous abortive campaigns in Somaliland, thought that our wish was father to the thought and that we were too optimistic. He was not prepared — and who could blame him? — to attempt anything on the cheap and risk yet another failure; and the plan which he submitted to the War Office visualised an expedition on a scale which was rejected by the Government on the score of expense. It looked as though the *status quo* was going to be indefinitely maintained, but rescue came from an unexpected quarter.

The RAF was in its infancy as an independent Service, and fighting for its very existence against the Navy and the Army. The Air Staff were always on the look-out for a chance to show what air power could do. They assured the Government that a handful of aeroplanes could finish off the Mullah on their own, and the Government decided that the experiment was worth a trial.

No sooner had this decision been made than the Mullah moved with his 'Privy Council' and about a thousand riflemen, from Tale to Medishe, twelve miles north-west of Jid Ali. The reason for the move has never been established. From the point of view of the RAF, it was unfortunate. The Medishe defences were less concentrated and would be harder to find than those at Tale. But from the point of view of the Camel Corps, the move was welcome. The Mullah would almost certainly try to escape into Italian Somaliland when we attacked him; and the greater the distance that he had to go, the better the chance of catching him.

The forces to be employed in the campaign were curiously assorted. The leading part was to be played by 'Z' Unit, RAF, whose striking force consisted of six DH 9 aeroplanes. Their speed was about 100 miles an hour; their endurance approximately four and a half hours; and their bomb load 460 pounds. It was expressly laid down that the air operations were in the first instance to be entirely independent, and that the RAF commander, Group-Captain Gordon, should take his orders direct from the Air Ministry. The idea of a Government Department in London exercising close control of a war in a remote corner of Africa had at least the merit of novelty.

The ground troops, commanded by Colonel G. H. Summers, were a job lot. They consisted of the Somaliland Camel Corps; a battalion of the King's African Rifles from Kenya; half a battalion of Indian infantry; about three hundred *illalos;* and an unruly mob, euphemistically called a tribal levy, of about fifteen hundred friendly Somalis, commanded by Captain A. Gibb. The Royal Navy were represented by HMS *Odin* and *Clio* under Captain G. G. P. Hewett, RN.

The plan was simple, though not very sensible. Early in January 1920, the Camel Corps and Indian infantry were to prepare a landing-ground and establish a supply depot at Eil Dur Elan. On 21 January, the six aeroplanes were to attack Medishe, and thereafter to continue to carry out independent air operations until the Air Ministry gave permission for them to co-operate with the rest of the performers. The Camel Corps were to be prepared to strike in any direction that might be required, but were forbidden to make any move eastwards until the air attack had been delivered, lest the Mullah might become suspicious and flee. We pointed out that we had frequently visited places a hundred miles further east than Eil Dur Elan without the Mullah getting excited, and that if we were not in the vicinity of the principal target when it was bombed, we would be unable to take advantage of the situation which might be created. But the Air Ministry turned a deaf ear to our protests. The King's African Rifles were to attack the fort at Baran and prevent the Mullah escaping east. Landing parties from the *Odin* and *Clio* were to attack the fort at Galbaribur as soon as combined operations were sanctioned. The tribal levy was to occupy the wells on the Mullah's line of retreat to Abyssinia, and the *illalos* were to be used for general utility purposes.

On the morning of the 21st the six aircraft duly flew over our heads on their way to bomb Medishe. We wished them the best of luck, but they did not have it. One of them had a forced landing, four failed to locate the target, and the attack was delivered by a solitary machine, whose pilot had got separated from his companions and happened to spot the objective. Extraordinary to relate, the first bomb singed the Mullah's clothing and killed his uncle, who was standing next to him. Thus it was only by inches that the campaign failed to achieve its object on the very first day. But to have deduced any lessons from such an amazing fluke would have been foolish.

The RAF continued to attack Medishe for the next three days, but the Mullah and his followers had taken refuge in deep caves, and no great damage was done. By 25 January the Air Staff in London were forced to the conclusion that nothing further was to be gained by independent air action, and gave permission for the rest of us to lend a hand. The Camel Corps moved at once on Jid Ali and arrived in sight of the fort early on the 27th, just in time to watch a couple of aeroplanes unloading their bombs on it. They were neither lucky nor accurate, and we moved up to the attack. The defenders, so far from being demoralised, fired away merrily and seemed in excellent heart and voice. The Stokes guns, our new toy, were brought into action at very close range, but the dervishes were still unshaken and full of fight. An assault would probably have been costly, and it was decided to break off the action and have another try next morning, with the explosives and hand-grenades which were on their way. But the dervishes saved us further trouble by fleeing during the night.

Meanwhile, there was no news whatsoever of the supreme objective of the expedition — the Mullah. We had no idea of where he was or what he was doing. The fog of war was complete, and I was delighted to be instructed to move on Medishe to try to clear up the situation. Just as we were about to march northwards, a deserter arrived at my bivouac and reported that the Mullah, with all his following and stock, had fled in a southerly direction. We gave chase at once. This is no place for a day to day account of a pursuit which took us from near the sea to the southern border of the Protectorate, but a few episodes will illustrate a type of scallywag fighting which is unlikely to recur.

We reached a central position at Hudin, a distance of 150 miles, in 72 hours, and from there I sent out strong patrols to the east and south in a vain search for information. The subsequent route of the Camel Corps is shown on the map on page 21, but there was no authentic news of the Mullah until the morning of 9 February, when one of his many sons arrived at my bivouac at Gaolo, about twelve miles west of Tale, and reported that his father was still in the fortress, though on the point of bolting. It was a relief to have at last located our quarry, but I was upset by the prospect of his immediate flight. He was almost certain to gain a long start by making a dash for it under cover of darkness, and my animals were in no condition for a long stern chase.

Gibb, with most of his tribal levy, now joined me, and we moved on Tale in the early afternoon; but scarcely were we in the saddle, when a report arrived that the bird had flown. By the time we got to the fortress it was pitch dark, and the hard gypsum surface made it impossible to follow the tracks by moonlight. We started at dawn the next day and rode until darkness closed in. As I had feared, many of my animals could no longer keep up the pace; and in addition, several of my officers were prostrated by vomiting and violent diarrhoea as a result of the more than usually filthy water. I therefore decided to continue the pursuit with half a dozen officers and a hundred and fifty of the fittest men and animals. We set off again as soon as the moon rose. We were very hungry, and I had the good fortune to find a piece of fat in my haversack, which must have fallen out of a sandwich which I had eaten several days previously. Unappetising though it looked and smelled, I was about to put it greedily into my mouth when decency compelled me to offer a portion to my adjutant,

James Beattie, who was riding alongside. He was as grateful as if I had given him a five course champagne dinner.

On and on we rode, hour after hour, mile after mile. The country was desolate and monotonous; the sun was without pity; the constant mirage was a mockery — it distorted vision and made us expend precious energy in chasing herds of wild asses which looked from a distance like enemy horsemen. The animals were flagging, and my own little pony, for all his lion heart, kept stumbling. The officers looked gaunt and hollow-eyed. The men were listless and unusually silent. Were we becoming resigned to failure? Or were we approaching the limit of physical endurance? I found myself wondering what I ought to do if we failed to overtake the enemy by nightfall, when a sudden commotion galvanised us all into life again. Our leading patrol had pounced on a dervish picket, who reported that a large number of men, women and children were resting in a dry watercourse about a mile ahead. The general lassitude disappeared; the men became animated and cheerful; even the camels entered into the spirit of the hunt and increased their pace perceptibly. When we reached the banks of the watercourse there was a scene of wild confusion, women and children screaming blue murder and riflemen firing in all directions. The latter had been specially charged by the Mullah with the protection of his wives and children, and they died fighting. The women and children were providentially unharmed and were soon being given titbits, and even an occasional cup of very weak tea, by my starving men. There is a rough chivalry among soldiers the world over.

The next morning a party of dervishes was espied moving in a southerly direction a few miles from our camp. We gave chase and accounted for most of them, and our captives included the Mullah's favourite wife. It looked as though the old fox himself was not far off. But while we were searching for him, a scout reported the tracks of a solitary horseman accompanied by about a dozen foot-men and two camels moving southwards. This might well be the Mullah himself, and Hornby and I moved on to the new trail with twenty pony-men — all that could now move faster than a walk. It took us more than two hours to catch up our quarry, only to find that the solitary horseman was an Abyssinian of some standing, who had been in the Mullah's camp for several years and had been given a special escort to his own country. We were not aware of his identity until he, and nearly all his bodyguard, had died fighting.

We had now mopped up three different parties of the enemy. Practically the whole of the Mullah's personal following had been killed, including seven of his older sons and several close relations. The captives included five of his wives and several of his younger sons and daughters. But the Mullah himself was still at large, and there was not a vestige of a clue as to his whereabouts. We had been on half rations for a long time, had less than one day's food for man and beast, and were over fifty miles from the nearest supply dump. Only a very few of the camels could carry a load, even at walking pace. The ponies were in an even worse plight. The men were ready to go on, food or no food, but where to? We would be looking for a small needle in a large haystack. Sick at heart, I decided to give up the chase. The fittest of the camels were given to the captive women and children. The rest of us trudged through the desert to the nearest point at which food and drink were to be found. It was only sixty miles, but it seemed like six hundred. The campaign was over. The Mullah was alive,[1] but dervishism was dead and would never again rear its ugly head.

The Government must have been relieved that the Somaliland problem had at last been settled, but the operations were so utterly insignificant as to arouse little or no public interest. Thus, the field was open for the Air Ministry to peg out claims for the efficacy of independent air action which no one in Whitehall had the desire or the knowledge to question. The most sweeping of their contentions was that a handful of aeroplanes had, in twenty-one days, settled a problem which had foiled the Army for twenty-one years. There was no mention of the fact that they would have been completely impotent if they had not been supplied with up-to-date and accurate information about the whereabouts of the Mullah, and the locations of his forts, and that this information had been gained as a result of many years' fighting and patrolling by ground troops, and could not, in those days, have been obtained in any other way. Even as it was, independent air action made a very slender contribution to the success of the campaign. All who visited Tale, Jid Ali, and Medishe after the

---

[1] He fled to Abyssinian Somaliland, and died of influenza before the year was out.

aeroplanes had done their worst could scarcely detect any traces of the bombardment.

Another of the Air Ministry's claims was that their bombing utterly demoralised the dervishes. I can only say that I attacked Jid Ali almost immediately after two aeroplanes had aimed all their bombs at it, and that I found no trace of demoralisation among the garrison. On the contrary, they were cheerful, utterly defiant, and grossly slanderous about my parentage.

There was even less justification for the claim that it was air attack that forced the Mullah to flee from Medishe, and later from Tale. An examination of the relevant dates points to a very different conclusion. The RAF bombed the Medishe on 21 January and the three following days. The only result was that the Mullah and his followers moved into caves in the vicinity. The Camel Corps arrived at Jid Ali on 27 January, and on 28 the Mullah fled helter-skelter to the other end of the country. At Tale the sequence of events was much the same. The RAF bombed the fortress on 1 February and subsequent days. The Mullah never budged. But as soon as the Camel Corps arrived in the vicinity nine days after the first air attack, he bolted for Abyssinia.

While, however, there can be no doubt that the Air Staff claims in regard to these insignificant operations were ill-founded, it is quite certain that they were justified a hundredfold if they did anything to strengthen the case for an independent Air Force. One shudders to think what would have happened in the Second World War if the Admiralty and War Office had had their way and the Air Arm had again become a mere auxiliary of the older Services.

Recovery from physical fatigue is far quicker than recovery from mental strain, and after a short rest at Tale, the Camel Corps was able to return to Burao by easy stages. Beyond writing my reports, there was now nothing to keep me in Somaliland, and in April I set sail for England.

I was thankful to see the last of the country in which I had been so unhappy; how constantly unhappy I never realised until I re-read my letters to my mother. I had never ceased to try to escape. Shortly after the outbreak of war, I applied to return to my regiment. My application was not even acknowledged. In 1915 Colonel Cubitt gave me permission to spend a few weeks at Gallipoli, in order to gain experience of modern war, if I could persuade anyone on the spot to give me a job. I wrote to an old friend, Major Cecil Allanson, whose exploits were soon to become famous,[1] and he replied that his regiment, the 6th Gurkhas, would gladly take me on their strength. But before I could start, an order went out banning Gallipoli as a holiday resort. Apparently too many 'tourists' had been killed in action. Later, Cubitt and Carton de Wiart, who were both commanding brigades on the Western Front, did their best to rescue me, but were told that I could not be spared. When I was in England on leave at the end of 1916, the War Office were willing to arrange for me to spend my leave in France, provided that my 'employers,' the Colonial Office, agreed. They refused point-blank. My last attempt at escape was made in the summer of 1918. I begged to be allowed to forgo the leave which was due to me and join my regiment in Mesopotamia for a few weeks. They had had heavy casualties and were short of officers. But the Colonial Office would have none of it. They ruled that if I was well enough to fight in Mesopotamia, I was well enough to stay in Somaliland. It was evidently not understood that a man might be a hundred per cent fit physically and yet be very sick at heart. Thus I had been frustrated for over five years. Nevertheless, as I rode out of the camp at Burao for the last time, I found myself echoing the words that Rudyard Kipling put into the mouth of the old galley-slave on the day that he was given his freedom.

'But to-day I leave the galley. Shall I curse her service then?
God be thanked! Whate'er comes after, I have lived and toiled
    with Men!'

While I was at Aden awaiting passage to England, a telegram arrived offering me a nomination to the Staff College at Quetta. It was a pleasant surprise to know that anyone in authority was even aware of my existence. But the idea of the Staff College appealed to me no longer. I had had no experience of modern war; a large number of my best friends had been killed; soldiering could never be the same again; and I was seriously thinking of resigning my commission and trying a new life. I returned a polite refusal to the offer.

[1] *See* Alan Moorehead: *Gallipoli.*

CHAPTER III

Staff Training

1920–1925

O N M Y A R R I V A L in London the Medical Board before whom I was ordered to appear diagnosed me as suffering from extreme war-weariness. They gave me twelve months' leave, with instructions to report again for a check-up in four months' time.

It was wonderful to be in civilisation again, and to meet friends whom I had not seen or heard of for nearly six years. I was over-joyed to find that so many of them were still in the land of the living, and soon gave up any idea of leaving the Army. I therefore plucked up courage to tell the War Office that I would like to go to the Staff College after all, only to be informed that the vacancy which had been offered to me had already been given away, but that I could sit for the examination for the course which started in February 1922. If I could get sufficient marks to qualify — which they appeared to think unlikely — there was a good chance of my being selected.

At the end of four months I reappeared before the Medical Board. Having become engaged to be married on the previous day, I told them that I had never felt better, whereupon they pronounced me fit for immediate service. This was a blow, and I ventured to point out that I had had only one third of the leave which had been granted to me. The doctors were sympathetic, but reminded me that there was a rebellion in Mesopotamia, and that regular officers were badly needed. There was nothing for it but to bow to the inevitable.

The following month I sailed for India, and was ordered to join my regiment at Bannu on the North-West Frontier. Much as I had hoped to be sent to Mesopotamia, it would be very agreeable, I thought, to serve with my own folk again on the familiar stamping-grounds. But it was a sad homecoming. The mess was full of ghosts. Fifty per cent of the brother officers to whom I had said good-bye in 1914 had been killed, or crippled. I was the only member of the pre-war polo team who would ever sit on a horse again.

I found that there had been great changes in the conduct of frontier warfare since my early youth. In those days, the transport consisted of camels and mules, and was cut down to the barest minimum. There were no amenities, and even the hospital arrangements were primitive in the extreme. Ammunition was jealously husbanded, and only definite targets were engaged. Now there was mechanical transport in abundance, fully equipped hospitals, plentiful rations, and even luxuries like bottled beer and soda water. The ammunition supply was apparently unlimited. To the disgust of my own hard-bitten regiment, units which were new to the Frontier used to indulge in 'prophylactic' firing — that is to say, filling a hill-side with lead on the off chance that hostile tribesmen might be harbouring there. But there was no serious fighting on our part of the front, and except for a very occasional brush with small parties of the enemy, I was free to play polo in the afternoons, and read for the Staff College in the evenings.

The examination was held in Rawalpindi in February, and I had an exciting journey. At one of the stations at which we stopped during the night, I was awakened by the unmistakable angry buzz of a riot, and shrill cries of 'Gandhi Ki Jai' (Victory to Gandhi). Having been in Egypt during the troubles of 1919, when one or two British officers were pulled out of trains and beaten to death, I took the precaution of barricading my doors with suitcases, and sat up, loaded pistol in hand, until the train drew out. I was not molested.

I found the examination papers on the conduct of operations in Europe fiendishly difficult, and was awarded the minimum marks. But I found those on frontier warfare absurdly easy, and was awarded the maximum. They levelled each other out, and my name duly appeared in the list of successful candidates. In April my regiment was moved from the turbulent frontier to peaceful Rawalpindi, the Aldershot of India, and I had no compunction in applying to complete the leave which had been cut short the previous year.

On my return to England I got married. I have been 'giving thanks always' ever since.

We joined the regiment at Rawalpindi in the autumn, and I have to admit that, for the next six months, I devoted more time to polo than to soldiering. There were four or five glorious weeks at Delhi, where about twenty or more polo teams, including two or three of almost international class, such as Jodhpur and Patiala, had collected for the big tournaments.

But all good things come to an end, and in February I joined the Staff College at Quetta. For the first time since I was eighteen years old, I had no official responsibilities and was free to try to improve my education. There was a well-stocked library, ample opportunity to read, and able instructors to put us on the right lines. In addition, there was much to be learned from discussions with fellow-students, many of whom had considerable war experience. At the end of the course we were required to write a memoir, not exceeding 15,000 words in length, about our ideas on the future conduct of war. I have found it interesting to compare the predictions of my first attempt at authorship with what actually happened when war came. My thoughts on the development of air power and armoured warfare were hopelessly wrong, as was my protest against the abolition of horsed cavalry. But some of my other guesses were much nearer the mark. I was insistent, for example, that the war of the future would be *total* war. 'National war is an affair of the whole people. It demands the conversion of the whole resources of the nation into actual power, and the utilisation of that power in a unified and predetermined manner.' I also had a good deal to say about the relations between statesmen and soldiers. 'Strategy is dependent on policy to an even greater extent than in the past, because, owing to the greater compactness of the world, more numerous interests are involved . . . It is essential that the statesman and the soldier should be in the closest touch with each other, and that they should work together frankly, openly and loyally . . . The soldier must realise that war is the instrument of policy, and that, in so far as any subservience is necessary, he must be subservient to the statesman.' By the end of the year, I felt that I was a good deal better educated than before, and that I had to some extent made up for what I had missed by not having had a university training.

I now set my heart on a tour of duty in England. Nearly sixteen of my seventeen years' service had been spent abroad, more than half of them on the North-West Frontier of India or in the wastes of Somaliland. It was time to exchange the circumference for the centre. There were also family reasons. I dreaded the prospect of continual separations, and I wanted to see more of my own children than my father had ever seen of me.

For Indian Army officers of my seniority there were only three, or perhaps four, appointments in England. I would have thought myself lucky to get any of them, but no vacancy was likely to occur for some time. I therefore applied for an appointment at Army Headquarters, India, and was posted to the Quartermaster general's Branch at Simla at the beginning of 1923. The building was a monstrosity. The architect may have had in mind a Swiss sanatorium, but the result looked like rows of wooden cow sheds built higgledy-piggledy on top of each other. In the stall next to mine there worked a young lieutenant-colonel for whom a great future was prophesied. His name, which will appear again in these pages, was Auchinleck.

Army Headquarters was one of those labyrinths which have been described as 'the glory of British administration.' Headquarters Staff consisted for the most part of men who were able, experienced and devoted, but the machine as a whole was impersonal and ponderous. There were too many bulky files, and too much long-winded minute writing. Problems which might have been settled by a five-minute talk between two or three men in authority, were bandied about for weeks at the lower levels. I had an eye-opener in my very early days. My staff clerk brought me a formidable-looking file and asked me to sign a minute which read as follows: 'General Staff Branch may see.' I observed, in my ignorance, that I saw no reason why the General Staff Branch should not see the gems which the file contained, but that I could not imagine how it would benefit them, or what contribution they could make to the solution of the problem with which it dealt. He looked at me pityingly. 'We must keep the files moving, sir.'

So, as Lord Curzon once wrote, 'round and round like the diurnal revolutions of the earth went the file — stately, solemn, sure and slow.' The procedure with which it was handled was more important than the arguments which it contained, or the decision to which it ultimately led.

It was a valuable experience to see how a large headquarters worked, and to learn a new side of staff duties under able chiefs. All the same, I counted myself fortunate that I did not have to complete my four years' tour of duty. When I had done a little more than a year, Air Vice-Marshal Sir Philip Game, who was then Air Officer Commanding in India, told me that the Air Ministry had allotted a vacancy on their next Staff College course at Andover to an Indian Army officer who had already graduated at his own Staff College. He strongly advised me to apply, and I jumped at it. It would mean a year in England. My application was approved, and we were soon homeward bound.

The course at the RAF Staff College was well worth while. Apart from learning the tricks of the trade of another service and making many new friends, with some of whom I was destined to work closely in future years, it gave me the opportunity for almost unlimited flying. I had no desire to learn to be a pilot, but I wanted to be able to feel just as much at home in an aeroplane as in a motor-car. The Staff College had their own quota of machines, and I made a practice of going down to the tarmac each day and offering myself as ballast. After a flight with an exceptionally fine pilot who had performed every kind of stunt imaginable, he warned me that it was silly to fly with our fellow-students indiscriminately. I protested that they had all got wings and a chestful of decorations, but he pointed out that several of them had been sitting on office stools for a long time. They could fly all right provided nothing went wrong, but if it did, they would probably wrap me around a tree. I quickly asked him for a black list, and thereafter I used to scan it very carefully before accepting any offers of a 'flip.'

My lucky star was still in the ascendant. The same Air Vice-Marshal Game, who had advised me to go to the RAF Staff College, told me that his brother-in-law, Colonel Walker, who happened to be a friend of pre-war days, was to vacate the appointment of Assistant

Secretary of the Committee of Imperial Defence at the end of the year. He suggested that I should see him at once. I took the next train to London. Charles Walker told me that he had always intended to ask me if I would like to succeed him, and I said that there was nothing that I should like better. So it only remained for him to approach his chief, Sir Maurice Hankey. I was vetted by the great man the following day, and told that, subject to the Prime Minister's approval, I could make my plans on the assumption that I would be joining his staff in December. It seemed almost too good to be true. I went back to India with a light heart, and at the end of six months at Army Headquarters, Simla, I was summoned home again.

CHAPTER IV

The Seats of the Mighty

1925–1930

O N A cold, dull morning in December 1925, I reported for duty at the offices of the Cabinet and Committee of Imperial Defence. Before I left for home that evening, I realised only too clearly that my new work bore no resemblance to anything that I had ever done before. I felt like a new boy at school, but I had the consolation of knowing that I would be learning the business under a past master. Sir Maurice Hankey, though still under fifty, already enjoyed an international reputation. He had started life in the Royal Marine Artillery, and had come to the notice of Admiral Lord Fisher when serving as a captain in the Mediterranean Fleet in about 1906. At that time the Committee of Imperial Defence was still in its infancy and having teething troubles. But Lord Fisher, realising its potentialities, dashed off a characteristic letter to Colonel Seely, then Secretary of State for War. It ran something like this: 'There is a captain of Marines called Hankey serving in the Mediterranean Fleet. He has a large forehead bulging with brains. He has been created by God Almighty for the express discomfiture of Kaiser Wilhelm II. Get him to the CID as soon as you can.' Hankey was duly appointed Assistant Secretary in 1908, and four years later he succeeded Admiral Sir Charles Ottley as

Secretary. He was therefore in that key post on the outbreak of the First World War. Throughout the war he was at the right hand of successive Prime Ministers, and when Mr Lloyd George set up a small War Cabinet, Hankey was the automatic choice for secretary. This was the first time in history that anyone other than a Minister had been allowed to attend Cabinet meetings. It was also the first time that any official records of those meetings were kept. When the war was over and peace terms were being discussed by the 'Big Three' of those days — President Wilson, Monsieur Clemenceau and Mr Lloyd George — Hankey was the only outsider present at their meetings. 'He knew everything; he could put his hand on anything; he said nothing; he gained the confidence of all.'[1] He became the sole recorder of the conclusions of the triumvirate.

When, in 1919, the War Cabinet was replaced by a peace Cabinet of normal size, and the CID reverted to a peace footing under its maiden name, Hankey was appointed Secretary to both bodies. As though that were not enough for this great glutton for work, he became Clerk of the Privy Council in 1923. Working under him was a wonderful training. He had a phenomenal memory, infinite tact, and tireless industry, and I can never be sufficiently grateful for all that he taught me.

Our office was situated in Whitehall Gardens — a cul-de-sac off Whitehall — and consisted of three private houses, rich in historical associations. No. 2 had been the home of Disraeli, and No. 3 that of Sir Robert Peel. Hankey's room, in which so many fateful meetings were held, used to be Disraeli's drawing-room, until the steep stairs proved too much for his gout. The gilt mirrors and the rather vulgar paintings of fat-tummied cherubim and pop-eyed fishes were exactly as he had left them; and in the garden below there still survived the mullberry tree beneath which King Charles II is alleged to have made love to Nell Gwyn.

Although within a stone's throw of Whitehall, it seemed far removed from the hurly-burly of that very official thoroughfare, and the atmosphere was as unlike that of a Government office as it was possible to be. The intimacy of the surroundings was matched by the diminutive size of the staff. The Military Secretariat of the Committee of Imperial Defence consisted of Hankey, who was a host in himself, and

[1] Winston S. Churchill: *The World Crisis: The Aftermath.*

four assistants, Commander Hermon-Hodge of the Royal Navy,[1] Lieutenant Colonel Macready[2] of the British Army, Wing Commander Norman Leslie of the Royal Air Force, and myself. The contrast between my new job and the job that I had just vacated in India was striking. It was like joining a small but highly prosperous family business after working in a mammoth publicly-owned multiple store. I was well content with the change.

From this point my narrative will include frequent references to the Committee of Imperial Defence, and the time has come to explain the origin of an institution which was destined to revolutionise the system of government control in peace as well as in war.

The conduct of the South African war at the beginning of this century brought little credit on the Government, and the War Office bore the brunt of the blame. Accordingly, when the war was over, a committee was set up under the chairmanship of Lord Esher to consider the reconstitution of that department. This committee quickly put their fingers on the weak spot in our armour. They pointed out that there were 'no means for co-ordinating defence problems or for dealing with them as a whole.' They suggested that apart from any question of War Office reform it was essential to set up machinery which could obtain and co-ordinate 'for the use of the Cabinet, all information and expert advice required for the shaping of national policy in war, and for determining the necessary preparations in peace.' They added that 'such information and advice must necessarily embrace not only the sphere of the War Office but also the sphere of the Admiralty and other Offices of State.'

The machinery which they recommended was a committee whose business it would be to advise the Cabinet on national and imperial defence in all its ramifications. It was to be of a novel and ingenious character. The Prime Minister was to be its 'invariable president' and to have 'absolute discretion in the selection or variation of its members.' Thus he would be free to invite anyone whose qualifications and experience were desired to take part in the Committee's deliberations — Ministers of the Crown, Service Chiefs, Civil Servants, members of the Opposition, representatives of the Dominions, in-

---

[1] Afterwards Rear Admiral the Honorable Claude Hermon-Hodge.
[2] Afterwards Lieutenant General Sir Gordon Macready, Bart.

dustrialists, 'Uncle Tom Cobley and all.' The committee was to be purely advisory and to have no executive authority whatsoever. Thus the constitutional responsibility of the Cabinet for deciding national policy, and the individual responsibilities of Government Departments for executive action in their respective spheres, would be unimpaired. At the same time, it goes without saying that the advice of a committee which was presided over by the Prime Minister, and whose meetings were attended by the Ministers primarily responsible for defence, and by the senior Service Chiefs, was likely to be accepted. There was to be a small permanent secretariat to maintain the records and secure continuity. This, as it turned out, proved to be the keystone of the whole edifice.

The Government approved the Esher Committee's recommendation, and the Committee of Imperial Defence was brought into being in May 1904. Like most innovations, it came in for a good deal of criticism at first, and it might have perished in its infancy if the then Prime Minister, Mr Balfour, had not been its stalwart champion. His first step was to nominate a panel of Ministers and officials who would receive all papers and attend all meetings; and this practice was followed by his successors. The membership of this hard core varied from time to time, in accordance with the personalities of the moment, but it always included the Ministers who were specially concerned with defence problems, such as the Secretaries of State for Foreign Affairs, Home Affairs, the Colonies, and War, the First Lord of the Admiralty, the Chancellor of the Exchequer, and the professional heads of the Navy and Army. Thus, for the first time, we find statesmen and Service Chiefs meeting regularly round the same table for the discussion of defence problems.

The Committee met once a week, and more often if necessary. In addition to advising the Cabinet on current defence questions, as and when they arose, they instituted enquiries into the manifold problems which would arise in the event of war with Germany. What were the risks of invasion? How large an army could the Germans land on our shores? What forces would be required to meet the threat? Should we intervene on the continent of Europe? If so, what should be the size of our expeditionary force? What was to be our naval strategy? How was blockade to be exercised? How were our military requirements affected by the need to defend India, Egypt, and so forth?

What arrangements were to be made for the control of enemy aliens and protection against sabotage? How could censorship of communications and of the Press be enforced from the moment war was declared? What was to be the policy as regards the treatment of neutral and enemy shipping? These and a hundred and one other problems were remitted to expert sub-committees for examination and report. Some of these were established on a permanent basis; others were appointed *ad hoc* and dissolved when their enquiries had been completed. Armed with all these reports, the Committee of Imperial Defence laid down the policy which should govern our action in all foreseen eventualities; and on that basis the Government Departments and the sub-committees concerned proceeded to make detailed plans and preparations covering a vast field.

In August 1914, ten years after the Committee's birth, its work was put to the supreme test. That it emerged from the ordeal with credit is clear from the Official History of Naval Operations: 'Among the many false impressions that prevailed, when after the lapse of a century we found ourselves involved in a great war, not the least erroneous is the belief that we were not prepared for it. Whether the scale on which we prepared was as large as the signs of the times called for, whether we did right to cling to our long-tried system of a small army and a large navy, are questions that will long be debated; but, given the scale which we deliberately chose to adopt, there is no doubt that the machinery for setting our forces in action had reached an ordered completeness in detail that has no parallel in our history.' [1]

The Admiralty, War Office and other Departments had done admirable work, but these results could not have been achieved without the initiative and central co-ordination of the Committee of Imperial Defence. Our country owes a deep debt to Lord Esher for having conceived the idea of the Committee, to Lord Balfour for having given it birth and to Lord Hankey for the uncanny foresight and measureless industry with which he nurtured it.

Far-sighted though the Committee had been, there were several problems which had not been thought out beforehand. For example, there were no preconceived plans for the provision of adequate reinforcements to the Army, with the result that 'our fighting strength did

[1] Julian Corbett: *Official History: Naval Operations.*

not reach its high-water mark until January 1917,'[1] i.e. two and a half years after the outbreak of war. Nor were there any plans for the conversion of industry to war purposes, with the result that it was not until the Battle of the Somme in June 1916 that the output of artillery ammunition became approximately adequate. Nor had it been foreseen that Cabinet control of the war could not be effective without a considerable reorganisation of the machinery of government. The reasons for these omissions are not far to seek. In the past, wars had been waged by professional navies, and armies, while the rest of the nation went about their ordinary peace-time avocations scarcely aware that hostilities were in progress. It was not sufficiently recognised that the impending war against Germany would be an affair of the whole people; nor had it been anticipated that it would last for over four years. On the contrary, the General Staff had calculated that the decisive battle would start on the nineteenth day after mobilisation, and that whichever side lost that battle, might be able to carry on a 'broken back' war for six months or so, but no longer. Many of the principal officers at the War Office, in their anxiety not to miss the fighting altogether, managed to get permission to leave their posts on the outbreak of war, and rush off to France. The chaos which this exodus caused in War Office administration may be imagined.

At the outset, the supreme control of the war was exercised by the Cabinet of twenty-one Ministers. It 'was too large to meet day in and day out, and too cumbrous to be called together rapidly at short notice. It did not work to an agenda and had no secretary and no records. Ministers sometimes misapprehended the decisions, and the staffs of the Admiralty and War Office and the Civil Service Chiefs were often in the dark as to what had been decided and what action they had to take.'[2]

After four months of confusion, Mr Asquith set up a body known as the War Council. Its composition and procedural methods were much the same as those of the Committee of Imperial Defence which it replaced. The main difference between the two was that the War Council had a limited measure of executive authority. At the same

[1] Lord Haig's Despatches.
[2] Lord Hankey: *Government Control in War*. Given as the Lees Knowles Lecture, 1945, and afterwards published in book form by Cambridge University Press.

time, Mr Asquith, in his insistence on maintaining the collective responsibility of the Cabinet, ordained that if the War Council proposed any major change in policy, the approval of the Cabinet must be obtained before it became effective. Later the War Council was replaced by the Dardanelles Committee, which, in its turn, gave way to a body known as the War Committee. Each of these was an improvement on its predecessor, but the fatal weakness of divided responsibility persisted.

Criticism of the higher direction of our war effort became increasingly vociferous and widespread, and in the Cabinet itself there was serious dissension. Towards the end of 1916, Mr Asquith fell from power, and Mr Lloyd George reigned in his stead. His first act was to combine the functions of the Cabinet and the War Committee into a smaller body known as the War Cabinet. This originally consisted of the Prime Minister (chairman) and four other Ministers, none of whom, with the exception of Mr Bonar Law, Chancellor of the Exchequer, had a Department to administer. It had full powers of decision, and henceforward no other Ministers of the Crown had any share in collective Cabinet responsibility for the conduct of the war. It was served by the Secretariat of the Committee of Imperial Defence, enlarged as required; and the procedural methods of that body were substituted for those of the peace-time Cabinet. Thus, Hankey himself, and such assistant or assistants as he required, were present at War Cabinet meetings and kept the records. Ministers who were not members of the War Cabinet were invited to attend those discussions in which their Departments were particularly concerned, and were allowed to bring their senior officials with them. The Chiefs of Staff of the Fighting Services were invited when military questions were under consideration.

The system was still far from perfect. There was no recognised machinery by which the War Cabinet could receive military advice, using the word 'military' in its broadest sense to embrace all the Fighting Services; nor was there any machinery for forward planning. Nevertheless, it was a vast improvement on anything which we had had before, and it carried us to victory.

It is astonishing that any machinery of supreme control should have been effective when one thinks of the deplorable disunity which prevailed in high places. According to the diaries and memoirs of some

of the leading personalities of those days, there were constant quarrels among Ministers, and there was no love lost between some of the
military chiefs. The politicians and soldiers regarded each other with
deep-seated mistrust and dislike, and treated each other with neither
consideration nor loyalty. To the Service Chiefs, their political masters
were 'frocks'; to the politicians, the generals and admirals were 'brass
hats.' Odious terms. We have it on the highest authority that a house
divided against itself cannot stand, and the abiding truth of that dic-
tum has been impressed upon me in diverse ways all my life. But no-
where can lack of unity be more fatal than in the machinery for the
supreme control of a war. A country may have powerful armed
forces, led by brilliant commanders; it may have statesmen of great
competence; it may have a civil population which is disciplined and
resolute; it may have immense wealth; it may have industries which
are most efficiently organised; but unless the statesmen and soldiers
at the summit work together in a spirit of mutual esteem, the essential
co-ordination between all these diverse elements of strength will be
lacking, and there is bound to be a deadly waste of blood and treasure. From my earliest days with the Committee of Imperial Defence,
I used to pray that if we ever got involved in a major war again, the
bitter animosities which had darkened counsel in the years 1914-18
would not recur. My prayer was answered when the time came.

In November 1919 the War Cabinet was replaced by a peace
Cabinet of the normal size, and the Committee of Imperial Defence
was revived in its original form. For the next few years there was no
lack of current problems to occupy their minds — the rebellion in
Iraq, the Chanak crisis, the creation of a base at Singapore, disarmament conferences, garrisons for the mandated territories, and a hundred and one other other matters. But in addition to the problems
which called for immediate attention, it was the responsibility of the
Committee of Imperial Defence to look ahead, and recast the defensive preparations which had proved so successful on the outbreak of
the First World War, in the light of the experiences of 1914-18 and the
changed conditions of the time. The atmosphere was not exactly favourable for studies of that kind. Everyone was war-weary. No one
could believe that, after all the world had just suffered, there would be
another convulsion within twenty-one years. There was no potential
aggressor in sight, and the idea of wasting time and energy on defen-

sive preparations was repugnant. Nevertheless it was important to make a start while those with first-hand experience of war conditions were still available.

The problems which confronted the post-war Committee of Imperial Defence were more far-reaching, complex and varied than those with which their predecessors had had to deal. Before 1914, war between sovereign powers had been regarded as the almost exclusive business of the Fighting Services. It had now been established that it was an affair of whole populations. Before 1914, our insularity, combined with our naval superiority, had justified us in assuming that we would have a time margin after the outbreak of war in which to organise our latent strength. Now, owing to the advent of air power, we no longer had the shield of time; we had got to be at immediate readiness. Before 1914, there had been only two Fighting Services, and there had been a clear-cut division of responsibility between them. Now the creation of a third Service had blurred all frontiers, and rendered the business of co-ordination at once more essential and more complex. Before 1914 the great civilian Departments of State had been only slightly concerned with national preparedness for war. Now the responsibilities of some of them were almost as great and varied as those of the Service Departments.

The Committee of Imperial Defence proceeded to resurrect those pre-war sub-committees which were still appropriate, and to set up such new ones as were deemed necessary. The only one of the latter that calls for special mention at this stage is the Chiefs of Staff Sub-Committee, which was brought into being in 1924. The chairman of the CID, i.e. the Prime Minister, was *ex officio* chairman, and the other members were the three Chiefs of Staff. As a general rule, however, the Chiefs of Staff met alone, with one of their own number, designated by the Prime Minister, in the chair. On assuming his appointment every new Chief of Staff was given a warrant signed by the Prime Minister which emphasised the collective character of his responsibilities in unequivocal terms: 'In addition to the functions of the Chiefs of Staff as advisers on questions of sea, land or air policy respectively to their own Board or Council, each of the three Chiefs of Staff will have an individual and collective responsibility for advising *on defence policy as a whole*,[1] the three constituting, as it were, a

[1] Author's italics.

super-chief of a War Staff in Commission.' Thus, for the first time in our history, we had recognised machinery for close and continuous consultation between the Fighting Services, for tendering collective advice to the Cabinet on defence problems as a whole, for the preparation of long-term military plans in time of peace; and, in the event of war, for acting as a battle headquarters.

We have become so accustomed to regarding the Chiefs of Staff Organisation as an integral and indispensable feature of our defence machinery that it is difficult to realise that it has existed only since 1924, and that it was not until very much later that it was provided with effective planning and intelligence staffs.

For the first few years of their existence, the Chiefs of Staff were not exactly a band of brothers. Inter-Service co-operation had never come their way, and each of them was intent on fighting for his own corner. I have a vivid recollection of a meeting at which I was acting for Hankey, when tempers got so heated and language so unrestrained, that I thought it discreet for a mere major to withdraw. However, a very different atmosphere soon grew up.

The title of my appointment — Assistant Secretary to the Committee of Imperial Defence — conveyed very little to most of my friends. Some of them thought that I had a big say in defence policy. They were entirely wrong. Others thought that I was leading a pleasant, idle life in England. They too were very wide of the mark. Never in my life had I had to work so hard or so fast. This perhaps is the place for a brief explanation. The four Assistant Secretaries were exactly what the title implies — assistants to Hankey. Our responsibilities were identical in character. We were all co-equal, and worked as a close-knit team. We all had direct access to everyone from the Prime Minister downwards. It was a strange experience to find oneself dealing directly with generals and admirals, instead of having to do this through all the recognised channels of the military hierarchy.

Our responsibilities fell into two broad categories. First, there was the day to day business. As soon as a problem appeared on the agenda of the CID, Hankey used to allot it to whichever of the Assistant Secretaries he thought the most suitable, or the least preoccupied at the time. It was the duty of the officer selected to attend the meeting at which the item in question was considered. If the Committee disposed of it at a single meeting, he had only to keep the record of the discussion and draft the conclusions. Frequently however it transpired that further study was required, and the matter was remitted to an *ad hoc* sub-committee for examination and report. In that event it was the responsibility of the Assistant Secretary concerned to take secretarial charge of the sub-committee, to arrange its meetings, see that members had the necessary documentation, keep the records, and finally draft the report for the Committee's consideration. Later in this account I will give examples of some of the more interesting problems that fell to my lot.

The second category of our work was to perform the secretarial duties for the numerous standing sub-committees which were engaged on long-term plans and preparations. In this field, we were expected to do much more than arrange business, maintain records, and draft reports. We had to supply the drive, initiate new ideas, and ensure that there was no overlapping with other committees. The chart on page 55, showing those which were in being when I joined the CID, gives an idea of the field which was being covered. Hankey divided the work between us as he thought fit, and to me fell the Sub-Committees on Censorship and War Emergency Legislation, the Principal Supply Officers Committee and its many subsidiaries, and the Sub-Committee on the Co-ordination of Departmental Action on the outbreak of war.

The Censorship Committee requires little explanation. It was their business to draft and keep up to date the regulations for enforcing postal, cable, wireless, telephonic and press censorship the moment war broke out, and to ear-mark the staffs who would be responsible for implementing these regulations, when the time came.

The business of the War Emergency Legislation Committee can also be explained in a few words. It was to ascertain all the special regulations which might be required in time of war and to have them drafted in legal language, so that they could be enacted by order-in-command, as and when the situation required. Lord Haldane, although a member of the Opposition, was Chairman — and an extremely enthusiastic one.

The Principal Supply Officers Committee was the most complicated and far-reaching of all my charges. The Chairman was the President of the Board of Trade (Sir Philip Cunliffe-Lister[1]) and the members

[1] Afterwards Earl of Swinton.

were the Principal Supply Officers of the three Service Departments
and a representative of the Board of Trade. The Committee was required first to ascertain the sum total of national requirements in a
major war in terms of raw materials and productive capacity; secondly, to determine how far these requirements could be met from
existing resources; and finally to make recommendations as to how all
the shortages which became apparent could be made good. It was a
tall order and involved the Secretary in the oddest investigations. In
the morning he might find himself listening to a group of experts engaged in discussing how to secure sufficient walnut wood for the man-
ufacture of rifle stocks: and the same afternoon he might find himself
listening to another group discussing what should be done to ensure a
sufficient supply of optical glass for the apparently unlimited war-time
requirements of the Services. It was a far cry from the days when a
morning was sometimes spent in an affray with border raiders, and an
afternoon playing polo.

Standardisation was one of the favourite expedients for simplifying
the supply problem. But it was difficult to induce the three Services to
agree to use the same pattern of anything, even of those simple stores
which were in common use, such as kitchen utensils, hardware, crockery, blankets, etc. A number of sub-committees were set up to deal
with each of these groups. I recall that the Chairman of the Hardware
Sub-Committee had a pretty wit. On learning that the Admiralty, War
Office and Air Ministry each had their own special pattern of hair-
brush, tooth-brush, clothes-brush, nail-brush, and broom, he secured
a specimen of each and laid them out side by side on tables in the
Committee Room. Before the discussion started, he casually picked
up a clothes-brush and handed it to the Admiralty representative,
saying, 'This seems to be a pretty good article. Surely it would
suit everyone.' The Admiralty representative, determined not to be
bounced, answered with some assurance, 'It won't do for the Navy.'
He looked a little abashed when the Chairman said, 'Well, it happens
to be the Navy's.' After that, matters went a little more smoothly; but
to this day the Services still cling jealously to many of their own
favourites.

The Committee for the Co-ordination of Departmental Action on
the Outbreak of War was responsible for seeing that all plans and
preparations made by Government Departments or sub-committees of

CABINET

COMMITTEE OF IMPERIAL DEFENCE 1926

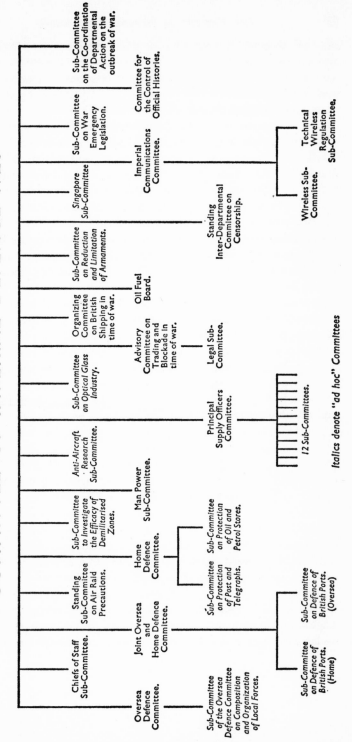

Italics denote "ad hoc" Committees

the CID to meet the eventuality of war, were incorporated under appropriate headings in a document known as the War Book. The purpose of this Book was to ensure that, if relations became strained or war broke out with a foreign power, every Department knew not only what it had to do itself, but also what other Departments were doing. Every order, letter, and telegram, every set of instructions, every piece of legislation was drafted and kept ready for issue. The Book which had proved so supremely useful on the outbreak of the First World War now needed to take into account several new features and several new problems, such for example as the creation of an independent Air Force, the necessity to include arrangements for civil defence, and the mobilisation of man-power and industry. To have continued to use the Book in its original form would have been like putting new wine into an old bottle, and my first act was to suggest the setting up of a small sub-committee to undertake the necessary revision. This was done.

In 1926, when I was still far from familiar with my new job, all long-term planning was abruptly interrupted. For some months past, a general strike had become increasingly probable, and in Whitehall numerous committees had been busily engaged in devising measures to keep the life of the country going in the event of such an emergency. How was public transport — the railways, the tubes, the buses — to be kept running? How was food to be cleared from the docks, and distributed? How were law and order to be maintained? By mid April the tragedy became imminent, and the Nation was seemingly rent in twain. On the one side were those who were going to strike, and on the other were those who were determined to break it. Many of my old friends seemed to be friends no longer. The cheerful greeting which I usually received from the conductor of my homeward-bound bus each evening was replaced by a sullen look. No longer did he ask me whether I had backed the winner of the 3 o'clock race; no longer was I regaled with stories of his experiences on the Somme, or at Ypres. I had been sent to Coventry. It was a hateful and unnatural situation. How would it end? Might there be civil war?

My vision of gloom was dissipated the moment that I emerged from my house on Campden Hill on the first morning of the strike. Kensington High Street was congested with every known type of vehicle — large opulent motor-cars with passengers perched on the roofs, small motor-cars of ancient vintage carrying half a dozen persons instead of the two for which they had been designed; horse-drawn vehicles of every kind; donkey-carts filled to overflowing: and even ancient two-seated pedal bicycles. Everyone was good-tempered, cheerful and extraordinarily helpful. The British public had evidently decided that, however much sympathy they might feel for the strikers' cause, they were not going to be coerced by unconstitutional methods. The traffic was moving at snail's pace, and it was quicker to walk the two miles to the office. Some of the staff had been told that, owing to the difficulty of providing transport for them, they need not attend until the strike was over; but, by the time I arrived, most of them had managed to turn up, including an aged messenger, who had been highly indignant at the idea that the office could carry on without him. He had walked six miles and was in a state of collapse.

It was difficult to take much interest in problems of industrial mobilisation, censorship and the like, and I felt at a loose end. There was an acute shortage of police, and I thought of asking for permission to enrol for part-time duty as a special constable. But I was soon to have a chance of more interesting work, and incidentally of having personal dealings for the first time in my life with Mr Winston Churchill.

On the third morning of the strike Hankey told me, on his return from a meeting of the Cabinet, that a committee had been set up to examine whether, and if so, how, the Territorial Army could be employed on police duties. It was to consist of Churchill, Chancellor of the Exchequer; Joynson-Hicks, Home Secretary; and Worthington-Evans, Secretary of State for War; and I was to be the Secretary. The first meeting was to be at 3 P.M. that day in Mr Churchill's room in the House of Commons.

The Committee duly assembled and Churchill put everyone at their ease at once. 'I have done your job for four years, Jix, and yours for two, Worthy, so I had better unfold my plan.' Whereupon he propounded the eminently sensible idea of asking territorial battalions, particularly those in London, to volunteer en bloc as auxiliary police. They would be paid at military rates, and given a reasonable subsistence allowance in lieu of rations. They would not be used individually, but in formed bodies; and they would have arm-bands instead of uniform, and truncheons instead of rifles. Joynson-Hicks intervened to enquire where the money for this extra expenditure was to come

from. The Home Office, he said, had no funds available. 'The Exchequer will pay,' retorted Churchill. 'If we start arguing about petty details, we will have a tired-out police force, a dissipated army and
bloody revolution.' Having delivered himself of that broadside, he
charged into the room of his secretary — who, at that time, was
P. J. Grigg[1] — taking me with him, and proceeded to dictate the so-
called conclusions of the committee in a voice which could certainly
be overheard by the Labour Party Opposition which happened to be
meeting in the next room. We then returned to his colleagues, and I
was told to read out the conclusions, as if I had been the draftsman.
They were immediately accepted, and Worthington-Evans undertook
to assemble a War Office committee at once to work out the details.
Churchill dismissed me with an injunction to attend the meeting, and
make sure that the scheme was announced by the BBC that night without fail. The War Office gripped the business with efficiency and
despatch; and, in spite of a rear-guard action by the financial adviser,
who tried unsuccessfully to whittle down the proposed subsistence allowance, full details were broadcast just before midnight.

I had no means of transport and was delighted to be told that a car
from the War Office pool would be available to take me home. I was
less delighted when I was confronted by an extremely small racy-
looking car and an extremely youthful driver. He cut short my apolo-
gies for turning him out at such an unearthly hour by saying that he
loved it; and away we went with an ear-splitting roar. We seldom did
less than sixty miles an hour; but the streets were deserted, and I got
home safely. Before leaving, my Jehu confided to me that he aspired
to the job of delivering the *British Gazette*[2] in Yorkshire, or even
farther afield; he could then really 'get cracking'! Secure in the knowledge that I would not again have to serve as ballast, I undertook to put
in a good word for him if I got an opportunity.

The strike ended after about ten days; and next morning I was able
to report to Mr Churchill at 11, Downing Street that all the Territorials
had been released from their voluntary duties, and all claims settled.
It had been a thrilling experience to see him in action, and I hoped

[1] Later Sir James Grigg, Secretary of State for War 1942-45.
[2] All newspapers ceased to be published during the strike, and the Government issued its own daily paper called the *British Gazette*. Mr Churchill was
particularly active in this venture.

that I might have a chance of serving him again. It was close on fourteen years before my hope was realised.

With the end of the strike we returned to the daily routine. I went full steam ahead on my standing committees, and in addition a current problem or two came my way in most weeks. A catalogue of these has no place in this narrative, but two or three examples may be given.

I will start with the question of the garrison at Aden. With no aggressor in sight, expenditure on defence was cut to the bone, and the Services were engaged in fighting each other to get the largest possible slice for themselves. The Royal Air Force were spreading their wings with a vengeance. 'Navies are obsolete, and the armies of the future will be aerodrome guards,' was a doctrine once propounded by a very high-ranking officer of the Royal Air Force in my hearing. The RAF claimed that in twenty-one days air power had solved the Somaliland problem, which had baffled the Army for twenty-one years. This claim was wholly untenable,[1] but the campaign was so utterly insignificant compared to the convulsion that had preceded it, that no one took the trouble to enquire into the facts. In 1921, the RAF had, with the backing of Mr Churchill, then Secretary of State for the Colonies, taken over from the Army the responsibility for garrisoning Iraq; and so far everything seemed to be going well there. The Air Staff now cast covetous eyes on Aden, and circulated a memorandum to the CID proposing that in future the RAF should be responsible for its defence. The Admiralty and the War Office were up in arms at once. The Admiralty claimed that Aden was an important naval base, and that it would be at the mercy of the Japanese Navy unless it was defended by coast-defence guns. The Army protested that the Imam of Sanaa, whose following amounted to a couple of thousand men, clad in loin-cloths and armed chiefly with flint-locks, would be able to overrun the place unless there were troops on the ground to stop them. In due course all these papers came before the CID. Churchill, always on the look-out for economies, was present. As a matter of fact he rarely missed a CID meeting, even if there was nothing on the agenda which directly affected the Treasury; and he was nearly always entertaining. After the representatives of the three Services had explained and amplified their papers, Churchill intervened. He pointed out that

[1] See page 35.

the distance from Tokyo to Aden was a matter of six or seven thousand miles, and dwelt upon a few of the risks which a Japanese Fleet would run in the course of their long voyage. Did anyone seriously imagine that the attempt would be made? Having demolished the Admiralty case to his own complete satisfaction, he proceeded to deal with the apprehensions of the War Office. 'And now I turn from the Mikado to the Imam,' was his opening gambit. There was no need for further argument. The committee disposed of the case in a single session. The Air Force had won.

The next problem which I have selected for mention took a matter of months to settle. It was the most interesting, important and difficult assignment which fell to my lot. From time immemorial, a Russian advance on India through Afghanistan had been regarded as the greatest and most probable threat to the Indian Empire; and after our little war with the Afghans in 1919, there were ominous signs of Russia's increasing interest in that country, notably the grant of a million rouble subsidy and the setting up of consulates in places where none had been before. It seemed that they might be paving the way for an encroachment into Afghan territory, or even perhaps an occupation of, say, the Northern Provinces. His Majesty's Government had to decide what they should do in order to ensure the predominance of British influence in Afghanistan, and what policy they ought to adopt in the event of a Russian violation of Afghan integrity. Should or should not the crossing of the Oxus be regarded as a *casus belli?* If not, what were the limits to be set on a Russian advance?

The Committee of Imperial Defence were asked for advice, and set up a powerful sub-committee to examine the whole problem. Lord Birkenhead, then Secretary of State for India, was chairman, and the members included Sir Austen Chamberlain, Lord Salisbury, Lord Balfour, Mr Winston Churchill, the three Chiefs of Staff, and Field Marshal Sir Claud Jacob, Military Secretary at the India Office. The committee met regularly for several weeks, and everyone who had experience which might contribute to the discussions was invited to give their views. First came Lord Reading, who had recently been Viceroy of India. Lord Haig, who had devoted considerable thought to the Russian problem when Chief of the General Staff in India, came all the way from Bemersyde to attend a meeting. Strange to relate, this was the first occasion on which his advice had been sought by any Government since he relinquished the appointment of Commander-in-Chief of the Armies in France. I got the impression that he was gratified. Instead of allowing me to wait upon him, he insisted on calling at my office an hour before the meeting was due to start, and he gave me two lengthy documents to read. One was a paper on the Russian problem, which he had written when he was in India: the other was the statement which he proposed to make to the committee. He said that he hoped that he would be allowed to speak without interruptions from Ministers. Could I drop a hint to the chairman?

On our way to the meeting, we passed the Cenotaph. It was covered with wreaths of poppies. Lord Haig looked at them — a little wistfully — and told me that when he first suggested an annual Poppy Day, he had been advised that it would have no popular appeal. He had therefore given his personal guarantee against a loss. 'Last year we got over a million pounds,' he added. As he entered the committee room, everyone rose to their feet. It was a spontaneous and graceful tribute to a commander who had led to overwhelming victory the largest army which the British Empire had ever placed in the field, but who had not always received the greatest consideration from his political masters.

Other expert witnesses were Sir Francis Humphrys, then Ambassador to Afghanistan, and Sir Esmond Ovey, formerly *chargé d'affaires* in Moscow. Among the papers circulated for the committee's consideration were two military appreciations by the British and Indian General Staffs respectively, and the conclusions which they reached were diametrically opposite. So far as I remember, the British General Staff thought that we should regard any significant violation of Afghan territory as a *casus belli*. The Indian General Staff, on the other hand, felt strongly that we should not go to war until and unless the Russian Armies had advanced as far as the Hindu Kush. Lord Birkenhead's comment was characteristic and illuminating. 'I am not in the least embarrassed by the fact that we are confronted with diametrically opposite advice from our expert advisers. Judges are constantly faced with comparable difficulties, and I have no hesitation in saying that, in my judgment, the British General Staff are right and the Indian General Staff are wrong.' The committee were in agreement with him.

There remained another difficult problem. Should we, or should we not, announce our policy in advance? If we did not do so, it could have no deterrent effect on Russia. If on the other hand we did so, Amanullah, the ruler of Afghanistan, might be deliberately provocative to the Russians in the knowledge that we were committed to go to his support. We would in fact be surrendering the issues of peace or war with the Soviet to the incalculable actions of an unscrupulous potentate. In the event, it was decided that no announcement should be made. I was instructed to draft the report on the basis of these two major decisions. It took me the best part of a fortnight.

The Defence of India Sub-Committee remained in being and discussed some of the organisational problems which would arise in the event of a war in Afghanistan. They decided, among other things, that the command of operations beyond the borders of India should be entrusted to a separate Commander-in-Chief appointed for the purpose, and should not be left with the Commander-in-Chief in India, who had other far-reaching responsibilities. It was of course recognised that the officer who happened to be Commander-in-Chief in India when the war broke out might be the best man to take command of the operations, but in that event he would give up his appointment as Commander-in-Chief, India, and be succeeded by another officer. In addition, it was agreed that the new Commander-in-Chief should have a staff entirely separate from Army Headquarters, India. Although this decision related to the North-West Frontier of India, the principle was equally applicable to the North-East Frontier. Nevertheless, when the occasion arose, it was neglected.[1]

My last example of day to day problems produced a situation which is probably unique. In 1930, Mr Ramsay MacDonald's Cabinet were confronted with one of the periodic agitations for the construction of a Channel tunnel. The question was referred to the Committee of Imperial Defence, who, as a first step, set up an expert sub-committee to study the military and economic implications of the project. When their report was ready, copies were sent, on Mr Ramsay Mac-Donald's instructions, to Lord Balfour, Mr Lloyd George and Mr Baldwin, accompanied by an invitation to attend the meeting of the Committee of Imperial Defence at which it was to be discussed. All

[1] See pages 309-310.

three accepted. A fortnight later there was a unique gathering at 2, Whitehall Gardens — a Labour Prime Minister, two Tory ex-Prime Ministers, and a Liberal ex-Prime Minister, sitting round the same table and applying their collective wisdom and experience to the solution of the same problem. It may be recorded, as a matter of historical interest, that they unanimously agreed that the construction of the tunnel should not be allowed.

In the winter of 1930, my five years at 2, Whitehall Gardens came to an end. It had been a very rewarding experience. My horizon had been considerably extended. I had acquired a good working knowledge of the machinery of government, and of the parts played by the great Departments of State. I had learnt much about the conduct and requirements of total war. I had worked at close quarters with some of the best brains in the land, both ministerial and official. In the past I had always regarded the politician as a man with few principles and little thought of anything but vote-catching and his own career. After seeing many Ministers in action for five years, my views underwent a change. The variety of tasks which I had had to tackle had given me confidence in myself, and my ability to express myself in speech and writing had greatly improved. Above all, I had made a host of new friends, many of whom were to be my colleagues in the days of trial which lay ahead.

I should not have liked to have been leaving the centre of affairs, if there had been any excitements in prospect, but the international sky was still almost cloudless. It is true that the spirit of Locarno had somewhat evaporated, that the Allied Control Commission had been withdrawn from Berlin, and that Germany under the Weimar régime was strongly suspected of having begun to rearm. Nevertheless our relative strength *vis-à-vis* Germany was so overwhelming that no one could seriously imagine that she would present any serious danger to us in the foreseeable future. I realised, too, that I was very tired of office work; and the prospect of spending less time at a desk and more time on a horse was attractive. All in all, I left the Committee of Imperial Defence in December 1930 with few regrets, the more so because Hankey had told me in confidence that I would probably be required to serve there again.

CHAPTER V

The Early Thirties

1930–1936

J U S T before I left Whitehall Gardens I was notified that the command of my own regiment would not be vacant for a couple of years, and that I was being transferred to the 12th (Sam Browne's) Cavalry, Frontier Force, with a view to taking over command almost at once. It was a wrench to leave the regiment which I had regarded as my second home for nearly a quarter of a century. But Sam Browne's Cavalry were old friends, and I looked forward to soldiering with troops again. However it was not to be. Scarcely had I been fitted for my new uniform, when I was offered the appointment of Military Secretary to Lord Willingdon, who was shortly leaving for India to succeed Lord Irwin as Viceroy. It was an attractive offer in many ways, but acceptance meant that I would never command a regiment in peace, and would presumably be disqualified for higher command. However the Commander-in-Chief in India, Field Marshal Sir Philip Chetwode, said that he wished me to take the job for two years, and assured me that it would make no difference to my future career. I obeyed.

The Viceregal party which left for India in April consisted of Lord and Lady Willingdon, the Miévilles, the Ismays and four aides-de-camp. It was my first introduction to 'pomp and circumstance' and *de*

64

luxe travel, and I liked it. Lord Willingdon was a most lovable chief. Having been Governor of Bombay, and later of Madras, he was familiar with the Indian scene, and he had a deep affection for the country and her people. He looked the part of Viceroy to perfection, and he was well endowed with the qualities which it called for — charm, judgment, and human sympathy combined with firmness. Lady Willingdon was an ideal helpmate. Her energy was dynamic, and to the staff she was sometimes exacting and difficult. But she had a heart of gold, and the courage of a lioness. She was a wonderful hostess. British and Indians, old and young, entertaining and boring, were all made to feel at home from the moment they set foot in the Viceroy's House.

The Willingdons had always set their faces against the social exclusiveness which did so much to poison relations between British and Indians. Not long after his arrival to be Governor of Bombay in 1913, Lord Willingdon had expressed a wish to show two of his guests, H.H. the Maharaja of Bikanir and H.H. the Jam of Nawanagar (better known to the cricketing public throughout the world as 'Ranji') over the Yacht Club. He was informed that, by the rules of the Club, no Indians could be admitted, even as guests. Willingdon was deeply shocked and immediately set to work to found a new club, the membership of which would be open to all suitable candidates, irrespective of class, colour, creed or sex. The Willingdon Club proved remarkably popular with all communities, and was still going strong when I went back to India in 1947.

The Private Secretary to the Viceroy was Eric Miéville, who had done the same job for Lord Willingdon in Canada. There were some heart-burnings that this plum, to which the 'Heaven-borns' [1] claimed an almost proprietary right, had been given to a man who had never been in India before. But it was not long before Eric won the confidence and esteem of everyone, from the highest to the lowest — from Indian Princes, Governors and members of the Viceroy's Council, down to junior secretaries. It was a joy to work with him, and we never had a cross word. I little thought that seventeen years later we would again be travelling to India together in the entourage of another Viceroy.

The title of my appointment was misleading. My military functions

[1] Sobriquet for members of the Indian Civil Service.

were confined to attending meetings of the Viceroy's **Executive Coun-**
cil, when military subjects were under discussion, and to acting as an
unofficial link between the Viceroy and the Commander-in-Chief.
But I had plenty of other responsibilities. I was in charge of the whole
personal staff, other than those of the Private Secretary's department.
There was a Comptroller of the Household, six aides-de-camp and a
surgeon, and we all wore the distinctive dress prescribed by Army
Regulations for the Viceroy's Staff. Now that uniforms have, as a
general rule, become drab and austere, it is interesting to recall the
variety and sartorial magnificence of our apparel. There were two full
dress tunics, one for mounted, and the other for dismounted occasions.
Both of them were covered with gold lace, and made us look like lion-
tamers. There was an elaborate military frock coat, special evening
dress, a special patrol jacket, and a special greatcoat. Even the trap-
pings, such as spurs, belts, and sword, were of a special pattern. I had
to spend more time — and more money — at my tailor's getting fitted
out with all this finery than a young lady would spend at her dress-
maker's buying her trousseau.

Another of my tasks was to organise all official functions such as
levees and investitures; and yet another was to arrange the Viceroy's
tours. These took him all over India, and since he had to be able to
deal with current business throughout the time that he was absent
from headquarters, the entourage which used to accompany him was
almost indecently numerous. To our long-suffering hosts, we must
have appeared like a swarm of locusts.

Finally, I was, by unwritten law, responsible for the safety of the
Viceroy's person. There was no attempt on his life during my tour of
office, but there was positive proof that a handful of hired assassins,
who were in the pay of a small but active terrorist movement, were always on the look-out for an opportunity to attack him. Consequently I
was never entirely free from anxiety except — paradoxically enough
— when we were in the somewhat elderly aeroplane which was purchased for the Viceroy shortly after our arrival in India. To provide
complete security against the fanatic or crack-pot, who was only too
ready to be apprehended and pay the extreme penalty, was out of the
question. To attempt to do so would have involved intolerable restrictions on His Excellency's activities. The hired assassin, on the other
hand, presented an easier problem. He had nothing of the martyr in

his make-up, and was most unlikely to attempt mischief unless he was fairly certain of making a getaway. It was therefore a golden rule that the Viceroy must never be in a position — such, for example, as the middle of a dense crowd — in which an assailant could attack him without serious risk of being apprehended.

An intercepted letter from one gunman to another throws an interesting light on the mentality and methods of the fraternity. The writer said that he had reconnoitred Viceroy's House carefully and that there was no chance of killing the Viceroy at night. He slept on the second floor, and in addition to the military guard outside the building, policemen were posted in the passages leading to his bedroom. The best chance was to adopt the disguise of a gardener and try a long shot at him while he was playing tennis. There was a postscript to the letter. 'I have also reconnoitred the Military Secretary's house. He sleeps on the ground floor. He does not carry a pistol, except when he is in attendance on the Viceroy. You can get him any time you like.' It was somewhat humiliating, though highly reassuring, to feel that the price upon my head was not sufficiently attractive to make an attempt worthwhile.

Before joining the Viceroy's staff my knowledge of Indians had been more or less limited to soldiers. The never-ending round of parties at Viceroy's House, and the much smaller and less formal parties at our own house, provided opportunities for meeting all sorts and conditions of Indian men and women; and my wife and I formed many friendships which we value to this day. Similarly the Viceroy's tours enabled me to see much more of the country and its inhabitants than had hitherto been possible. The outstanding impressions which these travels left on my mind were that India was a land of infinite diversity, that there was as much disunity between its various parts as between the States of Europe, and that such sense of nationalism as existed was entirely of British creation.

As for the general political situation in the early thirties, suffice it to say that Congress were peristent in their demands that we should quit India, and that Mr Gandhi was a constant thorn in our flesh. His spells of imprisonment, during some of which he added to the embarrassment of the Government by going on hunger strike, were punctuated by trips to Simla for personal discussions with the Viceroy. I saw a good deal of him when I returned to India in 1947.

Much as I enjoyed life on the Viceroy's staff, I was relieved when the Commander-in-Chief, true to his word, told me on Christmas Day 1932 that he had been authorised to offer me a first-grade appointment in the Intelligence Directorate of the War Office. This meant immediate promotion to full colonel and another spell of duty at home, and I said 'yes' with almost indecent alacrity. Four months later we left India with mixed feelings. It was a joy to be returning to our three children, but my wife and I were sad to say good-bye to a life which had been very pleasant. Our houses in Delhi and Simla had been lovely: we had been served by faithful and devoted servants: we had made many good friends, both British and Indian: and we had been members of a Staff which had been the happiest of families.

In May 1933 I duly reported for duty at the War Office. In days gone by I had frequently visited that mausoleum-like building on my lawful occasions, and I knew the geography intimately. Now, for the first time, I was an immate. During my time at the Committee of Imperial Defence I had seen many memoranda which had emanated from the War Office, but I had never known the processes by which they were produced. Now I was to learn, and indeed to lend a hand. I had always been childishly amused by a passage in Philip Guedalla's *Palmerston:* 'There is an ineptitude about the War Office which it has never lost.' Many a true word is spoken in jest, though this was something of an overstatement. Nevertheless I must confess that my first impressions of my new Department were not favourable. It struck me as hidebound, unimaginative, impersonal and over-populated. When I expressed this opinion to friends whose judgment I respected, they told me that my criticism was unjustifiable, and that the rarefied atmosphere of the CID had spoilt me. They were probably quite right, but my opinion of the War Office was to some extent confirmed when war broke out. Field Marshal Montgomery's account of the shortcomings of the British Expeditionary Force in 1939,[1] not only in equipment but also in organisation and training, makes sorry reading. Nor can the whole blame be attributed, as is sometimes done, solely to successive British Governments.

But whatever the faults of the War Office machine, there was no question of the individual ability of its personnel, both civilian and

[1] *The Memoirs of Field Marshal Montgomery*: Chapter 4.

military. Many of my superiors of those days were destined to gain richly-deserved distinction in the war, and the calibre of the more junior officers may be gauged from the fact that, out of the dozen or more lieutenant-colonels and majors who served under me in the Directorate of Intelligence, not one failed to reach the rank of at least major-general.

Intelligence is perhaps the most interesting of all Staff work in time of peace, and I enjoyed my taste of it. My business was to collect, analyse, evaluate and disseminate all information, particularly information of a military character, regarding the Middle East, the Far East, America, Russia, Poland and the Baltic States. Colonel Paget had similar responsibilities for the rest of the world. His area was much smaller than mine, but his problems much more involved. It has always seemed to me that Paget has never been given sufficient credit for his immense contribution to our victory. As Commander-in-Chief, Home Forces, from the end of 1941 onwards, he fashioned the Army which under Montgomery's leadership was to prove itself perhaps the finest that we have ever marshalled.

I should have liked to pay visits to all the countries in my charge, but a trip to Poland in 1935 was the only one that I could manage. Never have I seen nationalism in such extreme form. After having been partitioned for a hundred and fifty years, their pride in their independence was almost pathetic. Of the three Powers between which their country had been divided, the Poles tolerated, and indeed almost liked, the Austrians: they hated the Germans: and they loathed the Russians with a bitter loathing. It is a thousand tragedies that their independence was so short-lived, and that they are now held in bondage by those whom they so cordially detested.

In April 1936, a new vista suddenly opened up. Hankey sent for me one day and told me that it had been decided that there was to be a Deputy Secretary, CID, to assist him in coping with the ever-increasing work involved in rearmament. He had been authorised by the Prime Minister to offer me the appointment. Would I care for it? Acceptance meant a final break with active soldiering; but I had been away from troops for fourteen years and it seemed improbable that I would ever be considered for high command. In any case, I had always hoped that, somehow or another, I might get a chance of working with the Committee of Imperial Defence again. I therefore accepted with scarcely a moment's hesitation.

A week later, I was astonished to receive a letter from India, offering me command of the First Cavalry Brigade. This brigade was stationed at Risalpur, on the North-West Frontier of India, and would be the spearhead of any major operations in Afghanistan or beyond. The offer would perhaps have attracted me, if the international situation had been different. But war in Europe within the next three or four years seemed inevitable, and I did not want to find myself again on the wrong side of the Suez Canal. I therefore begged to be excused. As I signed the letter, I felt a momentary pang at the thought that my days of real soldiering were over. It was like saying good-bye to the dreams of my youth. But reason quickly banished sentiment, and I have never regretted my decision.

PART TWO

THE CRUCIAL YEARS

CHAPTER VI

Three Years of Suspense

1936–1939

T H E spring of 1936 marked a turning-point in the defence policy of His Majesty's Government. For some years past they had — to quote the White Paper of 3 March 1936 — 'deliberately taken the course of postponing defence expenditure which would certainly have been justified, and might indeed have been regarded as necessary, in order to give the best possible opportunity for the development of a new international order in which such expenditure might be avoided.' [1]

It was now only too clear that England's example of unilateral disarmament had not been, and was not going to be, followed by others. On the contrary, defence expenditure in many countries had been increased, and Germany in particular was rearming as fast as she could. Meanwhile conditions in the international field had deteriorated, and the Government realised that the appalling risks which they had taken for peace had done nothing to remove the danger of war. In the circumstances, they felt that the time had come when they had 'no alternative but to provide the necessary means both of safeguarding ourselves against aggression and of playing our part in the enforcement by common action of international obligations.' [2]

[1] Statement relating to Defence — 3 March 1936.
[2] *Ibid.*

73

The White Paper went on to outline the Government's proposals for strengthening the armed forces. Modest though they were, they were evidence of a determination to try to recover the ground which had been lost through their well-meaning efforts to lead the world towards general disarmament. Four days after the White Paper was issued, Hitler marched into the Rhineland. The alarm had certainly not been sounded too soon. Indeed it was probably already too late. But we would at least be better prepared to meet the fury of the storm.

Simultaneously with the decision to strengthen the armed forces, a number of steps were taken to improve the higher organisation of defence. The most important innovation was a new ministerial appointment, which was designed to take some of the load of responsibility for defence off the shoulders of the Prime Minister. The new Minister was to have the title of Minister for the Co-ordination of Defence. He was to exercise, on the Prime Minister's behalf, day-to-day supervision of the Committee of Imperial Defence; to consult with the Chiefs of Staff as necessary, and to have the right of convening the Chiefs of Staff Committee under his own chairmanship whenever he or they thought desirable; he was also to be the Chairman of the Principal Supply Officers Committee. He was to have no Department, and no executive authority. In fact it was specifically laid down that his appointment would neither affect the final responsibility of the Prime Minister in regard to defence matters, nor weaken the authority of the individual Service Ministers.

It was generally expected that Mr Winston Churchill, with his unique experience not only of all three Fighting Services but also of the Ministry of Munitions, would be given the new appointment; but Mr Baldwin is said to have felt that to bring him into the Government would damage the chances of peace, and raise awkward questions of succession to the Premiership when he himself retired.[1] He may also have felt that Churchill was unlikely to be content with the restricted authority which the new Minister was to exercise. But whatever may have been the reasons, his choice fell upon Sir Thomas Inskip, who was a distinguished lawyer and gifted parliamentarian but had no experience of defence matters. The selection caused a

[1] Keith Feiling: *The Life of Neville Chamberlain.*

good deal of surprise. 'The most remarkable appointment since the Emperor Caligula made his horse a consul' was the comment over-heard in a certain club.

Churchill himself has placed it on record [1] that 'this definite and, as it seemed, final exclusion from all share in our preparations for de-fence was a heavy blow.' But he goes on to say that it saved him from 'becoming involved in all the Cabinet compromises and shortcomings of the next three years,' and that in the long run, it was 'a blessing in what was at the time a very effective disguise.' As things turned out, this is undoubtedly true. On the other hand, is it not possible that events might have taken a very different course if Winston Churchill, instead of Thomas Inskip, had been appointed Minister for the Co-ordination of Defence in 1936? Perhaps he would have protested that the appointment was so limited in scope as to be a mere façade, and insisted that it should be supported by a considerable measure of authority? Perhaps our rearmament programme would have been pressed forward with greater vigour? Perhaps there would have been closer consultation, and a better understanding, between the French and ourselves? Perhaps Hitler would have realised more clearly that we meant business and that we would be redoubtable enemies, if he forced us to go to war? Perhaps he might not have made the exorbi-tant demands on Czechoslovakia which ended in Munich? Or con-versely, if he had made them, perhaps we would have taken up the challenge at the time? All this is in the realm of speculation, but I am on less controversial ground when I say that it is unfair to blame Inskip for having failed to make any significant contribution to our war-making capacity, or to suggest that if he had had greater famil-iarity with the problems of defence, he would have done better. After all, Lord Chatfield, who suceeded him in his thankless task early in 1939, found it equally impossible to get things done, in spite of his vast experience in the politico-strategic field. The root of the matter was that no living man — not even Winston Churchill — could have made a success of the appointment, unless he had been given not only a clear mandate that the rearmament programme was to have the highest priority, regardless of the dislocation of peace-time industry,

---

[1] Churchill: *The Second World War.*

but also an assurance that he would have the whole-hearted support of the Prime Minister and his colleagues in the Cabinet in any steps which he thought necessary.

Another decision announced in the White Paper was the reinforcement of the Joint Planning Committee. At that time this consisted of the Directors of Plans of the three Services, Captain Tom Phillips, RN,[1] Colonel Sir Ronald Adam,[2] and Group-Captain A. T. Harris.[3] But these officers were so preoccupied with the particular work of their own Departments, that they had little time to devote to combined planning. It was therefore decided that each of them should have a deputy who would be employed whole-time on that type of work. Thus it came about that Captain Daniel, RN,[4] Colonel R. H. Dewing[5] and Group-Captain Hugh Fraser were allotted a common room in 2, Whitehall Gardens. It was there that they spent most of their time working with each other, sitting round the same table; but they continued to maintain close contact with their own Departments, and particularly with their own Departmental Chiefs from whom, and from whom alone, they took their instructions. They were provided with a whole-time secretary from the Secretariat of the CID. Major L. C. Hollis, the officer selected for this duty, was appropriately a Royal Marine — 'soldier and sailor too.' This seemingly minor adjustment of our defence set-up resulted in an immediate acceleration of the business of combined planning, and paved the way for the expansion of the Joint Planning Staff which was to take place during the war, and prove of immense value.

In August I moved from the War Office to 2, Whitehall Gardens. It was like coming home again — the same chief, the same Civil Service colleagues, the same clerical staff, the same messengers. In the old days they had nicknamed me 'the galloping major,' because of my habit of running upstairs two at a time. But six years had passed, and in the interval I had had a severe polo accident. I was approaching my fiftieth year, and on the verge of promotion to major-

---

[1] Later Vice Admiral Sir Thomas Phillips, who was in command of H.M.S. *Prince of Wales* and H.M.S. *Repulse* when they were sunk in the China Sea.

[2] Later General Sir Ronald Adam.

[3] Later Marshal of the Royal Air Force Sir Arthur Harris.

[4] Later Admiral Sir Charles Daniel.

[5] Later Major General R. H. Dewing.

general. I now preferred to use the lift. Nevertheless they gave me a warm welcome.

To outward appearance everything looked much the same as when I had left in 1930, but I was immediately conscious of a very different atmosphere. During my first tour of duty there had been no aggressor nation in sight, and the possibility of a Second World War in my lifetime had seemed remote. But a sinister transformation had taken place. The skies, so far from being cloudless, were now heavily overcast. We had earned the undying hatred and contempt of Mussolini by our attitude over his Abyssinian adventure. The menace of Nazi Germany was growing daily. She was spending at the rate of 1,000 million pounds sterling per annum on armaments; and in air power she was already far ahead of us. Six months previously, she had occupied the Rhineland in defiance of her treaty obligations, and started to build the Siegfried Line. No one had lifted a finger to stop her. In Spain, a ferocious civil war had broken out; one side was backed by Germany and Italy, the other by Russia, and the British Mediterranean fleet had moved from Alexandria to Barcelona. In the Far East, Japan had defied, and left, the League of Nations. She was now engaged, as Churchill said, in eating up China 'like an artichoke, leaf by leaf.' A wide gulf had grown up between us and our former ally.

Churchill's *World Crisis* had always been one of my favourite books. I knew a good deal of it by heart, and I now read and re-read his account of the events leading up to the war of 1914-18. 'Events got on to certain lines and no one could get them off again. Germany clanked obstinately, recklessly, awkwardly, towards the crater, and dragged us all in with her.' Was history going to repeat itself?

My responsibilities for the last three years at the War Office had been limited and clear-cut. From now onwards I was to be concerned with every aspect of planning and preparation for a war which seemed imminent. Even though my functions would be more or less restricted to co-ordination and conciliation, the magnitude, complexity and responsibility of the task appalled me. Henceforward all family life would have to take second place. No longer could we make private engagements with any certainty — or even much hope — of being able to keep them.

There was little comfort to be derived from the papers which were given to me to study on my arrival, and I was particularly depressed by the records of two meetings which had taken place a week or two before I joined, between the Government, represented by Mr Baldwin and Sir Thomas Inskip, and a powerful deputation from both Houses of Parliament, which included Lord Salisbury, Sir Austen Chamberlain, Mr Churchill, Admiral of the Fleet Sir Roger Keyes, Marshal of the Royal Air Force Lord Trenchard and Field Marshal Lord Milne. The Prime Minister had agreed to have their representations and questions carefully examined, and to have a further meeting with them after the summer recess. Since I would have to lend a hand in preparing the Government reply, it was necessary for me to get into the picture as quickly as I could.

Mr Churchill's comprehensive and carefully reasoned statement on our shortcomings was particularly impressive. It ended on an alarming note. 'We are in danger as we have never been before.' Was this a deliberate exaggeration, intended to frighten the Government into more vigorous action? Or did it represent his genuine appraisal of the situation? Surely there were some redeeming features? Our naval superiority was overwhelming. The French Army was the most powerful in Europe. Perhaps Hitler was having his difficulties? Perhaps the German strength had been over-estimated? Perhaps there would be time to put our house in order? But, however much I tried to look on the bright side, I could not escape the feeling of impending calamity. It never entered my mind that we could be conquered; but grievous humiliation and suffering seemed almost inevitable.

Mr Baldwin and Sir Thomas Inskip again received the Parliamentary deputation towards the end of the year. The burden of Inskip's statement was that everything was being done which could be done without causing alarm and despondency and upsetting industry. The deputation was obviously unconvinced.

When we entered the First World War, we still enjoyed — as we thought — the immeasurable advantages of being an island. We reckoned on being able, as in the past, to take as much or as little of the war as we wished. Our armies might sustain shattering defeats abroad, but, so long as Britannia ruled the waves, the security of the homeland was assured. It was not until the war had been in progress for some time that the extent to which our insularity had been neutralised by scientific development was brought home to us. Despite our naval superiority, we came within measurable distance of being strangled by unrestricted submarine warfare. Eventually we devised ways and means of conquering the U-boat, and we breathed again. Since that time, a device called the Asdic, for detecting submerged submarines by means of sound waves, had been fully developed, and it seemed that under-water attack was no longer a mortal threat. On the other hand, the development of air power had revolutionised the position. Over two years had passed since Mr Churchill had pleaded that our Air Force should at least be equal to that of any nation within striking distance of our shores. But His Majesty's Government had not been as vigilant or as far-sighted as they might have been. Hitler had stolen a march on us, and the air power of Germany already greatly exceeded our own. It was now probably too late to bridge the gap, but it was a matter of life and death that we should make the best possible arrangements for meeting this new and awful peril with whatever resources we could muster in time.

The questions which called for the urgent and unremitting attention of the CID were novel, complicated and almost innumerable. How many fighter squadrons, A-A guns, balloons, searchlights and Observer Corps formations were necessary? How many could be provided, and by what date? Where should they be located? How were their operations to be co-ordinated? How many RDF (Radio Detection Finding) stations were required? Where should they be located? How would they be linked up with the various fighter headquarters? What arrangements should be made for the organisation and protection of the civil population? What form of shelters should be provided and where? Should women and children be evacuated to country districts from larger cities? What arrangements, if any, could be made to move the seat of government out of London if it should become impossible for it to function there? What hospital accommodation would be required to deal with civilian casualties? What should be done to meet gas attack? A complete list of all our puzzles would resemble a catalogue of the Army and Navy Stores. I will therefore confine myself to those problems with which I myself was closely concerned.

The Home Defence Committee had originally been responsible for advising on the measures that should be taken in such matters as the protection of vulnerable points against sabotage, and the control of aliens. Later, its terms of reference were extended to include Home Defence against air attack; and in that capacity they were required to advise on such matters as the number of fighter squadrons, A-A guns, etc., which should be maintained and where they should be sited. The Secretary of the CID had always been *ex officio* Chairman, but in order to lighten Hankey's load, I was appointed to that office when I became his deputy. The membership included representatives of the three Service Departments, the Treasury, the Home Office, the C.-in-C. Fighter Command and the GOC Anti-Aircraft Artillery.

Looking back upon the discussions of those days, I am struck by the extraordinary modesty — or even inadequacy — of the recommendations which we put forward from time to time to the CID. Economy had become so ingrained in us that we asked for no increases which could not be justified in the greatest detail. Never, for example, did we put forward a recommendation for additional A-A guns, unless we could specify the exact sites for which they were required — six more for Birmingham, twelve more for Southampton, and so forth; this at a time when the Germans already had four thousand modern guns in fixed positions, and a further twelve hundred modern mobile guns, whereas we only had about five hundred all told, many of them obsolescent. We continued to think in hundreds, while Hitler was producing in thousands.

I shall never forget the first meeting of the CID at which, in my capacity as Chairman, I had to introduce a report of the Home Defence Committee recommending the provision of an additional hundred guns or so. I was a junior officer, and it was the first occasion on which I had ever opened my mouth in that august assembly. After I had made my case, the Chancellor of the Exchequer, Mr Neville Chamberlain, recalled that scarcely a year had passed since a substantial increase of A-A artillery had been approved. Was there to be no end to this importunity? After a short homily on the need for economy he said that he was prepared to agree to the additional guns now proposed, but that he sincerely hoped that the last word had been spoken and that there would be no further demands. I felt it only honest to say that if the numbers, range, and bomb-carrying capacity of the German bomber force were to increase — as they almost certainly would — the Home Defence Committee would have no option but to recommend a corresponding increase in our defences. My purpose in relating this trivial episode is to give an idea of the atmosphere of those days in regard to rearmament. We may have been blameworthy for having failed to put our case sufficiently forcefully, but we were not sure enough of our ground. The problem was unprecedented, and we were groping in the dark.

It is easy to criticise peaceful democracies for their habitual lack of preparedness when a war breaks out, but it is only fair to recognise that the dice are loaded against them. Dictators, bent on aggression, have no need to consider parliamentary or public opinion, or to worry about the effect which vast expenditure on defence will exercise on the national economy. If they decide that guns must come before butter, there is no one to say them nay. They are masters of their own time-table. They are free to decide when to strike, where to strike, and how to strike, and to arrange their armament programmes accordingly. Their potential victims, the democracies, with their inherent hatred of war, are in a very different position. If their Governments propose a large increase in expenditure on defence, before the practical certainty of war is generally recognised, they are criticised for dislocating the economic and industrial life of the nation, and accused of endangering the prospects of peace by starting a race in armaments. Worse still, they do not know when or where the blow will fall, or what manner of blow it will be. Amid all this criticism and uncertainty, preparation for war is a complex and difficult business for democracies at any time; and in the days about which I write, the complexities and difficulties of the Government were greatly aggravated by the development of the air weapon as one of the decisive instruments of war.

Another CID sub-committee which was closely concerned with the problem of defence against air attack was the Air Defence Research Committee. This had already been in being for about two years and, as its name implies, it was responsible for exploring all the possibilities of applying science to the problem of air defence. The Chairman was Sir Philip Cunliffe-Lister, then Secretary of State for Air, and one of its most active, imaginative and vocal members, almost from the beginning, was Mr Winston Churchill. That such a persistent and outspoken critic of the Government should have been admitted to their secret deliberations is yet another example of the infinite flexibility of the CID.

The Air Defence Research Committee were assisted by an Air Ministry technical sub-committee consisting almost exclusively of scientists. The latter supplied the scientific knowledge; the former exercised a general supervision, and ensured that the necessary funds were made available to drive forward all promising experiments with the utmost vigour. When I arrived on the scene, these committees were busy following up Mr Watson Watt's ideas on the detection of aircraft by radio echoes, and they are entitled to a large share of the credit for the installation of the chain of radar stations which were destined to play so vital a part in the Battle of Britain and after.

In order to inform myself of what was happening in the strategic field I paid frequent visits to the room which was shared by the triumvirate of deputy planners. Their task was unenviable. It is one thing to be charged with the preparation of plans for specific offensive operations in accordance with a clear-cut directive: it is a very different thing to be expected to prepare plans of a purely defensive character when there is no certainty of the identity of the aggressor, or of the timing or form of the offensive which he will launch. The only instructions which the planners received, or indeed could receive, from the Chiefs of Staff in 1936 were to assume that Germany would be Enemy No. 1, and that Italy and later Japan might join her, while our only ally would be France. It was left to them to select a hypothetical date for the commencement of hostilities, and it so happened that they chose the autumn of 1939. That was a good guess. For the rest, the most that they could do was to draw up a series of broad appreciations setting out, on the one hand, the strength of the enemy and the various alternative courses open to them, and on the other, the strength which France and Great Britain could muster to oppose them, and what could be done to meet the hypothetical contingencies envisaged. Their appreciations were not reassuring, leading as they did to the inevitable conclusion that our potential enemies, in addition to having the priceless advantage of the initiative, were incomparably stronger than us in almost every respect, and that all that we could do was to try to bridge the gap as quickly as possible, regardless of expense or of the dislocation it would cause in the economic and industrial life of the nation.

In the midst of much that was uncertain and depressing, it was encouraging to find that most of the sub-committees, which had been my old familiar friends in bygone days, were still flourishing, and that those which were responsible for the administrative arrangements which would be necessary on the outbreak of war had made particularly good progress. The Censorship Committee had finished its work. Regulations for postal, cable and wireless, and press censorship had been prepared and only needed to be kept up to date. The staffs which would be necessary to implement them had been instructed in their tasks and could be assembled at a moment's notice. The War Emergency Legislation Committee had also completed its labours. All the special regulations that were likely to be required in time of war had been drafted in legal language and only needed Parliamentary sanction to be put into force when the necessity arose. The War Book, which I had started to revise in 1926, had been improved out of all recognition. Every Department of State now knew exactly what administrative action it was required to take, both during the precautionary period and on the outbreak of war. All the necessary telegrams were already in draft, with only the dates to be filled in, and all the recipients had been warned what to expect. A smooth transition from a state of peace to a state of war seemed assured. This would not of course save us from the consequences of our lack of military strength, but it would at least give the general public the feeling of firm and coherent direction.

The Air Raids Precaution Committee, which had been set up as far back as 1924 under Sir John Anderson,[1] then Permanent Under-Secretary of State at the Home Office, had surveyed an immense range of civil defence problems of all kinds. At first they had been hampered by the Cabinet ruling that their enquiries must be confined to government circles for fear of scaring the public. But the ban had been removed in 1934, and from that time onwards planning began to take a more practical form. In the following year a Civil Defence department was set up in the Home Office and took over the responsibilities hitherto borne by the ARP Committee.

[1] Afterwards Viscount Waverley.

Everything was still on a voluntary basis, but the foundations had been well and truly laid by that wisest of wise men, Sir John Anderson, and the problem was being realistically tackled.

The Principal Supply Officers Committee, with its Supply Board and rabbit-warren of sub-committees, had been my special charge during my first tour of duty. They were still going strong, and had made a good deal of progress in their plans for the conversion of industry to war purposes. Mr Churchill was insistent that these somewhat amorphous bodies, whose functions were advisory, should give way to a Ministry of Supply with executive authority; but, for the time being, the Government were adamant against the proposal. Since I myself thought that the time had come to make the change which Mr Churchill advocated, I found it a little difficult to prepare briefs for ministerial speeches based on arguments with which I was in almost total disagreement. But a staff officer has no option but to follow with absolute loyalty the directions of those who bear the ultimate responsibility. It was not until the rape of Czechoslovakia in March 1939 that a Ministry of Supply was created, and then only to deal with the requirements of the Army and the supply of those articles which were in common use in all three Services.

The three years from 1936 to 1939 were more difficult and anxious than the three years of almost uninterrupted disaster which followed them. Once the war started, we lived in a world of reality. There were concrete problems to deal with. But in the years before, we lived in a world of imagination, and the preparations on which our very existence might depend had to be based on forecasts which might prove to be entirely wrong. Many were the hours spent trying to pierce the veil of the future. If one could only divine German intentions correctly, there would be a solid basis for our own counter-preparations. My crystal-gazing led me to a number of conclusions which I committed to paper. It seemed that the Germans were bound to be influenced in their overall strategy by what had happened in the First World War. They would say to themselves, 'In 1914 we concentrated in the first instance on France and contained Russia. We had no means of getting at the third partner in the entente, Great Britain, owing to the unchallengeable authority of her navy. And what happened? The British had time to organise the latent strength of their whole Commonwealth and Empire. Their sea power enabled them to import all the food and raw materials that they needed and at the same time to exercise a relentless blockade of the Fatherland. Their industries, so unready at the start of hostilities, were converted to war purposes. Their "contemptible little army" was expanded into a mighty host of five million men and played a decisive part in the destruction of the Germany of Kaiser Wilhelm II. We must never let this happen again. Thanks to air power with its suddenness of strike, the Island Kingdom is now no longer untouchable. It must be attacked immediately on the declaration of war, or even before, with all the air strength at our command. Simultaneously every ship in our navy, both surface and submarine, must from the outset wage intensive war on British commerce, regardless of losses. Better to lose ships in that way than to scupper them ignominiously in Scapa Flow, as we had to do last time. As for our army, it can remain on the defensive behind the Siegfried Line until the Luftwaffe has disposed of the British, and is available to co-operate in the conquest of France.'

If this estimate of German thinking for the initial phases of the war was anything like correct, the counter-measures that we should take were fairly obvious. First and foremost, we should give priority to the defence of our island citadel against air attack. Secondly, we should maintain sufficient reserves of food, fuel-oil and all other necessities to enable us to do without imports until we had got the measure of the German Navy. Thirdly, we should build up our bomber force in as great a strength and as quickly as possible with a view to carrying the war into Germany itself from the outset of hostilities. Fourthly, we should make all preparations to send an expeditionary force to France to take post alongside the French Army on the outbreak of war, and we should expand it as fast as possible with a view to an all-out advance into the heart of Germany when the time was ripe. In the event, my prognostications of German action proved hopelessly wrong; but since the paper to which I had laboriously committed my thoughts never got further than Hankey's desk, no harm was done.

But whatever the course of the war in its initial phases, there was no doubt that we should find ourselves confronted with all sorts of unprecedented situations and that all sorts of unprecedented arrangements would be required to meet them. In the Committee of Imperial Defence Secretariat we used to rack our brains as to what these should be. Our labours were not altogether in vain.

One of the projects for which we were responsible — I cannot recall which of my colleagues gave birth to the idea — was that the Cabinet and Chiefs of Staff should be provided with protected accommodation in which to hold their meetings when London was under heavy bombardment. Having secured the blessing of the Chiefs of Staff to the idea, we persuaded the Treasury to authorise the very modest expenditure that we contemplated. Jo Hollis and Lawrence Burgis were put in charge of the project, and they were ably aided and abetted by Sir Eric de Normann, the Deputy Secretary to the Office of Works, who had just graduated at the Imperial Defence College and was fully alive to the importance of the work. Some of the cellars beneath the large block of Government offices which in those days housed the Ministry of Health, Office of Works and Board of Trade were selected for our purpose. They were cleared of archives and air-conditioned, and their roofs were shored up by lengths of crude timber. Steel would have been preferable, but this was all required for other more urgent purposes. The principal features of the stronghold were a small room for the Chiefs of Staff, a larger room for the Cabinet, and between the two a still larger room, called the Map Room, in which the latest information on all aspects of the war situation was to be available at all hours of the day and night. It was connected by telephone with the Admiralty, the War Office, the Air Ministry, the Ministry of Home Security and the Foreign Office, and the telephones were to be manned on a twenty-four-hour basis by retired officers of the three Services, who would be specially ear-marked for this duty. In the event, all these officers reported for duty on the day before the outbreak of war, and the Map Room functioned from that date, night and day, without a break, until Japan surrendered. It proved an unqualified success.

It is very doubtful whether this protected accommodation would, in its original form, have stood up to a direct hit; but it was at least proof against noise, and enabled the Cabinet to hold their meetings there undisturbed by the clatter of bombs and anti-aircraft artillery fire. The only interruptions to their deliberations that I can recall were due to a very different cause. Whenever the Duty Officer in the

Map Room reported that a very heavy air-raid on London was in progress, the Prime Minister used to insist on an adjournment in order that we all might watch the proceedings from the Air Ministry roof. It made an admirable, though not very safe, grandstand. As time went on, the War Room area was considerably strengthened by an overhead reinforcement of several feet of concrete, and enlarged to include a canteen and sleeping quarters for all the staff employed on night duty.

Another example of the initiative on the part of the CID Secretariat may be mentioned. Some ten years previously Hankey had prepared a paper setting out the various forms of machinery for the supreme control of war which had been set up in 1914-18, together with comments based on his own personal experience of the advantages and disadvantages of each system. His paper was duly placed before the CID who recorded the view that, in the event of total war, it would almost certainly be desirable to institute from the very outset a small War Cabinet on the Lloyd George model. At the same time, they felt that this was a question which must be left for decision by the Prime Minister of the day in the light of the then existing circumstances. An entry was therefore made in the War Book that, when hostilities seemed imminent, the Secretary of the Cabinet should bring Hankey's memorandum and the conclusions of the CID to the attention of the Prime Minister. On 1 September 1939, Sir Edward Bridges and I obeyed these instructions; there and then Mr Chamberlain decided, as we all expected, to set up a small War Cabinet.

There remained the question of machinery for the supreme control of the Allied war effort, and Lord Chatfield, who had succeeded Sir Thomas Inskip as Minister for Coordination of Defence in February 1939, instructed me to put up proposals. It seemed to me that we could not do better than to repeat the arrangements which were made towards the end of the First World War, and I proposed that as soon as hostilities started, an Anglo-French Supreme War Council should be brought into being. This was to consist of the Prime Minister of France and the Prime Minister of Great Britain, together with such persons as they desired to have with them. The CID approved and I was sent to Paris to sound General Gamelin on the views of the French Government. They agreed without demur. And so it came to pass that a few days after the outbreak of war the Supreme War Council held its first meeting at Abbeville.

Time passes astonishingly quickly when every moment of the day is occupied, and as the year 1937 drew to its close, it seemed more like eighteen weeks than eighteen months since I had returned to the centre of our affairs. It was impossible to feel satisfied with the progress of rearmament, and neither Parliament nor public opinion seemed to have any idea of the vital need for urgency. Germany was arming at a breathless rate, and the relations between the dictator powers and the democracies were growing steadily worse. At the same time, there was as yet no sign of an immediate storm, and I dared to hope that the Second World War might still be some way off.

The hope was short-lived. Within three months, Hitler marched into Vienna and proclaimed the annexation of Austria to the German Reich. It was a sign of the times that this example of rapine was almost taken for granted. Russia's proposal to have a conference was ignored. France contented herself with reaffirming her guarantee to Czechoslovakia. Great Britain, who had always contemplated some sort of union between Germany and Austria, did nothing except register disapproval of Hitler's methods. And Mussolini, so far from moving troops to the Brenner Pass, earned Hitler's undying gratitude by his acquiescence in the Anschluss.

Czechoslovakia was now militarily and economically isolated, and the excuse of a German minority of about three and a half millions in Bohemia made it extremely likely that she would be Hitler's next victim. His solemn assurance that he had no designs on her integrity made it a practical certainty. It was the kiss of death. Sure enough the Sudeten Germans soon increased the violence of their agitation for Home Rule, and Hitler added fuel to the flames by a particularly inflammatory speech on the subject. There were reports of German movements towards the Czech frontier, and the Czech Army was partially mobilised. The situation became daily more explosive, and M. Daladier, Prime Minister of France, confirmed his country's engagement to support Czechoslovakia if she were attacked. We ourselves had no commitment of any kind, but if France honoured her pledge and fighting started, we were certain to be drawn in. It looked as though we might soon be at war.

It was at about this time that Hankey told me that he intended to retire in July 1938. It would be idle to pretend that I did not give more than an occasional thought as to how this would affect my own future. Hankey had been Secretary of the Cabinet for twenty years (the first Secretary that there had ever been), and Secretary of the Committee of Imperial Defence for more than a quarter of a century. The question of the succession to these posts raised a difficult problem. There were some, including Hankey himself, who thought that the business of the Cabinet and of the Committee of Imperial Defence were so closely interlocked that it was essential for them both to be served by the same secretary. There were others, including myself, who thought that it was no longer possible for any one man to cope with the dual burden. For some time past the Cabinet had been meeting several times a week, and Hankey had had to spend a great deal of time before these meetings in arranging the agenda and studying the papers, and still more time in drafting the minutes and conclusions after the meetings were over. Thus he had had little time to devote to the Committee of Imperial Defence, whose work had already increased and was still increasing. There was the further argument that the two appointments called for very different training and experience. It would be difficult to find a soldier who would make a good Secretary of the Cabinet, and equally difficult to find a civilian who would make a good Secretary of the Committee of Imperial Defence and the Chiefs of Staff Committee. As *The Times* put it: 'Hankey's versatility cannot become a heritable organisation.'

The Prime Minister, to my great relief, decided to separate the two appointments and it was announced that, on Hankey's retirement at the end of July, Sir Edward Bridges was to be Head of the Combined Office and Secretary of the Cabinet, and I was to be Secretary of the Committee of Imperial Defence. Hankey's third hat as Clerk of the Privy Council was given to Sir Rupert Howorth, who continued in addition to be Deputy Secretary of the Cabinet.

I was unfeignedly thankful to be given this chance of service, and I was delighted by the appointment of Bridges to the Cabinet post. It was an ideal selection. For some years past, he had been in charge of the division of the Treasury which dealt with defence matters, and I had seen a good deal of his work at close quarters. I already had a great admiration not only for his clarity of mind, but also for his unfailing helpfulness and selfless devotion to duty. It gave me confidence to know that we would be working together in the great days that lay ahead.

Shortly before Parliament went into recess at the end of July, Hankey attended the CID for the last time, and richly deserved tributes were paid to his services. I suddenly felt very lonely at the thought that the next time the Committee met, my revered chief would no longer be there, and that the responsibility would rest fairly and squarely on my shoulders. His retirement marked the end of an era in more ways than one. The offices in Whitehall Gardens, in which so many famous men had discussed fateful problems, were shortly to be demolished to make room for the vast modern building which now houses the Air Ministry and the Board of Trade, and a block of private houses in Richmond Terrace, almost directly opposite Downing Street, was taken over as our new office. It suited our purpose admirably, but the Blitz of 1940 forced us to move to a more solid and, alas, typical Government building.

The clouds were gathering and I wanted to get into my new saddle as quickly as possible. I therefore went without a summer holiday and returned to the office early in August. I learned on arrival that 'incidents' were becoming more and more numerous in Sudetenland, and that Lord Runciman had just left for Prague to try to mediate between the Sudeten Germans and the Czech Government. From the outset his reports gave little grounds for optimism, and German troop movements continued. The climax seemed to be approaching, and the Service Ministers and Chiefs of Staff had a number of meetings to consider what, if any, preparatory measures should be taken. Their proposals were reported to a meeting at 10, Downing Street on 13 September, the day after Hitler had delivered a particularly violent speech at Nuremberg. But Mr Chamberlain, who presided, was reluctant to take any action which might tend to send up the temperature. In particular, he was not prepared to agree to the mobilisation of the Fleet without consulting the Cabinet.

Before this could be done, there was a startling and unexpected development. Mr Chamberlain decided to fly to Germany and see Hitler. My first reaction to the plan was resentment at the idea of a British Prime Minister seeming to go hat in hand to an unscrupulous gangster; but on further reflection I was immensely relieved to think that we had a leader who was not prepared to let us drift into war without taking great personal risks and making supreme efforts to avert it. I had seen Chamberlain in action at the Committee of Imperial Defence for nearly three years, and he had always struck me as persistent, single-minded and very self-confident. Perhaps Hitler would get a surprise.

For the next fortnight it seemed that the whole world held its breath, while Chamberlain had three separate encounters with Hitler. The proposals which he brought back from his first visit to Germany were tough enough in all conscience, but not absolutely intolerable. Sudetenland was to be ceded to Germany, and France and Britain were to guarantee what was left of Czechoslovakia. The Czech Government at first refused to agree, but finally gave way under extreme pressure from her friends. It looked as though peace had been secured — at a price; and Chamberlain flew back to Germany to get agreement on the implementation of the plan. To his dismay and astonishment, he was greeted by a raving creature, who announced that he was going to occupy Sudetenland by military force at once. Chamberlain pointed out that public opinion in Great Britain would be deeply shocked and that the Czechs would almost certainly fight; but the only concession that he managed to wring out of Hitler before he left for London, was an undertaking to postpone military action until 1 October. The Cabinet, on hearing the Prime Minister's story, were in no mood to submit to Hitler's ultimatum. The hopes to which the first visit had given birth had been killed stone dead, and it seemed that we should be at war within a week.

I was extremely worried that nothing had as yet been done to call up either the territorial anti-aircraft units, which were responsible for the defence of London, or the fighter squadrons of the Auxiliary Air Force, which might be urgently required at any moment. While Mr Chamberlain was still wrestling with Hitler at Godesberg, I voiced my uneasiness to my Minister, but he felt that no immediate action was necessary. The next morning there were headlines in the press that trenches were being dug in the parks for protection against air attack. I immediately rang up Sir Thomas Inskip, only to find that he had already started walking to the office. I joined him as fast as a taxi could carry me, and suggested that there was not a minute to be lost. The digging of trenches in the Royal Parks would convince friend and foe alike that the Government thought that war was almost inevitable. London might be attacked at any moment. If this were to happen before even the elementary defences which we possessed were in position, I could see myself strung up on one lamp post, and my Minister on another. On arrival at 10, Downing Street, Inskip looked in to see the Prime Minister who had just got back from his ordeal in Germany, and a few minutes later emerged with the permission to implement the precautions that I was advocating. I ran to Richmond Terrace as fast as my legs would carry me, and telephoned the necessary instructions to the Secretary of State for War and the Secretary of State for Air.

The sands were running out, but that very afternoon Chamberlain made his dramatic announcement in the House of Commons that he was making yet another journey to Germany at Hitler's invitation. Once again one dared to hope that war might be avoided; and when Chamberlain returned two days later with the news that all was settled, the sense of relief was overpowering and almost universal. For myself, I gave little thought at that moment to the price that had been paid, or to the probability that the reprieve was only temporary. All that mattered was that the dreaded explosion, which had seemed so imminent, had at least been postponed. I was in no mood for further work that evening and went home feeling light of heart. My reception was unexpected. My wife, so far from sharing my feelings, was highly critical of my attitude. How could I defend an arrangement which may have saved our own skins for the moment, but which had betrayed a smaller nation? The story of the family squabble which ensued need not be told. Suffice it to say that, on that evening, I defended Munich with the greatest vigour, and that ever afterwards I was so ashamed of it, that I deliberately put my head in the sand. I refused to allow myself to think about it, still less to discuss it.

There are those who say that we would have done far better to fight in 1938, rather than postpone the struggle until 1939. There are others who say that the year's breathing space saved us. It seems to me that, from the purely military point of view, it would have paid us to go to war in 1938. It is true that we were hopelessly unready, but German preparations were by no means complete, and in war it is relative strength which counts. It is also true that we had an extra year to rearm, but everyone knows that Germany made much better use of those twelve months than we did. Nor can there be any argument that Munich lost us the support of the fine Czech Army and placed the great Skoda Works at the service of our enemies instead of our friends. On the other hand, when one remembers the almost hysterical reception accorded to Chamberlain on his return from Munich, and the flood of congratulatory messages which he received from all sorts and conditions of men the world over, it seems very doubtful whether, if we had fought at Munich time, we would have done so as a united nation. It is still more doubtful whether we would have done so as a united Commonwealth and Empire. We now know from Field Marshal Smuts' lips that South Africa would have remained neutral; and Mr Mackenzie King, that great Prime Minister of Canada, told Mr Churchill during the war that he very much doubted whether his country would have rallied to us at once.

Lack of unity on the home front in time of war may well be more disastrous in its consequences than inferiority of armaments in the zone of battle; and there is therefore a good deal to be said for the view that, on the whole, the advantages which we ultimately derived from our surrender at Munich outweighed the disadvantages. But however that may be, there was complete agreement even among the most peace-minded, that Munich was not the sort of thing that any great nation could afford to do twice, and that rearmament must be pressed forward with all possible speed and almost regardless of financial considerations. An edict to that effect went forth, and the Service Ministries proceeded to add a nought or two to this or that requirement, and to increase their orders proportionately. But clearly nothing that could be done at this stage would make an appreciable difference to our state of readiness within the succeeding twelve months.

Mr Chamberlain, according to his biographer, Keith Feiling, was not altogether without hope that Munich and the relationship which he thought that he had established with Mussolini might postpone the war for a considerable time, and some of his more wishful-thinking adherents were even more optimistic. They were quickly disillusioned.

In March, Hitler seized the whole of Czechoslovakia and a week or so later he occupied Memel.

Mr Chamberlain had always had his suspicions about the Führer's integrity. He was now completely convinced that he was a consummate liar and blackguard, whose word could never again be trusted. Consequently, when Hitler started to turn the heat on the Danzig Corridor, and there was the usual agitation for self-determination for the German minority, Chamberlain at once gave a guarantee to Poland that if her independence were threatened, the British Government would lend them all the support in their power. Simultaneously he doubled the Territorial Army from thirteen to twenty-six divisions. Curious to relate, this decision was taken without any consultation with either the Committee of Imperial Defence or even the military authorities at the War Office. The decision was all the more extraordinary when one recalls the arguments which there had been about the size and role of the Army. Ever since the end of the First World War, the Army had lived from hand to mouth without any coherent or consistent policy. When, in 1936, rearmament became the order of the day, there were people in high places who argued that the cost of maintaining a mechanised army large enough to play a significant part in a continental war would be a prohibitive addition to the cost of maintaining an adequate Navy and Air Force. It was therefore seriously suggested that the role of the Army should be limited to providing garrisons overseas and anti-aircraft artillery for home defence, and that the French should be told that our contribution to the Alliance would be limited to naval and air forces. This proposal was reinforced by the shocking argument that the women of England would not tolerate the possibility of a repetition of the blood baths of Passchendaele and the Somme. It was difficult to believe that sensible people could be so hopelessly unrealistic. Did they imagine that a great nation could engage in total war, and take as much or as little of it as it wished? What did they suppose would be the reaction of our allies to our refusal to take any share of the burden of operations on land? They might be reproachful if we insisted that our original force must be small, but they would at least have the assurance that it would commit us to reinforcing it as fast as we could. Marshal Joffre, before the First World War, had expressed the feelings of his countrymen when he observed that he would be quite satisfied if the British Expeditionary Force consisted of a single soldier; he added that he would make sure that this soldier was killed. And what an insult to British womanhood to imagine that they would grudge any sacrifice or shrink from any ordeal which was demanded of them! I should have felt less worried about these here-sies if I had known at the time that the Prime Minister himself, while realising that we could not afford an enormous army to start with, thought that we 'should aim at an army of four divisions plus one mobile division and the necessary drafts to maintain its strength.' [1] It was not until early in 1937 that the question was set-tled. It was then decided that the Regular Army, 'armed cap à pie with the most modern equipment,' [2] should consist of six divisions, including two armoured, and that the Territorial Army should consist of thirteen divisions, of which two would be equipped to go over-seas. Now, by a stroke of the pen, these thirteen divisions had been doubled. Shortly afterwards conscription was introduced. Never in our history had there been compulsory service in time of peace, and the passage of the Bill at least showed the world that we were now in deadly earnest.

Meanwhile, the Dictators were evidently determined to cure the British of their week-end habits, and Mussolini selected Good Friday for the date of his surprise attack on Albania. Mr Chamberlain's riposte was to give guarantees to Greece and Roumania similar to that which he had given to Poland. At last he had adopted the policy which Churchill had always advocated of building up deterrents against aggression and accelerating rearmament. But it was now very late in the day.

There was not long to wait before the identity of Hitler's next victim became painfully apparent. Even before the rump of Czech-oslovakia had been digested the German minority in the Danzig Cor-ridor became more and more vociferous in their demands for self-determination; and on 28 April Hitler formally denounced the 1934 Non-Aggression Pact between Germany and Poland. The course of future events was now obvious. Hitler would, in his own good time, threaten Poland with war unless the question of the Corridor was set-

[1] Keith Feiling: *The Life of Neville Chamberlain.*
[2] *Ibid.*

tled as he demanded; the Poles would refuse to submit to blackmail, and Great Britain and France would be bound by their guarantee to lend them all the support in their power. The shooting had yet to be started, but the Cold War was on us. The Germans had a name for it — *Kriegpermanenz* (undeclared but standing war). Henceforward preparations for the inevitable struggle had priority over all else. Reserves of food, oil, and many essential war materials had to be increased, and storage arranged; a variety of evacuation schemes had to be planned and prepared in detail; the organisation of civil defence in all its ramifications had to be pressed forward; any amount of printing had to be undertaken in advance — ration books by the million, proclamations, emergency regulations, etc.; staffs had to be ear-marked for the many new activities which the Government would have to undertake, and office accommodation arranged; the War Book had to be scrupulously checked to ensure that all was up to date and that nothing had been forgotten. There was no end to it. Fortunately there were admirable records of all that had been done in the First World War. These provided an excellent guide; but the probability of intense air attack on the homeland raised innumerable problems which were completely novel.

It was at about this time that I had an interesting experience of Nazi mentality. One of the Secretaries at the German Embassy, Herr von Selzem, had been a good friend of mine in Calcutta, and we had seen quite a lot of him and his American wife in London. One day he asked me to lunch to meet a member of the faculty of the Technische Hochschule at Danzig. The Professor spoke perfect English, and we had scarcely sat down before he embarked upon a long rigmarole about the Danzig situation. When he had finished, I told him that I was already familiar with the problem, and that it seemed to me that there was plenty of room for patient discussion. On the other hand, the use or even the threat of violence would achieve nothing, and might lead to terrible consequences. 'But surely England would not fight for Danzig?' he asked. I replied that this was a matter for the Government, but that personally I devoutly hoped that we would. Carton de Wiart, who was living in Poland, had just written to me to say that Danzig was 'no longer a place but a principle,' and I used those words to describe how public opinion in England regarded the matter. I expected this to enrage the Professor, but he merely looked patronising. 'What could you do to save Poland?' he asked. This was exactly what I had been waiting for. I readily acknowledged that we could probably do very little to prevent Poland from being overrun in the first instance, any more than we had been able to prevent Belgium from being overrun in 1914. But we had hoped then, and we hoped now, that the knowledge that Great Britain would go to war if the integrity of countries to whom we had given a guarantee was violated, would restrain any aggressor. The Germany of Kaiser Wilhelm II had disregarded the warning and had paid the penalty. Surely Hitler's Germany would not repeat the mistake! By this time I was worked up and forgot my manners. 'Let there be no mistake about it, Professor. If you force us to go to war, we will get you in the end, as we got you last time.' After that there was not much more to be said. The party broke up.

On 4 August, the twenty-fifth anniversary of the outbreak of the First World War, Parliament went into recess for two months, and a few days later I left for Scotland on what was likely to be my last holiday for a long time. Saturday, 19 August, is one of the days that will always live in my memory. The sun was shining, we were a family party, there were plenty of grouse, and we all shot adequately. As I drove back to the lodge, I remarked, half jokingly, that it was too good to last; and sure enough there was a message from the Cabinet Office instructing me to return to London at once. It was impossible to get to Aberdeen in time to catch the train that night, and we spent most of the next day playing cricket on the lawn with my cousins' very young children. In that haven of peace it was difficult to realise that it was now certain that all hell was shortly to be let loose. The storm would probably be over before our playmates were old enough to be cannon fodder, but what sort of a world would it be by the time they entered into man's estate!

On the day of my return to London, we heard the news of the Russo-German Pact. This was a complete surprise to me, and, I fancy, to most people. I had never expected that our own belated and low-powered mission to Moscow would achieve anything, but who could have imagined that two gangsters, who had been heaping the vilest abuse on each other for many years, would kiss and make friends overnight? The implications of their infamy were transparent. Germany, relieved of all anxiety about her eastern front, was free to strike at Poland at once, and it seemed certain that we should find ourselves at war in a matter of days. The time had obviously come to institute a number of preparatory measures. The War Book, which I had started to revise and re-shape thirteen years previously, was now in charge of my RAF assistant, Bill Elliott. Lately he had been working on it day in and day out, and it was ready to the last comma.

The despatch of a single telegram of three words, 'Institute Precautionary Stage,' would have set in motion innumerable measures of infinite variety all over the world. From the practical point of view, its immediate despatch was highly advisable, but Mr Chamberlain had not yet given up all hope of reaching an accommodation with Germany, and the Cabinet were determined to avoid doing anything which might hot up the temperature or give the impression that war was thought to be inevitable. Accordingly it was ruled that the Heads of all Government Departments should meet daily under Bridges's chairmanship, and make recommendations as to the minimum precautionary measures which could not safely be postponed any longer. Day after day we met, and combed the War Book, and evening after evening the Cabinet authorised a further series of measures. By 31 August, practically all the action contemplated for the Precautionary Stage had been taken. The process had not been as tidy as we had hoped, but it was at least effective.

Following on Mr Chamberlain's decision to set up a small War Cabinet on the Lloyd George model, the Secretariats of the Cabinet and the CID were merged into a single body known as the War Cabinet Secretariat, headed by Sir Edward Bridges. It was organised in two wings — the civil and the military, the latter under my control. The hard core of my staff was Major (later General Sir Leslie) Hollis, Captain (later Rear Admiral) Angus Nicholl, Wing Commander (later Air Chief Marshal Sir William) Elliott, Major (later Lieutenant General Sir Ian) Jacob and Captain (later Brigadier) Cornwall-Jones. Immediately on the outbreak of war, the War Office let me have Lieutenant (later Captain Lord) Coleridge, R.N., who served with me throughout the war and was a tower of strength when I became Secretary General to NATO. Subsequent reinforcements and replacements who served in the Defence Office for varying periods included Captain (later Brigadier) Antony Head, who was Secretary of State for War from 1952 to 1956; Captain (later Major General) C. R. Price; Captain (later Colonel) Duncan Sandys, M.P., who has held numerous ministerial offices, including Supply, Housing, Defence and Civil Aviation; Major (later Sir George) Mallaby; Wing-Commander (later Marshal of the R.A.F. Sir Dermot) Boyle; Captain (later Vice Admiral Sir Eric) Clifford; and Group-Captain (later Air-Marshal) A. Earle. I have never been able to find words to express the gratitude which I owe to all these officers and also to the other members of my staff whom I have not been able to mention by name.

Before Munich I had hoped against hope up to the very last moment that peace might be preserved. Now I prayed that we should spring to arms the moment that Hitler laid hands on Poland. If we did so, we might or might not be destroyed. But if we failed to do so, we would be dishonoured for ever. I was not frightened or even excited, but I was furious — furious with ourselves as well as with the Nazis. Less than twenty-one years had passed since the Germans had lain prostrate at our feet. Now they were at our throats. How had we been so craven or so careless as to allow this to happen? The Cenotaph was almost on the doorstep of our office, and every time I passed it I felt a sense of guilt that we who had survived the First World War had broken faith with those who had died.

> 'To you from failing hands we throw
> The torch; be yours to hold it high.
> If ye break faith with us who die
> We shall not sleep, though poppies grow
> In Flanders fields.' [1]

They had given their lives in the belief that they were fighting the war which was to end wars. And now their sons and grandsons were about to be sent to the slaughter.

---

[1] John McCrae: *In Flanders Fields.*

CHAPTER VII

The Twilight War

1939–1940

ON SUNDAY morning, 3 September, the Chiefs of Staff were still in session in their underground war room at 11. At that moment, I thought it my duty, as Secretary, to bring it to the formal notice of the Committee that the British ultimatum had expired and that we were now at war with Germany. My intervention was received without comment. We emerged from the nether regions just in time to hear the wailing of the banshee, and when I reached my office in Richmond Terrace my staff had disappeared and locked away all my papers. The instructions laid down had been faithfully observed for the first — and probably the last — time; and there was nothing for it but to follow them to the shelter in the basement. It was very crowded and one or two of the girls were in tears. A year later they were to be seen stepping out into the fiercest blitz without a qualm. I assured them that it was a false alarm. This was true. And I added that in any case the shelter in which they had taken refuge provided complete security. This was probably very far from the truth. In point of fact I never visited this depressing cellar again until the night blitz started a year later; and on the only occasion that I tried sleeping there, I thought its security doubtful and its discomfort intolerable, and returned to my camp-bed on the second floor.

The war news was catastrophic. The Polish forces were evidently much less powerful than we had supposed and were being pulverised. It was painful and humiliating to be unable to do anything to help them. The Royal Navy were of course already hard at it protecting our sea lanes, capturing enemy shipping and enforcing the blockade. But none of these activities could bring any immediate relief to Poland. One might have expected the French Army, on which such high hopes were placed, to have drawn off some of the weight of the *Blitzkrieg* on Poland by an attack from the west. But the French insisted that their army was nothing like ready, that their aviation was deplorably weak, that the fortifications of the Siegfried Line were immensely strong, and that an immediate attack could only lead to complete disaster. In the light of the knowledge that we now have, their estimate was mistaken, but who were we, without even a platoon as yet on the Continent, to argue the matter? The Royal Air Force was hampered by the distances involved, and hamstrung by the condition that none but strictly military targets were to be attacked. They were nevertheless determined to act offensively; and on the day after war was declared, 4 September, twenty-nine bombers were dispatched to attack German naval units in Brunsbüttel and Wilhelmshaven harbours. From the moment that they were due to return I started badgering Air Marshal Richard Peirse, Deputy Chief of the Air Staff, for news. He sounded as much on tenterhooks as I was, and suggested that I should keep him company at the Air Ministry. I gladly accepted, and at last reports began to filter through. The results were insignificant and our losses were seven bombers. The time was not very far distant when the departure of more than a thousand of our aircraft to Germany on a single night did not rob one of a moment's sleep. It was not that one had become callous. It was because one realised that emotions had to be kept under control if one was going to do one's work properly. All through that first winter nothing but leaflets were dropped on Germany, and it was not until the war had been in progress for over six months that the first bomb was dropped on a land target — the sea-plane base at Hörnum on the island of Sylt.

The arrangements which were made with the French Government in 1938 for the inter-Allied direction of the war have already been described. Let us now see how they stood the test of war. The first meeting of the Supreme War Council was held at Abbeville early in September. Mr Chamberlain took Lord Chatfield and me with him, and M. Daladier, Prime Minister of France, was accompanied by General Gamelin. There was no agreed agenda, and the discussions were discursive and not very profitable. Subsequent meetings of the Council, held now in England and now in France, were attended by more representative national delegations and proved very useful. Those which took place after the Twilight War had ended will be described in some detail in their proper place. Those which took place before that time were instrumental in reaching a number of decisions of vital importance in both the political and military fields. In the military field, the Council agreed at its meeting on 17 November to approve the plan recommended by General Gamelin that in the event of a German violation of Belgian territory, the Allied forces should at once move forward into Belgium in order to hold the Germans as far east as possible. This became known as Plan D. In the political field, the Council recorded a solemn agreement at the meeting on 28 March 1940 that neither side would make a separate peace or armistice.

It should be noted that the Supreme War Council was an advisory body, and its conclusions were not binding unless and until they were confirmed by both Governments. Of course it stands to reason that, if the conclusions reached were within the framework of instructions which the two Prime Ministers had already agreed with their ministerial colleagues, they could be implemented without further reference back. It also stands to reason that the advice of a Council which consisted of the Heads of both Governments, and such eminent advisers as they desired to have with them, was extremely likely to be accepted by their ministerial colleagues. Nevertheless it is important that the constitutional position should be correctly understood.

The Council meetings during the Twilight War were not always productive, but they provided a pleasant change from the daily routine, and I particularly enjoyed an occasion on which we went to France by destroyer. We were a large party — the Prime Minister, Lord Halifax (then Foreign Secretary), Mr Churchill, the three Chiefs of Staff and myself. Mr Churchill, attired as an Elder Brother of Trinity House, made it clear from the outset that the journey was a naval occasion, that he, as First Lord, was our host, and that 'a good time was going to had by all.' He must have travelled in scores of destroyers and crossed the Channel on almost innumerable occasions, but his enthusiasm that morning was spontaneous and infectious. The Prime Minister and Halifax were led directly to a post of honour on the bridge, and the rest of us were given to understand that we would be missing a great treat if we retired to the ward-room instead of staying on deck. As luck would have it, a stray mine was spotted, and the order went forth that it was to be destroyed by rifle fire. Churchill insisted on planting a steel helmet on Mr Chamberlain's head to protect him against the splinters. The combination of this ill-fitting head-gear and the well-known, badly rolled umbrella was somewhat incongruous. At the Council Meeting that morning, Churchill was scrupulously careful to leave the lead in Chamberlain's hands. Indeed I cannot remember that he intervened in the discussion at all. That night the whole embassy party took themselves to bed at an early hour, but Lord Halifax told me the next morning that just as he was about to turn out his lights, Churchill had arrived in a dressing-gown and observed that it was very seldom that two intelligent people got the chance of a nice uninterrupted talk. Halifax did not say how long the talk lasted, but he looked extremely sleepy on our return journey.

There can be no doubt that on the whole the Supreme War Council served a useful purpose, but the lack of a permanent Anglo-French secretariat to maintain records, preserve continuity, and ensure systematic procedure was a grave defect. As will be seen later in my account, this omission was rectified with the happiest results when the time came for setting up Anglo-American machinery for the supreme direction of the war.

About ten days before Christmas I accompanied Mr Chamberlain to Lord Gort's headquarters at Arras in France. During the first day he was told about the military situation, the progress of our defences, and various problems of general administration. He listened attentively, but unlike his successor as Prime Minister, asked very few questions. The next day was spent inspecting the troops and defences on the Belgian frontier. The construction of pill-boxes and anti-tank ditches was proceeding apace, but there seemed a great deal still to be done, and I could not help feeling thankful that the Germans were unlikely to attack in the winter months. It also struck me as somewhat odd that in the event of a violation of Belgian territory, we were to leave those elaborate defences and fight an encounter battle in Belgium, but both Governments had agreed that this was the right policy. For most of the day I drove in the same car as General Dill. He was depressed. He appeared to have a very high opinion of the German forces and a correspondingly low one of the French; and he expressed grave anxiety about our lack of armour, or of any effective means of stopping enemy armour.

After two days with Gort, we drove to Rheims by car and had discussions with Air Marshal Barratt, the commander of the 'Air Striking Force.' The chain of command seemed very peculiar. Barratt was entirely independent not only of Gort, but of the French High Command, and received his orders from the Commander-in-Chief, Bomber Command, in England. It almost seemed as though the Air Staff would prefer to have their forces under Beelzebub rather than anyone connected with the Army. When one recalls the views which were then held by the General Staff on the employment of air power, one can scarcely blame them. That night we went in Gamelin's extremely comfortable train to Verdun, and the next day we visited the Maginot Line in Lorraine. This was a depressing experience. The fort over which we were shown looked more like an underground city with its garrison living like troglodytes. All the guns in the world could fire at them, and all the aircraft bomb them, without the inmates even hearing the noise. One would imagine that a few days in that sort of environment would sap the offensive spirit of even the bravest soldier. There was a good deal of new construction going on in the rear of the fort, and my enquiry from the French Army commander who accompanied us, elicited the reply that these new works were designed to secure '*profondeur*.' It seemed a little late in the day to have realised that elementary necessity. The only bright spot in a bitterly cold and utterly dismal day was the receipt of the news that the *Graf Spee* had scuttled herself in Montevideo harbour. Our French friends were very correct in offering their congratulations, but clearly had little enthusiasm for naval affairs. What they wanted from us was a bigger and better army, and a much, much bigger air force.

For some time before September 1939 we had been nominally at peace but practically at war. Now we were at war — but, except at sea, practically at peace. Our bombers occasionally sallied forth at night to drop leaflets over Germany, but no one tried to stop or hurt them. The blackout added to our discomforts, but not to our security. The staffs of the Service Departments multiplied exceedingly, and London was full of officers in uniform. At the start we all obediently carried gas-masks, but this tiresome practice was soon discarded by senior officers, except those with an exaggerated sense of discipline. So much so that a young naval officer who found difficulty in identifying army badges of rank was advised to salute everyone who did not carry a gas-mask.

It is hardly going too far to say that 'business as usual' seemed to be the prevailing mood. Food rationing was not started for several months after the outbreak of war, and then only in limited form. Conscription was applied by slow stages, and at the turn of the year there were over a million unemployed. Generally speaking, the normal working hours of peace-time were observed and war production was lagging. In Whitehall planning continued unceasingly, but was almost exclusively defensive: for, except at sea, we had not the wherewithal to carry the war into the enemy camp. The British Government and people were profoundly uneasy, but for the most part there seemed to be little conception of what the Fates had in store for us, and little recognition of the supreme exertions and sacrifices which would be required if we were to survive. I am ashamed to admit that at first I welcomed the lull. I thought, in my folly, that time was on our side, and was inclined to agree with Mr Chamberlain's unfortunate observation that Hitler had 'missed the bus.' As it turned out, we were falling further and further behind the Germans in strength of armaments.

From time to time I accompanied the Chiefs of Staff on their visits to General Gamelin's headquarters in the Château de Vincennes. Sometimes the Supreme Commander was alone with his *'famille militaire'* headed by Colonel Petibon: sometimes he was supported by Admiral Darlan and General Vuillemin, the Commander of the French Air Force: and on one occasion General Georges, who commanded the Northern Group of Armies (including the BEF), Gort and Pownall were also present. But the impression left on me by all these meetings was that our allies were getting more and more despondent as the weeks passed.

The shops in Paris were full of scarves, handkerchiefs and favours inscribed *Il faut en finir,* and the references at the *Folies Bergère* to what was going to happen to Hitler and the Siegfried Line were received with hysterical applause. But it was all make-believe. The soldiers in the trenches were being methodically rotted by the German propaganda campaign, of which the key-note was that the British would fight to the last Frenchman, and there seemed to be a grave lack of confidence in the High Command. Every offensive action that we proposed was vetoed on the grounds that it would result in German retaliation on undefended France. It seemed a little late in the day to realise that if one engaged in war one was liable to get hurt. On my return from a visit to Paris in the early months of 1940, my wife remarked that I was looking more exhausted and depressed than she had ever seen me, and demanded to know what was the matter. At first I said that it had been a very long day, but I ultimately confessed that I had come to the conclusion that the French were not going to fight seriously. I quickly added that I had no grounds for my pessimism, and that I should probably feel quite differently when I had had a good sleep.

Throughout my years of duty in Whitehall I had nearly always lunched at the United Service Club and had much enjoyed this interlude in the daily grind. But from the first day of war it ceased to be enjoyable. Generals of the days of my youth used to waylay me with the observation that I was 'just the boy to tell them all about the war.' I was sorry for these old war-horses who had been put out to grass, and would not have offended them for the world. Other retired friends, who were my contemporaries, would beg me almost on bended knee to find them a job, protesting that they were still physically fit and mentally alert. Was not there any niche, however humble, poorly paid, or even unpaid, which they could fill? But for good fortune, I myself might have been in similar plight, and I used to listen sympathetically, and promise to do what I could. Alas it was only rarely that I could help. I was less sympathetic with another sort of inquisitor — the type of man, and there were many of them, who had a big idea for winning the war. He would lurk about the entrance to the club and buttonhole me as soon as I crossed the threshold. After explaining that he had rung me several times in my office and always been told that I was either out of the building or at a committee meeting (how I blessed my staff for being such vigilant watch dogs!), he would launch into an interminable dissertation on his latest brain wave. Once it was the flying tank; another time a pilotless aeroplane; another time a plan for burning down German forests. As a rule I used to listen to these men with what patience I could muster and promise to forward any ideas which they might send to me in writing to the proper quarters; but occasionally I could endure it no longer and fled to the peace of my office with my lunch unfinished. In the end I was compelled to go elsewhere for my midday meal. White's proved ideal. All the young, and many of the not-so-young members were away fighting, and those who were too old to be accepted had no bright ideas for winning the war, and were careful not to embarrass me by asking questions which it would have been difficult to answer. One or two of them did not follow the war very closely. General Alexander, fresh from his triumphs in Italy, came into the Club one day in a flannel suit, and was greeted by a contemporary who lived in Ireland: 'Hullo Alex, I haven't seen or heard of you since the war started. What have you been doing with yourself?' To which Alexander replied: 'I'm still soldiering.'

CHAPTER VIII

Mr Chamberlain's Machinery of War Direction

1940

T H E First World War had been in progress for some two and a half years before an effective machinery of war direction was set up. In the Second World War the time-lag was not so long, although we had our teething troubles. Since I was one of the few who were closely concerned with every stage in the evolution of this machine, I deem it my duty to tell the story in some detail for the benefit of the student of war and of such of my readers as may be interested in these matters.

On the outbreak of war, Mr Chamberlain set up a small War Cabinet on the Lloyd George model. But now there was an entirely new feature to be fitted into the mechanism. In the war of 1914-18, the two Chiefs of Staff advised the War Cabinet on matters connected with their respective services independently of each other. The situation had now been fundamentally changed by the creation of the Chiefs of Staff Committee,[1] charged with the collective responsibility for advising His Majesty's Government on defence policy as a whole. In a time of peace, the Chiefs of Staff Committee used to report to the Cabinet through their parent body, the Committee of Imperial Defence; but when, on the outbreak of war, the latter went into sus-

[1] See page 51.

pense, they reported to the Cabinet direct. As a result, the Cabinet found themselves involved in the formulation of military policy at too early a stage and in too much detail, and it was felt that there should be some smaller ministerial body, which could concentrate on defence and form a link between the Cabinet and the Chiefs of Staff Committee. Accordingly, the Standing Ministerial Committee on Military Co-ordination was set up at the end of October. Its terms of reference were 'to keep under constant review on behalf of the War Cabinet the main factors in the strategic situation and the progress of operations, and to make recommendations from time to time to the War Cabinet as to the general conduct of the war.' The Chairman was Lord Chatfield, Minister for the Co-ordination of Defence, and the members were the three Service Ministers and the Minister of Supply. Curiously enough, the Committee included no authority on foreign policy.

Even in the comparative lull of the Twilight War, this system of supreme direction did not work satisfactorily. The Chiefs of Staff, after considerable discussion of a problem, would report their conclusions, or differences, to the Ministerial Co-ordination Committee. There the whole ground would have to be gone over again, and perhaps a new set of conclusions or differences would be reached. The matter would then go to the War Cabinet, and once more the process of explanation and disputation would have to be repeated. I believe that most of us, whether Ministers or officials, who were cogs in the machine, felt that it would fail to secure the necessary speed of decision once the war started in earnest. But even before that happened an obvious change suggested itself.

The position of the Minister for the Co-ordination of Defence had always been anomalous. On the one hand, he was held by Parliament and the public to have responsibilities covering the whole field of defence. On the other hand, he had no executive authority whatsoever. Looking back, one cannot escape the feeling that the creation of the post had been a compromise, dictated by political rather than practical considerations. Nevertheless, by dint of goodwill on the part of all concerned, it had undoubtedly served a useful, if limited, purpose in time of peace. But when war broke out and the three Service Ministers were included in the War Cabinet, a military co-ordinator, without a vestige of power, became redundant. Lord

Chatfield felt his position keenly, but I never heard a word of complaint pass his lips. One evening at the beginning of April 1940 he told me in confidence that Mr Chamberlain had asked for his resignation. He looked sad, as well he might; and I shared his sadness. His whole life had been spent in the service of his country. Only a few weeks before the outbreak of war, we had gone to the theatre together. Our seats were in the middle of a row, and owing to pressure of work we were late. There are few things more maddening than having late-comers climbing across one's feet when one is watching a good play. We both felt guilty, and we apologised profusely; a hardbitten-looking man seemed very cross until he recognise Lord Chatfield, when he said to me: 'Don't worry. We would do anything for *him*.' That was how he stood in public opinion. And now, in the eyes of the world he was going to appear a failure and there would be an abrupt ending of the devoted service of a lifetime.

The more I thought about it, the more convinced I was that the Prime Minister's decision was right. So, greatly daring, I wrote to Lord Chatfield that same evening to say how relieved I was for his sake. Up to the present, we had suffered no major disasters, but the Twilight War would not last for ever. When the storm broke, it seemed highly probable that, owing to our relative weakness and general unpreparedness, we would suffer dire forfeits in the first instance. For these the blame would inevitably, albeit most unjustly, be laid at the door of the Minister for the Co-ordination of Defence. Little did I suspect that we were to receive our first shock within a week.

Lord Chatfield resigned on 3 April. The next day we learned that his post was not going to be filled, but that the Chairmanship of the Military Co-ordination Committee would in future be undertaken by the First Lord of the Admiralty, as the senior Service Minister. I had always hoped that Mr Churchill's unrivalled experience of war and his unique qualifications would be given more scope, but I felt instinctively that this new arrangement was another compromise which would not work. I could not see how any man, even a Winston Churchill, could run the Service Department which was at that time far the most actively engaged in hostilities, and at the same time exercise effective supervision over the Committee which was responsible for advising the War Cabinet on the conduct of the war as a whole. But, having learnt by experience that it is unwise to be dogmatic on questions of this kind, and that the success of any organisation depends in the ultimate issue on the human element, I was quite prepared to see it work out all right. Anyway, I hoped it would.

The Ministerial Co-ordination Committee held its first meeting under Churchill's chairmanship on 8 April. On the very next day, Hitler fell upon Denmark and Norway, but for the sake of clarity, I propose to conclude my account of Mr Chamberlain's machinery of war direction before dealing with the Norwegian episode. Directly the Twilight War ended, the meetings of the Military Co-ordination Committee became at once more frequent, more controversial and — may I say — more acrimonious! After a week's trial, Mr Churchill represented to Mr Chamberlain that in present circumstances nobody except the Prime Minister himself had the authority to ensure the necessary rapidity of decision and action. Accordingly, Mr Chamberlain agreed that, in future, he would himself preside over all meetings at which matters of exceptional importance relating to the general conduct of the war were under discussion. This ended in his having to preside at no less than nine out of the next ten meetings.

The Ministerial Co-ordination Committee was not the only feature of our machinery which was proving unsatisfactory at this juncture. It had always been visualised that in time of war the Chiefs of Staff Committee would constitute a Battle Headquarters, and that as such they would have the responsibility, *inter alia,* for the selection of commanders, for issuing directives and subsequent instructions to these commanders, and for receiving their reports. But in the flurry of the Norwegian campaign, nothing of the sort happened. On the contrary, the worst shortcomings of the First World War, as exemplified by the conduct of the Dardanelles campaign, were faithfully repeated. The Chief of the Naval Staff and the Chief of the Imperial General Staff acted with sturdy independence. They appointed their respective commanders without consultation with each other; and, worse still, they gave directives to those commanders without harmonising them. Thereafter they continued to issue separate orders to them. Thus confusion was worse confounded. The best that can be said is that we learned, at not too prohibitive a cost, how things should not be done.

Perhaps it was this lack of inter-Service co-operation which in-

spired a tale which gave us food for laughter, at a time when there
was not much to laugh about. A New Zealand major arrived in London and was instructed to report to the War Office. He found Whitehall easily enough, and approached a naval lieutenant for further
directions. 'Which side is the War Office on?' he asked. The young
sailor looked puzzled. 'I'm afraid I don't know for certain,' he replied. 'At the beginning of the war we thought that they were on
ours, but now we are not at all sure.' It is satisfactory to be able to
record that the weaknesses in our machinery of supreme direction
were soon remedied, and that the Chiefs of Staff organisation developed in course of time into the most efficient Battle Headquarters in
our history.

At the end of April, Mr Chamberlain summoned me to No. 10. He
told me that it had been decided that in future Mr Churchill would
not only take the chair at all meetings of the Ministerial Co-ordination Committee at which the Prime Minister himself did not preside,
but would also be responsible *on behalf of that Committee* for giving guidance and direction to the Chiefs of Staff Committee. Mr
Churchill was to be assisted by a suitable 'Central Staff' under a
senior staff officer, who would be an additional member of the Chiefs
of Staff Committee. The officer in question was to be myself!

These arrangements seemed rather odd. How would the Secretary
of State for War and the Secretary of State for Air feel about their
respective Chiefs of Staff taking orders from the First Lord of the
Admiralty? Would they be prepared to be excluded from meetings of
the Chiefs of Staff Committee summoned by Mr Churchill? As for
Mr Churchill's chairmanship of the Ministerial Co-ordination Committee, this had already been tried and abandoned after a week's
trial. The proposed staff arrangements seemed even more odd. Presumably the Military Wing of the War Cabinet Secretariat would continue to be responsible for the secretarial arrangements of all military
committees, including the Military Co-ordination Committee and the
Chiefs of Staff Committee. It was therefore difficult to see exactly
what duties would fall to the special Central Staff responsible to Mr
Churchill alone. I voiced some of my misgivings to Mr Chamberlain,
but he left me in no doubt that the decision was final, and instructed
me to report to Mr Churchill forthwith.

My feelings as I walked to the Admiralty were mixed. On the one hand I was to have the chance, for which I had always longed, of serving directly under Churchill; on the other, it seemed to me that his position was going to be just as unsatisfactory and nebulous as Lord Chatfield's had been. As I saw it, he would not be able to give the Chiefs of Staff the guidance and direction which he himself thought best, but *only such guidance and direction as the Military Co-ordination Committee approved.* In other words, he was to have responsibility without any real authority. As for myself, I had no idea of the reason for my having been made an additional member of the Chiefs of Staff Committee, or of the functions which I and the new Central Staff were expected to exercise. Were we going to be advisers? Surely not. And what was to happen to my trusted staff in the War Cabinet Secretariat? Would they still be under me, or would I be altogether divorced from them? I profoundly hoped that Mr Churchill would be able to enlighten me.

He was obviously expecting me, as I was shown straight into his presence. To my surprise he gave the impression of being enthusiastic about the new arrangements. Anyway, he was clearly determined to lose no time in giving effect to them, and he had already had a spacious room adjoining his own office prepared for my exclusive use. I expressed suitable gratitude, but suggested that my permanent location must be in the War Cabinet Secretariat building. Unless I were in the middle of the Whitehall 'web,' with my own chosen staff around me, I would be unable to function effectively. This argument was brushed aside, and he proceeded to discuss the personnel of my Central Staff — Oliver Lyttelton for supply problems, Desmond Morton on the political side, Professor Lindemann for scientific research and statistical work, and so forth. I ventured to recall the confusion that there had been when Lloyd George had set up a special private staff in the grounds of 10, Downing Street. This had come to be known as the 'Garden Suburb' and had caused nothing but friction with all Departments. I pleaded that the War Cabinet Secretariat, the Military Wing of which was under my control, could, with certain adjustments and perhaps reinforcement, give him all the service he required to discharge his new responsibilities, and that the creation of a special high-power staff of the type that he contemplated not only was unnecessary and undesirable but would also create immense confusion. Mr Churchill turned a deaf ear to my protest and instructed me to submit proposals 'on one page' showing exactly what my Central Staff was to consist of and how we were to work. I went away filled with gloom, and proceeded to write a paper which proved, conclusively as I thought — that the best, indeed the only, practical arrangement was to use the existing machinery. Incidentally I failed to compress my argument into less than three foolscap pages. I was to become more adroit in later years.

Having despatched my paper I was unhappy. My close association with Churchill looked like being short-lived. He was not the sort of man to suffer a chief of staff who made difficulties. But I was saved by the pressure of events. The new arrangements were announced on 1 May, but there were so many urgent questions demanding immediate decision that no one, least of all Mr Churchill, had time to worry about problems of organisation. Consequently, in the absence of orders to the contrary, I continued to work in the middle of the 'web' at 2, Richmond Terrace with my trusted colleagues around me, and made no attempt to recruit the Central Staff. On the other hand, I spent increasingly long periods of the day, and more especially of the night, in the company of Mr Churchill, and the meetings of the Military Co-ordination Committee were generally held at the Admiralty, instead of at Richmond Terrace as heretofore. It is possible, though in my view extremely unlikely, that the new arrangements might have been made to work. But momentous changes were imminent.

When one is working anything up to fourteen hours a day within the confines of Whitehall, one tends to lose touch with the outside world. I therefore had no idea of how deep-seated or widespread was the dissatisfaction of Parliament with the conduct of the war, and in particular with the failures and frustrations in Norway, until the stormy debates of 7 and 8 May in the House of Commons. Both days were packed with drama — Amery lashing Mr Chamberlain with his vitriolic peroration, in which he quoted Cromwell's words to the Long Parliament: 'Depart, I say, and let us have done with you. In the name of God, go!'; Lloyd George begging the Prime Minister to set an example of sacrifice by giving up the seals of office; Mr Chamberlain appealing to his friends; Admiral Sir Roger Keyes denouncing the Admiralty Staff, some of them his old shipmates, and protesting that he had begged the War Cabinet to allow him to 'take all the responsibility and lead the attack' (on Trondheim in Norway).

No one who reads the full account of the debate can fail to be impressed by the part played by Mr Churchill. He was — as he had recently told Mr Chamberlain — most unhappy about the complete failure of our methods of conducting the war. He had heard many of the fiercest critics of the Government doing their utmost to exculpate him and to drive a wedge between him and his colleagues; and he must have sensed that a large body of parliamentary opinion passionately desired his leadership. He felt in his heart of hearts — as he afterwards wrote — that if it fell to him to lead the nation, he would not fail. The temptation to play for his own hand must have been overwhelming. A lesser man might have succumbed. Not so Churchill. Not for nothing had Lord Birkenhead written twenty years earlier, 'There is no man in public life with a loyalty so unswerving and so dependable.' [1] Not for nothing had Mr Chamberlain, within the last few days, described him as 'absolutely loyal.' To Lloyd George's suggestion that the First Lord was not entirely responsible for what had happened, Churchill at once retorted, 'I take complete responsibility for everything that has been done by the Admiralty, and I take my full share of the burden.' And, in winding up the debate, he ferociously attacked not only the Opposition for insisting on a division but also those Conservatives who had turned against the Government in its hour of trial. Nor did he stop there. When the debate was over, he tried to convince Mr Chamberlain that he still had a good majority and ought not to resign. There are those who might say that, in the national interest, he was wrong to carry loyalty so far. Be that as it may, loyalty is a noble and a lovable trait.

Two days later, on 10 May, we learned in the early hours of the morning that Hitler's long-awaited assault on the Low Countries had started, and in the evening that Mr Chamberlain had resigned and that Mr Churchill reigned in his stead. The idea is prevalent that backroom boys know everything that is going on behind the scenes. I can only say that, although I was in almost constant attendance on Mr Churchill during those days, my first intimation that he was to be Prime Minister was his summons to Buckingham Palace. And so it

[1] Birkenhead: *Contemporary Personalities.*

came to pass that, on the very day that Hitler launched his attack on the Low Countries, the man who was to prove the greatest war Prime Minister in our history took over the leadership from the man who might well have been one of our greatest peace Prime Ministers, if only the war could have been averted. He was, as he said of himself: 'a man of peace to the depths of my soul,' [1] and no one who knew him can doubt that he would have gladly laid down his life to preserve it.

The change in leadership may have given rise to a few misgivings in Whitehall. There is a type of senior official, both civil and military, who get more and more set in their ways as they ascend the ladder of promotion. These able, upright, worthy men do not like the even tenor of their lives disturbed, and resent dynamic ministerial control. This is precisely what they were likely to suffer at Churchill's hands. But, whatever misgivings there were in Whitehall, certainly the nation as a whole acclaimed his leadership with enthusiasm. Almost overnight the British public took him to their hearts. Here was a man whom they understood and who understood them; a man who would not be content with merely warding off the enemy's blows, but would 'give it them back' with all the power at his command. Two or three days after he became Prime Minister, I walked with him from Downing Street to the Admiralty. A number of people waiting outside the private entrance greeted him with cries of 'Good luck, Winnie. God bless you.' He was visibly moved, and as soon as we were inside the building, he dissolved into tears. 'Poor people,' he said, 'poor people. They trust me, and I can give them nothing but disaster for quite a long time.'

Personally I was thrilled by the turn which events had taken. For some reason, which I have never been able to explain, I had never thought that we could lose the war. At the same time I had never been able to see how we were going to win it. Here was the one Englishman who would provide the answer to that question, and who, I was sure, would lead us to ultimate victory, however long and hard the road might be. Mr Churchill has said that, at that moment, he felt as though he was 'walking with destiny.' [2] I, in my lowly sphere, felt much the same. I did not know exactly what sort of ma-

[1] Mr Chamberlain's broadcast to the nation on 27 September 1938.
[2] Churchill: *The Second World War.*

chinery he would set up for the conduct of the war, but it seemed pretty certain that he himself would exercise a personal and continuous direction over the whole field, and that I would have the chance of serving him very closely. At the same time, my joy at the prospect was tempered by the fear that I might prove unequal, or unsuited, to the job. Churchill was reputed to have a preference for men who were imaginative and unorthodox. I could lay claim to neither of these qualities. I have never been gifted with much imagination, and although I had seen a good deal of scallywag fighting I had always been a very orthodox scallywag. On the other hand, I had a few assets. I had worked and formed friendships with many leading personalities, both civilian and military. I had an intimate knowledge of the workings of Whitehall. I had a robust constitution, and, perhaps most important of all, a burning desire to be of service to the one man who could pull us through. The first time that I saw him after he had become Prime Minister, I was too shy to congratulate him. But my whole heart went out to him in his superhuman task, and I made a silent vow that whatever he asked of me, I would do my utmost to give — with one reservation. However much he pressed me, I would never say that I agreed with him on any question of consequence unless I in fact did so. If once I said 'Yes' when I thought 'No,' I would be no more use to him. Later in the war, we had an argument on some point or other, and I stuck obstinately to my opinion. He scolded me for not agreeing with him, so I told him of the vow I had made at the outset of our association. His reaction was characteristic. 'You should forget these outmoded Staff College shibboleths.' This, with simulated ferocity, betrayed by an endearing twinkle, indicated that the argument was closed — for the time being.

CHAPTER IX

The Rape of Norway
and Denmark

1940

T H E changes which Mr Churchill made in our machinery for the
conduct of the war will be described later in my narrative. Meanwhile, let us return to the events which were the occasion for the downfall of Mr Chamberlain.

The Twilight War ended for me in a most unexpected and dramatic way. In the very early hours of 9 April, I was wakened out of a
deep sleep by the telephone bell. It was the Duty Officer at the War
Cabinet Office. I could not make head or tail of what he was saying,
in spite of frequent requests for repetition; so, suspecting the trouble,
I suggested that he should draw the blackout curtains, switch on the
lights, find his false teeth and say it all over again. My diagnosis was
evidently correct, because after a pause, he started speaking again
and was perfectly intelligible. His report was brutal in its simplicity.
The Germans had seized Copenhagen, Oslo, and all the main ports of
Norway. My first reaction was mechanical. 'I am coming to the office
at once. Ring up the Chief of the Air Staff [1] and tell him that, in anticipation of his instructions, I am arranging a meeting of the Chiefs of

---

[1] Marshal of the R.A.F. Sir Cyril Newall who was then Chairman of the
C.O.S. Committee.

118

Staff Committee for 6.30 A.M. Directly you have his agreement, tell the other two Chiefs of Staff.'

As I hurried into my clothes I realised, for the first time in my life, the devastating and demoralising effect of surprise. I had always thought that Hitler's next move would be either an invasion of the Low Countries and France, or alternatively an air attack on the British Isles. The idea of an operation of this scope against Scandinavia had never entered my head. It was only recently that the Chiefs of Staff had recorded the opinion that any sea-borne operations against the western seaboard of Norway would be impracticable, in view of our great naval superiority.

We had suspected, it is true, that some mischief was brewing in Norwegian waters, for there had been reliable information two nights previously that a sizable German naval force was on the move northwards, and at the War Cabinet meeting the next morning the First Lord had reported that a few hours previously the destroyer *Glow-worm* had signalled that she was in action against a superior force, that her signals had suddenly ceased, and that she had evidently been overwhelmed. This was confirmation that a German force was at sea, but it was thought that their objective was probably limited to forestalling any action that we might take at Narvik. Now it transpired that without the slightest warning, without the semblance of an excuse, they had laid violent hands on an innocent, neutral country, with whom they had no quarrel whatsoever. One did not expect Hitler to stop at much, but this was an outrage beyond all bounds. The infamy which had inspired the operation, the immensity of its scope, and the rapidity and precision with which it had been executed were staggering. So far as I knew, we had not a vestige of a plan to deal with it. All the same, we surely had the means of effective counter-attack. Our naval superiority was overwhelming. Could we not harry the lives out of the German forces stationed along that long coast line? Could we not at once bomb the German forces in the ports which they had seized before they had had time to instal A-A Defences? Had not Hitler over-reached himself in a reckless gamble? These were the thoughts that jostled each other in my mind as I hurried off to Richmond Terrace. But they were nothing like so coherent or so orderly as might appear from this record.

The gathering that assembled in my office at 6.30 A.M. was not exactly inspiring. I had hoped that one or other of the Chiefs of Staff would have a plan of action, but so far as I can remember not a single constructive suggestion had been put forward by the time that we had to break up the meeting and join the War Cabinet at 10, Downing Street. I have little recollection of what transpired, but Mr Churchill has recorded that the War Cabinet decided that he 'should authorise the Commander-in-Chief of the Home Fleet to take all possible steps to clear Bergen and Trondheim of enemy forces, and that the Chiefs of Staff should set on foot preparations for military expeditions to recapture both those places and to occupy Narvik.' [1]

Amphibious operations are a very specialised form of warfare. They have 'to fit together like a jewelled bracelet,' as Churchill once said. They require highly-trained personnel, a great variety of technical equipment, a detailed knowledge of the points at which the landings are to take place, accurate information about the enemy's strength and dispositions, and, perhaps above all, meticulous planning and preparation. In the case of the projected Norwegian expeditions, none of these requirements could be fulfilled. The resources available were inadequate and unsuitable; we had to make the best of whatever we could scrape together. Our information about the enemy's strength and dispositions was vague in the extreme. Our knowledge of the Norwegian ports was incomplete, and there was no time for meticulous planning. In the circumstances, the hazards of the operations were generally recognised, but no one was in doubt that, in spite of them, we must do what we could to help poor little Norway. The business of war would be far less complicated, if only purely military considerations had to be taken into account.

The principal fractions of the plan of intervention were the capture of Narvik in the far north and a direct assault on Trondheim in central Norway. This was to be preceded by subsidiary landings at Namsos, one hundred miles to the north, and Andalesnes, one hundred and fifty miles to the south. To my great joy the command of the Namsos operations was given to my friend of Somaliland days, Major-General Carton de Wiart. For some years before the war he had been living in Poland, where his name was renowned. We had cor-

1 Churchill: *The Second World War.*

responded from time to time. Shortly before Hitler invaded Poland, he had been recalled to the active list, and given charge of our military mission in that country. He had retreated with the Polish Army, escaped into Roumania, and made his way to London. It was a tonic to see the old war-horse again, and absorbingly interesting to learn about modern German technique from one who had seen and felt it. No better man could have been chosen to lead untried and not too highly-trained troops in an adventure of this kind.

Both the Namsos and Andalesnes landings were successful, and the plans and preparations for the attack on Trondheim were being pressed forward with the utmost vigour, when suddenly the Chiefs of Staff unanimously and unequivocally urged that the idea of a frontal assault should be abandoned. They said that there was not enough time to prepare for an intricate operation of this kind, that much of the information that was essential was lacking, that the Home Fleet would have to operate under concentrated air attack, and that the landings were bound to be prohibitively costly. Accordingly they recommended that Trondheim should be enveloped by the forces which had been successfully landed at Namsos and Andalesnes. The War Cabinet had no option but to agree.

In the event, it soon became obvious that the expeditions to Namsos and Andalesnes were helpless in the face of air attack which they had no means of countering, and orders for evacuation from both places were issued. Facilities for re-embarkation were primitive, and there was no air cover. The evacuations were bound to be hazardous. My principal recollection of those days is my sense of relief when we got away from both places early in May with far less loss than could have been expected.

Nor is there much to be said about Trondheim that has not already been said. Even in the light of the knowledge that we now have, it is difficult to say whether it was right or wrong to call off the attack on that key strategic point. It may well be that the risks of the operation were exaggerated. Military advisers generally err on the side of caution. They tend to overrate the enemy's strength and underrate his difficulties. When, for example, we captured all the ports in Italian Africa, it was found that their coast defence armament was only just over half of what our Intelligence Service had estimated. Having been an Intelligence Officer myself, I have every sympathy with the error. When so much is at stake, it is only natural to want to be on the safe side. This applies equally to Planning Staffs. If, for example, they estimate that two brigades might be just sufficient for an operation, who can blame them if they advise that a minimum of three brigades is required? That their tendency to over-insure was not due to any lack of fighting spirit was not always understood by Mr Churchill, and his description of the Joint Planning Committee as the 'machinery of negation' was far from just. On one occasion he was so exasperated by what he termed their prohibitive demands, that he wanted them all sent back to their ships and regiments. Fortunately it was possible to convince him that nothing would give greater pleasure to the 'offenders,' and that the officers brought back from the Front to succeed them would probably make even more prohibitive demands in the hope of similar 'punishment.' Perhaps we could have taken Trondheim without serious loss; but, even if we had done so, we should have been bled white in trying to maintain ourselves there.

I have mentioned that, when the Government's military advisers hardened against the direct attack on Trondheim, Admiral of the Fleet Sir Roger Keyes, one of Mr Churchill's oldest friends, begged to be allowed to *'take all the responsibility and lead it.'* [1] His statement made a deep impression upon the House of Commons during the debates on Norway. I have never understood why. There is no shadow of doubt that Keyes, one of the bravest of the brave, would have given his very soul for the chance of leading the attack, and that he would have led it superbly. There is equally no doubt that every single flag officer in the Royal Navy, including those who had advised against the operation, would have been delighted to have been selected to command it — however forlorn the prospects. For them, there would have been nothing to lose except life; and in war that does not count too much. But the responsibility for deciding whether the operation should or should not take place was a matter for the Government, and the Government alone. How could they delegate it to anyone else? Who was to defend the decision in Parliament, if it proved disastrous? Was the Prime Minister to plead, 'No

[1] Author's italics.

blame attaches to the Government. The Admiral took all responsibility?'

The Norwegian episode was not yet over. There was still Narvik. But by the time that it was captured, every ounce of our strength was required elsewhere, and it was evacuated almost at once.

CHAPTER X

Assault on the West

1940

O N T H E morning of 10 May the long-awaited whirlwind broke in all its force. I was again wakened by a telephone call from the Cabinet Office. The same officer who had rung me up about the attack on Norway happened to be on duty. But this time there was no doubt about his meaning; nor did his message come as a surprise. The German attack on the Low Countries had started. Here, at any rate, was something for which we were prepared. Nor were any immediate decisions required in London, since the Supreme War Council had decided as far back as November 1939 that in the event of a German violation of Belgian territory, the plan known as Plan 'D' would automatically be put into operation. This meant that without any further instructions the British Expeditionary Force would very soon be on the move at top speed into Belgium.

On my way to the office, I pictured the scene at Gort's headquarters at Arras, which I had visited the previous December with Mr Chamberlain — Gort, delighted that the period of inaction had ended, rubbing his hands together and chuckling over his favourite French slogan, *'tout le monde à la bataille.'* My mind went back thirty-five years to the days when he and I were cadets at the Royal Military College, Sandhurst. Even then he had seemed sure to go far.

He had certainly done so. With him, as Chief of Staff, was Henry Pownall, one of the best brains of my vintage in the Army, courageous, competent and cool as a cucumber. How wise he had been to leave the Committee of Imperial Defence in 1936, and go back to troops. I envied him.

The outlook would have been more hopeful if there had been any agreed plans for co-operation with the Belgian and Dutch forces. But all our requests for Staff conversations had been consistently refused by both those Governments. It seemed odd that the Belgians should have imagined that Hitler was more likely to respect their integrity than Kaiser Wilhelm had been in 1914, but the attitude of the Dutch was easier to understand. Not having been dragged into the First World War, they hoped to be able to keep out of the Second. Their chances of being able to do so were remote. In January, Churchill had addressed a warning, forcefully descriptive, to all neutrals. 'Each one hopes that if he feeds the crocodile enough, the crocodile will eat him last.' His words were unheeded. Only a month previously, the world had seen the violation of strictly neutral and wholly innocent Norway and Denmark. Even this example of Nazi frightfulness was ignored. Presumably the only reason which prompted the Dutch to persist in holding the Allies at arm's length was the fear of giving Hitler any justification for picking a quarrel with them. It seemed extraordinary, after the events of the past two years, that anyone could have been so simple as to imagine that the Führer required justification before indulging in aggression. Any lie, however brazen, would be invented to serve his purpose.

When I reached my office, information from the Front was dribbling in. This time Holland was not being by-passed as she had been in 1914. German forces had crashed across her frontiers; the Luftwaffe was relentlessly bombing her towns; and the German fifth column, assisted by traitors, was playing havoc here, there and everywhere. Appeals from the Dutch soon started coming in; but, except for the very little that the Royal Navy could do, it was impossible to help them. They did not blame us; nor was it our fault. But it was none the less painful to be so powerless. It was not the first time that we had been unable to help a friend in trouble; nor was it to be the last.

Throughout that first day of the German onslaught, it was difficult to take much interest in anything else, and we wasted a lot of time poring over maps, and speculating how things were going. Towards midnight, Mr van Kleffens, the Foreign Secretary of Holland, who had escaped by the skin of his teeth from The Hague that morning, arrived in my office to see the Chiefs of Staff. He had two requests. Could we direct bombers to destroy the Moerdijk bridges? And could we, by any means, despatch to Holland a military force sufficiently strong to be of real help? As regards the first, we had to point out that the range of our fighters was insufficient to provide the necessary escort. As regards the second, we were equally helpless. Even if the troops had been available, we had no means of getting them there in time. I remember observing that, alas, we had no magic carpet.

Three days later Mr van Kleffens rang me up at about midnight from Buckingham Palace. He had just had an audience with Queen Wilhelmina, and wanted to see the Prime Minister at once. I said that Mr Churchill had just gone to bed, and that I would prefer not to disturb him unless absolutely necessary. Could Mr van Kleffens come to my office and tell me what he had in mind? If it were something of vital urgency with which I could not deal, I would of course arouse the Prime Minister. Mr van Kleffens agreed. Meanwhile, anticipating that air support was likely to be one of the points which he would raise, I asked Air Vice-Marshal Sholto Douglas, the Deputy Chief of the Air Staff, to join me.

Within half an hour Mr van Kleffens arrived, accompanied by a Dutch colonel who had just escaped from Holland after some hair-raising experiences. His communication was short and simple. Here is the text: 'The possibilities in the Netherlands are the following: (1) Effective help is at once rendered. In that case, effective resistance can be carried on. (2) If effective help is *not* given, the General Commander-in-Chief will be empowered to act as in his judgment he deems best, having regard to the military forces and the civilian population.' Mr van Kleffens enquired whether the British High Command would agree that this was the right course. Sholto Douglas and I had no hesitation in giving him the assurance that he sought. We suggested that when his Commander-in-Chief felt that no further damage could be inflicted on the enemy, and that the continuance of fighting would merely involve further loss of civilian life, it would be his duty to capitulate.

As Mr van Kleffens was leaving, his companion collapsed in a dead faint. The crash of his forehead on the table sounded like a pistol shot. I had nothing wherewith to revive him, and it was some time before he came round. I made a mental note that in future a small first aid box, including a small bottle of brandy, should be part of the equipment of my office; but I forgot all about it until I came to write these memoirs. Fortunately the need never again arose in such acute form. After five days' bludgeoning, Holland capitulated. But the Queen and Government were safely in England, irrevocably determined to continue the struggle with every man, woman, ship and aeroplane that had succeeded in escaping from the clutches of the Nazis.

For the first three or four days such information as we received of the battle in Belgium suggested that everything was going according to plan; but on 14 May we learned that the Germans had crossed the Meuse at Dinant and broken through at Sedan. The next morning the Prime Minister had a personal telephone message from M. Reynaud that the break-through at Sedan was on a wide front, and that 'the battle was lost.' At the time this message seemed somewhat hysterical, but on the following day we received information which left no doubt as to the extreme gravity of the situation. Mr Churchill decided to fly to Paris at once, taking Dill and myself with him. He always preferred to see things for himself and to learn what was happening at first hand.

From the moment we set foot on Le Bourget airfield, there was an unmistakable atmosphere of depression. Colonel Redman, who was in charge of my small liaison mission at General Gamelin's Headquarters, told me that things were much worse than I appeared to imagine, and even hinted that the Germans might be in Paris itself pretty soon. I was flabbergasted. 'But they never got here last time in more than four years,' I protested. 'You will find it is different this time,' was his reply. As we drove through the streets, the people seemed listless and resigned, and they gave no sign of the passionate defiance that had inspired the cry, *'Ils ne passeront pas,'* in the previous struggle. They showed little interest in our heavily-escorted cavalcade, and there were no cheers for Churchill. Some four years later, half a million Parisians were to acclaim him with a frenzy of enthusiasm such as perhaps even the Champs Elysées had never witnessed. But on that Thursday afternoon, how could they know that this was the man whose voice would bring them comfort and hope in the days of their bondage, and who would ultimately encompass their deliverance?

Our first port of call was the British Embassy. In the past I had always admired that imposing building, and had spent many happy hours there. But now it all seemed different. It was like a shell. The cheerful, lived-in atmosphere seemed to have departed, and the rooms felt as though they had been empty for years. They seemed to know that they would soon be deserted by their friends. I am sure that houses have feelings and memories. Since the war I have been to many cheerful parties at the Embassy and greatly enjoyed myself. But even now I cannot enter the building without recalling the depression which I felt on that summer afternoon.

The Quai D'Orsay, where we went after a cup of tea or something stronger, was even more depressing. M. Reynaud, M. Daladier and General Gamelin were awaiting us in a very large room, looking out on to a garden which had appeared so lovely and well kept on my last visit, but which was now disfigured with clusters of bonfires. The French archives were already being consigned to the flames. This was the first meeting of the Supreme War Council at which Churchill had headed the British delegation, and I was interested to see how he would handle the situation. He dominated the proceedings from the moment he entered the room. There was no interpreter, and he spoke throughout in French. His idiom was not always correct, and his vocabulary was not equal to translating all the words which he required with exactitude. But no one could be in any doubt as to his meaning. 'Things seem pretty bad,' was his opening gambit, 'but this is not the first time that we have been in a mess together. We will get out of it all right. What is the situation?' M. Reynaud called on General Gamelin to reply. When he had finished his tale of unmitigated woe, the Prime Minister slapped him heartily on the shoulder (the General winced) and said: 'Evidently this battle will be known as the Battle of the Bulge.' (On the spur of the moment, "Boolge' was the nearest he could get to this in French.) 'Now, my General, when and where are you going to counter-attack — from the north or from the south?' General Gamelin replied dejectedly that he had nothing with which to counter-attack, and that, in any case, he suffered from inferiority of numbers, equipment, method and morale. That was a terrible shock. The Commander-in-Chief seemed already beaten.

For all his simulated cheerfulness, Mr Churchill made it clear that his whole heart went out to his beloved France in her agony, and that we would do all in human power to aid her. Time and again the French insisted that the help which they needed above all else was more fighter squadrons. Indeed I understood General Gamelin, who was no optimist, to say that the battle might yet be saved if we could give them a sufficiency of that kind of support. Mr Churchill undertook to explain the situation to his colleagues in the Cabinet and seek their consent to the despatch of additional fighter squadrons. With that the meeting broke up.

Mr Churchill was convinced that, on both political and military grounds, we ought to send the French ten squadrons of fighters, instead of the four squadrons which the Cabinet had authorised him to offer; but it was never his habit throughout the war to take any major decision without the express approval of his ministerial colleagues. He therefore proceeded to draft a telegram of his recommendations immediately we got back to the Embassy, and he instructed me to arrange for the Cabinet to be summoned at once to consider it. Before leaving London, I had taken the precaution of asking that my Indian Army assistant, Captain Cornwall-Jones, should be available in the office at all times, in case I should want to telephone to him in Hindustani. The transmission of operational information by this means would of course have been too risky; but it might be useful for matters of a lesser order of secrecy. And so it proved. I was able to tell Cornwall-Jones in Hindustani, first, that a very important top secret telegram was being enciphered for despatch; secondly, that the Prime Minister wished the Cabinet to be summoned at once so as to be able to discuss it immediately it was deciphered; and thirdly, that he was to telephone me their decision before midnight.

Within a couple of hours, Cornwall-Jones telephoned the single word '*Han*' (Hindustani for Yes). This was quick work, and I was congratulated on my ingenuity. Alas, candour compelled me to admit that the idea was not original. Mr Lloyd George had done the same thing at one of the post-war conferences, except that he had arranged for a Welsh instead of a Hindustani speaker to be standing by in Whitehall.

Mr Churchill was delighted that the War Cabinet had endorsed his recommendation so promptly, and we thought that he would telephone the good news to M. Reynaud at once. But not at all. He was determined to tell it to him face to face. This was in character. We all know the delight that it gives to some of our friends, especially our younger friends, to watch our expressions as we open their gift parcels. That was Mr Churchill's motive at this moment. He was about to give Reynaud a pearl beyond price, and he wanted to watch his face when he received it.

It was now close on midnight and Reynaud, somewhat to Churchill's surprise, had already left his office, so we made our way to his flat. He appeared slightly disgruntled at the intrusion, but was obviously delighted when he heard the reason for it. He did not look too well pleased however when it was suggested that M. Daladier, who was at that time Minister of National Defence and War, should be invited to come over and learn the good news at first hand. Socially they were not on speaking terms. Nevertheless Mr Churchill was at his most persuasive, and Daladier duly arrived. He, too, expressed profound gratitude.

Churchill spent the night at the British Embassy, while Dill and I slept at the Crillon Hotel. As we left at daybreak on our homeward journey, I wondered how long it would be before I saw Paris again. It was to be in only five days.

After the shock of all that we had seen and heard in Paris, it was a relief to be home again in a world in which everyone seemed calm, cheerful and resolute; and as I drove through the familiar streets, London seemed like a much-loved old nanny, gathering me to her ample bosom and saying, 'Don't fuss and fidget, dearie; it will all come out all right!'

All the same, it was difficult not to fuss and fidget. The news from France got worse and worse, and it was obvious that the wide and ever-deepening penetration of the German armour at Sedan had placed the British Expeditionary Force in dire peril. Their retirement had already been ordered, and the refugee problem was adding immensely to their difficulties.

It is always difficult to get accurate information about a fast-moving battle, and for those who have to wait far from the scene, there is nothing for it but to exercise patience, and to remember that the commander in the field is preoccupied with the conduct of the engagement, and often has neither the time nor the knowledge to report details of its progress. This truism was never fully accepted by my impetuous Chief; nor did he always make sufficient allowance for the fact that, in the fog of war, the commander himself does not know from hour to hour what is happening at every point on an enormous front.

All the same we in London felt that we were being harshly treated by the French High Command. We had placed our Expeditionary Force under their orders, and we had the right to be kept informed at least as to the tenor of the instructions under which it was operating. They had told us nothing, and we were almost completely in the dark. The Prime Minister decided that he must go to Paris himself and find out what was happening.

So back we went on 22 May. The primary purpose of this meeting was to discuss military matters; and it was held at the Headquarters of the French Supreme Commander in the Château de Vincennes, where the necessary maps and latest information from the Front were available. General Gamelin had been relieved, and General Weygand reigned in his stead. But the *Beau Geste* flavour of the old fort was just the same — spahis with white cloaks and long curved swords, on guard duty, and the floors and chairs covered with oriental rugs. Weygand's appearance was a pleasant surprise. He gave the impression of being a fighter — resolute, decisive and amazingly active, in spite of his wizened face and advanced years. He might have been made of India rubber. One dared to hope that the Allied armies would now have the leadership that had hitherto seemed lacking.

The meeting was short and businesslike. Weygand opened it with a description of the situation as he had found it, and then proceeded to unfold his plan. This, in summary, was that the French First Army and the British Expeditionary Force should attack south-west, while a new French Army Group that was now being formed from here, there and everywhere, under the command of General

Frère, was to attack northwards from south of the Somme and join hands with them. The plan met with general agreement, and the meeting ended on a note of restrained optimism.

Some of us were not nearly so happy, however, when we had had time to consider the implications of the decision. For one thing, the operation demanded of Gort, already heavily engaged, was bound to be extremely complicated and hazardous, even if it were practicable. How could he disengage and move south? For another thing, we could not see where the divisions for the new French Army Group were coming from. Even if they materialised, it was doubtful if they could arrive in time.

These doubts were to prove only too well-founded. By 25 May there was still no sign of any French movement from the Somme. Meanwhile the British Expeditionary Force, and indeed the whole of the Allied Northern Armies, were in mortal danger owing to the rapid advance of the German Panzer divisions in their rear. Their lines of communication were cut; most of their ammunition dumps had been captured; and they were completely encircled except for a narrow corridor leading northwards to the sea. Calais and Dunkirk were still in our hands. Therein seemed the only hope of saving something out of the wreck. Lord Gort, to his undying credit, took the fateful decision on his own responsibility, and issued orders for an immediate withdrawal towards the coast.

For some days Boulogne and Calais had been the only ports through which the British Expeditionary Force could be supplied, and troops had been sent from England to garrison them. Boulogne had held out until the night of 22-23, when the garrison was withdrawn by destroyers. But Calais was still ours, and when it was known that Gort was making for Dunkirk, the grim decision was taken that it must be held to the last ounce of our strength, in order to guard for as long as possible the flank of the corridor to Dunkirk. Accordingly, on the night of the 26 May, a telegram was sent to the commander at Calais, Brigadier Nicholson, telling him that his force would not be withdrawn, and that he must fight it out to the bitter end. The number of troops involved was relatively small, but it is a terrible thing to condemn a body of splendid men to death or captivity. The decision affected us all very deeply, especially perhaps Churchill. He was unusually silent during dinner that evening, and he ate and drank with evident distaste. As we rose from the table, he said, 'I feel physically sick.' He has quoted these words in his memoirs,[1] but he does not mention how sad he looked as he uttered them.

And now began one of the worst periods of the war. I was destined, before it ended, to suffer on many occasions the anguish of waiting, and to realise, as never before, what women have to suffer in a war in which their menfolk are engaged. But the wait at Dunkirk time was the hardest to bear. It was the first of these horrors, and so many of my closest friends were involved. I used to think how lucky we had been to survive the First World War and to have risen to fairly high and responsible positions: and I had especially envied those who had gone to France with the Expeditionary Force. Now they were faced with the choice of either fighting it out to the death, or surrendering. There was no doubt which of these alternatives they would have preferred, if their choice had been unfettered. But commanders have no right to call on their men to continue the struggle when the point has been reached at which no further damage can be inflicted on the enemy. Perhaps it was our friends who had fallen in 1914-18 who had been the lucky ones? Of course, if the corridor to Dunkirk could be kept open, a fraction of the BEF might get away. But the flower and also the seed-corn of our army seemed almost certain to be lost.

A staff officer should always pay the greatest attention to his demeanour. However pressed he may be, he must never appear too busy to give his undivided attention to any problem which may be brought to him — especially by junior officers. However black the situation may be, he must never look as if he is rattled or lacking in confidence. In fact he must always give the impression of having time on his hands and a song in his heart. All my life, and especially since the war started, I had done my utmost to live up to these precepts; but at Dunkirk time I must have failed to conceal my feelings. For I have preserved a note slipped furtively into my hand by Angus Nicholl, my naval assistant: 'I know what you are going through and I just wanted to offer my heart-felt sympathy in the ordeal our chaps have got to face — the finest chaps in the world and so many of them your close friends.'

[1] Churchill: *The Second World War*: Vol. II.

*   *

Operation DYNAMO started slowly. By the second day, 28 May, about 25,000 had been brought safely back. When we heard the score that night, the Prime Minister asked me how I would feel if I were told that a total of 50,000 could be saved. I replied without hesitation that I would be absolutely delighted, and Churchill did not upbraid me for pessimism. But by the next evening that limit had already been passed, and by the following night, 30 May, over 120,000 British and Allied troops had been landed in England. Unfortunately only a very small proportion of these were French, and there was a good deal of misrepresentation and recrimination in French circles. 'Gort has refused to obey the orders of the Commander of the Northern Armies and is moving independently to the coast.' 'There go the British, running away as fast as they can and leaving their friends in the lurch.' 'Priority in evacuation at Dunkirk is being given to British troops, and the French are being refused passage.' These were the sort of charges that were being bandied about in France, and the Prime Minister decided that he must go there again at once, in order to remove misunderstandings and explain exactly what was happening.

We flew to Villacoubly on the morning of 31 May, and the Supreme War Council met immediately after lunch at the Ministry of War. As we were standing round the table waiting for the discussion to begin, a dejected-looking old man in plain clothes shuffled towards me, stretched out his hand and said: 'Pétain.' It was hard to believe that this was the great Marshal of France, whose name was associated with the epic of Verdun, and who had done more than anyone else to restore the morale of the French Army after the mutinies of 1917. He now looked senile, uninspiring, and defeatist.

On the British side there were two new figures at the Conference — Mr Clement Attlee and Brigadier-General Spears. Attlee, who had been Leader of the Opposition up to the time that Mr Chamberlain resigned, was now Lord Privy Seal, and Deputy Prime Minister. He was brave, wise, decisive, and completely loyal to Churchill. His integrity was absolute, and no thought of personal ambition seemed to enter his mind. His appearance was deceptive: he looked somewhat meek and mild. That he was neither has been proved by his record during two wars, and as Prime Minister from 1945 to 1951. He was a grand chief to serve, and a great servant of his country.

The presence of Spears calls for explanation. As will appear time and time again in this narrative, Churchill believed that good teamwork between allies could be achieved only if the principals kept in close and continuous touch with each other. The more frequently that they could meet and discuss their war problems face to face, the better for everyone. But clearly he and M. Reynaud could not sit in each other's pockets all the time, and they therefore decided to appoint a special intermediary between them in their capacities as Ministers of Defence. Brigadier-General Spears was the obvious choice for this appointment. Bilingual in French and English, he had proved one of the most brilliant and gallant liaison officers of the First World War. After the war, he had retired from the Army and entered Parliament. He had become Chairman of the Parliamentary Anglo-French Committee, and he had recently led a delegation to Paris to meet the corresponding committee of the Chamber of Deputies. Thus he was known by, and had the entrée to, most of the principal political and military personalities in France, and could count on facilities that would not have been afforded to most people. There was some feeling in the Foreign Office that Spears' appointment would be an embarrassment to our Ambassador, Sir Ronald Campbell; but what Churchill and Reynaud required was someone who could move freely between France and England, and who had the necessary background of military knowledge. In the event, Spears and Campbell got on like the proverbial house on fire. In the War Office too there were a few murmurs. It was said that Spears was out of date and that someone with modern experience should have been selected. But where was the serving officer who could have had the entrée to men like Reynaud, Pétain and Weygand in the same way as Spears, or have been so candid with them? He knew exactly how to handle them, and very soon made himself indispensable, in spite of the difficulties of the situation. The Front was crumbling before he got there, and many of the French High Command had already lost all hope. But he himself was undaunted. Personally, I found it invaluable to have in Paris someone who had access to the highest French authorities, and we communicated with each other regularly, sometimes in writing and sometimes by telephone in guarded language. He has since told me that one day, when we were trying to wrap up our meaning and did it so successfully that neither of us could make head or tail of what the other was driving at, I reproached him for not knowing Hindustani. But I cannot believe that I was so unjust.

The conference ranged over a number of topics — the evacuation of Narvik, the need to strike at Italy the moment she entered the war, the battle in France, and particularly the evacuation from Dunkirk. The Prime Minister was at pains to point out that orders had been given that the French and British were to be rescued in equal proportions. They were, as he described it, to be brought away *bras dessus, bras dessous* — arm-in-arm. His generosity and transparent honesty had a marked effect.

We returned to London to find that operation DYNAMO was prospering beyond all hope and expectation, and before nightfall the aggregate had reached nearly 200,000. I told the glad tidings to my wife when I got back to our flat in the early hours of the morning. 'Yes,' she said. 'I have seen the miracle with my own eyes.' She had done a Red Cross job in the West Country that morning and had had a long wait at Oxford Station for her connection. It was a hot evening, and the crowd on the platform were listless and seemingly resigned to misfortune. Suddenly a train drew in. It was full of soldiery — unkempt, unshaven and in tattered uniforms. Some of them were bandaged — all of them looked exhausted. The people on the platform suddenly realised the significance of this apparition. The refreshment room was rushed, and everything eatable or drinkable was purchased and thrust into the hands of the weary passengers. Scarcely a word was spoken on either side. When the train drew out, there was not a dry eye to be seen on the platform. The tears were tears of relief and gratitude. My wife's train was shunted into sidings at Didcot and Reading, while train-load after train-load of soldiers went past. She had arrived at Paddington five hours late and had been lucky enough to find a taxi. Otherwise she would have walked the two miles to our flat. Nothing would have induced her to telephone to me for help.

DYNAMO went on and on, and it was not until the afternoon of 4

June that the Admiralty put out the announcement that it had been completed. Over 350,000 British and Allied troops had been brought safely to England.

Throughout the country there was a sense of deliverance and pride. The Army had shown those same qualities of patience, determination, humour and courage which had characterised them in the First World War. The Royal Air Force had fought heroically against overwhelming odds and terrible difficulties, and had made a noble contribution to the salvation of the BEF. It was hard that their fierce battles in the air over the Channel went unobserved by their comrades in the Navy and Army. In the early days of Dunkirk, a young air commodore came to my office with a report. As soon as we were alone, he burst into tears. 'I was on the platform with a lot of soldiers from Dunkirk this morning,' he said, 'and they pointed at me and called the RAF bloody cowards.' Churchill gave the lie to such cruel and unfounded insinuations in his next speech in Parliament. But at the end of it all, DYNAMO was a naval occasion. It was the sort of operation in which the Royal Navy excels itself. They are past masters at improvisation. I have never wanted to be a sailor, but I have always been inordinately proud of their Service.

It is difficult to understand why the Germans did not make more determined efforts to prevent our escape from the Continent, and the exact truth may never be established. Personally I take the view that *au fond* the blame should be laid at the door of the German High Command, the much-vaunted OKW. Admittedly, they were highly skilled in the 'set piece.' The planning and execution of the Norwegian campaign had been a model of efficiency, and the co-operation of the three Fighting Services had been well-nigh perfect. But OKW were riddled with personal jealousies and had neither the team spirit nor the flexibility which are needed to cope with an unexpected situation such as our improvised escape from Dunkirk. It is apt to be forgotten that in the First World War the German High Command was very far from being the perfect machine which some people thought. 'The machinery in Berlin was very clumsy,' wrote Ludendorff in his memoirs. 'The right hand did not know what the left hand was doing.' The position was much the same in the Second World War, and it was aggravated by Hitler's personal interventions.

CHAPTER XI

The Last Days of France

1940

THE 10 June was a ghastly day. Italy came into the war; the French Government left Paris; and the French Army seemed on the point of collapse. Churchill pressed for an early meeting of the Supreme War Council, and Reynaud agreed to meet him at Briare, on the Loire, about sixty miles east of Orléans. So after lunch on 11 June, we boarded the Flamingo once more. I got into trouble on this journey. Early in the morning the Prime Minister had told me that I had better stay behind and 'mind the shop.' Presumably some well-meaning friend had said that I was worn out and needed a rest. Since this was untrue, I did not take the instructions too seriously, but to be on the safe side I got to Hendon well ahead of Churchill and hid behind the aeroplane. As soon as he embarked, I followed close on his heels, and sat in the seat immediately behind him. I felt like a stow-away, and it was a relief when we took off. After we had been flying for about five minutes, Churchill turned round and barked out, 'You're here, are you?' There was not much that I could say, so I remained silent. He turned his back on me and continued reading. After a further pause he turned round again and, with an expression of fury, said, 'I knew you'd come.' Another pause, and he was handing me papers to read and comment upon. I was forgiven. But we were not yet out of the wood. The Prime Minister suddenly realised that we were heading west instead of south. He protested that he wanted to get to Briare as quickly as possible. 'Why don't we fly direct over France?' I suspect that he had a faint hope of being able to see something of the battle! However, the pilot was able to convince him that both he and the fighter escort had had precise instructions from the Air Ministry, and that it was impossible to change the route.

We got a depressing reception at Briare airfield. As Spears has written in his description of the scene,[1] 'It was like walking into a house thinking one was expected, to find one had been invited for the following week. Our presence was not really desired.' However, when we arrived at the château in which the meeting was to be held, Reynaud did his best to make us at home. In spite of the apparent hopelessness of the situation, and of the defeatism around him, he was, as ever, friendly, militant and a bundle of energy. Weygand, on the other hand, looked a very different Weygand from the brisk, confident commander who had greeted us at Vincennes only about a fortnight previously. He seemed to have abandoned all hope; and Marshal Pétain looked more woebegone than ever.

This was the first occasion on which I had any talk with Brigadier-General de Gaulle. M. Reynaud had summoned him from the fighting line, where he had led a regiment of tanks with judgment and gallantry, and had appointed him Under-Secretary of State for National Defence. My first impression of him was that, with all his courage and efficiency, he was frigid, humourless and probably prickly. It never occurred to me that he had the warmth or personality to inspire a great movement and become a symbol of resistance and hope to his countrymen. His first appeal broadcast from London immediately after the capitulation showed how wrong I was. 'Whatever happens, the flame of French resistance must not and shall not die.'[2] Churchill himself could not have sounded a clearer call to honour. On the only occasion that de Gaulle uttered a word during the conference at Briare, Weygand made it only too plain that he resented his translation into the political world.

It was late in the afternoon before we got to business, and the start was not a happy one. A few days previously we had arranged with the French High Command that if Mussolini came into the war he

[1] *Assignment to Catastrophe*: Vol. II.
[2] De Gaulle: *The Call to Honour* (Documents).

should be shown at the earliest possible moment that he was not going to have it all his own way. Two sets of operations had been planned. The first, a joint air and naval operation against Turin and Genoa, the French supplying the naval forces and Britain supplying the air forces flying direct from the United Kingdom. The second operation was to be a night attack on the same area by a number of RAF Wellington aircraft which had been sent over for the purpose to the airfield at Salon, near Marseilles. Reynaud opened the meeting by asking, rather shamefacedly, that our joint air and naval operation should be cancelled, since it would inevitably invite retaliation on Marseilles and Toulon, which were practically defenceless. I did a quick calculation. According to my arithmetic, our bombers had already started from England, and it was impossible to countermand them. On Churchill's instructions, I explained this elementary but decisive fact. There was nothing more to be said. Weygand looked pained.

The conference then addressed itself to the situation in France. The story has been told in some detail by Churchill and others; but since it was, in my view, one of the most critical moments of the war, I ask the reader's indulgence to give my own version of the gist of the discussion. Weygand started off by giving a picture of the plight of the French Army. It was at its last gasp. Unless it was immediately provided with a considerable reinforcement of air support, the end would come very soon. He insisted that it was a cardinal principle of strategy to concentrate all available forces at the decisive point. 'Here,' he exclaimed, 'is the decisive point. Now is the decisive moment. The British ought not to keep a single fighter in England. They should all be sent to France.' There was an awful pause, and my heart stood still. The Prime Minister and the Cabinet had only recently been solemnly warned by Air Chief Marshal Dowding, Commander-in-Chief Fighter Command, that if any more fighter squadrons were sent to France, he could not guarantee the defence of the British Isles. That was clear enough. It was a terrible position for a man like Churchill — generous, warm-hearted, courageous and with a pronounced streak of optimism — and I was terrified lest he might be so moved as to promise that he would ask his Government to send some additional air support. Thank God my fears were groundless. After a pause, and speaking very slowly, he said, 'This is not the decisive point. This is not the decisive moment. The decisive moment will come when Hitler hurls his Luftwaffe against Britain. If we can keep command of the air over our own island — that is all I ask — we will win it all back for you.' After another long pause, he continued magnificently, 'Of course if it is best for France in her agony that her Army should capitulate, let there be no hesitation on our account. Whatever happens here, we are resolved to fight on and on for ever and ever and ever.' Reynaud, obviously moved, said: 'If we capitulate, all the great might of Germany will be concentrated upon invading England. And then what will you do?' Whereupon Churchill, with his jaw thrust well forward, rejoined that he had not thought that out very carefully, but that broadly speaking he would propose to drown as many as possible of them on the way over, and then to *'frapper sur la tête'* anyone who managed to crawl ashore.

It was after 9 P.M. before the conference adjourned, and the Prime Minister insisted that he must have a bath and change before dinner. Consequently we did not sit down until about 10 P.M. We had had an early lunch and I was very hungry; but before I had finished my soup I was summoned to the telephone to speak to Air Marshal A. S. Barratt, the RAF commander in France. He was in a rage. 'The local French authorities will not allow my bombers at Salon to take off against Italy,' he complained. I told him that, in addition to the Prime Minister, Eden, Dill, Reynaud and Weygand were all close at hand and that I would report to them and give him a reply as quickly as I could. I begged him not to let go of the telephone at his end, because the only instrument available to me was in the 'Gents' and there was little hope of making contact again if we were cut off. I reported to the Prime Minister, and four or five of the principals left the table and discussed the matter in a small group in the passage. The upshot was that Reynaud undertook to send orders that the British bombers were to be allowed to proceed. I duly telephoned the good news to Barratt, and hoped for the best. But I was woken up at 4 A.M. next morning by a message from him to say that the French had driven farm carts on to the airfield and that it had been physically impossible for our bombers to get into the air. Later Barratt joined me, and we went off together to report to the Prime Minister. I expected an explosion, but he took the news philosophically.

The Council had a second short session that morning. The only conclusions that need be mentioned were the agreement to try to organise a redoubt in Brittany, and the undertaking given by the Prime Minister to despatch divisions from England, as soon as they could be equipped and organised.

As I said good-bye to my friends of the *Grand Quartier Général,* it seemed unlikely that I would see them again until after the war. We had worked closely together for a long time and I ought to have felt sad at the parting. But I am bound to admit that I felt no pang. The French refusal to allow us to bomb Italy had been the last straw. Not content with being unable or unwilling to fight themselves, they seemed to want to stop us fighting. Ever since the Battle of France had started, they had blamed us for practically everything that had gone wrong. This, I thought, was grossly unfair. After all, it was they who had insisted upon Plan D, which had meant leaving our prepared defences on the Belgian frontier and rushing forward into Belgium. It was they who had insisted that a German attack through the Ardennes was impossible. It was their troops which had broken at Sedan and placed all the rest of us in mortal jeopardy. They had continually pressed us to send them all our fighters, and thus deprive ourselves of any hope of defending our island and continuing the struggle. It almost seemed that because they themselves were heading for ruin, they wanted to pull us down with them. And now they had persuaded us to agree to send them the only equipped divisions in Britain to help them to build a castle in the air in Brittany.

Even before I reached the airfield at Briare I realised that I was being churlish. As Churchill had never ceased to impress upon me, our contribution to the battle in France had been niggardly. So far the French had had nine-tenths of the casualties — inconsiderable though they were by the standards of the First World War — and endured ninety-nine-hundredths of the suffering. As for their demand for our fighters, was there not a perfectly natural reason? They were continentals, who had no idea of amphibious strategy, and no notion of the priceless value of the twenty miles of salt water which separated us from the Continent. In their view, the result of the war would be decided by the battle in France. If that was lost, all was lost. The battle for Britain would merely prolong the agony: it would not affect the result. Britain would have 'her neck wrung like a chicken'[1] within the month. Why not, then, adhere to the cardinal principles of strategy and concentrate everything at the decisive point in France? I believe, and my belief has been endorsed by several French friends since the war ended, that if they had had any confidence that we could win the Battle of Britain and that our island would remain inviolate, they would never have pressed us to render ourselves defenceless. What is more, I believe that they themselves would have continued to fight in North Africa, backed by a fierce guerrilla warfare in metropolitan France. But anyway, it was unworthy to judge too harshly a friend who had fought with us so loyally, and lost over one and a half million of the flower of her manhood in 1914-18. I regretted that I had said good-bye so casually.

All the same, I was appalled at the prospect of throwing away more of our precious remaining strength on the Brittany fantasy. The French Army was no longer capable of coherent effort, and the forces that we had on the spot, or could get there in time, were far too small to achieve anything by themselves. On the Prime Minister's arrival at the airfield I voiced my misgivings to him. I pleaded that the Brittany project, however attractive in theory, had not got the ghost of a chance of success. The best we could hope for was yet another evacuation. The greater the numbers that set foot in France, the greater would be our losses in men and material. We must of course keep our promise to send reinforcements to France soon: but need we be in too much of a hurry? Could we not unobtrusively delay their departure? Churchill would have none of it. 'Certainly not. It would look very bad in history if we were to do any such thing.' Some twenty-five years earlier, Lord Birkenhead had written of Churchill: 'He has never in all his life failed a friend, however embarrassing the obligation which he felt it necessary to honour.'[2] I should have known better than to suggest that he should default on his promise to the French, even though he knew in his heart of hearts that his efforts to sustain them at almost any cost were certain to be in vain. And so it proved.

At almost the exact moment that this conversation was taking place on Briare airfield, General Sir Alan Brooke, who had done so magnifi-

[1] Weygand's words to Reynaud at Briare.
[2] *Contemporary Personalities.*

cently in the withdrawal to Dunkirk, was embarking for Cherbourg to take command of all the British forces which remained in France, and such reinforcements as could be rushed to their aid. He realised almost at once that any attempt to hold a bridgehead in Brittany was bound to be suicidal, and that the situation was becoming hourly more desperate. Within three days he was able to convince the Prime Minister that the only hope of salvation lay in orders for immediate evacuation, and over a hundred and thirty thousand British troops were saved.

Briare airfield was a desolate spot, and it was depressing to be told by the RAF commander that there was ten-tenths cloud over the Loire valley, and that it would be impossible for the fighter escort to accompany us. But it was important for the Prime Minister to get back to England as quickly as possible; and it seemed reasonable to assume that if the clouds made it impossible for our fighters to keep contact with us, they would make it equally impossible for the German Air Force to spot us. So off we went in our slow, unarmed machine. As we came out over the sea there was bright sunlight, and our pilot observed a commotion beneath us. It was a single German aircraft — or it may have been two — bombing some Allied shipping. The German pilot did not look upwards, and we went on our way unobserved.

Later in the war one of the Planning Committees was instructed by the Chiefs of Staff to put themselves in the position of the German High Command and make plans from their view-point. The Committee's report included the following passage: 'The elimination of Churchill must be an essential feature of any attack on British morale . . . There is no other statesman who could possibly take his place.' If that was true in January 1942, as I firmly believe it to have been, how much truer it was in June 1940! If the German aviator had spotted the Flamingo on that brilliant Wednesday morning, the course of history might have been changed. As it was, Churchill landed safely, and was making his report to the Cabinet by lunchtime.

Scarcely were we back in England before we were off again to France — this time to Tours. The Prime Minister sensed that Reynaud was under great pressure from Weygand, backed up by Pétain, to ask for an armistice, and that he needed all the encouragement and support that could be given to him. Tours airfield had been heavily bombed the night before; but we landed safely and taxied around the craters in search of someone to help us. There was no sign of life, except for groups of French airmen lounging about by the hangars. They did not know who we were, and cared less. The Prime Minister got out and introduced himself. He said, in his best French, that his name was Churchill, that he was Prime Minister of Great Britain, and that he would be grateful for a *'voiture.'* They lent us a small touring car, which took us to the *Préfecture* in considerable discomfort. The party included Halifax, who had very long legs, and Churchill took up more than his share of the room. No one at the *Préfecture* recognised or took the slightest notice of us, and we wandered through the dreary building, jostled by swarms of refugees. Evidently the members of the French Government had not yet arrived, but fortunately a staff officer — blessings on his head — espied us and escorted us to a near-by restaurant. The manager cleared a small private room, and we sat down to a welcome meal of cold chicken, cheese and Vouvray wine.

We went back to the *Préfecture* as quickly as possible, and a little later M. Reynaud arrived. I was shocked by his appearance — he looked so changed. He started the meeting by saying that the plight of the French Army was now absolutely desperate, and that Weygand was insistent on the necessity for an immediate armistice. He referred to the pledge which both Governments had taken at the meeting of the Supreme War Council in London on 28 March that they would 'neither negotiate nor conclude an armistice or treaty of peace, except by mutal agreement'; and he asked that, in view of the sacrifices which France had made and the hopelessness of their position, Britain should release her from her promise. The Prime Minister said that this was a question which he must discuss alone with his colleagues, and we trooped out into the garden. It was wet under foot, ill-kept and matched our spirits. The talk did not take long. Churchill said that the capitulation of the French Army was a military question which France was entitled to decide without reference to her partners: but that the conclusion of an armistice was a political matter of such deep concern to ourselves that we ought to refuse to be a party to it. Halifax and Beaverbrook were in complete agreement. Back we went to the conference room, and the Prime Minister told Reynaud that, much as Great Britain appreciated the agony of France, she could not release her from her pledge. He suggested that Reynaud should make one more appeal to President Roosevelt and await his answer before considering such extreme measures. Reynaud agreed to do so.

Just before the meeting broke up I reminded Churchill about the four hundred German aviators who had been shot down by the British and French, and were held prisoners in France. Reynaud had promised at Briare that they would be handed over to us for safe custody in England, but we had heard nothing more about them. Once more he undertook to see to the matter, but that was the last we ever heard of it. It was not his fault. He was always loyal and helpful. But sinister influences were at work all round him, and he could no longer command obedience.

We left the battered airfield that afternoon, and by 10 P.M. the Cabinet was assembled to be told the sad story. Thus ended our fifth visit to France since the battle started. The physical and mental strain on all of us had been intense, but the Prime Minister, who had had by far the most grievous burden to carry, never looked harassed or tired. He had, as he afterwards admitted, suffered real agony of soul; but he never gave a sign of it.

I had now been away from my office for most of the last three days, and there was a large pile of papers awaiting me. This was a merciful dispensation. The heavier the work, the less time there was to worry. On the afternoon of 15 June, M. Jean Monnet, who had been the Chairman of the Franco-British Purchasing Commission for some time, and was now one of de Gaulle's principal advisers, called at my office. He started by telling me of a proposal that was being thought out for an indissoluble union between France and Britain. This seemed to me to be so divorced from reality that I wondered whether he was serious. Then he turned to the main purpose of his visit. Could not the decision about fighter support for France be reconsidered? It was the only hope for both of us. All I could do was to repeat what Churchill had said at Briare, and again at Tours. 'The fate of both of us depends upon the Battle of Britain. We believe that we have just sufficient strength, but with no margin whatsoever, to defend our island, and win it all back for you.' Monnet was unconvinced and disappointed. He repeated the appeal to the Prime Minister later in the day.

The next afternoon there was a Cabinet meeting. To my amazement the first item to be discussed was a draft 'Declaration of Union,' which had been prepared by Sir Robert Vansittart,[1] M. Corbin, M. Jean Monnet, and others. To my still greater amazement, the Cabinet approved it after less than two hours' discussion. If the idea had been mooted in peace-time, innumerable difficulties and objections would have been raised, endless memoranda would have been written, and the arguments would have dragged on for years and years. But now His Majesty's Government were prepared at a moment's notice to go to almost any lengths to keep France in the ring. The French Government did not accept the proposal, but I wonder whether the War Cabinet of those days has ever been given sufficient credit for the single-mindedness, courage and generosity which it showed at this frightful moment.

Before the Cabinet dispersed, it was decided that the Prime Minister, accompanied by the leaders of the Labour and Liberal Parties and the Chiefs of Staff, should meet Reynaud next day at Concarneau, off the coast of Brittany, to discuss, among other things, the draft Declaration of Union. We were to go by special train to Southampton, and from there by cruiser. After a hasty dinner, we hurried off to Waterloo, and we were actually sitting in the train waiting to start, when a message arrived from the British Ambassador at Bordeaux, saying that there was a ministerial crisis and that the meeting was now impossible. I returned to my flat *en route* to the office, to tell my wife that I would after all be sleeping at home. When she saw me she thought that it was my ghost.

On the following day Pétain, who had replaced Reynaud as Prime Minister, sued for the armistice which he and Weygand had long demanded. We were now alone. So far from being alarmed, we were relieved, nay, exhilarated. Henceforward everything would be simpler. We were masters of our own fate. Just before Dunkirk, the Prime Minister had asked the Chiefs of Staff for a formal expression of their views as to our ability to continue the war with any hope of success, if France were to collapse. There was no doubt in any of our

[1] Later Lord Vansittart.

minds as to what the answer would be, but it was less easy to state the reasons on which that answer was to be based. Consequently the report produced by the Chiefs of Staff was a curious document. The first twelve paragraphs were devoted to showing that the enemy had the whip hand in almost every sphere, and the summing-up set out in the thirteenth and final paragraph seemed somewhat inconsistent. 'Our conclusion is that, *prima facie,* Germany has most of the cards; but the real test is whether the morale of our fighting personnel and civil population will counterbalance the numerical and material advantages which Germany enjoys. We believe it will.'

The report contented Churchill, and the conclusion undoubtedly represented the views of the nation as a whole. Shortly after the fall of France, Mr Bevin had to address a somewhat restive audience of Trade Unionists. He started off by saying that although things looked bleak, the Government, on the advice of their military experts, had decided to carry on the fight. Whereupon a voice from the front row shouted: 'We'd knock your bleedin' 'ead off, Ernie, if you'd decided anything else.'

It was grievous and ironical that our first offensive action after the fall of France should have had to be directed against our late allies. Some people thought at the time, and may still think, that the decision to attack the French ships at Mers-el-Kebir (Oran) was not only unprincipled but also unnecessary. My readers must judge for themselves.

Thanks largely to Admiral Darlan, the French Navy at the outset of war was probably stronger than it had ever been in the past. There were, in particular, the battle cruisers, *Dunkerque* and *Strasbourg,* which were thought to be more powerful than Germany's *Scharnhorst* and *Gneisenau,* and faster than any of our big ships, except perhaps the *Hood.* There were also two of the very latest battleships, the *Jean Bart* and the *Richelieu,* which were nearing completion. If these powerful units were to fall into enemy hands, the whole balance of sea power would be seriously affected, and we would find ourselves in mortal danger. When therefore M. Reynaud begged to be released from his promise not to make a separate armistice, and to be allowed to make enquiries from the Germans as to the terms which they would offer, the War Cabinet ultimately agreed, on 16 June, to tell him that he could go ahead provided, and only provided, that the French Fleet was sailed to British harbours pending negotiations. But events moved too fast. Marshal Pétain came into power on the very next day. He broke his predecessor's promise without any reference to us, and asked the Germans for their armistice terms, without stipulating any reservations whatsoever. So far as the French Fleet was concerned, the German reply demanded that all their ships should be ordered to sail to German or Italian ports where they would be disarmed and demobilised; the Germans, for their part, promising not to use them for their own purposes.

The War Cabinet thought that it would be criminal folly to place any trust in Hitler's promise when our very existence was at stake, and decided that the French Navy must either be demilitarised or brought under our control at the earliest possible moment. It has been suggested that we should have trusted Darlan to redeem the promise which he had given to Mr Churchill at Briare, that he would never allow his ships to fall into German hands. But apart from the fact that one of his own compatriots had warned us that the admiral had political ambitions and hated the British, what could he have done, even with the best will in the world, to save ships which lay at anchor in German and Italian ports?

It was anticipated that the French ships in British ports would give little trouble, and this anticipation proved correct. It was also anticipated that the French ships under the command of Vice-Admiral Godfroy at Alexandria, could be looked after by Admiral Sir Andrew Cunningham, who had superior forces, and what was even more important, enjoyed the esteem and confidence of his French colleague. This anticipation also proved correct. There was no immediate hurry about the *Jean Bart* and the *Richelieu,* since both of them would have to be sailed to French ports for completion before they were fit for action. But the French fleet at Mers-el-Kebir, including as it did the battle cruisers *Dunkerque* and *Strasbourg,* presented a hideous problem. The nearest British fleet was Force H at Gibraltar, under Admiral Sir James Somerville. This included the battle cruiser *Hood,* the aircraft carrier *Ark Royal,* and two old battleships, the *Valiant* and the *Resolution.* Here was sufficient force, but how was it to be applied? After prolonged discussion, the Cabinet agreed that Somerville should be instructed to offer the French admiral at Mers-el-

Kebir a number of alternatives. He could either join us and continue the fight against Germany and Italy; or he could sail with reduced crews to a British port; or he could sail to some French port in the West Indies — such as Martinique — where the ships would be de-mobilised or perhaps entrusted to the United States, and the crews repatriated to France. The message which Somerville was instructed to present to Admiral Gensoul explained these various proposals, and ended on a grim note: 'If you refuse these fair offers, I must, with profound regret, require you to sink your ships within six hours. Finally, failing the above, I have the orders of His Majesty's Govern-ment to use whatever force may be necessary to prevent your ships from falling into German or Italian hands.'

I pictured the horror on the face of James Somerville, a typical British sailor and the soul of chivalry, as he read these instructions; and his distress was very evident from the signals which he sent in reply. There was nothing for it but to give him a peremptory order to carry out the repugnant task without further question. But all who were present when that message was drafted could not but feel sad and, in a sense, guilty. To kick a man when he is down is unattractive at any time; but when the man is a friend who has already suffered grievously, it seems almost to border on infamy. To Churchill, with his deep love of France, it must have been an agonising moment. But he never flinched. I admit that I was at first inclined to disapprove, not only on ethical grounds, but also because of the risk of a declara-tion of war by the Vichy Government. In the end, however, I was completely convinced that we had no option. At the same time I clung to the hope, up to the very last moment, that Admiral Gen-soul would feel that honour had been satisfied by his protests, and that in the circumstances he would be justified in yielding to *force majeure*. But he was adamant. It speaks volumes for his stubborn courage, and for the robust discipline of the French Navy that, in spite of the hopelessness of their position, they did their duty as they saw it.

The unhappy Somerville had to do the deed before nightfall. He went into action just before 6 P.M. and the firing lasted for less than a quarter of an hour. The *Dunkerque* ran aground; the *Bretagne* blew up; and the *Provence* was beached. Only the *Strasbourg* managed to escape to Toulon, suffering casualties on the way. The danger that we had feared was over. Our command of the sea was secure. Parliament and the Press warmly approved the action; but they did not 'glory in it,' as General de Gaulle has unfortunately alleged in his war memoirs.[1] Neutrals were impressed, and astonished, by this evidence of the British determination to stop at nothing. The Vichy Government broke off relations with us, but did not declare war, and we now know that by no means all Frenchmen in occupied France condemned our action. Churchill has told a story which is so revealing that I venture to repeat it. The *Strasbourg,* as I have said, escaped to Toulon. Among her dead were two young sailors whose homes were in that port. Both their families asked that at their funeral service the Union Jack should lie upon the coffins side by side with the Tricolour. This was done. 'In this,' writes Churchill, 'we may see how the comprehending spirit of simple folk touches the sublime.' [2]

Shortly after the action, Somerville received a letter signed by a very large number of French naval officers, reviling him for his treachery, and accusing him of having brought disgrace on the whole naval profession. He pretended to take the rebuke light-heartedly, but I am sure that it cut him to the quick.

[1] *The Call to Honour,* 1940-1942.
[2] Churchill: *The Second World War*: Vol. II.

CHAPTER XII

Retrospect

1940

T H E war had now been in progress for just on ten months. It was about to enter upon a new and, as it then seemed, decisive phase. For Hitler, everything, or practically everything, had so far gone according to plan. His successes had been phenomenal. His one military failure had been to prevent the British Expeditionary Force escaping from Dunkirk. Only Britain now stood between him and the domination of Europe. If she were so foolish as to refuse to come to terms, she would be first assailed from the air and then invaded. She was now within such easy reach that this would not be difficult. All that he needed was a brief pause in which to refit, reorganise and re-group his forces for their crowning triumph.

For Britain the future seemed stormy indeed. Practically nothing had gone according to plan, and the situation bore no resemblance to anything that had been visualised in our pre-war studies. It was mortifying to realise that so many of our forecasts had proved wrong. It had always been assumed that in the French Army and the British Navy, we had two decisive assets for all time. The French Army had already collapsed, and the limitations of naval power in the new age had been painfully revealed by the Norwegian campaign. Basing ourselves on the experiences of 1914-18, we had concluded that in modern war an offensive could not succeed unless it had a superiority of three to one over the defence in the zone of impact. We had now seen numerically inferior forces of German armour tear the French armies to pieces. There was a general conviction that the Germans would start the war with air attacks on England, and the Air Staff had estimated that one night's bombing of London would cause one hundred and fifty thousand casualties. The London hospitals had therefore been drastically cleared on the outbreak of war, in order to leave as many beds as possible available to receive them. So far, the civilian population had been unscathed and the beds had lain empty. The tank was a British invention, and one might have expected that we would, in that respect at least, be well-equipped. Yet we went to war devastatingly outclassed in armour. We had never contemplated that Hitler would assault Scandinavia; in fact the Chiefs of Staff had specifically dismissed as impracticable any idea of German sea-borne operations against Norway. The whole of Denmark and Norway were now in German occupation.

For more than three centuries it had been one of the most cherished and consistent features of British foreign policy to prevent the ports of northern Europe falling into the hands of a great military power. It was primarily for that reason that we had fought Philip II of Spain, Louis XIV, Napoleon, and Kaiser Wilhelm the Second. When Ludendorff made his last desperate lunge in March 1918, there was apprehension in well-informed circles that if the Channel ports were lost, Britain would be unable to continue the war. The position was now incomparably more serious. Not only all the ports of northern Europe, but also the Biscay and Norwegian ports, were in the firm grip of the enemy. To make matters worse, the Southern Irish ports, which had proved so valuable in 1914-18 for the conduct of the anti-U-boat war, were denied to us by the Government of Eire, in spite of the promises which they made when we handed them over in April 1938. Our plans for air defence had been based on the assumption that the hostile air forces would be operating from Germany. Now the Germans had airfields within twenty-five miles of our shores. With a naval superiority infinitely greater than we had enjoyed in the First World War, the possibility of invasion of Britain had scarcely entered our thoughts. It now seemed highly probable that it would be attempted within a matter of weeks.

The situation overseas was just as different from our pre-war conceptions as the situation in Europe. Our plans for the Mediterranean and the Middle East theatres had been based on the assumption that if Italy came into the war we could rely on the co-operation of French forces in North Africa, Syria and French Somaliland. But now that all these territories considered themselves bound by the French armistice and remained faithful to the Vichy Government, a new set of dangers had arisen and a new set of plans had to be made.

If, in August 1939, the Chiefs of Staff had had reason to think that this was going to be the situation after less than twelve months of hostilities, I believe that they would have unhesitatingly warned the Cabinet that to go to war would be to invite overwhelming disaster, and that somehow or other time must be bought to put our house in order, even at the expense of humiliating concessions.

My wife has reminded me that I told her on my return from Tours that the fall of France was inevitable, and that she asked me to tell her candidly what I thought of our chances of survival. My reply was: 'Three to one on.' Lest it be thought that I was whistling to keep up her courage and my own, let me give the reasons for my confidence.

The British people were united as perhaps never before in their history. 'Be one people,' had been Chatham's exhortation when we were in dire peril. Churchill had said the same thing in different words. The Navy had answered every call that had been made upon them. It had maintained our sea communications against the assaults of U-boat, surface raider and magnetic mine; and it had already given the enemy a taste of its mettle on several occasions. The German Navy would not relish the responsibility of protecting the sea passage of the invading forces.

Thanks to the escape from Dunkirk, we had a larger army in our island than ever before in our history. Admittedly, a considerable proportion was untrained, and most of the men had nothing but their rifles to fight with. There were scarcely five hundred field guns, and less than two hundred medium or heavy tanks, in the country. But the factories were working full blast, and large quantities of equipment purchased in America were on the way. The troops themselves were convinced that man for man they were every bit as good as the Germans, and could be relied upon to give a good account of themselves. They would be backed up by the Home Guard, already more than half a million strong and increasing in numbers every day. Some of these were old men and most of them were poorly armed, but they were tough and resolute, and knew every inch of the country. The Royal Air Force had foiled the Luftwaffe against heavy odds over Dunkirk, and they would have the great advantage of 'playing the final on the home ground,' as the hall porter of a London club put it. The eight-gun fighter might well prove a match winner, and our radar screen would give the Luftwaffe an unpleasant surprise.

It was said that we were 'alone,' but we were not really alone. The great self-governing Dominions were with us body and soul, and were rushing forces to our help. Canadian soldiers already stood on guard in the island. Australia, New Zealand and South Africa had all sprung to arms, and their forces were moving to the sound of the guns. For the defence of our overseas territories there were the mighty armies of India and the troops of the Colonial Empire. In addition, we had on our side the men, women and military equipment that had been salvaged from the countries which Hitler had overrun — Poland, Norway, Holland, Belgium, Czechoslovakia, and Free France. We had, too, the moral support and sympathy of nearly the whole of the free world.

But all these things might have been of little avail had it not been that in Churchill we had found a leader to match the hour. 'Without a moment of hesitation, without a twinge of diffidence,' [1] he had set himself at the head of his countrymen; and it is no reflection on others to say that in less than two months he had revolutionised the situation. From the outset he had done the right thing and struck the right note. 'I have nothing to offer but blood, toil, tears and sweat,' he told the House of Commons in his first speech as Prime Minister. His definition of our policy was in the simplest terms: 'It is to wage war with all our might and with all the strength that God can give us.' When asked what we were fighting about and whether it was worth it, his retort was uncompromising. 'If we stopped fighting, you would soon see.' To those who were looking for scapegoats for our defeats, his warning was unmistakable: 'If the present tries to sit in judgment on the past, it will lose the future.' He never encouraged false hopes or used smooth words. When France was tottering, he told the country to 'prepare itself for hard and heavy tidings.' And when the es-

[1] Macaulay: *Essay on the Earl of Chatham.*

cape from Dunkirk was successful beyond all our dreams, and there was a tendency to indulge in unrestrained rejoicing, he brought us down to earth again. 'We must be very careful not to assign to this deliverance the attributes of a victory. Wars are not won by evacuations.' His spirit of defiance set the whole kingdom on fire. 'We shall defend our island whatever the cost may be. We shall fight in the fields and in the streets. We shall fight in the hills. We shall never surrender.' And after the collapse of France his call to duty resounded to the uttermost ends of the earth: 'I expect that the Battle of Britain is about to begin. Upon this battle depends the survival of Christian civilisation . . . Let us therefore brace ourselves to our duty and so bear ourselves that, if the British Commonwealth and Empire lasts for a thousand years, men will still say, "This was their finest hour." ' That message happened to be supremely well-timed. It was delivered on the hundred and twenty-fifth anniversary of the Battle of Waterloo.

It is extraordinary that Churchill could find the time in those days of turmoil for the preparation of these masterpieces. They were dictated without the aid of a note; they came straight from the heart. Some three months later I was walking with him in the garden at Chequers, after dinner. London was under bombardment, and we could see the glow of the fires from afar. Churchill was sad at all the suffering and said that he wished that he could do more 'for the poor people.' I reminded him that, whatever the future held, nothing could rob him of the credit of having inspired the country by his speeches. 'Not at all,' he retorted, almost angrily. 'It was given to me to express what was in the hearts of the British people. If I had said anything else, they would have hurled me from office.' [1] I had never attributed to him the quality of humility, and it struck me as odd that he failed to realise that the upsurge of the national spirit was largely his own creation. The great qualities of the British race had seemed almost dormant until he had aroused them. The people then saw themselves as he portrayed them. They put their trust in him. They were ready to do anything that he asked, make any sacrifice that he demanded, and follow wherever he led.

[1] Churchill put the same thought into other words on his eightieth birthday. 'It was the nation and the race living all around the globe that had the lion's heart. I had the luck to be called on to give the roar.'

But Churchill's inspiration and example extended far beyond the borders of his own country. He had established close personal relations with the Prime Ministers of the Dominions, and had been at pains to keep them continually and closely informed of all that was happening. He had gained their confidence, and they were ready to leave the day-to-day conduct of the war to the Cabinet under his leadership, and to place their armed forces under British operational control.

To the occupied nations in Europe, he was already the living symbol of resistance and hope. Only if Britain was victorious could they regain their freedom, and they felt that if anyone could bring about that victory, it was Churchill. Travelling in Scandinavia and the Low Countries after the war, this was the sort of thing that I heard on all sides: 'You in England had no idea what Churchill meant to us. We used to sit in dark cellars with the wireless turned on as low as possible, and while one of our number patrolling the streets would keep a look-out for the Gestapo, we would strain our ears to catch his every word. His voice was the only ray of light in an otherwise completely dark and hopeless world.'

His impact on the United States of America was of immense consequence. It was once said that he was 'half American and all British,' and that was a fair description. Even before he became Prime Minister, he saw more clearly than anyone else the overriding necessity of securing the goodwill and material assistance of America. He had pinned his faith on President Roosevelt, and had carried on a regular correspondence with him from the very beginning. The mutual confidence which had grown up between them was now to prove of cardinal value. Our refusal to give way to the repeated appeals to send more fighters to France had been misunderstood by people who did not know all the facts of the case, including President Roosevelt, and even that wisest of wise men, Field Marshal Smuts. Consequently, when Mr Bullitt, United States Ambassador to France, reported to Washington that Britain might be conserving her Fleet and Air Force as bargaining counters wherewith to get better terms with Hitler, the results might have been serious. It would have been foolish of the Americans to continue to sell munitions, which they might sorely need for their own defence, to a country which was on the point of making peace with Germany. But Churchill's private correspondence with Roosevelt and his public speeches convinced the President and his principal advisers that so long as he was Prime Minister, any accommodation with the enemy, even on the most favourable terms, was out of the question. They continued to send us precious equipment as fast as it could be shipped.

Even the Russians, who at that time regarded Churchill as the most implacable enemy of Communism, were forced to recognise the unique quality of the man. 'There have been few cases in history,' said Marshal Stalin at a dinner party at Yalta over four years later, 'where the courage of one man has been so important to the future of the world.'

As for the German people, the very word 'Churchill' struck a chill into their hearts. They regarded him as the sole obstacle to the peace for which they longed. They knew that he would never give in, and they heaped abuse on him at every turn. He stood alone as Public Enemy No. 1. After the war, I happened to be with him at Chartwell when the results of the Nuremberg trials of the Nazi war criminals were published. 'It shows,' he remarked, 'that if you get into a war, it is supremely important to win it. You and I would be in a pretty pickle if we had lost.' He certainly would have been.

Arrian, in his *History of Alexander the Great,* pays his hero a remarkable tribute: 'I believe that there was in his time no nation of men, no city, nay, no single individual with whom Alexander's name had not become a familiar word. I therefore hold that such a man, who was like no ordinary mortal, was not born into the world without some special providence.' How truly these words could have been written of Churchill in 1940.

CHAPTER XIII

Mr Churchill's Machinery
of War Direction

I N Chapter VIII, I have described the development of our Machinery of War Direction up to the date when Mr Chamberlain resigned. This is the place to tell the story of its further development under Mr Churchill. His first and most far-reaching change was to assume, with the approval of the King, the title of Minister of Defence. He did not attempt to define the scope or the powers of his new office; he himself would decide what was required in the light of experience, subject of course to the approval of the War Cabinet. Nor did this change involve special legislation or the creation of a full-blown Ministry, such as has since[1] been set up. All that Mr Churchill wanted was what he called a 'handling machine'; and, fortunately for me, he decided that the Military Wing of the War Cabinet Secretariat — comprising perhaps a dozen officers all told — would meet his needs. Overnight therefore we became known as the Office of the Minister of Defence, but we continued to be members of the War Cabinet Secretariat, of which Sir Edward Bridges was the head, and to work hand in glove with our old friends and colleagues on the civil side. The only difference was that henceforward we were to have direct personal contact with the Prime Minister himself, and to perform

[1] In 1948.

such additional duties as he demanded. Our path was not going to be smooth, but it would at least be clear-cut. Many of my friends said at the time, and others have written in their memoirs, that they would not have had my job for the world. I can only say, in all sincerity, that I would not have exchanged places with any of them for a king's ransom.

Another change made by Churchill was the replacement of the Ministerial Committee for Military Co-ordination by the Defence Committee under his own chairmanship. This committee worked in two panels called the Defence Committee (Operations) and the Defence Committee (Supply) respectively. My comments are confined to the former. The composition of the committee varied from time to time, but always included the Deputy Prime Minister, the three Service Ministers and later, the Foreign Secretary. In addition, other Ministers, such as the Minister for Home Security, and the Minister of War Transport, were invited to meetings at which problems affecting their departments were to be discussed. The Chiefs of Staff were always in attendance.

It might seem on the face of it that these two innovations made little change in existing arrangements; but the practical effects were revolutionary. Henceforward the Prime Minister himself, with all the powers and authority which attach to that office, exercised a personal, direct, ubiquitous and continuous supervision, not only over the formulation of military policy at every stage, but also over the general conduct of military operations. There was a remarkable intensification of national effort in every field. All the considerations affecting any problem — political and economic, as well as military — could now be brought into focus more readily, and thanks to Mr Churchill's personal exercise of the wide powers given to him by the War Cabinet, and to his astonishing drive, firm decisions could be reached and translated into action far more quickly than had hitherto been the case. For the first time in their history, the Chiefs of Staff were in direct and continuous contact with the head of the Government, and were able to act as a combined Battle Headquarters — 'a superchief of a War Staff in Commission' — as had always been contemplated.

Another innovation introduced by Mr Churchill shortly after becoming Prime Minister was prompted by the offensive spirit which always animated him. After the fall of France, it was painfully evi-

DEFENCE MACHINERY 1942

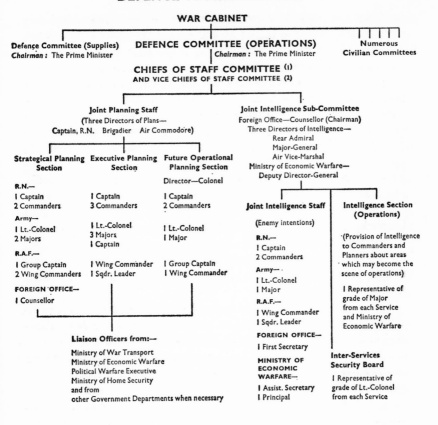

WAR CABINET

Defence Committee (Supplies)
Chairman : The Prime Minister

DEFENCE COMMITTEE (OPERATIONS)
Chairman : The Prime Minister

Numerous Civilian Committees

CHIEFS OF STAFF COMMITTEE (1)
AND VICE CHIEFS OF STAFF COMMITTEE (2)

Joint Planning Staff
(Three Directors of Plans—
Captain, R.N.   Brigadier   Air Commodore)

Joint Intelligence Sub-Committee
Foreign Office—Counsellor (Chairman)
Three Directors of Intelligence—
Rear Admiral
Major-General
Air Vice-Marshal
Ministry of Economic Warfare—
Deputy Director-General

Strategical Planning Section	Executive Planning Section	Future Operational Planning Section
		Director—Colonel
R.N.—		
1 Captain	1 Captain	1 Captain
2 Commanders	3 Commanders	2 Commanders
Army—		
1 Lt.-Colonel	1 Lt.-Colonel	1 Lt.-Colonel
2 Majors	3 Majors	1 Major
	1 Captain	
R.A.F.—		
1 Group Captain	1 Wing Commander	1 Group Captain
2 Wing Commanders	1 Sqdr. Leader	1 Wing Commander
FOREIGN OFFICE—		
1 Counsellor		

Liaison Officers from:—
Ministry of War Transport
Ministry of Economic Warfare
Political Warfare Executive
Ministry of Home Security
and from
other Government Departments when necessary

Joint Intelligence Staff
(Enemy intentions)
R.N.—
1 Captain
2 Commanders
Army—
1 Lt.-Colonel
1 Major
R.A.F.—
1 Wing Commander
1 Sqdr. Leader
FOREIGN OFFICE—
1 First Secretary
MINISTRY OF ECONOMIC WARFARE—
1 Assist. Secretary
1 Principal

Intelligence Section (Operations)
(Provision of Intelligence to Commanders and Planners about areas which may become the scene of operations)
1 Representative of grade of Major from each Service and Ministry of Economic Warfare

Inter-Services Security Board
1 Representative of grade of Lt.-Colonel from each Service

NOTES

(1) COMPOSITION OF CHIEFS OF STAFF COMMITTEE.

Chairman:
General Sir Alan Brooke (Chief of the Imperial General Staff).

Members:.
Admiral of the Fleet Sir Dudley Pound (First Sea Lord and Chief of Naval Staff).
Air Chief Marshal Sir Charles Portal (Chief of the Air Staff).
Major-General Sir Hastings Ismay (Representing the Minister of Defence and directing the Defence Secretariat).
Vice-Admiral the Lord Louis Mountbatten (Chief of Combined Operations)—present when major strategical issues or specific operations are under discussion.

(2) THE VICE-CHIEFS OF STAFF.

In order to ease the burden of the dual task which devolves on the Chiefs of Staff of advising His Majesty's Government on defence policy as a whole, and at the same time directing the work of their own individual Services, each Chief of Staff has a Vice-Chief of Staff as his *alter ego.* The Vice-Chiefs of Staff hold regular meetings at which they deal, in the name of the Chiefs of Staff Committee, with such matters as are delegated to them.

Members:
Vice-Admiral H. R. Moore (Vice-Chief of the Naval Staff).
Lieut.-General A. E. Nye (Vice-Chief of the Imperial General Staff).
Air Chief Marshal Sir Wilfrid Freeman (Vice-Chief of the Air Staff).

The Chairmanship varies according to the nature of the business.

dent that our immediate concern must be Home Defence, and that some time must elapse before we could have the necessary resources for an offensive on any considerable scale. Nevertheless, Churchill was determined that we should not fall into a completely defensive habit of mind, and on the very day on which the evacuation from Dunkirk was completed, he gave instructions that raiding forces of 'say, one thousand up to ten thousand' men should be organised as quickly as possible in order to harry the Germans all along the coasts of the countries which they had conquered. He followed this up three weeks later by setting up a Directorate of Combined Operations under Admiral of the Fleet Sir Roger Keyes. This organisation rendered invaluable services, first under Keyes, then under Vice-Admiral Lord Louis Mountbatten, and finally under Major-General Laycock. The Combined Operations Directorate was also charged with the responsibility of devising all the special equipment required for amphibious operations in general and opposed landings in particular. That they discharged their task supremely well will be evident as my narrative unfolds.

The only other development in our War Machine that need here be mentioned was the reorganisation and expansion of the Joint Planning and Joint Intelligence Staffs. This enabled intensive study to be simultaneously devoted to a large number of different plans. It also ensured the closest co-operation, not only between the Service Departments themselves, but also between those Departments and the Civilian Departments particularly involved in war planning, such as War Transport, Home Security and Economic Warfare.

The Machinery in the form in which it existed after the changes which I have mentioned, is described in greater detail on page 161.

In addition to the permanent Machinery, Churchill made a practice of setting up *ad hoc* committees, over which he himself presided, whenever he wanted to turn the heat on to any particular aspect of our war effort. In March 1941, for example, when sinkings in the Atlantic were extremely heavy, he set up the Battle of the Atlantic Committee. Its meetings were attended by all whose experience of this or that aspect of the problem could contribute towards its solution. Questions of strategy, tactics, co-ordination, command, equipment and scientific devices, were thrashed out round the table. The presence of the Prime Minister in the chair not only enabled decisions to be taken on the spot, but also ensured that they were put into effect at once. He was perhaps too impatient and self-willed to be an ideal chairman in the generally accepted sense, but his enthusiasm, drive, imagination and readiness to accept responsibility more than made up for all. The Battle of the Atlantic gradually turned in our favour, and at the end of six months, there was no more need for the Committee to meet. Similarly the Tank Parliament, the Night Air Defence Committee and other committees were set up to fulfil specific purposes, and dissolved when these purposes had been achieved.

From time to time Churchill's conduct of the war was severely criticised in Parliament. When things go badly there is always a tendency to attribute to faulty direction the blame for failures which are due to very different causes. The House of Commons was not at its best in these debates. One speaker suggested that the appointment of the Minister of Defence should be abolished and the conduct of the war entrusted to a superman drawn from one of the Fighting Services. He was to have no responsibility to Parliament. But he was to have unfettered control of the armed forces of the Crown, and the right to resign at once if the Cabinet did not give him everything for which he asked. Needless to say, the prospect of a virtual dictatorship did not commend itself to the Mother of Parliaments.

There was another proposal which was also aimed at Churchill. It was argued that no one man could combine the offices of Prime Minister and Minister of Defence, and it was proposed that Churchill should surrender the latter appointment to someone else. Considering that most of the important decisions which have to be taken in time of war relate to military operations, there is much to be said for the principle that the Prime Minister should be intimately connected with the formulation of defence policy from its inception, and at every stage. That, at any rate, was a lesson of the First World War. But apart from the question of principle, a nation which is so fortunate as to produce a Winston Churchill at the critical moment would surely be insane if it did not give the fullest rein to his unrivalled experience and qualifications. He was a 'war man' if ever there was one, and his whole life had been a preparation for the task which now confronted him. In his youth he had seen a lot of rough-and-tumble fighting in India, the Sudan, and South Africa; and in the First World War he had commanded a battalion in France. Admittedly the mechanics of war had changed out of all recognition by the time that the Second World War broke out, but fighting experience of any kind, especially in the front line, is a valuable asset to anyone charged with the higher direction of war.

In addition to having seen a great variety of front-line fighting, Churchill's ministerial experience in the military field was unique. For three years before the outbreak of the First World War, he had been First Lord of the Admiralty; and he had proved himself a brilliant war-time Minister, until the failure of the Dardanelles campaign brought about his downfall. For the last year of the war he had been Minister of Munitions; and after the armistice he held office for a short time as Secretary of State for War and Air. On the outbreak of the Second World War he was once again appointed First Lord of the Admiralty, with a seat in the War Cabinet. 'Winston is back' was the cheerful signal sent to all ships under the white ensign by the Board of Admiralty on 3 September 1939.

From his early youth he had been a student of military history, and his many books on military subjects, notably *The River War, Marlborough* and *The World Crisis,* are rightly regarded as classics of their sort. His knowledge of the campaigns of the great Captains of the past was phenomenal, and in his grasp of the broad sweep of strategy — 'the over-all strategic concept,' as our American friends called it — he stood head and shoulders above his professional advisers.

It has always seemed to me extraordinary that Churchill earned the reputation of being a wild and unrealistic strategist because of the failure of the Gallipoli campaign. In the after light there can be no doubt that his conception of forcing the Dardanelles and joining hands with Russia was admirable. Nor can there be any doubt that if the Government had been effectively organised for the conduct of war, the expedition would either have been completely successful or would not have been attempted. It might, perhaps with justice, be said that Churchill was blameworthy in continuing to press for the Gallipoli campaign long after it was clear that his ministerial colleagues and his principal technical adviser, Lord Fisher, had not got their hearts in it. But to blame him for the strategic conception is manifestly absurd.

The reader may care to consider how the business would have been handled if an expedition such as the Dardanelles had been proposed in 1941, instead of 1915. The ball would have been opened by a minute from the Prime Minister to the Chiefs of Staff explaining his ideas and requesting their views. The first question to which they would have addressed themselves would have been, 'Is the plan practicable and desirable from the military point of view?' If their conclusions had been unfavourable, they would have reported to the Prime Minister to that effect. If their objections were found unconvincing, they would have been subjected to a searching cross-examination and perhaps to heavy pressure, by the Prime Minister, and possibly by the Defence Committee. The discussion might have been heated, and hard words might have been used. But if the Chiefs of Staff had stuck to their guns, there would have been no expedition.

If, on the other hand, the Chiefs of Staff, instead of dissenting, had agreed that the expedition was advisable from the military point of view and had thought that the necessary resources could be found, the Joint Planners would have been instructed to prepare an outline plan giving their views as to the form the expedition should take, the resources that it would require, and the date at which it could be launched. The results of their studies would have been examined by the Chiefs in the first place, and then by the Prime Minister and Defence Committee. Once the plan had been 'finalised,' the War Cabinet would have been informed in general terms, and their approval sought. Thereafter the commander of the expedition would have been nominated, given the necessary staffs, and instructed to go ahead with detailed plans and preparations.

A proposal which Churchill put forward in the latter half of 1941 will serve as an object lesson. Shortly after Germany attacked Russia, he pressed for an expedition to capture northern Norway. It would have to some extent satisfied the importunate demands of the Russians, and the clamour of public opinion in Britain and America, for a second front in Europe; and it would have gone a long way towards eliminating the risks which the Arctic convoys had to run, thus saving hundreds of lives, many precious ships and thousands of tons of equipment and supplies. It was in fact an 'Arctic Gallipoli' designed to keep Russia in the fight. But the Chiefs of Staff were adamant that, apart from the hazards of the operation, we had not got adequate resources to undertake it. They were almost certainly right. The Prime Minister continued to press them for some time, but did not persist. Not once during the whole war did he overrule his military advisers on a purely military question.

After that long digression, let me examine some of the other suggestions which were put forward in Parliament for improving the War Machine. One of these was based on the argument that the Chiefs of Staff could not combine the proper performance of their departmental duties with their collective responsibility for advising the Government on defence policy as a whole. It was, therefore, proposed that they should be restricted to their departmental work, and that their collective responsibility should be assigned to three other military personages of similar calibre.

The authors of this suggestion were seemingly unaware of the fact that, in April 1940, the Chiefs of Staff had been 'double-banked' by the appointment of a Vice Chief of Staff in each of the Service Departments. The innovation had relieved the Chiefs of Staff of much of their departmental work, and proved a great success. But apart from that the idea of three men of genius living in splendid isolation and divorced not only from the harsh realities of administration but also from any responsibility for the execution of their brainwaves, would not find many supporters among men of experience. The prime virtue of our war system was that the men who were responsible for advising on defence, were in actual control of the armed forces. As Field Marshal Sir William Robertson is reported to have said to Mr Lloyd George, 'I could give you a hundred plans for winning the war if I had not got the responsibility for carrying them out.'

The only proposal which need be mentioned was based on the argument that no one man could discharge the immense responsibilities of a Chief of Staff and at the same time be an effective chairman of the Chiefs of Staff Committee. It was therefore suggested that a Service figure of independent mind should be selected for that appointment. He would have no departmental responsibilities and be able to devote his whole time, energy and experience to the task. In principle, there is a good deal to be said for this idea. Before the war it had always been the practice for the Chairman of the COS Committee to come to meetings with two briefs; one, prepared by his own Staff, dealt with the problems on the agenda from the point of view of his own Service, while the other, prepared by the Secretary of the Committee of Imperial Defence (who was *ex officio* Secretary of the COS Committee), dealt with the problems from more general points of view. In the pressure of war this practice of a general brief lapsed, with the result that the three war-time Chairmen of the Committee — Marshal of the RAF Sir Cyril Newall, Admiral of the Fleet Sir Dudley Pound, and Field Marshal Sir Alan Brooke — were perhaps prone to see problems through the eyes of their own particular Services. The proposal for an independent chairman was strongly advocated by *The Times,* and received support from many men of experience. It has now been implemented,[1] but it remains to be seen whether it would prove satisfactory in time of war. However that may be, the arrangement was unacceptable to Churchill. Under his régime the responsibility of the Chairman of the Chiefs of Staff Committee was confined to taking the chair at meetings, acting as spokesman for reports to the Defence Committee or Cabinet, and advising on matters relating to *his own* Service. He was not the principal strategical adviser in the accepted sense of that term. Churchill always believed in going to the root of a problem himself, and in dealing with the man, or men, who not only knew all the details but also bore the responsibility. If, for example, he was studying the details of an essentially naval problem, he would deal direct with the First Sea Lord. He was criticised for having refused to give a trial to the suggestion of an independent chairman; but surely he was entitled to argue that he had been allotted an almost superhuman task, and that he must be allowed, within reason, to use whatever tools suited him best.

The House of Commons as a whole were clearly content with Churchill's methods and machinery. They gave him overwhelming majorities on every occasion that he was challenged on the subject, and his arrangements remained unchanged in essentials until the end of the war. They may not have been perfect, but they at least achieved their primary purpose — victory. They suited the genius and temperament of the extraordinary man who presided over them, and it can be claimed that, on the whole, they worked smoothly and harmoniously.

It may also be claimed that there were none of the hateful intrigues or bitter amimosities which disfigured the councils of the First

[1] In 1957.

World War. Of course there were moments when tempers were frayed; of course there were occasional quarrels, such as often occur in the best-regulated families; of course there were times when the soldiers resented the continuous, but not always unsalutary, prodding of their political Chief; and of course there were also times when the Prime Minister became, not always unjustly, impatient. But it is my sincere hope that too much attention will not be paid by posterity to stories of taunts uttered in moments of irritation, or to private diaries which were never intended for public scrutiny. I spent the whole war in the middle of the web; I had a legitimate foot in every camp — naval, military, air, as well as political. I did not have a finger in every pie, but it was my duty to know about all the pies that were being cooked and how they were getting on; and I can testify that the War Cabinet was a band of brothers, and that the relations between Churchill and his official advisers, both civil and military, were characterised by mutual understanding, esteem and affection.

Mr Churchill's account[1] of how the War Machine worked is written from the point of view of the man who controlled it. Mine will be written from the personal point of view of one of the cogs in the machine. I had three sets of responsibilities. I was Chief of Staff Officer to Mr Churchill; I was a member of the Chiefs of Staff Committee; and I was head of the Office of the Minister of Defence. Thus I was a cog which had to operate in three separate though intimately connected mechanisms.

With regard to my personal responsibilities to Mr Churchill, many people seemed to think — and some still think — that I was his military adviser. On one occasion, indeed, when our fortunes were at a particularly low ebb, I was flattered to see myself discribed in print as his 'Eminence Khaki.' This was of course a travesty of the truth. Nothing would have been more certain to dislocate the Machine and to bring discredit on myself than an attempt on my part, however cunningly concealed, to usurp advisory functions which properly belonged elsewhere. Once, at the outset of our association, Churchill asked me, in the presence of the three Service Ministers, what I thought of a certain military figure. Actually I had a poor opinion of the man in question, but I begged to be excused from expressing any

[1] *History of the Second World War*: Vol. II, Chapter I.

opinion on the grounds that this was a matter on which the Minister concerned was his responsible adviser. I submitted that, if it were thought that I was trying to exert influence on matters outside my province, I would forfeit all confidence and be useless to him.

At the same time, it is not easy to define my precise position in relation to my chief. His own description of me as the 'head of his handling machine' seems pretty near the mark, but I prefer the term 'agent.' Anyhow, that is how I interpreted the part. An agent cannot do his job properly unless he knows the thoughts and the wishes, the hopes and the fears, of the man for whom he is working. With Mr Churchill this presented little difficulty, since he took all of us who were in his inner circle into his complete confidence. An agent must also be at his master's beck and call at any hour of the day or night, week-day or holiday. I therefore tried to be my chief's shadow, whatever he did and wherever he went. If I could not accompany him myself, I always tried to arrange for one of my trusted deputies, Hollis or Jacob, to do so.

Perhaps my principal function was to be a two-way channel of communication on military matters between the Prime Minister and everyone in Whitehall who was concerned with military business. On the one hand, I was required to communicate and, if necessary, amplify and explain his views to those concerned, and on the other, to obtain for him all the manifold information which he needed. His instructions were invariably given in writing, for he was a firm believer in the written word; and his unequalled clarity of expression left no doubt as to what he wanted. But his thirst for information was unquenchable. There was no limit to the number, variety or range of the problems remitted to me. By way of example, I was called upon on 2 August 1940 — a date which I have selected more or less at random — for reports on the following:

1. The Air Staff's most recent scheme for increasing the number of pilots.
2. The programme of lectures on tactics to the Army.
3. The collection of scrap (report to be on one page).
4. The work of the Salvage Department in the Admiralty.
5. The functions of Police and ARP personnel in case of invasion.

6. The future organisation of the Armoured Division (report on one page).

7. A forecast of deliveries of uniforms to the Home Guard.

Neither I nor any member of my Staff could, out of our own knowledge, have given the answers to any of these conundrums, but it was our business to obtain them from the person or persons who were qualified to do so. At the same time, I was not merely a glorified Post Office. Many of my informants had an exact knowledge of all the facts but were unable to present them in a form that would have been acceptable to a busy and exacting Minister. The presentation — or co-ordination, if there were more than one informant — of the reply had therefore to be done by myself or one of my staff. And it was not always easy to translate the technical jargon in which Whitehall delighted into the English on which Mr Churchill insisted, or to boil down several foolscap pages into the one sheet of paper to which I was so often restricted. 'Clarity and cogency can be reconciled with a greater brevity,' was one of his favourite admonitions; which, if unheeded, was followed up by a more direct reproof. 'It is slothful not to compress your thoughts.' I got round the difficulty by a technique which bordered on subterfuge. I used to compress the salient facts of the case into a short minute of the prescribed length, and attach thereto the fuller information, on which the facts were based, in the form of Annexures A, B, C, etc. etc. To these there was no limit imposed by my chief, and I recall that I once needed all the letters of the alphabet as far as T, and that Annexure L alone covered two pages of foolscap.

Another of my functions related to Churchill's speeches on military matters. He seldom asked me for material, but he almost invariably sent me his drafts to be checked on questions of fact. His tendency to leave the preparation of these drafts to the last moment required special arrangements. When an important speech was in the offing, I used to keep in continuous touch with all the officers whose collaboration in checking it was likely to be required, and we used to fall upon the draft the moment that copies were received from the Prime Minister's Private Office. We never failed to get a full commentary into his hands in time; but there were some hairbreadth escapes. On one occasion he was in bed in his room at the White House in Washington making amendments to the speech which he was to deliver to Congress that morning in the light of the commentary which I had just brought to him. The confusion of paper strewn all over the place was indescribable. Suddenly Leslie Rowan[1] came into the room in a state of agitation. 'Do you realise, sir,' he asked, 'that you are due at Congress in twenty minutes?' Churchill shot out of bed, and papers flew in every direction. 'Mind you get the pages in the right order. My life depends upon it,' was his parting shot as he disappeared into the bathroom. 'What about mine?' retorted Leslie. It may seem frivolous to recall these trivialities, but no picture of the brilliant creature whom I am trying to portray would be complete without them. His puckishness may at times have been exasperating, but I can vouch for it that those who served nearest to him were thankful that in some ways he had never quite grown up.

He took a delight in gadgets; the 'klop' which he used to punch tag holes in his paper was always near at hand, as was a supply of special labels inscribed, 'Action This Day,' or 'Action Within One Week,' which he used to affix to his minutes as the mood moved him. In point of fact it made very little difference to the speed with which they were handled, since it was a point of honour in our office to provide him with the answers in the shortest possible time, irrespective of whether they were, or were not, specially labelled. Our colleagues in the other offices co-operated nobly.

I now turn to my role as Mr Churchill's representative on the Chiefs of Staff Committee. This appointment was unprecedented, and gave rise to not a little suspicion and resentment. My duties were never specifically defined, and it was left to me to interpret them as best I could. First and foremost, I made it my business to express, and if necessary explain, Churchill's views to the Chiefs of Staff Committee, and to inform him of their reactions. Now and then a certain amount of tactful expurgation was necessary. To have passed on the identical language used by either party in unguarded moments would have led to trouble. I had to be not only an interpreter, but a mediator. For the rest, I was determined that the change in my status should make as little difference as possible to my functions. In particular, there could be no question of my membership of the Com-

---

[1] Assistant and later Principal Private Secretary to the Prime Minister, 1941-1945. Subsequently Sir Leslie Rowan.

mittee impinging upon the individual and collective responsibility of the three Chiefs of Staff for advising on defence policy as a whole. That triumvirate must remain inviolate, and all military advice tendered to ministerial authority, and all orders and instructions issued to commanders in the field, must continue to bear their signatures, and theirs alone. I did not therefore sign any Chiefs of Staff documents; nor, it may be mentioned, did Admiral Lord Louis Mountbatten when, as Chief of Combined Operations, he was made a member of the Chiefs of Staff Committee for meetings at which major strategical issues or opposed landings were under discussion. In effect I remained the Head of the Chiefs of Staff Secretariat; and, as such, I continued, in collaboration with my colleagues and particularly the man who had succeeded me as Secretary of the Committee, Jo Hollis, to assist in drafting reports, preparing statements of the case, and reconciling differences of opinion.

My functions in my third field of responsibility, namely the headship of the Office of the Minister of Defence, remained precisely the same as they had been when the war started. In spite of the ever-increasing load of business, I kept our numbers to the absolute minimum, on order not to lose the personal touch which was so essential to our type of work. But we continued to provide the secretaries who arranged the business, drafted the reports, and maintained the records of *all* military committees, from the Defence Committee downwards. Thus my office served as a focal point where an answer could readily be found to almost any question relating to the conduct and progress of military operations.

For Commanders-in-Chief a special room was set apart in the Defence Office in which all war information which was too secret to be circulated in the ordinary way, was maintained under the able supervision of Miss Bright.[1] This 'Secret Intelligence Centre' enabled Commanders-in-Chief visiting London to be brought fully up-to-date about the situation in theatres other than their own. They took full advantage of the facilities, and the experiment proved a great success.

In addition, a number of foster-children, for whom there was no obvious parent, were placed in my charge. The first of these was the War Room Staff, whose functions have already been explained. Whenever a big battle or critical movement was in progress, it was a

[1] Later Mrs Philip Astley.

temptation to find pretexts for going to the War Room at all hours of the day and night, in order to get the very latest information. The sensation was not unlike visiting a friend in hospital. One entered the room hoping for the best, but fearing the worst. 'How is the Malta convoy going?' one would ask, trying not to appear unduly anxious. The nature of the answer could generally be guessed from the expression of the officer on duty. If he looked cheerful, one expected something like this: 'Splendidly. Only one ship has been hit and she is keeping up with the convoy.' But if he looked strained, one was prepared for bad news: 'Two ships have been sunk by U-boats and six by air attack.' My visits often coincided with those of a sturdy figure in a siren suit, and I began to understand why my chief was always so embarrassingly up to date with every detail of the situation.

Another of my foster-children was one of Churchill's pet creations. He maintained that, during the First World War, the War Office had been dismally slow and unimaginative in addressing their minds to the provision of special mechanical devices to meet the conditions of static warfare on the Western Front; and, in particular, he had never forgotten the official obstruction which had caused such inordinate delay in the production of his dream child, the tank. Accordingly, as soon as he became Prime Minister, he insisted on having a small experimental establishment of his own, which was to work in the closest touch with Professor Lindemann. Major Jefferis, whose inventive genius had come to Churchill's notice early in the war, was placed in charge; and I was instructed to 'take him under my protection,' lest the Ordnance Board and the Ministry of Supply, who were unlikely to approve of free lances, should make things difficult for him. Jefferis, with continuous support and encouragement from 'the Prof' and the Prime Minister himself, did valuable work, but his start was not a happy one. He was trying his hand at producing a small bomb which could at short range be thrown at a tank and stick to it, thus ensuring a powerful explosion when it detonated. Unfortunately his first trial bomb failed to stick, and was about as effective as a damp squib. I was sorry to think of Jefferis's disappointment, but I much enjoyed the receipt later in the day of a minute warning me that 'any chortling by officials who have been slothful in pushing the bomb would be viewed with great disfavour.' How to convey this warning to the persons for whom it was intended, or even to identify them, were puzzles which I failed to solve. But, anyway, the 'sticky' bomb eventually proved completely successful, as did other inventions of the ingenious Jefferis.

Needless to say the supervision of the experimental section under Jefferis was only one of the many responsibilities which the Prof undertook on behalf of the Prime Minister; but it was certainly one that he found very attractive. Churchill used to say that the Prof's brain was a beautiful piece of mechanism, and the Prof did not dissent from that judgment. He seemed to have a poor opinion of the intellect of everyone with the exception of Lord Birkenhead, Mr Churchill and Professor Lindemann; and he had a special contempt for the bureaucrat and all his ways. The Ministry of Supply and the Ordnance Board were two of his pet aversions, and he derived a great deal of pleasure from forestalling them with new inventions. In his appointment as Personal Assistant to the Prime Minister no field of activity was closed to him. He was as obstinate as a mule, and unwilling to admit that there was any problem under the sun which he was not qualified to solve. He would write a memorandum on high strategy on one day, and a thesis on egg production on the next. He seemed to try to give the impression of wanting to quarrel with everybody, and of preferring everyone's room to their company: but once he had accepted a man as a friend, he never failed him, and there are many of his war-time colleagues who will ever remember him with deep personal affection. He hated Hitler and all his works, and his contribution to Hitler's downfall in all sorts of odd ways was considerable.

Another group which came under my wing at a later date and added a spice of variety to our daily round was the handful of planners who were responsible for inventing cover plans for mystifying and deceiving the enemy. They did a magnificent job, and examples of their handiwork will be given in their proper places.

The story of a typical Churchillian day in Whitehall may serve to put a little flesh on the bare bones of the organisation which I have tried to describe. On most mornings I used to report to the Prime Minister in his bedroom about half an hour before the daily meeting of the Chiefs of Staff Committee. Sometimes he would give me last minute instructions on one or two of the questions which the Committee was about to discuss; sometimes he would refer to one of the latest telegrams and say that he would like to know what the Chiefs of Staff thought of it; sometimes he would hand me a minute, which he had perhaps just dictated, with orders to bring it to the immediate notice of the Chiefs of Staff and to let him know their reactions as soon as the meeting was over. He might spend the rest of the morning either at a Cabinet meeting, or in interviews, or in continuing to read official papers, and dictate minutes, speeches, etc. Wisely he used to do as much of his work as possible in bed.

Often I had occasion to report to him again before lunch. If, by way of example, the Chiefs of Staff had agreed to a draft telegram of his, I would report accordingly, and the telegram would be duly initialled and despatched. If, on the other hand, the Chiefs of Staff had not seen eye to eye with him, he might accept their suggestions, or he might address them a further minute on the subject; or again, he might decide to discuss it personally with them at an early meeting. The system was completely flexible. Men of genius are unpredictable, and Mr Churchill was never amenable to regular routine.

He almost invariably had people to lunch, generally those with whom he wished to discuss this or that war problem. In the afternoon there might be a meeting of the Cabinet or of one of the numerous committees over which Churchill presided, such as the anti-U-boat Committee, or the Tank Parliament. But whatever his arrangements, he invariably got between the sheets for an hour or so. His capacity for dropping off into a sound sleep the moment his head touched the pillow had to be seen to be believed. There was no fixed time for his siesta. It would start when the spirit moved him, with the result that his afternoon engagements had to be readjusted at the eleventh hour. This upset the programmes of other people and led to a certain amount of grumbling. Such grumbling may have been only natural but it was unreasonable. If an afternoon sleep enabled the one and only man in the country who was indispensable to 'get the last scrap out of the human structure,' it ill became people of less consequence to object to the dislocation of their own arrangements.

Dinner, like lunch, was nearly always devoted to war business, and discussions continued throughout the meal — and maybe long after. Finally, there were his nocturnal habits. Much has been written about them; and on at least one occasion they were the subject of adverse criticism in Parliament. This, too, seems unreasonable.

Churchill's job was never-ending, and he was surely entitled to discharge it in whatever way and at whatever time suited him best. Apart from that, the grumblers might have borne in mind that we were fighting for our very lives, and that the troops in the front line did not invariably enjoy a full night's rest in comfortable beds between linen sheets. Surely it was not too much to expect those who were living in comparative comfort and safety to sacrifice a few hours' sleep, if their chief required it. I myself was frequently summoned after dinner; but on the days that no summons came, I used to make a point of calling at the Prime Minister's office between eleven and twelve P.M. to find out what he was doing. If he was engaged with others on business which did not require my presence I went thankfully to bed. But, on nights when I was told that he was alone dealing with his papers, I used to join him and keep him company until he retired for the night. I was under no illusion about the value of my contribution to the war during these sessions. Occasionally I could give him information which he wanted, or receive his instructions on this or that question. Occasionally I could persuade him to tone down a harsh minute or telegram, or postpone its despatch until he had had time for further reflection, or for the facts to be checked. But as a rule the most that I could hope was that the mere fact of my presence and of my unspoken desire to help him, gave him a grain of support. Once in his room, it was almost impossible to get away. If I tried looking pointedly at my watch, his usual reaction was that I could go to bed if I liked, but that he was going to do his duty. His hour of retirement was seldom earlier than 1 A.M., and usually very much later. Sometimes he was too exhausted to do constructive work towards the end of these night watches; and on those occasions I used to feel aggrieved at having lost precious sleep to no good purpose. Perhaps, if I had kept a diary, the entries on those unproductive nights would have been querulous and critical. And how sorry I would have felt when I read them the next day!

But now and then he would give birth to a brainchild at a moment when he looked too exhausted to be capable of coherent thought. I remember in particular an October night in 1940. We were alone in the Hawtrey Room at Chequers, and the clock had just chimed midnight. Mr. Churchill looked tired out and I had visions of an early bed. But suddenly he jumped up, exclaiming, 'I believe that I can do it.' Bells were rung; secretaries appeared; and he proceeded to dictate his first broadcast to France. He had no notes; but slowly and steadily, for a space of some two hours, the words poured forth. The result would have been a *tour de force* by any standards and at any time; but, in those circumstances, it was a most remarkable triumph of mind over matter. The impression of that broadcast on our French friends has lasted through the years. To this day they cannot recall it without emotion.

Churchill's thoughts, whether lunching or dining, whether waking or even, I believe, sleeping, were concentrated on the war. Except for an occasional film, he allowed himself no respite. Week-ends were to him exactly the same as week days, except that he spent the latter at Downing Street and the former at Chequers or Ditchley or, very occasionally, at his own beloved Chartwell[1]. His brain and nerve and sinew were driven relentlessly forward by his indomitable will. If there was work to be done, he seemed impervious to fatigue, physical or mental. The idea of a holiday never crossed his mind. When the war had been going on for nearly three years, I told him that my staff were getting somewhat stale, and suggested that we should all take a few days' leave. He agreed without much enthusiasm, and a little later I sent him a note saying that I proposed to go to the country for a week on the next Friday. But when Thursday came round, he said, 'I shouldn't take leave if I were you. No one requires leave. All that the human structure requires is change, and we will probably be going to Washington very soon.' I felt sore at the time, but I believe that he was right.

His most fervent admirers would not say that he was considerate, but neither could his fiercest critics deny that, so far as waging war was concerned, he was more inconsiderate of himself than he was of others. Even when he was really ill, perhaps running a high temperature, he insisted on continuing to work. Just before leaving for the Second Quebec Conference, he was in the throes of a serious bout of pneumonia, and the doctors had forbidden him to see anyone or to read papers. Not having heard this, I obeyed a summons to his bedside which was delivered to me by his valet; his secretaries knew the

[1] Chequers is the official country home of the Prime Minister; Chartwell is Churchill's private country home; Ditchley is the home of his friends, Mr and Mrs Ronald Tree, where he often visited.

doctors' orders and would not have passed on the message. He looked desperately ill and did not seem to understand what I was saying. Seriously frightened, I rang up Brendan Bracken (then Minister of Information and one of Churchill's closest friends), who was always a magnificent stand-by on occasions like this. He came along post-haste, and marching into the bedroom, asked Churchill whether he had informed the King that it might be necessary for His Majesty to send for someone to form a new Government. Churchill snorted. Of course he had done no such thing. Why should he? He was not going to die. Whereupon Brendan retorted, 'That is exactly where you are wrong. If you go on playing the fool like this, you are certain to die.' That kept him quiet for a bit, but not for long.

CHAPTER XIV

Assault on Britain

1940

I USED often to feel homesick when serving overseas, and the first sight of the white cliffs of Dover after a long absence never failed to give me a thrill of pride and thankfulness. The greyer the skies, the more homely seemed the welcome. And when I left for abroad again, I always uttered a silent prayer that I might come back again in due season to the land of my fathers. But I never realised how precious England was to me until she was in imminent danger of violation. That she would be invaded was highly probable; that she would be subjected to frightful air bombardment was certain. The very thought gave me a spasm of almost physical pain.

It seemed unlikely that invasion would be attempted for at least a few weeks. Hitler could not in his wildest dreams have anticipated the rapidity of his victory over France, and it was very doubtful whether his plans for landing in England were as yet complete. In any case, it would take some time to assemble the necessary shipping and other paraphernalia. We could therefore count on a respite of at least a couple of months, in which to improve our defences against invasion.

But air attack was a very different proposition. The Luftwaffe could be at our throats almost any day, and we were by no means unprepared to meet them. The Air Staff, with splendid assistance from

179

our men of science, had rendered great service to the country by the ingenuity and thoroughness of their preparations for the defence of the homeland. Mr Baldwin was possibly right, though not perhaps well advised, when he told the House of Commons in 1932 that 'the bomber would always get through.' But since then the modern fighter, modern A-A guns, the Observer Corps, and radar, working under unified control from ingeniously equipped and well protected operation rooms, had drastically changed the situation. We could now be pretty certain that in daylight the attacker — be he bomber or fighter — would be detected and engaged, provided, of course, that there were sufficient fighter squadrons for home defense. But were there? That was the question on which our survival depended.

Looking back on all the arguments that we used to have in our pre-war planning, I believe that the Air Staff were, on the whole, nearer the mark than either of the older Services in their conception of the war of the future. They had already proved correct in the contention that naval forces, operating without air cover, would be very seriously handicapped; and they were to prove equally correct in resisting the demands of the General Staff for a separate allocation of air forces to the Army. Nevertheless, there was one point on which their attitude was open to question.

As the speed, range, and bomb-carrying capacity of the German Air Force continued to increase, and war loomed nearer and nearer, it was proposed from time to time that the number of fighter squadrons for home defense should be increased. But the Air Ministry were opposed to this, unless the number of bomber squadrons was simultaneously increased in proportion. They said that multiplication of fighters was a heresy which appealed only to those who were ignorant about air power, and did not understand that the counter-offensive by bombers must always be our crowning aim. In theory they may have been perfectly correct, but to the layman it seemed that the particular circumstances of those days justified a departure from the text-books. The vital need was to ensure that the Citadel could be effectively defended until such time as we could build up the necessary apparatus — including, of course, large numbers of bombers — to assume the offensive. As things turned out, the number of fighters available for Home Defence in July 1940 was the barest minimum. There was no margin whatsoever.

Before the Battle of Waterloo, the Duke of Wellington is alleged to have pointed to a lone British soldier standing near-by and to have said: 'There, it all depends on that article whether we do the business or not. Give me enough of it, and I am sure.' Substitute the Hurricane or Spitfire pilot for the lone British soldier, and Air Chief Marshal Dowding might have used much the same words. He must have felt intensely thankful that the solemn warning which he had given to the Cabinet in the previous month about the danger of sending more fighter squadrons to France had been heeded.

The German Air Force had been at full stretch throughout the Battle of France, and it was not until the first week in July that the Battle of Britain started in earnest. As usual, the Prime Minister took every opportunity to go and see things for himself, and I accompanied him on many of his visits to fighter stations in Kent and Sussex. From the moment one set foot on the tarmac, one sensed the tension in the air — the pilots standing by 'on readiness,' waiting to 'scramble' into their machines at a moment's notice. It was impossible to look at those young men, who might within a matter of minutes be fighting and dying to save us, without mingled emotions of wonder, gratitude, and humility. The physical and mental strain of 'the long hours at dispersal, the constant flying at high altitudes (two or three sorties a day were normal, six or seven not uncommon),' [1] must have been prodigious. And yet they were so cheerful, so confident, and so obviously dedicated. They were always thrilled to see Churchill, and they gave me a kindly welcome. But they seemed a race apart, and I felt an intruder. They brought to my mind something that I had once read in the Old Testament. I looked it up when I got home. 'And they shall be mine, saith the Lord of hosts, in that day when I make up my jewels.' [2]

The Operations Room of No. 11 Group, Fighter Command, was Churchill's favourite port of call at this period. It was the nerve centre from which he could follow the course of the whole air battle. The sequel to a visit in mid-August must be told. There had been heavy fighting throughout the afternoon; and at one moment every single squadron in the Group was engaged; there was nothing in reserve, and the map table showed new waves of attackers crossing the coast. I felt sick with fear. As the evening closed in, the fighting died down,

[1] *The Royal Air Force,* 1939-1945, published by H.M. Stationery Office.
[2] Malachi III: 17.

and we left by car for Chequers. Churchill's first words were: 'Don't speak to me; I have never been so moved.' After about five minutes he leaned forward and said, 'Never in the field of human conflict has so much been owed by so many to so few.' The words burned into my brain and I repeated them to my wife when I got home. Churchill, too, had evidently photographed them in his mind; for, as everyone knows, he used them in a speech that was heard throughout the world.

Except for these occasional excursions, it was my lot to remain in Whitehall and await the results of each day's fighting. Mercifully, there was never any shortage of work to provide distraction, and now and then there was the minor excitement of seeing formations of enemy planes over London. But it was almost impossible to get the air battle out of one's mind. Everything that we held dearer than life itself was at stake. All London, nay, all England, could think of little else. 'What is the score today?' was the question on every lip in bus, tube, factory and office. The hall porters at hotels and clubs had to supply the answer a dozen times a day.

To learn of large numbers of enemy aircraft destroyed was of course encouraging, but equally important was the tally of our own losses. Our survival depended on whether they could be made good sufficiently quickly by new production and repairs. It was at this juncture that Churchill's insistence on the creation of a Ministry of Aircraft Production, and his selection of Lord Beaverbrook to take charge of it, paid handsome rewards. This is no reflection on the splendid work done by Air Chief Marshal Sir Wilfrid Freeman, Air Member for Development and Production in the immediately pre-war years. Without the solid foundations which he laid, neither Beaverbrook nor anyone else could have achieved very much by the time the Battle of Britain had to be fought. Nevertheless, desperate situations call for desperate remedies, and Beaverbrook had just the qualities which were needed. He was in his element. His dynamic energy and remarkable flair for improvisation brushed aside all obstacles. In the pursuit of anything which he wanted — whether materials, machine tools, or labour — he never hesitated — so rival departments alleged — to indulge in barefaced robbery. His office was pandemonium, especially in the night watches. But the results were astounding. Even so, it was not possible to satisfy the men who were doing the fighting, and an enjoyable, though perhaps apocryphal, story went the rounds of Whitehall. An outraged squadron leader, who had been disappointed by the non-arrival of some badly needed spare parts, rang up the Air Ministry and peremptorily demanded to speak to the appropriate person. As soon as he was connected, he embarked on a violent tirade against the negligence and uselessness of the Air Ministry and all who dwelt therein. When he paused for breath, the voice at the other end asked, 'Do you know who you are speaking to?' 'No,' came the reply. 'Well, it's Air Chief Marshal Sir So and So,' said the voice. 'Do you know who you are speaking to?' asked the squadron leader. 'No,' came the reply. 'Thank God,' said the young man, and abruptly rang off.

Gradually, as the days passed, we seemed to be getting on top. Between the beginning of the battle and mid-September, we had destroyed over 1,100 German aircraft, and lost less than 650 fighters in the process. Göring was no longer prepared to face the RAF in daylight. The Battle of Britain had been won. It had 'been a damned nice thing; the nearest run thing you ever saw in your life.' [1]

Personally I always felt that if we won the Battle of Britain the Germans would not invade, and that if we lost it, they would have no need to invade. It would be a case of 'Movement Tables' and 'Occupation Instructions' instead of 'Operation Orders.' That over-simplification must be explained.

So long as Fighter Command were able to operate effectively, invasion on a large enough scale to hold out good hopes of success would involve overwhelming difficulties and prohibitive casualties. As a prelude to the operation, masses of shipping and landing craft of every description would have to be assembled in the ports of northern Europe. This would take a matter of days, if not weeks; and all the time this closely packed and highly vulnerable mass would be attacked night and day by the Royal Air Force. The next problem for the enemy would be to embark large numbers of troops and masses of heavy equipment under continuous air attack. I was astonished to hear it argued at about this time that the escape of our army from Dunkirk had shown what could be done, even in the face of a vastly superior air force, and that the embarkation of a German army in the face of attack by our numerically inferior air forces would not be too

[1] The Duke of Wellington to Mr Creevey on the day after the Battle of Waterloo.

difficult. There is no parallel between the two cases. Our men left Dunkirk as naked individuals, in no semblance of formation, and without any equipment except their rifles. The Germans, on the other hand, would have to embark in formed bodies, ready to fight immediately on landing, and with all the paraphernalia that the modern army requires. Then would come the sea passage in the face of vastly superior naval forces. The German Navy would have little stomach for this trial of strength. Finally, there would be the hazards of disembarkation by those who had survived the attentions of the Royal Air Force while they were embarking, and the attentions of both the Royal Navy and the Royal Air Force while they were on passage. They would find the beaches heavily mined and wired, and the exits from them obstructed by every kind of obstacle; and they would be subjected to a deadly fire from defenders on the ground and in the air. It is therefore my considered opinion that, with Fighter Command still in being, a German invasion would have suffered much the same fate as the Spanish Armada.

Now let us consider what would have happened if the Battle of Britain had been lost. The Luftwaffe could have proceeded to wipe out in their own time and without any significant hindrance, first our air stations, then our aircraft factories, then perhaps our other munition factories, then our ports, and so on. The point would have been reached, perhaps quite soon, when we would have been bereft of all means of serious opposition. We could have continued the war from Canada — I hope that we would have done so. But the physical occupation of Britain would have presented no serious difficulty.

When I was thirteen years old, I won as a prize a book called *Fifteen Decisive Battles of the World* by Sir Edward Creasy. It seemed a curious book to present to an undersized boy who had no intention in those days of being a soldier, and it remained unopened for several years. In later life I read it many times from cover to cover, and I often wondered whether I agreed with the author's choice. If I were now asked to name the battles which had had the greatest influence on the history of the world, I should unhesitatingly put the Battle of Britain very high on my list.

Having failed to subdue the Royal Air Force in daylight fighting, Hitler decided to break the spirit of the British people by night bombing. Thus the Battle of Britain gradually merged into what became known as the Blitz. In the first place the Luftwaffe concentrated on London, the finest target in the world for indiscriminate attack. There was no precedent for this kind of warfare. It might be immediately and overwhelmingly successful or it might completely fail in its purpose. All would depend — as it always does in war — on the human element. Would the civilian population, however brave, resolute, disciplined, and well-organised, be able to stand up to the casualties and sufferings that were bound to be their lot? London, and later other cities in Britain, were soon to give the answer to that question.

The Blitz started in earnest on 7 September. At first we could do little, save take our punishment, but it was not long before the Prime Minister set up the Night Air Defence Committee under his own chairmanship; and ministers and airmen, A-A gunners and scientists sat together regularly to thrash out ways and means of combating the danger. Within a few months, the most promising solutions had been identified and pressed forward with the utmost vigour. Soon there was a progressive increase in the number of enemy aircraft destroyed, and those that survived were kept at a respectful height by the improved efficiency of the A-A guns. The situation improved out of recognition.

Churchill lost no opportunity of visiting the stricken areas, and I had my first experience of the effects of air bombardment on a big scale when I accompanied him to the London Docks immediately after the first heavy attack. The destruction was much more devastating than I had imagined it would be. Fires were still raging all over the place; some of the larger buildings were mere skeletons; and many of the smaller houses had been reduced to piles of rubble. The sight of tiny paper Union Jacks which had already been planted on two or three of these pathetic heaps brought a lump to one's throat.

Our first stop was at an air-raid shelter in which about forty persons had been killed and many more wounded by a direct hit, and we found a big crowd, male and female, young and old, but all very poor. One might have expected them to be resentful against the authorities responsible for their protection; but, as Churchill got out of his car, they literally mobbed him. 'Good old Winnie,' they cried. 'We thought you'd come and see us. We can take it. Give it 'em back.' Churchill broke down, and as I was struggling to get to him through the crowd, I heard an old woman say, 'You see, he really cares; he's crying.' Having pulled himself together, he proceeded to march through dockland at breakneck speed. I could never understand how he managed it. He was no longer a young man, and normally he never took any exercise at all. If he had been asked to walk from Downing Street to the House of Commons, he would have refused indignantly. And yet, on his inspection visits, he would cover miles of ground at a remarkable pace.

On and on we went until darkness began to fall. The dock authorities were anxious that Churchill should leave for home at once, but he was in one of his most obstinate moods and insisted that he wanted to see everything. Consequently, we were still within the brightly-lit target, when the Luftwaffe arrived on the scene, and the fireworks started. It was difficult to get a large car out of the area, owing to many of the streets being completely blocked by fallen houses, and as we were trying to turn in a very narrow space, a shower of incendiary bombs fell just in front of us. Churchill, feigning innocence, asked what they were. I replied that they were incendiaries, and that we were evidently in the middle of the bull's-eye!

It was very late by the time we got back to No. 10, Downing Street, and Cabinet Ministers, secretaries, policemen and orderlies were waiting in the long passage in great anxiety. Churchill strode through them without a word, leaving me to be rebuked by all and sundry for having allowed the Prime Minister to take such risks. Fatigue and fight are not conducive to patience, and I am alleged to have told the assembled company, in the language of the barrack room, that anybody who imagined that he could control the Prime Minister on jaunts of this kind was welcome to try his hand on the next occasion.

London was bombarded for the next fifty nights on end. The attack generally started directly it was dark, and the all-clear seldom sounded before daylight. Considering that Civil Defence had been on a voluntary basis until a few years before the war, and that even then it was starved of money, the arrangements proved a good deal better than we deserved, and they were progressively improved in the light of experience. But the decisive factor was the spirit of the Londoners. They were helpful, adaptable, cheerful, fearless, and utterly defiant. The womenfolk in particular were amazing. The courage of the charwoman who used to clean my office was typical of her sex. She generally arrived before the last German bombers had left, and for the first fortnight or so she was full of cheerful gossip when she awakened me. But one morning she was in floods of tears. She said that nearly all the houses in her street had been destroyed, that her sister had been killed, that she never got any sleep, and that she could not stand it any longer. I told her that I was just as frightened as she was, and that the only solution that I could think of was to tell Hitler that we could not take it, and that he had better come over and occupy England. Whereupon the old lady gave vent to a flood of the most sulphurous language that I have ever heard. Her description of Hitler's ancestry to the third and fourth generation was a masterpiece. The outburst evidently gave her relief; anyhow, there were no more tears or grumblings.

It was at this time that a letter written by a young working girl to a friend came into my hands. One or two extracts must be preserved: 'What's happened in London simply defies description, "Dante's Inferno" must have been a picnic in comparison . . . None of us are afraid to die, in fact we expect any minute to be our last but this is not a despairing attitude, it is more one of defiance; let them do their damnedest they can't and won't get us down. We'll stand on our feet to the end of this murderous fight and we will come out on top. We've all got our blood up I feel I could strangle a thousand Germans and enjoy doing it. I am going to get the shelter ready for tonight before I write any more of my murderous thoughts. I can't cry over anything but I've learned to swear like a Billingsgate porter.'

Early in November Göring switched his attack from London, first to the great industrial cities and then to our principal ports. I have never understood his reason. One would have thought that to continue to concentrate on London would have paid a better return. But if he imagined that the inhabitants of his new target areas might not show the same fortitude and adaptability as the Londoners, he was grievously mistaken. They were one and all completely undaunted.

From the moment that the Germans were in occupation of the northern coast of Europe, supreme efforts had to be made to put the whole island into a state of defence. Churchill interested himself in every detail and paid frequent visits to the threatened areas. At the start it was a very depressing experience. The amount of equipment was negligible. Tanks, artillery, Bren guns, anti-tank rifles and anti-tank guns were few and far between. The construction of fixed defences, the protection of the beaches by mines and obstacles, the obstruction of open spaces against parachute landings, seemed to progress, but slowly. Most of the troops were less than half-trained, and there were not nearly enough of them. From time to time Churchill would suggest to a commander that the defence of such and such an area ought to be strengthened. The commander would wholeheartedly agree, but point out that this could only be done by weakening some other equally important sector. Churchill used to say that he felt like a man trying to go to sleep on a very cold night with a blanket which was too small for him. If his feet were covered, his shoulders got cold; and if he pulled up the blanket to cover his shoulders, some other part of his body had to suffer.

Dover exercised a particular attraction for him. Apart from the fact that it seemed certain to be in the 'invasion area,' and therefore required special supervision, there was always the chance of seeing an air battle or of being on the spot when the heavy guns on both sides of the Channel were in action. Our own heavies had been manufactured in 1918, when Churchill was Minister of Munitions, and had, on his insistence, been carefully maintained ever since. It was on his orders that they had been installed at Dover as a counter to the German heavies at Calais and Cap Gris Nez. It is doubtful whether these monsters had any significant practical effect, but they were good for the morale of their respective sides. It is consoling to a man who is under bombardment to know that his enemy is catching it too.

One day while we were visiting Ramsgate there was a tip-and-run raid by a couple of German aircraft, and we were hustled into a public shelter. No smoking was allowed and Churchill obediently sacrificed his newly-lit cigar. The first thing that we saw on coming to the surface again was a tea shop which had been wrecked by the last of a bomb. Part of the roof had fallen in, and there was a shambles of broken crockery, chairs and tables. The aged proprietress, her livelihood gone, was sobbing her heart out. Directly we got into the train to return to London, Churchill said: 'Arrangements must be made for poor people like that to be given immediate compensation in order that they may be able to start up their businesses again.' And there and then he dictated a minute to the Chancellor of the Exchequer asking for a scheme to be worked out at once. This was done; and I have an idea that the proposal got through the Treasury in record time. Churchill used to say that power for the sake of lording it over our fellow creatures was base, but that power which enabled a man to give the right orders and have them obeyed was a blessing. In Shakespeare's words: 'It is excellent to have a giant's strength, but it is tyrannous to use it like a giant.' [1]

On one of his earlier visits Churchill espied a party of middle-aged men in civilian clothes wearing armlets marked, 'LDV' (Local Defence Volunteers). He had already proposed that this uninspiring title should be changed to 'Home Guard,' and the sight of those armlets decided him to press the point again. Within a few weeks the 'LDV' badges were called in, and 'HG' badges issued in their place. What a difference that change made to the *esprit de corps* of that gallant company of veterans.

Churchill was always insistent that there was much more in a name than many people seemed to think. On learning that Communal Feeding Centres were about to be established, he addressed a protest to the Minister of Food. 'It is an odious expression, suggestive of Communism and the workhouse. I suggest you call them "British Restaurants." Everybody associates the word "restaurant" with a good meal, and they may as well have the name if they cannot get anything else.'

His interest in terminology even extended to the selection of code names for operations. Facetious names met with vehement disapproval. How would a mother feel is she were to hear that her son had been killed in an enterprise called BUNNY HUG? Much better use the names of 'heroes of antiquity, or figures from Greek and Roman mythology.' The titles of the six volumes of his *Second World War* show his flair for finding appropriate phrases. *The Gathering Storm, Their Finest Hour, The Grand Alliance, The Hinge of Fate, Closing the Ring, Triumph and Tragedy.* There, in nineteen words, is a panorama of the origin, the course and the aftermath of the war.

I often wondered why he did not insist on changing the name of the War Office, which, to the uninformed, tends to convey the impression that it is the Department responsible for running a war. Why not substitute the title 'Army Ministry'? This would be a faithful description of its function, and the only objection which I have heard is

[1] *Measure for Measure*: Act II, Sc. 2.

that it would be a break with tradition. Considering the traditions that have had to be sacrificed by the disbandment of famous regiments or their amalgamation with others, this argument is scarcely conclusive. Many of us have had tears in our eyes when watching the ceremonial laying up of Regimental Colours, but I have yet to meet the soldier who would feel the slightest pang if he were told that his destiny would be controlled by the Army Ministry instead of the War Office.

Churchill used to hold periodic invasion conferences throughout the summer and autumn. He himself presided, and in addition to the Chiefs of Staff, all the Commanders-in-Chief were present. The Army had only one — the Commander-in-Chief, Home Forces: the Navy had five Commanders-in-Chief — the Home Fleet, the Nore, Portsmouth, Plymouth, and Western Approaches: and the Royal Air Force had three — the Commanders-in-Chief of Bomber, Fighter, and Coastal Commands. Suggestions were made that in the event of invasion, a Supreme Commander would be necessary; but it is difficult to see how any military figure could have performed the duties of Generalissimo not only of all those Fighting Services, but also of the civilian population which would be inextricably involved. The large number of political and domestic issues that would arise could not have been decided by anybody except the War Cabinet. Thank God no decision on this problem had to be taken, but it seems likely that, if the worst had come to the worst, the Supreme Command over the whole field would have been exercised by the Chiefs of Staff under the direct and continuous supervision of the Prime Minister.

An incident which occurred at one of the earliest Invasion Conferences must be related. The problem under discussion was the part to be played by the Home Fleet in the event of invasion, and the Commander-in-Chief asked that it should be clearly understood that his heavy ships could not, in any circumstances, operate south of the Wash. Everyone expected an explosion from Mr Churchill, and his reaction was surprising. He said, with an indulgent smile, that he never took much notice of what the Royal Navy said that they would, or would not, do in advance of an event, since they invariably undertook the apparently impossible without a moment's hesitation whenever the situation so demanded. If, for example, two or three nurses were wrecked on a desert island, the Navy would rush to their rescue, through typhoons and uncharted seas; and he had not a shadow of doubt that if the Germans invaded the south coast of Britain, we would see every available battleship storming through the Straits of Dover. Most of the meeting agreed with Churchill, and I am sure that the German admirals would have considered his forecast of our naval action most realistic.

CHAPTER XV

Middle East See-Saw

1940–1941

M USSOLINI had always had ambitions of a Mediterranean empire with access to the Atlantic Ocean, and perhaps that thought was uppermost in his mind when he hitched his wagon to Hitler's star by the 'Pact of Steel' in May 1939. The outbreak of war four months later placed him in a dilemma. To honour his obligation to Hitler and intervene at once might be disastrous. Italy was ill prepared for war, and her possessions in Africa would be at the mercy of her enemies. On the other hand, if Mussolini were to leave his intervention too long, Hitler might win the war without him and refuse him any share of the loot. His perplexities were resolved by the rapidity of the French collapse, and on 10 June, the very day on which the French Government left Paris, Italy declared war on Britain and France. Garibaldi must have turned in his grave, and all decent Italians felt bitterly ashamed that their leader had chosen this moment to strike 'the dagger into his neighbour's back.' [1] But to a man with no principles, it was certainly 'the chance of five thousand years,' as Ciano wrote in his Diary.

The combination of Italy's entry into the war and the capitulation of France transformed our whole position in the Middle East. The Medi-

[1] Roosevelt's address of 10 June 1940.

192

terranean route to the East was practically closed; Malta was isolated, exposed to attack by the Italian metropolitan air force, and in danger of invasion; Egypt, the Sudan, Kenya and British Somaliland were threatened by numerically superior enemy forces. Our preconceived plans had to be entirely recast, and our intelligence arrangements considerably revised and supplemented. The outlook was so bleak that many people thought that we should be attempting too much if we tried to hold the Middle East. But Churchill, with the full backing of the War Cabinet, the Chiefs of Staff and the commanders on the spot, was determined to fight it out to the very last ounce of our strength.

Egypt was the prize which Mussolini coveted above all else, and in July 1940 it seemed within his grasp. The Italians had over two hundred thousand men assembled in Tripolitania, Cyrenaica, and along the Egyptian border. Now that the French troops in North Africa had declared for Vichy and need no longer be taken into account, all of these were available for the invasion of Egypt. To oppose them, the British could muster fifty thousand men at most. With a numerical superiority of four to one, Mussolini must have thought that his vision of a triumphal entry into Cairo, riding a white charger, would soon come true.

At the outset our small but magnificently-trained covering force assumed the offensive, and proceeded to harry the enemy unceasingly. It soon established a moral ascendancy over them, inflicting casualties and taking several hundred prisoners. But in the main, our initial strategy had to be defensive. Even Churchill had to submit to this; but he was, as ever, on the look-out for a chance to attack and, as usual, his thoughts turned to the possibilities of amphibious action. Could we not, for example, strike at the enemy's long line of communications from Tripoli by landing a brigade or so from the sea at some suitable point? But neither the Chiefs of Staff nor General Wavell, Commander-in-Chief Middle East, thought the idea practicable with the slender resources then at our disposal. Churchill did not insist.

At this point the Prime Minister introduced a new feature into our machinery for the conduct of the war, in the shape of a standing ministerial committee on the Middle East. The chairman was Mr

Eden, Secretary of State for War, and the members were Mr Amery, Secretary of State for India, and Lord Lloyd, Secretary of State for the Colonies. The new committee caused not a little duplication and, so far as I am aware, achieved nothing that could not have been equally well achieved without it. It had a short life. The shortcomings of the Dardanelles Committee set up by Mr Asquith in 1915 should have warned us that it is a mistake, in a world-wide war, to introduce special machinery to deal with individual theaters of operations. Foreign policy and strategy are not susceptible to treatment in watertight compartments.

A year later Mr Churchill tried another innovation with very different results. He appointed Mr Oliver Lyttelton, then President of the Board of Trade, to be Minister of State Resident in the Middle East, with the task of representing the War Cabinet and presiding over the whole war effort in that area. No better selection could have been made. Lyttelton had had a splendid fighting record in the First World War, and had gained considerable business experience in the years between the wars. He had been an admirable President of the Board of Trade, and knew the ways of Whitehall inside out. He quickly gained the confidence of the Commanders-in-Chief in the Middle East and was able to relieve them of most of their political, financial and economic burdens, and to settle questions affecting several departments which would otherwise have had to be referred home. When he was recalled to London in the following February to become Minister of Production, the Commanders in Chief represented that the appointment of a Minister of State was indispensable, and requested an urgent replacement. Later in the war, this experiment of Mr Churchill's was repeated with equally successful results in other theatres.

At the end of July 1940, the Italians were still engaged in building up their forces on the Egyptian frontier, and establishing supply dumps along the road from Tripoli; but there was no sign of any forward move. The opportunity was therefore taken to invite Wavell to come to London for discussions. Churchill had never met him before, but from now on they saw a good deal of each other. It was soon apparent that they did not see eye to eye on every point; but Churchill was evidently convinced by Eden and Dill that Wavell was the right man for the job. What Wavell thought of Churchill, I have no idea. He was the soul of loyalty and did not carry his heart on his sleeve. Anyway, the events of the next few months were to bring them much closer together.

During Wavell's three weeks in England there were many discussions as to how the forces in the Middle East could be strengthened, and it was before he returned to his post that the decision was taken to send half of our total tank strength in Great Britain round the Cape to the Middle East. Considering the risk of imminent invasion, the boldness of this strategic stroke deserves high praise. The original idea was put forward by Dill, after conferring with his brother Chiefs of Staff, and was ardently supported by the Secretary of State for War, Mr Eden. Churchill not only welcomed it enthusiastically, but wanted to go one better. He could not bear the idea of this priceless equipment being out of action for three months on a long voyage round the Cape, and strongly urged that it should be sent direct through the Mediterranean. But the First Sea Lord considered the risk unjustifiable, while the CIGS said that the urgency was not sufficient to warrant it. Churchill was disappointed, but acquiesced in the decision.

While Wavell was still in London, Mussolini was presented with a small but gratuitous triumph. It was recognised before the war that if Italy came in against us she could invade British Somaliland with incomparably larger forces than we could afford for its protection; and that she would have little difficulty in capturing Berbera, the capital of the country and its only harbour. It was therefore decided that, in the event of an Italian attack, the country should be evacuated. This meant the abdication of our treaty obligations to protect the Somali tribes; the virtual disbandment of a fine regiment, the Somaliland Camel Corps, since Somali troops could not be expected to leave their families and property to the tender mercies of the Italians; the desertion of all Somali Government servants; and a great loss of face, in a country where face has a very special importance.

Was there no alternative to a policy which involved such serious consequences? Of course there was. Berbera was little more than a primitive roadstead, which had little war value for us, and could have no war value whatsoever to the enemy. The proper course would have been to evacuate the capital but not the country — to quit Berbera and withdraw, not northwards across the Gulf of Aden, but *southwards* to the Somaliland plateau. There were any number of places which would have been suitable for the headquarters of the Government. Supplies could have been assured by dumps established beforehand and by imports from Aden through the numerous inlets east of Berbera; and the Somaliland Camel Corps, with their great mobility and intimate knowledge of the country, would have been admirably placed to harry the Italians by continually raiding their long line of communications from Abyssinia. This single unit, properly handled, could have made their lives a burden to them.

But in September 1939 the original policy of evacuation was superseded by one that made it reasonably certain that we would get the worst of all worlds. It was decided that the country should not be evacuated, and that Berbera should be defended. Reinforcements, amounting eventually to five battalions of infantry and a battery of light artillery, were sent piecemeal to Somaliland, and plans were drawn up for opposing the Italians in a position sixty-five miles southwest of Berbera. It should have been obvious that this could not be held for long, if the enemy were to invade the country with the vastly superior numbers at their disposal.

On 3 August an Italian force of about seventeen battalions, with tanks and armoured car units, crossed the Somali frontier, and attacked our position a week later. The result was a foregone conclusion. Our troops put up a stout resistance, and inflicted severe casualties on them; but at the end of five days' fighting, withdrawal was the only alternative to annihilation. Our troops retired on Berbera, and with the exception of the rank and file of the Camel Corps, embarked for Aden. British Somaliland passed into the hands of the Italians.

This unhappy episode attracted little attention; but to me, with my long association with Somaliland and my affection for her soldiers, it was very painful. The picture of the British officers of my old regiment saying good-bye on Berbera beach to the men whom they had so recently led in battle, and leaving them to fend for themselves, was not a pretty one.

Within eight months the Italians were thrown out of the country, and we resumed our responsibilities there. But I wonder whether our prestige in the Horn of Africa has recovered to this day.

*   *

Mussolini's appetite was whetted by his cheap victory in Somaliland, and he now exerted the greatest pressure on Marshal Graziani to start the invasion of Egypt. It was not however until mid-September, 1940, that the Marshal could be induced to cross the frontier. Advancing reluctantly and nervously, he reached Sidi Barrani four days later, while our forces withdrew on Mersa Matruh. The first serious clash now seemed imminent. But the weeks passed and, in spite of vigorous prodding from Rome, Graziani made no move.

Meanwhile, Mr Eden, Secretary of State for War, had been on an extended visit to the Middle East. He returned to London on 8 November, bringing tidings of a deadly secret but extremely welcome character. To a restricted meeting of the Defence Committee, at which only the Prime Minister, the three Service Ministers, the three Chiefs of Staff, Jacob and I were present, Eden disclosed that Wavell had decided not to await Graziani's attack at Mersa Matruh, but to take the offensive himself at an early date; and he followed up this startling announcement with an explanation of Wavell's plans. Every one of us could have jumped for joy, but Churchill could have jumped twice as high as the rest. He has said that he 'purred like six cats.' That is putting it mildly. He was rapturously happy. 'At long last we are going to throw off the intolerable shackles of the defensive,' he declaimed. 'Wars are won by superior will-power. Now we will wrest the initiative from the enemy and impose our will on him.'

Needless to say, Wavell's plan was approved without a moment's hesitation, and even before the meeting broke up Churchill started estimating the spoils. He was always prone to count his chickens before they were hatched, and as a rule his estimates erred on the generous side. But on this occasion the results were to exceed his most optimistic expectations.

While we were all agog for Wavell's drama to start, Admiral Sir Andrew Cunningham provided a most welcome curtain-raiser. On the night of 11 November, his Fleet Air Arm aircraft attacked the Italian fleet at anchor in Taranto Harbour, and sank or severely crippled no less than three battleships. It was now the turn of the army. We had not tasted victory on land since the war had started. On 9 December, Wavell struck. The Italian Army had little stomach for the fight, and within a week, Marshal Graziani, who had continually warned his political masters of the risks they were taking, was writing to his wife in Rome that 'one cannot break steel armour with finger nails alone.' Within nine days there was not a single Italian soldier left in Egypt, except as a captive in our hands. Within two months the equivalent of nine Italian divisions had been ripped to pieces, with a loss of one hundred and thirty thousand prisoners, four hundred tanks, and nearly thirteen hundred field guns. The Army of the Nile was now in possession of all the ports on the coast of Cyrenaica as far west as Agheila. There let us leave them for the moment, and turn to an enterprise which was destined to rob us of most of our hard-won territorial gains, and to lead to other grievous misfortunes.

In October 1940 Mussolini attacked Greece, and the Greek Government at once invoked the guarantee given them by Mr Chamberlain in April 1939. There was general agreement in both London and the Middle East that a failure to redeem our undertaking would have a deplorable effect in Turkey and Yugoslavia and destroy all hope of establishing a Balkan front against Germany, and the Prime Minister immediately promised that we would do all in our power to help. This he would undoubtedly have done, guarantee or no guarantee. To start with, all that could be spared was four squadrons of aircraft, and a military mission. But by the turn of the year, Wavell's resounding victories in the desert had put a very different complexion on the situation, and it seemed that we could afford to be much more generous. 'It is quite clear to me,' Churchill wrote on 6 January 1941, 'that supporting Greece must have priority *after the Western flank of Egypt has been made secure.*' [1] Here was the first warning to Wavell that the Desert must continue to have first call on his resources.

On 12 February 1941 the Prime Minister repeated the warning. *'You should therefore make yourself secure in Benghazi*[1] and concentrate all available forces in the delta in preparation for movement to Europe.'

The Cabinet now asked Mr Eden and General Dill to proceed to the Middle East in order to examine, in consultation with the Commanders-in-Chief, what measures, both diplomatic and military, should be taken against the Germans in the Balkans. The despatch of these exceptional envoys was evidence of the determination of His Majesty's Government to get the best possible advice on every aspect of the

[1] Author's italics.

politico-strategic problems which confronted them, before making final decisions.

Scarcely had Eden and Dill arrive in Cairo when the Prime Minister warned them that the Cabinet were in no mood to press the matter of help to Greece. 'Do not feel yourselves obligated to a Greek enterprise, if in your hearts you feel it will only be another Norwegian fiasco; if no good plan can be made, please say so.' Meanwhile the envoys, accompanied by the three Commanders-in-Chief, had already visited Athens and taken an optimistic view of the possibilities. 'We believe,' Eden telegraphed, that there is 'a fair chance of halting a German advance and preventing Greece from being overrun.' Thereupon preparations were pressed forward for assembling a strategic reserve in the Nile delta; but the decision as to how it should be used was left open.

On 5 March a bombshell reached London in the shape of a report from Eden that he and Dill had visited Athens again, and found 'a changed and disturbing situation and an atmosphere quite different' from that of their last visit. General Papagos now offered only sixteen to twenty-three battalions for the defence of the Aliakmon line, instead of the thirty-five that we had been led to expect; and he was no longer prepared to order any withdrawals from his Albanian front. Nevertheless, the military advisers on the spot still 'did not consider it by any means a hopeless proposition to check and hold the German advance.'

The Chiefs of Staff, who had never shared the optimism of Cairo, met at a moment's notice to consider this disturbing message. They now regarded the successful outcome of an expedition to Greece as more remote than ever; and they felt that the failure of Papagos to redeem his promises gave us the opportunity to withdraw with honour from the adventure. There is little doubt that, left to themselves, they would have advised its abandonment, but they were not as yet prepared to disregard the advice of the men on the spot, who included one of their own number, in the person of Dill. In submitting an immediate report to that effect, they made it clear that, in their own judgment, the military prospects were extremely hazardous. The hazards which they had in mind related solely to the expedition itself, and not to any consequences which it might involve elsewhere. In particular, they took it for granted that the security of the desert flank of Egypt was receiving first priority, and that the despatch of help to Greece would in no way prejudice that security. If they had had any doubt on that score, it is pretty certain that they would have advised against the enterprise. And it is even more certain that if the Prime Minister had felt the slightest anxiety that the forces remaining in Egypt would be inadequate to cope with any attack which could be made upon them from the West, he would have insisted that the idea of sending substantial help to Greece should be abandoned.

Churchill telegraphed the report of the Chiefs of Staff to Eden and, at the same time, gave him a clear hint that the Cabinet would probably decide against intervention on the Greek mainland. This warning brought instantaneous and vigorous protests. A telegram from our Minister in Athens, Sir Michael Palairet, was the first to arrive, on 6 March:

> . . . How can we possibly abandon the King of Greece after the assurances given him by the Commander-in-Chief and Chief of the Imperial General Staff as to reasonable chances of success? This seems to me quite unthinkable. We shall be pilloried by the Greeks and the world in general as going back on our word. There is no question of 'liberating the Greeks from feeling bound to reject the ultimatum.' They have decided to fight Germany alone if necessary. The question is whether we help or abandon them.

Eden also stuck to his guns:

> The Chief of Imperial General Staff and I, in consultation with the three Commanders-in-Chief, have this afternoon re-examined the question. We are unanimously agreed that, despite the heavy commitments and grave risks which are undoubtedly involved, the right decision was taken in Athens.

The searching telegram which the Prime Minister sent the next day, 7 March, almost invited a negative reply:

> . . . We must not take on our shoulders responsibility of urging Greeks against their better judgment to fight a hopeless battle and involve their country in probable speedy ruin. If however . . . they resolve to fight to the death, obviously we must . . . share their ordeal. It must not be said, and on your showing it cannot be said, that, having so little to give, we dragged them in by over-persuasion. I take it, from your attitude and Athens telegrams, that you are sure on this point.
>
> It happens that most of the troops to be devoted to this solemn duty are the New Zealand Division and after March the Australians. We

must be able to tell the New Zealand and Australian Governments faithfully that this hazard, from which they will not shrink, is undertaken not because of any commitment entered into by a British Cabinet Minister at Athens, and signed by the Chief of the Imperial General Staff, but because Dill, Wavell, and other Commanders-in-Chief are convinced that there is a reasonable fighting chance. This I regard as implied by your positive reactions to our questioning telegrams.

Please remember in your stresses that, so far, you have given us few facts or reasons on their authority which can be presented to these Dominions as justifying the operation on any grounds but *'noblesse oblige.'* A precise military appreciation is indispensable.

The 'precise military appreciation' required by Churchill never materialised, but Eden's reply testified to the unshaken unanimity of the men on the spot:

Whole position again fully reviewed with the Commanders-in-Chief and Smuts . . . We can find no reason to vary our previous judgment. There has been no question of urging Greece against her better judgment . . . We are all agreed that the course advocated should be followed and help given to Greece.

That settled it. The Prime Minister telegraphed immediately that in view of the steadfastly expressed opinion of the Commanders-in-Chief on the spot, the Chief of the Imperial General Staff and the commanders of the forces to be employed, the Cabinet had decided to authorise the Operation to proceed, and by so doing accepted for itself the fullest responsibility.

The expedition, under the command of General Wilson, started to move to Greece on the 4 March, and a month later, the Germans invaded the country. Within the space of a fortnight the Greeks were forced to surrender, and our troops had to undertake yet another evacuation. Namsos, Andalesnes, Narvik, Dunkirk — it was already a long list. Once again the Royal Navy achieved the seemingly impossible in the face of overwhelming air superiority. Meanwhile we had already sustained a very severe defeat in the Western Desert and were shortly to lose Crete. Before dealing with these misfortunes, let me attempt to draw conclusions from the story which I have just told.

It may be claimed that to have fought and suffered defeat in Greece was less damaging to us than to have left the Greeks to their fate. A military failure may be excused, but failure to keep a promise to help a friend in trouble is not easily forgiven, or forgotten. It may also be claimed that, on a long-term view, our action was vindicated in that it delayed the German attack on Russia for four or five weeks. Nevertheless, there can be no doubt that the immediate military results of the decision to intervene on the mainland of Greece were disastrous, and that the ultimate responsibility for that decision rested with the Prime Minister and Cabinet. To that extent they may justifiably be blamed. On the other hand, they cannot be blamed — indeed they deserve not a little credit — for the processes by which their decision was reached. Their first step was to send two great figures, the one political and the other military, to examine the problems on the spot, in consultation with the Commanders-in-Chief. They then proceeded, as the dates of the telegrams testify, to keep in almost hourly touch with them, in order to ensure that foreign policy and strategy moved hand in hand, both in London and Cairo. They gave instructions that first priority must be accorded to the security of our desert flank in Egypt, and that help to Greece must take second place. They expressly warned our envoys that they must not regard themselves as in any way obligated to an overseas expedition and that if a good plan could not be made, they should not hesitate to say so. Later, when they heard of the change of atmosphere in Athens and of the inability of the Greeks to give us the minimum support which had been anticipated, they went so far as to advise Cairo that the Chiefs of Staff at home took a very poor view of the military prospects, and that it would probably be decided to give up all idea of an expedition. Finally, they sought and received categorical assurances. first that the Greeks themselves sincerely desired our help and, secondly, that there was a reasonable chance of preventing Greece being overrun. Then, and then only, did they decide to give the expedition their blessing. And having taken that decision they did their best to fortify the men on the spot by assuming full responsibility.

Let us now return to the Egyptian desert. Towards the end of February 1941 there was some concern in London at the reports that considerable enemy reinforcements, including German armoured units, were arriving in Tripoli. But Wavell was reassuring. On 2 March he reported in a telegram that owing to 'shipping risks, difficulty of communications, and the approach of the hot weather,' no large-scale attack was likely to develop against him *before the end of the summer*. It was therefore a shock when, on the last day of March, General Rommel, now in command of the German contingent in North Africa, fell upon Agheila. His original intention was a limited advance; but finding us weaker in armour and less well-organised than he expected, he exploited his initial success to the utmost. The story of the battle has been told in the official histories and elsewhere. Suffice it here to say that in less than a week, the desert flank, which all had thought so secure, had been driven in, and the whole of Cyrenaica except for Tobruk was again in enemy hands.

This disappointment was grievous. But there were no reproaches; only the firm resolve to win it all back. One could imagine the imperturbable Wavell reciting one of his favourite poems:

> 'Oh yesterday our little troop was ridden
> > through and through,
> Our swaying, tattered pennons fled,
> > a broken beaten few,
> And all a summer afternoon they hunted us and slew;
> > But tomorrow,
> By the living God, we'll try the game again!' [1]

Churchill was buoyant as always. 'We seem to have had rather bad luck,' he telegraphed to Wavell. 'I expect we shall get this back later. Every good wish.'

The 20 April was a Sunday, and I had arrived at my home in Gloucestershire in the early hours of the morning, hoping for a day's rest. But I was wakened by a message from the Prime Minister at Ditchley, the home of Mr and Mrs Ronald Tree, that he wanted to see me at once. I found him extremely disturbed by Wavell's latest reports to the effect that he was dangerously weak in tanks, and that Rommel was likely to be reinforced by a German armoured division in the fairly near future. He thought it absolutely imperative that a large number of our best tanks should at once be sent to the Middle East direct through the Mediterranean, and instructed me to place a minute to that effect, which he had already dictated, before the Chiefs of Staff at once. My submission that it was Sunday, that the

[1] John Masefield: *Tomorrow.*

Chiefs were probably scattered all over the country, and that it would be difficult to assemble them until the next morning, was summarily and rightly dismissed. 'Are there no telephones? Are there no motor-cars?' At this point his hostess came into the room, but he forestalled her question. 'Pug will not be able to stay to lunch. He is starting for London at once.' I did.

The Chiefs of Staff met in the afternoon. They did not seem too well pleased at having their one day of rest interrupted, and at first they showed little enthusiasm for the Prime Minister's proposal. It was argued that the despatch of a large number of tanks would dangerously weaken our Home Forces, and that their passage direct through the Mediterranean would involve unwarrantable risks. By the time that we adjourned for dinner, no decision had been reached. But I got the impression that the Chiefs of Staff would end by opposing the project, and I was worried. It did not seem likely that they would press the argument about the danger of sending so many tanks out of the country, since it was fairly certain that Hitler was preparing to launch an attack on Russia, and obviously could not invade us at the same time. On the other hand, it seemed more than likely that they would pronounce the risks of sending the convoy direct through the Mediterranean prohibitive. In that event, the Prime Minister, feeling as strongly as he did, might obtain the support of the Cabinet to overrule them. This would be a thousand pities, whatever the result of the operation. If it succeeded, the Chiefs of Staff might feel that having been proved wrong, they ought to resign; and if it failed the outcry against the Prime Minister would be formidable. In any case, the relations between the Prime Minister and his military advisers would never be quite the same again.

My fears proved groundless. At the after-dinner session of the Committee, the Chiefs of Staff had evidently weakened on their objections as a result of discussions with their advisers. They still thought that the operation proposed by the Prime Minister was very hazardous, but agreed to recommend that, in view of the vital importance of providing Wavell with an immediate reinforcement of armour, the risks should be accepted. The Prime Minister was delighted, and his optimism proved to be justified. TIGER, as the operation was called, was almost completely successful, and the convoy arrived at Alexandria before the middle of May with the loss of only one ship. The next essential was to have the 'tiger cubs' [1] made desert-worthy in time to enable Wavell to attack Rommel before reinforcements of German armour could reach him. For the sake of chronology, I must now leave Egypt, and record the events which were taking place elsewhere in the Middle East.

The melancholy sequel to the Greek adventure must first be recorded. When the Italians invaded Greece, the Greek Government invited us to occupy Crete, and we jumped at the chance. The Prime Minister had always attached great strategic value to this island, and he gave orders that it should immediately be put into a state of defence. In particular, he wished Suda Bay to be made into 'another Scapa.' His instructions were not implemented as thoroughly as they might have been, perhaps because the chances of an attack on the island seemed so remote at that time. But now that Greece had fallen, the outlook was very different. Indeed we learned from unimpeachable sources, even before our troops were out of Greece, that the Germans were preparing for a full-scale attack on Crete in the near future. Our information, which proved accurate in every respect, led us to believe that the exploitation of overwhelming air superiority was the keynote of the German plan. They would start the battle with intensive bombing attacks, and when the defences had been softened up, assaults by airborne and seaborne troops would follow. Kesselring's air circus was a *corps d'élite,* which had been under training for this very type of operation for a long time.

The Prime Minister at once took a lively interest in every detail of the arrangements for defending the island. His first thought was to find a commander, and there was no need to look further than General Freyberg, the bravest of the brave, who was on the spot. The suggestion that he should be appointed was warmly approved by Wavell.

Churchill realised that in the battle for Crete, we would be completely outmatched in the air, and that it was therefore absolutely vital for us to retain possession of the three airfields. If this could be done, the numbers of the attackers would be limited to what could be dropped by parachute or landed in gliders. With these the garrison

[1] Churchill's nickname for the tanks sent in TIGER convoys. Out of 295 despatched, 238 arrived.

might be expected to cope. On the other hand, if the enemy could capture even one airfield, they would be able to land troops by engine-driven aircraft which could return to their bases and bring successive contingents to the field of action. The attackers could then be reinforced until their strength was overwhelming. Churchill argued that parachute and glider-borne troops would not have the equipment to deal with good Infantry tanks, and that any airfield which was protected by a dozen or so of these vehicles would defy capture. He developed this argument to me on several occasions, and the only flaw in it which I could detect was that bombers enjoying complete air superiority might be able to knock out the tanks and clear the way for their lightly-equipped troops. Be that as it may, Churchill pressed with all his might for a few of our most modern tanks to be sent to Crete. Perhaps the air blockade, which the Germans had already established, rendered their despatch impossible, but the fact remains that they never arrived.

The battle opened on 20 May. The fighting was ferocious and the Germans suffered very severe losses; so much so, that at one moment Kesselring thought of crying off. But on the second day, the airfield at Maleme fell into German hands. A continuous stream of reinforcements could now be flown in by engine-driven aircraft. It was the beginning of the end. After seven days' struggle, yet another evacuation was the only alternative to annihilation. The Navy, which had done magnificent work in preventing any sea-borne landings on Crete, had already had heavy casualties. They were now faced with another desperate adventure. Once again they achieved the impossible, albeit with further heavy loss. The moment came when there were only about five thousand ill-equipped, disorganised men remaining on the island; and at a Commander-in-Chiefs' meeting held in Alexandria, the Army spokesman said that he could not ask the Navy to attempt any further evacuation. Admiral Cunningham would not hear of it. 'It takes three years to build a ship, but three hundred years to rebuild a tradition,' he said. 'The Navy will go.' It might have been Nelson speaking. The Navy went. The sequel must be told. As one of our destroyers was steaming out of Alexandria harbour on its errand of rescue, an able-bodied seaman was heard to observe as he blew up his Mae West: 'This is all the ruddy air support I am likely to get this trip.' There was no sourness in the remark.

It merely showed the carefree spirit that was in the tradition of Nelson's Navy.

The naval losses had been crippling. Three cruisers and six destroyers had been sunk, and three battleships, one aircraft carrier, six cruisers, and seven destroyers had been damaged. The army casualties had been close on twelve thousand. But Kesselring's air circus had been torn to pieces. If it had been reserved for the invasion of Russia, its influence must have been very considerable. And if it had been available to be used against Malta a year later, it might well have been decisive. The victory of Crete had been dearly bought.

Even before the Battle of Greece had been decided, there was a distraction which proved little more than vexatious, but which might have had disastrous consequences. Ever since the end of the First World War, Great Britain had enjoyed a special position in Iraq, and the 1930 Treaty gave us the right to maintain bases at Habbaniya and Shu'aiba in time of peace, and to have freedom of transit of all kinds throughout the country in time of war.

It had been known since the war started that there was a considerable anti-British element in Iraq and that the Germans and Italians were doing their best to acquire influence in the country. But it came as a shock when information arrived towards the end of March 1940 that a revolution had been staged by the pro-German Rashid Ali, supported by a group of generals who were known as the 'Golden Square,' and that the pro-British Regent had fled the country. There was every possibility that German aircraft and possibly German parachute troops would appear on the scene at any moment, and it was necessary to act at once to restore the situation.

At the Prime Minister's request the Government of India despatched a brigade group, which happened to be on the point of sailing for Malaya, to Basrah, and the troops disembarked at that port without opposition on 19 April. Initially Rashid Ali gave orders that they should be given all facilities; but shortly afterwards he stipulated that they must move across Iraq at once, and that no further troops must be landed until they were clear of Iraqi territory. This was contrary to both the spirit and the letter of the 1930 Treaty, and was ignored. A second brigade from India arrived at Basrah towards the end of the month.

At this juncture an Iraqi force of about 10,000 men, including tanks and artillery, moved on the RAF Base at Habbaniya, and occupied the high ground which dominated the cantonment. The RAF strength numbered about eighty aircraft, mostly of obsolete types, with only thirty trained pilots to fly them; and the garrison consisted of 1,200 levies, an armoured car company and half a battalion of infantry which had recently been flown in from Basrah. Their artillery consisted of two elderly howitzers. A perimeter of seven miles could not be defended by a garrison of this size, and it was clear that Habbaniya must succumb to any serious attack unless it was immediately reinforced. No help could reach them from Basrah owing to the fact that the railway to Baghdad was under the control of the Iraqi Army. Reinforcement from the west was therefore the only hope, and Wavell was directed by the Chiefs of Staff to despatch a relief column from Palestine with all possible speed. Wavell's protest was vehement. He pointed out that his forces were already strained to the limit, and beyond it, by his other commitments, and that the conduct of prolonged operations in Iraq would endanger both Palestine and Egypt. He begged that a political settlement should be negotiated.

To this the Chiefs of Staff, with the support of the Prime Minister and Cabinet, replied that no political settlement was possible, and that there was no option but to crush Rashid Ali by military action before the Germans appeared on the scene. They added that they had informed His Majesty's Government that they themselves were 'prepared to accept responsibility for the despatch of a force to Habbaniya from Palestine at the earliest possible date.' This was the first occasion in the war on which the Chiefs of Staff overruled the commander on the spot, and took full responsibility for the consequences.

Wavell, as always, responded gallantly, and the rest of the story can be told in a few words. On 1 May, Air Vice-Marshal Smart, the commander at Habbaniya, with the strong support of Colonel Ouvry Roberts, who had just flown in from Basrah, took the matter into his own hands. He demanded the withdrawal of the Iraqi troops from their threatening positions, and having received no reply, his improvised bombers attacked them at dawn the next day. They were met by some desultory and ineffective artillery fire, but the Iraqi Army appeared uninterested and there was no move by the infantry or tanks. After four days, they withdrew eastwards, and suffered the indignity of appreciable casualties at the hands of a sortie by the tiny garrison which they had set out to destroy. The danger to Habbaniya had passed. Meanwhile Wavell's flying column from Palestine reached Baghdad with very little opposition, and the Royal Air Force knocked out those elements of the German Air Force which had established themselves at Mosul. Rashid Ali and his friends, the German and Italian Ambassadors, fled the country. The revolt was over. The situation in Iraq had been restored by a mixture of bluff, courage and determination.

It is difficult to understand why the Germans let such a golden opportunity slip through their hands. If they had sent a military mission to Baghdad, directly Rashid Ali had usurped power, they could have vitalised the Iraqi Army and arranged for their reinforcement by German aircraft and possibly air-borne troops. Habbaniya could have been overwhelmed without much difficulty, and the troops at Basrah compelled to evacuate the country. The control of the pipeline from Iraq to the Mediterranean would have passed out of our hands, and we would have been hard put to it to protect the oil refineries at Abadan in Persia. We were in fact saved from a disaster of some magnitude by the ineptitude of the German High Command. One can only suppose that their minds were full of their impending attack on Russia.

The overstrained, long-suffering Wavell was soon to be handed yet another tiresome baby. Axis designs on Syria were beginning to take shape, and before the end of May about a hundred German aircraft and a few Italian aircraft had established themselves on Syrian airfields, with the approval of the Vichy Government. Somehow or other, Syria had to be saved and Wavell was ordered to prepare a force to do so. Not unnaturally, he once again entered a protest, but on learning that the Chiefs of Staff were adamant, he set to work to organise an expedition under the command of General Wilson. Initially this consisted of one Australian division, a handful of commandos, and a few battalions of Free French. On 8 June, Wilson advanced. The Vichy troops fought stubbornly, and, sad to relate, resisted their own countrymen with particular bitterness. Wavell scraped the pot for reinforcements, and after a campaign of just over a month, an armistice was signed. Syria was ours.

Throughout these days the Prime Minister kept in almost hourly touch with Wavell and his fellow Commanders-in-Chief, Admiral of the Fleet Sir Andrew Cunningham, and Air Chief Marshal Sir Arthur Longmore. Telegrams of congratulations, exhortation, questions, and advice followed each other in rapid succession. Those who criticise him for this habit of bombarding commanders in the field with a never-ending stream of messages fail to understand his motives. Obviously he wanted to keep in close touch with all that was happening or going to happen; obviously he wanted to be assured that everyone was on his toes, and that all available resources were being put to the best use. But he wanted, perhaps above all else, to impart to the commanders his own 'impetuous, adventurous and defying character.' [1] He wanted them to feel that they were always in his thoughts, and that he was sharing their problems and their difficulties, their hopes and their fears, their failures as well as their successes. He wanted them to tell him in what way he could help them, and he wanted them to understand that, provided they showed a sincere desire to engage the enemy, he would back them to the limit, whatever the result. 'All acts and decisions of valour and violence against the enemy will, whatever the upshot, receive the resolute support of His Majesty's Government.' [2] Could any commander wish for more?

It is perhaps natural that Commanders-in-Chief should have sometimes resented his continual prodding. The higher a soldier rises in his profession, the more sheltered his life becomes. He is surrounded by a large and loyal staff, whose aim it is to do their utmost to spare the chief from unnecessary trouble or unpleasantness. Without being in any way 'yes men,' their sense of discipline does not permit them to oppose his wishes too forcibly, or to state their own case too baldly. Thus, the commander becomes more and more accustomed to having his own way and more and more prone to resent criticism. The life of the politician is a very different one. The higher he goes, the better

[1] Macaulay: *Essay on the Earl of Chatham.*
[2] Telegram from the Prime Minister to Wavell just before the first major offensive against the Italians in December 1940.

the target which he presents for criticism, and the harder he has to fight for his purposes.

All this time Wavell had been girding up his loins for his next trial of strength with Rommel. The operation was given the name of BATTLEAXE. Churchill had high hopes that this would redeem all recent failures, and was all impatience for it to start. He was furious to hear of the long time that it was taking to get the new tanks battleworthy; bitterly disappointed that the battle could not start until mid-June; and critical as ever of the tendency of commanders to insist on having the last button sewn on the last gaiter before attacking. More than once in those days he told the story about the man who set out to kill a bear by blowing a poisonous concoction down its throat. The man spent hour after hour in making sure that he had exactly the right mixture; he then packed it slowly and methodically into a paper funnel; and, at long last, he raised the funnel to the level of the bear's mouth, and was just about to blow. But the bear blew first.

On 15 June, BATTLEAXE was duly launched. After two days' fighting it was obvious that it had failed, and our forces withdrew to their old positions. The casualties on either side were relatively small, but the failure to defeat Rommel meant that he could continue to build up on the Egyptian frontier, with a view to an all-out attack on Egypt in the autumn.

Wavell had been Commander-in-Chief of the Middle East since July 1939. He had found himself conducting five campaigns at one and the same time, much as a juggler keeps five balls in the air at once. He had won splendid victories. His first campaign in the Western Desert had resulted in the capture of the whole of Cyrenaica. He had conquered Eritrea and Italian Somaliland. He had thrown the Italians out of Abyssinia and enabled the Emperor to return to his throne. He had retaken British Somaliland. He had shown strategic genius of a high order. His withdrawal of the Fourth Indian Division from the battle still raging in the Western Desert, and their despatch to the Sudan, a distance of over 1,000 miles, was a master stroke. Rommel rated him as the most redoubtable of the commanders who were pitted against him.[1] He had gained the complete confidence of his troops. He had a happy knack of turning up at the critical mo-

[1] Edited by Liddell Hart: *The Rommel Papers.*

ment of a battle; and the flying risks that he took to get there nearly cost him his life on several occasions. But there are limits to human endurance, and it was now felt by many people in London, including some of his close friends and ardent admirers, that Wavell was mentally and physically tired, and in need of a respite from the tremendous responsibilities which he had borne so resolutely for so long. Accordingly the Prime Minister decided to offer him the appointment of Commander-in-Chief in India, and to replace him in Cairo by General Auchinleck. Wavell's reaction to the Prime Minister's telegram breaking the news of this change was typical of his modesty and selflessness. He said that the Middle East theatre needed a new eye and a new hand, and that Churchill's decision was quite right. Many people who did not know the facts, and particularly the troops, who loved and trusted Wavell, were astonished and indignant. They could not understand why he was being superseded. It was even suggested that, having been compelled by the politicians to send an expedition to Greece, he was now being made the scapegoat for the disasters which flowed from that decision. My narrative has shown that this accusation was groundless. But one and all were grieved to see the departure of a fine soldier whose niche among the great commanders of our country was already assured.

Wavell flew to India without having a single day's leave, and took up the reins of his new appointment. But before six months had passed, he was once more called upon to undertake a desperate assignment. When the Japanese assailed us in the Far East, it was decided, on the initiative of President Roosevelt and the American Chiefs of Staff, that Wavell should be asked to take supreme command of all the American, British, Dutch and Australian forces (ABDA) assigned to the south-west Pacific area. There was no time to collect a Staff; there were practically no resources; everything was crumbling; and it was only a matter of time before every important strategic point was overrun by the enemy. Wavell was under no illusions, but he accepted the appointment without hesitation. Within six weeks of his taking control it was all over and his command was dissolved. He must have been through agony of mind, but his Chief of Staff, Henry Pownall, told me that never once did he hear him grumble.

CHAPTER XVI

Early Contacts with the United States

1941

T H E year 1941 was to bring us two mighty allies, the one a godless despotism, the other a democracy of our own faith and way of life. Soviet Russia had never ceased to hope for our downfall up to the moment that she was attacked by the very country with whom she had only recently signed a non-aggression pact. Then, in the twinkling of an eye, the slogan: 'Stop This Imperialist War,' which had been crudely scrawled up all over the place by her dupes in Britain, was replaced by 'Second Front Now.' Until that moment, an icy silence had been maintained between His Majesty's Government and the Soviet Government.

The attitude of the United States Government and the majority of the American people had been very different from the outset. 'Let the British move up; God bless your arms' was the welcome, though somewhat unneutral, message that I received from Washington from my old friend, Brigadier-General Raymond E. Lee,[1] on the day that England declared war on Germany. We in Britain took comfort in the thought that his sentiments were shared by large numbers of his fellow countrymen. The United States Government had kept in the closest touch with His Majesty's Government from the begin-

---

[1] Brig.-General R. E. Lee had been Military Attaché in London, and had later been appointed Director of Army Intelligence in Washington.

ning of the struggle, and official communications had been powerfully reinforced by the stream of personal messages which had passed between the President and the Prime Minister. Even before France collapsed, the Americans had raided their own reserve stocks of military equipment up to the limit permitted by the law of the land, and sent us a generous consignment of rifles, ammunition and artillery. They had allowed us to purchase from their munition factories vast quantities of equipment of all kinds which they would have liked to keep for their own use. In September 1940 they handed over fifty old destroyers, and as a quid pro quo they were given 99-year leases of a number of bases in the West Indies. The year 1941 was to see the two nations draw closer and closer together, and the United States move nearer and nearer to war, until the infamy of Pearl Harbor on 7 December made us comrades in arms.

Shortly after New Year's Day, Mr Roosevelt sent his close friend and confidant, Harry Hopkins, to England with the style and title of 'the President's personal representative.' Hopkins had no authority to negotiate, and no instructions except to talk with everyone who mattered, to see everything that he could, and to report back to his chief. He said that his role was to act as a 'catalytic agent' between the President and Prime Minister. He played his part to perfection.

Churchill at once recognised the importance of this unusual type of envoy and decided to constitute himself Hopkins's personal guide, philosopher, and friend. The order went forth that he was to be treated as one of ourselves — only better — and Brendan Bracken went all the way to Poole, in Dorsetshire, to meet his aeroplane. At first there was no sign of him, and it was thought that he must have been left behind. But eventually he was found still sitting in his seat, too exhausted to move. He was brought on to London by special train and arrived in the middle of a brisk air-raid. He was too tired to dine at Downing Street that night and it was not until the next day that I first set eyes on him. He was as unlike one's picture of a distinguished envoy as it was possible to be. He was deplorably untidy; his clothes looked as though he was in the habit of sleeping in them, and his hat as though he made a point of sitting on it. He seemed so ill and frail that a puff of wind would blow him away. But we were soon to learn that in that sickly frame there burned a fire which no flood could quench. He was completely selfless. All his life he had been a champion of the weak and downtrodden; he was now to prove himself a fanatical fighter for freedom. He loathed Hitler and all his works with a bitter loathing. Not even Churchill was more single-minded than Harry Hopkins in his determination that Nazism should be remorselessly crushed. In personal relationships he was a human, lovable character with a delightful, if somewhat waspish, sense of fun.

Churchill was attracted to Hopkins at once and scarcely let him out of his sight. The first tour on which he took him was to Scapa Flow. The purpose of the tour was twofold: first, to give a special send-off to Lord Halifax, our new Ambassador to the United States, who was sailing in HMS *King George V;* and secondly, to inspect the Home Fleet.

'Light-heartedness is essential if you would take your work seriously' was a piece of advice given to me in my youth: and the reader will forgive me if I place on record some of the lighter incidents of the trip. To start with, Hopkins got muddled between King's Cross and Charing Cross, and only arrived at the former in the nick of time. He had a good deal to say about British nomenclature. Then, to my surprise, I found Sir Charles Wilson[1] sitting in the train. He looked miserable and I asked him why he was there. He said: 'About three-quarters of an hour ago, the Prime Minister sent for me to Downing Street and told me that he had a bad cold. Would it be all right for him to go to Scotland? I naturally replied "No," to which he retorted: "Well, I am going and you are coming with me!" So here I am, without even a toothbrush.'

At Thurso we boarded the mine-sweeper that was to take us on the last leg of our journey. It was bitterly cold and pouring with rain, but as we turned into Scapa Flow, the sun broke through the clouds, and the first sight of the Home Fleet riding at anchor was inspiring. I wanted Harry to see the might, majesty, dominion and power of the British Empire in that setting and to realise that if anything untoward happened to these ships, the whole future of the world might be changed, not only for Britain but ultimately for the United States as well. I found him disconsolate and shivering with cold in the wardroom, but he cheered up when I provided him with an extra sweater and my fur-lined flying boots. He was too cold to be enthusiastic about

[1] The Prime Minister's medical adviser. Later Lord Moran.

the Home Fleet, and too tired to fall in with my suggestion that a brisk walk might be good for us. I therefore went off alone. A few minutes later, he came up to me and said with a shy smile that, hardly had he found a sheltered place to rest when a petty officer had told him most politely that it was unwise to sit on a depth-charge.

I had a little trouble myself before the day was over. The luggage of the Halifax party had been taken from the mine-sweeper to *King George V*, while the luggage of the Prime Minister's party was supposed to have been sent direct to HMS *Nelson*, in which we were to spend the next two or three days. We all lunched together on board *King George V*, and having said good-bye and god-speed to Lord and Lady Halifax, the Prime Minister's party proceeded to leave for the *Nelson* in the Admiral's barge. Churchill was always a stickler for naval etiquette and it was his right and duty, as senior officer, to be the last to leave. I was just in front of him, and as I turned to salute the quarter-deck, I was horrified to see my one and only suitcase lying near the gangway. The prospect of spending the next few days in the same predicament as the unhappy Charles Wilson, without even a toothbrush, was too bleak to contemplate; so I dived past the Prime Minister towards my luggage. He imagined that, as an ignorant soldier, I did not know the naval code and exclaimed sharply: 'Go on; I come last.' 'My luggage,' I gasped, and ducked under his arm. He thought I was mad.

The next two days were spent in inspecting naval establishments; but snow was on the ground and Hopkins was persuaded to stay in bed for most of the time. On the day of our departure, the sea was choppy, and it was difficult to transfer from the Admiral's barge to the destroyer which was to take us back to Thurso. Churchill climbed aboard first, according to rules, and I heard one of the steps of the ladder crack ominously under his weight. I was careful to avoid that particular rung when my turn came, but Harry Hopkins was not so lucky. The step broke under him, and he fell through. Two large seamen held him by the shoulders, as he dangled helplessly, and Churchill encouraged him by saying, 'I shouldn't stay there too long, Harry; when two ships are close together in a rough sea, you are liable to get hurt.'

On the way to London, Churchill took the opportunity of visiting various cities which had been subjected to bombardment. The first of these was Glasgow, where there was a large parade of Civil Defence workers — fire brigades, ARP personnel, police, WVS, Red Cross, etc. They were drawn up in serried ranks, and Churchill started his inspection with Harry Hopkins following in his footsteps. To each rank he was proudly introduced as the President's personal representative. After a little, Harry got tired and hid in the crowd instead of following Churchill. But there was no escape. 'Harry, Harry, where are you?' came the call; and poor Harry had to reappear.

In the evening, the Secretary of State for Scotland, Mr Tom Johnston, gave a dinner in the Prime Minister's honour, and Hopkins was persuaded to say a few words. After a tilt or two at the British Constitution in general, and the irrepressible Prime Minister in particular, he dropped his voice almost to a whisper, and quoted from the Book of Ruth. 'Whither thou goest, I will go; and where thou lodgest, I will lodge . . . where thou diest, will I die . . .' It may have been indiscreet for him to show his partisanship in this way, but it moved us all deeply. It was a small party, and the story never leaked.

Hopkins stayed in England for nearly three weeks, instead of the one week which had been his original intention. He accompanied Churchill on many other visits and spent a lot of his time at Chequers. The only corner in which he could keep warm was the gentlemen's cloakroom, and I often found him there muffled up in his greatcoat, sadly reading his papers. From various talks with him I gathered that he had not always been an Anglophile, and that he deplored what he called British colonialism; but he left me in no doubt of his conviction of the vital importance of the United States and Great Britain keeping in the closest step on all important questions of foreign policy. When the time came for him to leave our shores, he had got right inside Churchill's mind, and gained his complete confidence; he had won the hearts of us all, from the highest to the lowest; he had seen everything. We felt sure that he would report to his chief that we were worth backing to the limit. Henceforward he was not only Roosevelt's principal adviser, but also a 'precious link' between his chief and Churchill.

Meanwhile, there had been an important development on the other side of the Atlantic Ocean. At the end of January 1941, Staff talks were started in Washington in deadly secrecy, and continued for two months. The British delegation consisted of Rear-Admirals R. M. Bellairs and V. H. Danckwerts, Major-General E. L. Morris, and Air Commodore J. C. Slessor. The American representatives were of comparable rank. Perhaps the most important result of the discussions was the agreement reached in regard to the over-all strategic concept for the conduct of the war, if both America and Japan became involved. This provided that the Allies should concentrate on knocking out Germany in the first instance, and that Japan should be contained until Hitler was beaten. The British delegation left Washington at the end of March, but joint Anglo-American missions were established there on a permanent basis, in order that the exchange of information and the co-ordination of ideas should be continued.

Shortly after the Staff talks had ended, there was a development of supreme importance in the economic field. As far back as 8 December 1940 the Prime Minister had written the President one of the most important letters that even he had ever been required to write. He pointed out that hitherto we had paid for all the munitions and ships which the United States had been able to send us, but that the time was approaching when our dollars would be exhausted. He felt sure that the Government and people of the United States would not wish to confine their help to such munitions as could be immediately paid for, and he begged the President to regard his letter, not as an appeal for aid, but as a statement of what was necessary to achieve the common purpose.

The President himself had always been anxious to give and not to sell us the help that we needed; but there was Congress to be considered. Shortly after the receipt of Churchill's letter, he publicly stated that there was no doubt that the best immediate defence of the United States was in fact the defence of Great Britain. Therefore it was important from a purely American point of view that the United States should do everything possible to help the British Empire to defend itself. The Lend-Lease Bill was prepared on that assumption, and passed through Congress in March. In future we were to have practically *carte blanche,* and there was to be no question of repayment. It was, as the Prime Minister described it in Parliament, 'the most unsordid act in the history of any nation.'

In the diplomatic field too, the United States Government were consistently helpful. When, for example, Darlan proposed to move the damaged *Dunkerque* from Oran to Toulon for repairs, and thus run the risk of the ship falling into enemy hands, President Roosevelt intervened, at our request, and persuaded Darlan to abandon the idea.

In the opening months of 1941, the Battle of the Atlantic was causing grave anxiety. U-boats, using wolf-pack tactics and operating in areas in which air cover could not be provided for our convoys, were causing grievous losses. Focke-Wulf aircraft, plying between the French Atlantic seaboard and Norway, were taking a heavy toll in the western approaches; and the surface ships, *Scharnhorst, Gneisenau, Hipper* and *Scheer* had raided far and wide and destroyed a large amount of shipping. The *Bismarck,* the most powerful battleship in the world, was almost ready to go to sea. We were finding it hard to breathe. The United States lent us powerful aid. They extended their security zone and patrol areas to a line covering all north Atlantic waters west of W. longitude 26°, and established bases in Greenland, Newfoundland, Nova Scotia, Bermuda and the West Indies. It was agreed that we should keep them fully informed about the movements of our convoys, and that they would let us have details of any German ships or aircraft operating in the prescribed area. A little later, Iceland[1] was included in the American zone and the British garrison there replaced by United States troops. Gradually the crisis was overcome. We continued to suffer heavy losses in the Battle of the Atlantic until mid-1943, but never again were we in quite such grave danger of strangulation. The appearance of the *Bismarck* in the Atlantic Ocean might however have made a great difference, if she had not been destroyed on her maiden voyage. This brings me to the story of the most exciting week-end that I ever spent at Chequers.

At the end of the Chiefs of Staff meeting on Friday, 23 May 1941, Admiral Sir Dudley Pound, the First Sea Lord, told us that the *Bismarck* and the new 8-inch-gun cruiser *Prinz Eugen* were almost certainly trying to break out into the Atlantic, and that there was a good chance of intercepting them in the Denmark Straits. He added that he proposed to take up his abode in the Admiralty War Room in order to direct operations and that he would not be able to attend Chiefs of Staff meetings until the German ships had been disposed of.

---

[1] A British force had occupied Iceland on the 10 May 1941.

This incident illustrates the essential difference between the functions of the Chief of Naval Staff, and those of the Chiefs of Staff of the other two services. Occasions sometimes arose when the former was required to assume command of the battle and to issue executive orders to all ships which could play a part in it. No comparable functions were ever required of the CIGS or the CAS.

That evening Henry Pownall, who was Vice-Chief of the Imperial General Staff, and I drove to Chequers together to spend the week-end. Mr Averell Harriman was another of the guests. Harriman had been sent to London by the President shortly after the successful passage of the Lend-Lease Bill, in order to expedite the business at the British end. No one could have done the job more sympathetically or effectively. His infinite capacity for taking pains and remarkable powers of concentration enabled him to acquire an intimate knowledge of all our needs; and the President's confidence in his judgment ensured that his recommendations on our behalf were treated with sympathy and despatch. He proved a staunch friend to us throughout the war, but we owe him a special debt of gratitude for all that he did for us in the time of our greatest need.

The situation in Crete was critical, but the conversation at Chequers that night was confined almost exclusively to the impending clash at sea, and we sat up even later than usual, on the chance of getting some news. But none came, and at last we went to bed. I had only just dropped off to sleep — or so it seemed — when I heard the sounds of conversation in Averell's room, which was opposite mine. I jumped out of bed to see the Prime Minister's back view disappearing down the corridor. Averell's door was ajar and I went in. He looked puzzled. 'Winston has just been in and told me that the *Hood* has blown up but that he reckons we have got the *Bismarck* for certain.' Neither of us could fathom the reason for his optimism; nor could Henry Pownall, whom I awoke to tell the news. Presumably it was based on the reasoning that the German monster could not get home again without encountering the whole might of British sea power. Anyway, it was cold comfort, and I returned to my room feeling miserable. I had gone aboard the *Hood* in Portsmouth only a few weeks previously and had been much impressed by her strength and the beauty of her lines. Now she was at the bottom of the sea, and the *Bismarck* was apparently still unharmed.

Meanwhile, under orders from the First Sea Lord, ships from all points of the compass were converging on the scene. The hunt was on. The next three days were exciting and confusing. First, we heard that the *Bismarck* was under close observation by our light cruisers; next, that she had been hit by a torpedo from an aircraft of the *Victorious;* next, and that was a grim moment, that our light cruisers had lost contact; next, that the *Bismarck* had been picked up again heading for Brest; next, the glorious news that aircraft from the *Ark Royal* had scored several torpedo hits and smashed her steering gear, and that the monster was now out of control. The following morning she was pounded to pieces by our heavy ships and sunk by a torpedo from the cruiser, *Dorchester*. The Prime Minister was able to intervene dramatically in the House of Commons with the brief announcement: 'I have just received news that the *Bismarck* is sunk'; and the First Sea Lord was able to emerge from his lair in the Admiralty and resume the chair at the daily meetings of the Chiefs of Staff Committee.

Before closing this tale, I permit myself a question which has always puzzled me. In most of the armies of the civilised world it is recognised that, once a point has been reached when there is no longer any chance of inflicting damage on the enemy, it is the duty of the commander to avoid fruitless sacrifice of life by capitulation. This code was observed at one time or another by most of the belligerent armies and there were numerous cases of surrender by large bodies of unwounded and fully armed soldiery. But the navies of the world had very different ideas. The *Bismarck* continued to defy her enemies long after she had become a blazing, helpless hulk, and went to the bottom with the loss of practically the whole of her complement. The French ships riding at anchor in Oran harbour had no chance whatsoever of inflicting damage on Admiral Somerville's overwhelming fleet, but they did not hesitate to join issue with them and scorned any idea of capitulation. In the first November of the war, the converted passenger liner *Rawalpindi,* armed with ancient six-inch guns, sighted a German battleship closing rapidly upon her. Her Commander, Captain Kennedy, R.N., knowing full well that his ship would be blown to pieces in a matter of minutes and that he could not inflict the slightest damage on his powerful adversary, accepted the challenge without demur and was sunk with all hands. It goes without saying that this discrepancy between the codes of the soldier and the sailor is not due to any discrepancy in their courage, but it would be interesting to know how and why it came into being and is still observed.

We must now return to the development of Anglo-American relations in 1941. On 9 August HMS *Prince of Wales* steamed into Argentia harbour, Newfoundland, with the Prime Minister and his party on board. The United States cruiser, *Augusta,* carrying the President and his party, was already riding at anchor there. The story of this Conference has been told by Churchill; and I, having been left behind in England 'to mind the shop' as the Prime Minister put it, can add no local colour. I was, however, concerned in an incident which provides an illuminating illustration of the working of the Cabinet machinery. At about 2 P.M. (GMT) on 11 August Churchill sent Mr Attlee a long telegram about the work of the Conference. It included the full text of the President's draft of the joint declaration, which was afterwards known as the Atlantic Charter, and the Prime Minister asked that the Cabinet should consider it at once and let him have their views. The telegram reached London about midnight GMT and Mr Attlee ordered the Cabinet to meet at 1.45 A.M. I was just about to go to bed and was not too pleased at the summons; others who had already been asleep for some time looked even more disgruntled. That however did not prevent the most meticulous consideration being given to the draft declaration. The upshot was agreement to recommend a small amendment, and the insertion of a new paragraph dealing with Social Security. A telegram to that effect was immediately despatched to the Prime Minister. Thus, within twelve hours of the despatch of his telegram from Newfoundland, he received the advice which he needed from the War Cabinet in London. They could hardly have done better if they had been in the same room, instead of thousands of miles apart.

Meanwhile the Americans continued to do their utmost to sustain us. Shortly after the Argentia Conference, we were experiencing great difficulty in finding the necessary shipping for reinforcing the Middle East, and the Prime Minister made a personal appeal to Mr Roosevelt. As a result, three United States naval transport vessels were placed at our disposal, and twelve United States merchant ships plied between the United States and the United Kingdom, thus releasing twelve of our own ships for the Middle East run. And when, towards the end of the year, the Italian Empire in Africa had ceased to exist, and the Red Sea was no longer a war area, American shipping was allowed by their Government to carry their precious cargoes of supplies for the Middle East as far as Suez.

Thus, in every sphere, and at all times, the Americans had, from the very outset of hostilities, befriended us with encouragement and material help. They were not yet our comrades in arms, but they had done all that was possible short of going to war.

CHAPTER XVII

A Strange Alliance

T H E word ally is generally associated with friendship, loyalty and helpfulness. In the mid-summer of 1941, we were to acquire an ally who was neither friendly nor loyal and who gave us no immediate help, though no one can deny that she made a mighty contribution to our ultimate victory.

As early as the beginning of April, we had positive information of Hitler's preparations to attack Russia, and the Prime Minister passed the news to Marshal Stalin. His message was not answered or even acknowledged. By mid-June, we were positive that the attack was imminent. At no time in his life had Churchill made any secret of his loathing of the Communist régime. He had done his utmost to strangle the new Bolshevik State at its birth, and had continued to proclaim that it was the mortal foe of free civilisation. Nevertheless he never had the slightest doubt that if Russia were attacked by Germany, we should at once make a public declaration that we would do all in our power to help her. 'I have only one purpose,' he told Mr Colville, one of his private secretaries, on the night before the German attack; 'the destruction of Hitler. If he were to invade Hell, I would make at least a favourable reference to the devil in the House of Commons.'

It must be admitted that the prospect of being allies with the Bolsheviks was repugnant. Apart from the revolting record of the régime, their treachery in signing up with Hitler in August 1939 could not easily be forgiven, and they had done their best to damage our war effort ever since. How could we be friends with people like that? Apart from ethics, there were grave doubts about their military value. During the period 1933-36, I had been responsible, *inter alia,* for military intelligence relating to Russia. By the end of my term of office, I had formed the conclusion that the Soviet forces were making great strides in equipment and training, and that armoured and parachute units were receiving special attention. But shortly afterwards, a number of their best generals, including Marshal Tukachevsky and General Putna, were purged; and it was generally assumed that this would greatly reduce the efficiency of the Red Army.

General Putna was the Soviet Military Attaché in London from 1934-36. He had been a private soldier in the Imperial Guard and joined the Revolution immediately it started. He quickly rose to the rank of major-general, and the division which he commanded in the Russo-Polish War in 1921 was the only one to get away with all its guns in the retreat from Warsaw. He and his wife used often to come to our house, and Putna and I went out *à deux* on two or three occasions. That he was completely and utterly loyal to his masters, there is no shadow of doubt. One night, after watching a performance of *Henry IV*, I took him to the United Service Club and showed him some of the mementoes. He inspected them with great interest and he expressed admiration for the way in which the British Army preserved their traditions. This prompted me to enquire whether the Russian Army did likewise. Were, for example, the traditions of his own famous regiment of Guards still maintained? He froze at once. 'Certainly not; those evil days are past and forgotten.' A few weeks later he wrote to tell me that he had been summoned to Moscow for consultation, but would soon return to London. In my reply I expressed the hope that our friendship would continue although our official relationship had ended with my departure from the War Office. So far from returning to London, Putna was thrown into the Lubianka prison, where he 'confessed' his crimes and was duly executed.

I was afraid that my letter might have been harmful to him, as evidence of the bad company that he had been keeping, and I was relieved when the German Military Attaché, General Baron Geyr von Schweppenburg, told me that one of the main charges against Putna had been that he had been very closely associated with a senior German officer in London — meaning of course himself. He denied that there was any truth in the allegation. Shortly afterwards, Geyr was appointed to command an armoured division in Berlin, and came to say good-bye. He said that he had grown very fond of England, and hoped to visit us again soon. I replied that we would always be delighted to see him, provided that he did not bring his legions with him. He professed to being so shocked at the very mention of such a fantastic idea, even in fun, that it was obvious that this was not the first time that the possibility had come into his mind. All the same, I believe that he was sincere in his admiration of England, and we now know that he did his best to persuade his political masters that we were not as soft as they thought us, and that war with Britain would be a dangerous business. Geyr was in command of 'Panzer Group West' — i.e. all the armour under Marshal Rundstedt — at the time of our return to the Continent in June 1944, but was removed from the appointment the following month. After the war, he wrote to ask me if I would give evidence for him at his trial, but I did not feel that I knew enough about his political views before the war, or his record during the war, to be of any help to him.

As the date of the German attack on Russia drew nearer, we had many discussions as to how the fight would go. The Red Army's recent performances in Finland had not been inspiring, and General Dill was not alone in thinking that the 'Germans would go through them like a hot knife through butter.' If this forecast was correct, Hitler, so far from being weakened by his attack on Russia, would in the long run be incomparably stronger. The help given to Stalin, at great sacrifice to ourselves, would have been wasted, and we ourselves would be in greater danger than ever. Nevertheless, in spite of these forebodings, it was recognised that there was no alternative to the Prime Minister's policy.

In the early hours of 22 June, the Germans launched their attack on a fifteen hundred mile front, and the Russians, in spite of the warning that Churchill had given to Stalin in April, and of the example of what had happened in Poland, were taken by surprise. Their covering forces were overrun and large numbers of their aircraft were caught on the ground and destroyed by the Luftwaffe.

That night, the Prime Minister, in one of the most effective broadcasts of his life, declared unequivocally that our policy would be to give whatever help we could to Russia and the Russian people. One would have expected the Soviet Government to welcome this declaration, but they maintained an icy silence. Churchill, undeterred, immediately set to work to try to establish friendly relations with Marshal Stalin. On 7 July, he sent him a telegram couched in a personal vein, and he followed it up two days later with a message of a more official character, suggesting a declaration of alliance between Britain and Soviet Russia.

At last Stalin deigned to reply; but his answer was confined almost exclusively to the demand that we should immediately establish a second front against Hitler in the west. He might as well have demanded the moon. Already the Kremlin were having the impertinence to complain that they had been fighting alone for eleven weeks. They showed neither penitence nor shame for having betrayed us in August 1939 by joining forces with what they now called 'the robber hordes of Hitlerite bandits,' or for having actively assisted Germany with supplies throughout the long months when we were fighting the Axis single-handed. They made no allowance for the many fronts on which we were already fully extended, and they scarcely said thank you for the supplies which we at once began to send to them at great sacrifice to ourselves. How tired we were to become of that slogan 'Second Front.' We got little else from the Soviet Government for the next three years, and the cry was taken up by a number of people in the United States and in Britain. Mr A. P. Herbert was constrained to express in rhyme[1] what most of us felt about those uninformed pressures:

> 'Let's have less nonsense, from the friends of Joe . . .
> In 1940 when we bore the brunt,
> We could have done, boys, with a Second Front.
> A continent went down a cataract,
> But Russia did not think it right to act.
> Not ready? No. And who shall call her wrong?
> Far better not to strike till you are strong.
> Better, perhaps (though this was not our fate),

[1] *Less Nonsense.*

To make new treaties with the man you hate.
Alas! These shy manœuvres had to end
When Hitler leaped upon his largest friend
(And if he'd not, I wonder, by the way,
If Russia would be in the war to-day?)'

The Germans drove deep into Russia, but it was soon clear that the Red Army was resisting stubbornly, and that the forecast that they would be beaten to their knees within a matter of weeks was very wide of the mark. In fact there was a glimmer of hope that they might be able to hang on to Moscow and Leningrad until the Russian winter set in.

Meanwhile President Roosevelt, while agreeing with Churchill that aid to Russia was the correct policy, made no public announcement. There was bound to be opposition in the United States, and before undertaking any definite commitment, he wanted to find out more precisely what form of help was required, and how it could be conveyed to Russia. Accordingly, in mid-July, he sent Harry Hopkins on a second visit to England, to discuss these and cognate problems with the Prime Minister and principal British authorities. Hopkins had not been long in the country before he became convinced that it was of vital strategic importance to keep Russia in the ring and to help her with munitions and supplies on a scale hitherto not contemplated. He therefore suggested that he should himself fly to Moscow, to find out from Stalin in person what assistance he required, and assure him of the utmost support of the United States. The President agreed, and the frail creature set out for Russia alone in a Catalina aircraft from Invergordon. His visit to Moscow must be regarded as an important milestone in the war. He found Stalin friendly, frank, and communicative; and he learned more about Russian requirements in three days than could have been ascertained through more conventional channels in three years. On 2 August he flew back to Scapa Flow, a shattered wreck, and was put to bed on board HMS *Prince of Wales,* which was to take the Prime Minister and his party to Newfoundland for the meeting with President Roosevelt. Two days later they set sail. Hopkins must have sensed my disappointment at being left behind in England, for he found time to write to me from aboard ship. 'I should so much have liked to tell you about the trip to Moscow. At least I was not air-sick, although the caviar and smoked salmon were almost too much . . . The Prime Minister failed to work yesterday for the first time in his life.'

Hopkins' account of his conversations with Stalin was fully discussed at the Argentia Conference, and there was general agreement that immediate aid to Russia on a gigantic scale was essential. It was therefore decided, on the Prime Minister's suggestion, that an Anglo-American Mission should be sent to Moscow as soon as possible, to discuss the problem with the Russian authorities and reach agreement on the provision of munitions and other supplies by the United States and Britain conjointly.

The American delegation was to be headed by Mr Averell Harriman and to include Mr William Batt, General Burns, General Chaney, Colonel Faymonville, and Admiral Standley. The British Mission was to be headed by Lord Beaverbrook and to include Mr Harold Balfour,[1] Under-Secretary of State for Air, Sir Archibald Rowlands, Major-General Macready, and myself. The reason for my unexpected inclusion in the party is implicit in the letter which Churchill gave Beaverbook to deliver personally to Stalin. 'General Ismay, who is my personal representative on the Chiefs of Staff Committee and is thoroughly acquainted with the whole field of our military policy, is authorised to study with your commanders any plans for practical co-operation which may suggest themselves.'

The two delegations had several meetings in London, and decided upon the programme of what was to be offered to Russia. Their requirements were so colossal that in order to meet them we would be compelled not only to draw heavily upon the output of our own factories and our own slender resources of raw materials, but also to forgo a significant proportion of the American equipment which had been promised us, and which we so sorely needed for our own forces. This meant, among other things, that we would be unable to do very much to strengthen our position in the Far East. It was like having all one's eye-teeth drawn out at the same time, but there was nothing to do but grin and bear it.

Before we left England elaborate cover plans had to be devised to explain the absence of the more senior members of the delegation. In my own case, it was given out that I was in bed with influenza at my home in the country, and my wife was banished from London to

---

1 Later Lord Balfour of Inchrye.

look after the imaginary invalid. About a week after we had said good-bye, she was relieved to be awakened one morning by an old retainer with the news that the BBC had announced our safe arrival in Moscow. 'We have all been so worried about the General,' she said. To my wife's astonished enquiry as to how they had known about my destination, she replied that the chauffeur who had come from London to collect my heavy underclothes had given them the idea. It speaks volumes for the good sense and discretion of the average British man and woman that during the war, if by chance they got to know important secrets, they never discussed them outside their own circle.

The King and Queen graciously received both delegations at Buckingham Palace on 21 September, and on the next day we sailed from Scapa Flow in HMS *London*. We took the same course as HMS *Hampshire* had taken with Lord Kitchener on board in 1915. The ship had been mined or torpedoed off the Orkneys, and there had been practically no survivors. With the enemy in occupation of Norway, and with the Luftwaffe as well as the U-boats on the search for prey, the hazards of the journey had not diminished. We had no destroyer escort and no air cover. The Arctic Sea looked most uninviting. But the voyage passed pleasantly enough, and we arrived at Archangel roadstead on 27 September. There we transferred to a Russian destroyer which took us to a rest camp a short way up the Dvina. Having always regarded the 'Bear' as an exclusively land animal, I was surprised to find a spotlessly clean ship and a smart crew.

The next day we set off at dawn for Moscow in a Russian airplane. The pilot was evidently not an expert navigator, for we flew at about five hundred feet following the line of road or railway. When we were about forty miles out of Moscow, a Russian anti-aircraft battery opened fire on us with all its guns. There were little black puffs all round us, but fortunately too far off to do any damage. Our pilot at once nose-dived to tree-top level, in the hope that other batteries on the route would recognise us. We flew at that height to the end of our journey. It was a relief, not to say a surprise, to land safely in Moscow.

Our reception at the airport by Molotov, Voroshilov, and a number of others was correct if somewhat frigid. The guard of honour was well turned out and their drill impeccable; but everything else looked shoddy, particularly the motor-cars which took us to the Hotel Nationale, just off the Red Square. The plumbing there left a great deal to be desired, but the food was good and the service efficient. Two or three of the waiters were old men who had worked in hotels in Paris and London in days gone by, but they did not dare to be more than coldly civil to their capitalist guests. In fact, the only people who seemed pleased to see us were the few foreign visitors who had been allowed to remain in the hotel. They would now have hot water every day instead of tepid water once a week.

Immediately on arrival we had a meeting amongst ourselves in Beaverbrook's room. It was impossible to talk freely, owing to the fact that microphones were almost certainly installed everywhere. We therefore evolved the techniques of turning on the wireless full blast, or tapping with a fork on a wine glass as we were talking, or pitching our voices so low that we almost had to lip-read.

In the evening, Beaverbrook and Harriman went off to the Kremlin to see Stalin. They returned well satisfied with the results. The next day the military members of our Mission had meetings with Soviet officials. The discussions were frustrating and achieved nothing. When we tried to elucidate the basis of their astronomical requirements of equipment, we could get no answer out of them. We asked, for example, how many anti-tank guns were allotted to a division, adding that our divisions had seventy-two. The reply was, 'It depends on what sort of division.' When we suggested that an infantry division might be taken as an example, the reply was, 'That depends on where it has to fight.' It became obvious that the Soviet Generals were not authorised to give information of any kind, and that to try to do business with them was a waste of time.

Beaverbrook and Harriman returned from their second meeting at the Kremlin in the depths of depression. For some unknown reason the atmosphere had been very different from that of the previous evening, and Stalin had been unmannerly and apparently uninterested. I wondered then, and I have often wondered since, whether we were right when confronted with that kind of behaviour to turn the other cheek, as we persistently did throughout the war. No one will deny that it was in our own interests to give the Russians the wherewithal to fight our common enemy; nor will anyone deny that the Red Army were making splendid use of what we gave them. But it was surely unnecessary, and even unwise, to allow them to bully us in the way that they did. Should we not have said something like this: 'Do not imagine for a moment that you are conferring a favour on us by accepting our generous help. The boot is on the other leg. If you persist in your attitude of taking everything and conceding nothing in return, we will leave you to deal with your recent friend, Hitler, as best you can.' The argument that was always put forward against this tougher approach was that it involved the risk that Russia would come to terms with Germany. But what sort of terms would they have been offered by the man whose consuming passion was the annihilation of Communism? Stalin was a realist, and knew perfectly well that the only alternatives open to the Russians were either to keep on fighting for their lives or to become slaves of Hitler.

On the next night, Beaverbrook and Harriman came back from their third visit to the Kremlin in high spirits. Everything had been agreed. Stalin had been forthcoming, and had even gone so far as to announce his intention of giving a banquet in our honour the next day. This did not seem much of a return for several billion dollars' worth of supplies, but I suppose that it could be taken as a symbol of unity at last achieved.

I had no discussions either with Stalin or any Russian officers about military matters, in spite of the fact that my inclusion in the delegation had been for that express purpose. But Beaverbrook and Harriman decided, probably rightly, that there was no point in talking about problems on which there was not the slightest possibility of agreement. I was not sorry to be spared an exasperating task.

Moscow was drab and depressing. The Muscovites, young and old, male and female, seemed solitary folk. One seldom saw them address a word to each other as they walked the streets or stood in seemingly endless queues waiting for a bus. Their faces were expressionless. They had the same look of resignation as cows coming in from the fields one by one at milking time. The only time that I ever saw them natural and happy and laughing and friendly to each other, was at the ballets at the Bolshoi Theatre. The performances were invariably superb, but to me the pleasure of the evening was to see the audience enjoying themselves and behaving like free people.

It was a surprise to find that the Russian soldiery, both officers and other ranks, were most punctilious about saluting. This caused my Royal Marine orderly some embarrassment. In his blue uniform, he was far the smartest member of our party, and the red band on his hat was apparently misleading. 'It is very awkward, sir,' he said, 'to be saluted by Russian generals.' The only advice that I could give him was to acknowledge their compliments handsomely.

All the senior members of the Mission had a couple of security officers permanently attached to them. They posted themselves outside our rooms in the hotel, one of them keeping awake all night. Whenever we went abroad, they followed us. It was irksome to have these permanent shadows.

On the afternoon of 1 October we assembled at the Kremlin to witness the signing of the agreement setting out the supplies which were to be allocated to Russia by the United States and Great Britain up to June 1942. It was a voluminous document, and included equipment which we most grievously needed for ourselves — tanks, aircraft, anti-tank guns, anti-aircraft guns. We were giving away our life's blood. The agreement stipulated that the supplies would 'be made available at British and United States centres of production'; and an undertaking was given that we would *help in their transportation to Russia;* help, and no more. In the event, we were a good deal better than our word. Ninety per cent of the merchant ships employed on the Arctic convoys in 1941-42 were British (including British controlled) and American (including American controlled). The escorts were supplied exclusively by the British and American Navies, chiefly the former. Occasionally small Soviet warships met the convoys as they approached their destination, but they never operated far from their bases. Our repeated requests for improved fighter protection at the terminal ports, for minesweeping, and for more anti-submarine escorts, met with very little result. Scarcely a convoy got through without loss, and the last straw came when in June 1942 twenty-three ships were sunk out of the thirty-four which had sailed from Iceland. Thereupon the Admiralty insisted that further convoys should be suspended until a time of the year in which there was not perpetual daylight. The Prime Minister had to break the news to Stalin. The reaction was characteristic — a flood of abuse about our refusal to take the ordinary risks of war, and the taunt that we were defaulting on our *contracted obligation*. Here was the chance for the Prime Minister to point out very forcibly that our contract was limited to *helping* with the transport of supplies to Russia, that our performance had far exceeded our promise, and that the

Soviet Navy and Air Force had scarcely lifted a finger to assist us. But he preferred once more to turn the other cheek. This may have been generous and shown a Christian spirit, but was it the best way to deal with a bully? In our determination to help Russia at almost any cost, we resorted to the experiment of sailing ships independently during the period that escorts could not be provided, owing to the needs of TORCH,[1] about which I shall have something to say later in my narrative. Thirteen ships left Iceland. Three turned back; five were sunk; and five arrived. Our Christian spirit cost us dearly.

The promised banquet at the Kremlin took place the next evening, and I set eyes on Stalin for the first time. He was in Russian civilian costume — long boots of fine soft leather, baggy trousers, and a well-cut blouse of a dove grey colour and obviously expensive material. He wore no medals or decorations. Later in the war, he used to look somewhat ridiculous in the uniform of a Russian Marshal, but on this occasion he was the best-dressed man of the party. From the pictures which were placarded up all over Moscow, I had imagined him to be tall and burly, and it was a surprise to find that he was diminutive. Presumably the photographers were under orders to magnify him to create a more formidable image. He moved stealthily like a wild animal in search of prey, and his eyes were shrewd and full of cunning. He never looked one in the face. But he had great dignity and his personality was dominating. As he entered the room, every Russian froze into silence, and the hunted look in the eyes of the Generals showed all too plainly the constant fear in which they lived. It was nauseating to see brave men reduced to such abject servility. The banquet dragged on until the early hours of the morning. There was too much food, too much vodka, too many speeches, and too much artificial bonhomie.

A couple of days before we left Moscow, an emaciated British soldier called James Allan turned up at the British Embassy. He had been washed, shaved, clothed, and let loose from the Lubianka prison that morning. He had a shocking story to tell. He had been captured by the Germans at Calais and imprisoned in Germany. After a few weeks, he had escaped into Poland, where he was kept in hiding and extremely well treated by friendly Poles. But, determined to try to get back to England, he had made his way into Russia, which was

[1] Anglo-American operation against French North-West Africa.

not then a belligerent. There his troubles started in earnest. He was accused of being a spy, thrown into solitary confinement on a starvation diet, and beaten almost daily. We took him back to England with us, and he was eventually awarded the DCM. But the citation of the deeds which earned him this distinction was not published. The courageous endurance of devilries perpetrated on a British soldier by an ally of his country could not have been divulged at that time. Allan subsequently wrote an interesting account of his experiences.[1]

Our return journey to Archangel was again made in a Russian plane. It was very rough, and two or three members of the party were compelled to use their tin helmets for a purpose for which they were never intended. At Archangel we boarded a British mine-sweeper which took us alongside HMS *London*. A heavy sea was running, and the two vessels kept bumping each other in alarming fashion. As I was awaiting my turn to walk the plank between them, I heard one of the mine-sweeper's crew say, 'Hurrah. One more bump like that and we will have to go home for a re-fit.' The rest of the journey was a delightful relaxation, and there were no alarms or excursions. What a relief it was to be once again in a free country!

The trip had been interesting and instructive. Beaverbrook and Harriman had shown dynamic and imaginative leadership, and the relations between the two delegations had been most harmonious. This was my first experience of working closely with Americans. I had found it extremely congenial, and I was to find it more and more congenial as the years went by and our partnership became ever closer.

I had been depressed by much that I had seen in Russia, but I came away with a firm conviction that the Russian Army and people were going to fight to the bitter end, and that Moscow would hold out. Both Beaverbrook and Harriman agreed, but most people thought otherwise. Hitler was quoted as having definitely promised the German people that Moscow would be captured by Christmas. Dill estimated the odds at five to four on. The Prime Minister put the betting at even money. I would have willingly laid ten to one against, and am on record as having said so.[2] In the event, the Germans never got nearer than twenty miles from Moscow. My forecasts were so often wrong, that I must be forgiven for recording this exception.

[1] James Allan: *No Citation.*
[2] Sir R. H. Bruce Lockhart: *Comes the Reckoning.*

CHAPTER XVIII

The Menace of Japan

THANKS to the Anglo-Japanese Alliance signed in 1902, there was never a moment's anxiety about our interests in the Far East throughout the First World War. Once German influence in that part of the world had been eliminated, our only commitments were small garrisons to look after the naval base at Hong Kong, and to maintain internal security in Malaya. But shortly after the end of the war, the Anglo-Japanese Alliance was annulled in deference to American opinion. Churchill has written that His Majesty's Government 'had to choose between Japanese and American friendship,' and that he himself 'had no doubts what our course should be.' [1] No responsible person would have disagreed with him. Nevertheless, to the peoples of Asia, it seemed that one of their number had been affronted by a European power, and our position throughout the East was significantly weakened. The Japanese themselves were mortally offended. So far from being the staunch friends that they had been in the past, they became, almost overnight, potential enemies; and the possibility of finding ourselves involved in war with them at some future date had to be taken into serious account.

In order to meet this contingency, remote though it then seemed, a

[1] Winston S. Churchill: *The Second World War*: Vol. III.

large naval base, which would enable us to exercise control of sea communications in the Indian and Southern Pacific Oceans, became a necessity; and in 1921, His Majesty's Government decided upon Singapore as the best site. The project was bound to be a lengthy and costly business, and after the ravages of war, money for defence was hard to come by. Nevertheless it was to start at once, and go ahead as rapidly as financial considerations permitted.

For the next fifteen years, the defence of Singapore was the subject of continuous study by the Committee of Imperial Defence. The crux of the problem was whether the primary defence against naval attack should be provided by aircraft or by heavy guns. Had we known then what the Norwegian campaign in April 1940 taught us, it would have been an easy question to answer. But in the 1920s, air power had not come into its own, the torpedo-bomber was still unproved, and most people outside the Royal Air Force believed that modern battleships would be able to look after themselves. Consequently it was decided, in 1926, to compromise by installing three 15-inch guns in the first instance, leaving the question of whether aircraft should take the place of the rest of the heavy armament to be considered at a later date.

The defence of Singapore soon became one of the stock exercises at all military academies, and I was first introduced to it as a student at Quetta Staff College in 1922. We were required to put ourselves in the place of the Japanese General Staff, and to make recommendations as to how Singapore was to be captured. My solution was to land a force of several divisions in the north of Malaya or the south of Siam, in order to attack the fortress from the north, while the fleet maintained a sea blockade. At the same time, I stipulated, in my role of a Japanese planner, that, so long as a British fleet was 'in being' and ready to proceed to the Far East at short notice, it would be an unwarrantable risk to base any such expedition on Japan — a distance of over three thousand miles. At the time, I derived a good deal of satisfaction from this optimistic conclusion. The possibility of our not having a 'fleet in being,' or of the Japanese being in a position to use Indo-China as a base, never entered my mind.

Following the annulment of the Treaty, Anglo-Japanese relations became progressively worse, and the Japanese became more and more aggressive. In 1931 they seized Manchuria, and flouted the order of the League of Nations to withdraw. Even though the League did not go so far as to impose sanctions of any kind, Japan withdrew her membership.

It was at about that time that I was appointed to the Intelligence Directorate of the War Office, with the Far East as one of my responsibilities. A few months after I had been in office, I put forward a proposal that Hong Kong should be demilitarised. I argued that, in the event of war against Japan, Hong Kong could not be used as a naval base, owing to the impossibility of maintaining air forces there, and that, for the same reason, it could not be held against a determined enemy for more than a limited period. Thus a garrison which could be usefully employed elsewhere, e.g. in Malaya, was being condemned to death or captivity for no useful purpose. I also mentioned the sentimental appeal which a beleaguered garrison always exerts on public opinion, and the danger of being stampeded into premature and dangerous attempts at relief. My proposal was not favourably received. Indeed surprise was expressed by my superior officers that I should hold such defeatist views. About three years later, the Air Staff raised the issue again, advancing much the same arguments as I had done; but they got no support from either of the other Services, or from the Foreign Office.

The garrison continued to be maintained at full strength, and was actually reinforced by two Canadian battalions only a few weeks before the Japanese attack on 7 December 1941. The fortress fell on Christmas Day. Our casualties were about twelve thousand killed, wounded and missing; and those of the defenders who survived suffered unspeakable horrors in Japanese prison-camps for over three and a half years. From the purely military point of view, the decision against demilitarisation had proved disastrous, but that does not mean that it was wrong. There may well have been overriding political considerations. It would undoubtedly have involved loss of prestige, and discouraged the Chinese in their struggle against Japan. But I have gone too far ahead of my story.

Towards the end of 1936 Japan joined Germany in the Anti-Comintern Pact, thus drawing further away from us, and nearer to the country which was so obviously bent on aggression. Henceforward our long-term studies in the Committee of Imperial Defence were based on the assumption that we and the French might find ourselves fighting Germany, Italy and Japan simultaneously. The silver lining to that black thundercloud was the probability that if Japan entered the war on the side of Germany and Italy, the United States would come in on our side. That would make up for all. But there was no certainty.

For the next three years the temperature in the Far East continued to rise; but, when war with Germany broke out, Japan made no move. She was busy devouring China, and not yet ready for the plunge. At the same time, it was clearly necessary to do all that we could to put our Singapore house in order. A trickle of army reinforcements was despatched from India, but very little in the way of air forces could be spared from England, in view of our own parlous situation and the demands of the Middle East. Air Chief Marshal Sir Robert Brooke-Popham, who had been appointed Commander-in-Chief, Far East, in November 1940, constantly represented the weakness of his position to the Chiefs of Staff. He had been Commandant of the RAF Staff College at Andover when I graduated in 1924-25, and he supplemented his official representations by personal letters to his former pupil. The only consolation that I could give him was that his needs were fully recognised by the authorities in London, but that at the moment the cupboard was bare. It was however hoped that as soon as we began to reap the fruits of American production and of the increased output from our own factories, we might be able to do something substantial for him. That hope never materialised because help to Russia had to be given priority. Thus we continued to be lamentably weak in Malaya, both in quantity and quality. To make matters worse, our naval commitments in European waters seemed to rule out any possibility of our being able to send a sufficiently strong fleet to Singapore, if trouble blew up in the Far East.

Meanwhile, the Japanese position had steadily improved, both militarily and politically. The collapse of France had enabled her to bring pressure on the Vichy Government to permit her to maintain troops in Indo-China on the plea that they were required for operations against Chiang Kai-Shek, and in September 1940 Japanese forces moved into that country. In the same month she joined the Tripartite Pact; and in the following April, she signed a neutrality pact with Russia. All this was very ominous.

From the outset, the Prime Minister had not allowed the ugly possibilities in the Far East to depress him unduly. He thought it unlikely that Japan would take the risk of fighting the two most powerful Navies in the world. If, on the other hand, they were so foolish as to do so, the entry of America into the war would more than compensate for everything. Nevertheless, when the USA imposed drastic economic sanctions on Japan, which might leave her no option but to resort to arms, he felt that we must do all in our power to deter her from putting a match to the fire. With this in mind, he conceived the idea of forming an Eastern Fleet. After a good deal of discussion with the Admiralty, it was decided that this should be done, and that the fleet should consist of the *Prince of Wales,* one of our latest battleships, the battle-cruiser *Repulse,* and the aircraft-carrier *Indomitable.* The Eastern Fleet was to be under the command of Admiral Sir Tom Phillips.

Tom Phillips had been successively Director of Plans, Deputy Chief of Naval Staff, and Vice-Chief of Naval Staff at the Admiralty. We had worked together for many years in peace and war, and I had always greatly admired his courage, industry, integrity and professional competence. His whole heart and soul were in the Navy, and he believed that there was nothing that it could not do. In particular, he refused to admit that properly armed and well-fought ships had anything to fear from air power. Nor was he alone in that opinion. Even Winston Churchill, whose forecasts were not often at fault, was one of the many who did not 'believe that well-built modern warships properly defended by armour and A-A guns were likely to fall a prey to hostile aircraft.' [1] The battles-royal which raged between Tom Phillips and Arthur Harris when they were Directors of Plans in their respective Departments, were never-ending, and always inconclusive. On one occasion, when the situation which would arise in the event of Italy entering the war on the side of Germany was under discussion, Tom Phillips insisted that our Fleet would have free use of the Mediterranean, however strong the Italian Air Force might be. Bert Harris exploded. 'One day, Tom, you will be standing on a box on your bridge (Tom was diminutive in stature), and your ship will be smashed to pieces by bombers and torpedo aircraft. As she sinks, your last words will be, "That was a . . . . great mine!" '

Tom Phillips came to say good-bye to me before he sailed. He was

[1] Winston S. Churchill: *Step by Step.*

blissfully happy at the prospect of flying his flag after so many years in Whitehall. As he left the room, I suddenly felt sad. I am not psychic, nor am I given to having presentiments. But for some unaccountable reason, I had a feeling that I would not see him again.

By the end of November, we were almost certain that Japanese forces were on the move, but we had no definite information as to what they were up to. I had intended to go to the country on Saturday, 6 December, but the First Sea Lord rang up in the afternoon to say that two convoys of Japanese transports with naval escort had been spotted sailing westwards from Saigon. A meeting of the Chiefs of Staff was called at once, and Sir Alexander Cadogan came over to represent the Foreign Office. We sat for two or three hours discussing the various possibilities, but no definite conclusions were reached. On the following day, there were Chiefs of Staff meetings in both the morning and the afternoon, but still there was no certainty about what was happening. That evening I was just finishing my supper at the Carlton Hotel Grill Room, when an excited waiter came up and said that the BBC had just announced that the Japanese had attacked Pearl Harbor. My first reaction was stunned surprise. It had never occurred to anyone in London, nor I believe in Washington, that such a thing was possible. My next reaction was thankfulness, for of course I had no idea of the grievous injury which the American Fleet had suffered. Indeed, had I not been in a public place, I would have shouted for joy. How I wished I could have been with the Prime Minister at that moment! To have the United States with us had been uppermost in his thoughts from the outset of the war; and now that it had come to pass, his relief was unbounded. 'So we had won after all . . . England would live . . . Once again in our long island history, we should emerge, however mauled or mutilated, safe and victorious . . . No doubt it would take a long time . . . I expected terrible forfeits in the East . . . But there was no more doubt about the end.' [1] Those were exactly my own feelings, but I could not express them so graphically. When Sir Robert Bruce Lockhart, Head of the Political Warfare Executive, came to consult me next morning about problems of collaboration with the United States, the best that I could do was to say that the entry of the United States into the war made ultimate victory certain, but that we must expect things to be

[1] Churchill: *The Second World War: Vol III.*

worse before they were better. Our eastern possessions, almost undefended, were now open to the Japanese. My optimism would have
been mitigated if I had known the fearful losses which had been
suffered by the United States Navy at Pearl Harbor, or realised the
cataract of disaster which lay ahead of us.

It was not until the early hours of 8 December that I learned that
the Japanese were attacking Hong Kong and had landed in Siam and
Malaya. By this time the fleet under Tom Phillips, minus the *Indomitable,* which had gone aground at Jamaica, had arrived at Singapore,
and on the following night the Prime Minister called a meeting of the
Defence Committee to consider the whole position in the Far East.
The principal topic of discussion was how the *Prince of Wales* and
Repulse were to be used. The Prime Minister suggested two alternatives. Either they should vanish into the ocean wastes and exercise a
vague menace like 'rogue elephants'; or alternatively, they should go
south and join the remnants of the United States Fleet. The discussion
continued far into the night without any definite decision being
reached, and it was agreed to have another look at the problem the
next day.

Hollis and I were both sleeping in our offices, and on our way to
bed, I confessed to him that I had dreamed the night before that the
Prince of Wales had been sunk and that I had wakened in a cold
sweat. At dawn the next morning, he came into my room looking
ashen-grey. 'Your dream about the *Prince of Wales* was true; and the
Repulse as well.'

Nature is merciful. She sets a limit to the amount of pain, mental or
physical, that she requires us to endure. When that limit is reached,
numbness sets in. It was some time before I could bring myself to try
to measure the situation to which five days of war with Japan had
brought us. The enemy had undisputed command of the eastern seas.
Hong Kong, Singapore, the Philippines and the Dutch East Indies —
all seemed doomed. Australia, New Zealand, Burma and India were
all in danger. It was a shocking start. Nevertheless there was still a
long way to go to the winning post: and there was a good deal to be
thankful for. Russia was holding fast, and the German armies had a
bleak winter in front of them. Above all, the Japanese treachery had
brought America into the war as a completely united nation. We were
now all in the same boat. It might be badly knocked about by the

storm, but it would not capsize. There was no doubt about the end.

The Prime Minister was always at his best when things were at their worst. 'In defeat, defiance,' was one of his favourite slogans; and he practised what he preached. There were many grave problems which called for his presence in London, but he saw that there was an over-riding need for him to consult with President Roosevelt at once, and settle not only the broad strategy which was to govern Anglo-American action but also the machinery by which that action was to be unified and directed. Within forty-eight hours of the disaster in the Gulf of Siam, he set out for Washington in HMS *Duke of York*, taking with him Pound, Portal, Dill and Jo Hollis. It was again my fate to be told to stay in London to 'mind the shop,' this time with General Sir Alan Brooke, who had just been appointed CIGS in place of Dill. How I hated being left behind!

The discussions in Washington led to two decisions of the highest consequence. The first was the confirmation of the policy which had been provisionally agreed at the Staff conversations earlier in the year: that the elimination of Germany should be our primary objective, and that Japan should be contained until that had been achieved. We had not expected our American friends to see eye to eye with us on this question without considerable argument, since it seemed probable that public opinion in the United States would clamour for the weight of American effort to be directed against Japan in the first instance. It was a great relief to us that agreement was reached so readily.

The second vital decision was the setting up of the Combined Chiefs of Staff Committee. Hitherto the United States had had no formal machinery for consultation between their Army and Navy. The President, after discussing the British arrangements with the Prime Minister, decided to set up a Chiefs of Staff Organisation on the British model. At the same time, the President and the Prime Minister decided to set up the Combined Chiefs of Staff Committee, consisting of the American Chiefs of Staff and the British Chiefs of Staff. They were to be responsible for the stategic direction of all the Allied forces, and for the allocation of man-power, munitions and shipping. They were to be served by a Combined Secretariat, and by Combined Planning and Intelligence Staffs. Their headquarters were to be in Washington, and they were to be in permanent session. Since the British Chiefs of Staff obviously had to be in London in order to be close at hand to the British Government, they were to be represented in Washington by three high-ranking officers, headed by Field Marshal Sir John Dill, who would reside there permanently.

Dill was the ideal man to head this Mission. He soon gained the complete confidence of President Roosevelt and established the closest relationship with his advisers, particularly General Marshall. They recognised in him a soldier of vast experience and exceptional competence. His sincerity, modesty and transparent integrity won all hearts. His simplicity was endearing. He had been in Washington only a few weeks when he was asked what his duties were. He replied that he was not yet quite sure, but that at least he provided neutral ground on which the American Army and Navy could meet. As the months went by, his position got stronger and stronger, until he became an almost indispensable link between the British and American High Commands. Later, he suffered much from ill health, and he told me at the Second Quebec Conference in September 1944 that the doctors had forbidden him to do more than half a day's work. Should he make way for someone who was one hundred per cent fit? I assured him that, even if he could work only one day a week, he would still be worth his weight in gold. Within four months he died in harness. President Truman attended his funeral, and the American Chiefs of Staff acted as pall-bearers. The Resolution passed by the American Congress recognising Dill's outstanding service to the Alliance, and the equestrian statue which his friends in America have erected over his grave in their national cemetery at Arlington, bear testimony to their esteem and affection for a noble officer and gentleman.

The conferences which took place in various parts of the world, under the chairmanship of President Roosevelt and Mr Churchill, provided many opportunities for the British Chiefs of Staff themselves to meet with their American opposite numbers. In point of fact, out of a total of about two hundred Combined Chiefs of Staff meetings, no less than eighty-nine were attended by the British Chiefs of Staff in person; and it is probably true to say that most of the particularly important decisions which governed the conduct of the war were taken at those meetings of principals.

General Marshall has said that the Combined Chiefs of Staff Committee secured 'the most complete unification of military effort ever achieved by two allied nations.' [1] But the members of that great team would be the first to admit that they could not have achieved what they did, if they had not been wisely guided and loyally sustained by President Roosevelt and Mr Churchill, who alone were in a position to focus all the issues — economic and political, as well as military — and who alone had the authority to take the necessary decisions. Whenever the British and American military experts were unable to reach agreement, their political chiefs stepped in and settled the problem between themselves. Thus the President and Prime Minister, with the Combined Chiefs of Staff as their military advisers, constituted in fact, though not in name, a supreme war council which directed the war efforts, not only of their own countries, but of *all* the nations engaged in war against the Axis, with the exception of Russia. In the face of the mortal danger which confronted them, proud sovereign States were ready to waive their claims to representation on the organ of supreme control, realising that a council consisting of a dozen or more Prime Ministers and a dozen or more sets of Chiefs of Staff would be hopelessly unwieldy. On the other hand, the fact that they were not represented in the supreme council did not deprive them of their right to veto any proposal affecting their own forces or territory of which they did not approve. An example may be given. After the disasters of Pearl Harbor and the Gulf of Siam, the Government of Australia demanded that their divisions in the Middle East should be sent back to Australia at once for the defence of the homeland. Their wishes were of course respected. It so happened that at the moment that the convoys carrying them were passing through the Indian Ocean, Japanese forces were moving in great strength to Burma from Siam. Accordingly, Mr Churchill, supported by President Roosevelt, informed the Australian Government that the only hope of saving Burma was for Australian troops to break their journey at Rangoon and assist in its defence as a temporary measure, until rein-

[1] General Marshall's Biennial Report to the Secretary of War. 1 July 1943 to 30 June 1945.

forcements could arrive from elsewhere. The Australian Government, in view of the threat to their own country, did not agree, and the convoys sailed direct to Australia. This episode shows that members of a coalition at war can waive their claims to representation on the organ of supreme control, without in any way surrendering their sovereign rights.

It may be asked why Russia was not represented on the Combined Chiefs of Staff Committee. Apart from the fact that no Russian military adviser would ever have been given authority by his political masters to engage in frank discussions or disclose any information of Soviet intentions, the Russians, until the very end of the war, had a far-distant and wholly independent theatre of operations. There was therefore no need for that intimate integration which was essential for Anglo-American forces. All that was necessary was to exchange information with each other on the broad sweep and timing of their operations.

It had been arranged that the Prime Minister and party should return to England in two stages — the first by air to Bermuda, and thence by sea in the *Duke of York*. But on the first leg of the journey, the Prime Minister decided to take the risk of flying the whole way. His reason for this last-minute change was perfectly valid; there was any amount of business at home which urgently required his presence. But his innate love of danger was undoubtedly a contributory factor. He never took wholly unjustifiable risks; but if he thought, or could persuade himself to think, that any benefit would result from his doing so, his sense of duty was powerfully reinforced by his natural inclination. He had all the instincts of the warrior. He had far too much imagination to be fearless, but he was pre-eminently brave. He would have liked to be in the forefront of the battle, instead of having to stay behind and make the decisions which sent others to their death.

The return journey was not without incident. His Boeing Clipper came within an ace of flying over Brest, where it would have been an attractive and not too difficult target for the German gunners; and later, it was momentarily mistaken for an enemy aircraft, owing to the direction from which it approached our shores, and might have been shot down by our own fighters. But, by the mercy of Providence, it arrived safely at Plymouth. Churchill had enjoyed himself hugely; and he was at pains to point out that he was able to grapple with vitally important business four or five days earlier than if he had returned by sea. So as usual he had the last word.

From my earliest youth, 19 January had always been rather a special date in my calendar as the anniversary of my mother's birthday. In 1942, it was a very dark day. When I reported to the Prime Minister in the morning, I found him in a towering rage. Why had I not told him that there were no defences on the north side of Singapore island? Before I could protest that he must have been misinformed, he thrust into my hand a telegram from Wavell reporting that little or nothing had been done in the way of constructing defences to prevent the crossing of the Johore States. I could scarcely believe my eyes. The Prime Minister continued: 'You were with the Committee of Imperial Defence for several years before the war broke out. You must have known the position. Why did you not warn me?' I was tempted to explain that the Committee of Imperial Defence had concerned themselves solely with the installation of heavy guns at Singapore to meet sea-borne attack, and with the period for which the fortress must be prepared to hold out until relief came, and that it had been taken for granted that the commanders on the spot would see to the local defences against land attack from the north. But I remained silent. What did my own feelings matter when so ghastly and humiliating a disaster loomed ahead?

The next few weeks were a hideous nightmare. On 15 February, Singapore surrendered unconditionally. Speaking in the House of Commons, Churchill called it 'the greatest disaster to British arms which our history records.' On 8 March, Java followed suit. Almost simultaneously Rangoon was abandoned, and Burma lay open to the invader. In addition to the *Prince of Wales* and the *Repulse,* our naval losses had been grievous; and the Dutch Navy had been annihilated. The Japanese had complete command of the Bay of Bengal, and both India and Ceylon lay wide open to attack. In India itself, political agitation inspired by Gandhi had led to a serious internal uprising. No one had ever expected that retribution for our unpreparedness in the Far East would be so swift or so catastrophic.

CHAPTER XIX

Anglo-American Strategy

1942

T H E reader will recall that it had been agreed at the secret Staff
conversations early in 1941 that, if America were to enter the
war, first priority should be given to the defeat of Germany and that
Japan should be contained until Germany had been knocked out. It
seemed possible however that public opinion in the United States
might be so outraged by the treacherous attack on Pearl Harbor as
to insist that immediate revenge be taken on Japan; and it was a great
relief to be assured, when Churchill visited Washington in December
1941, that there was no intention of making any change in the over-
all strategic concept. The next step was to determine what specific
operations should be undertaken to give effect to it.

The Americans were the first to make up their minds, and their
plans were brought to London in April 1942 by General Marshall
and Mr Hopkins in person. Their main proposal was that there
should be a massive invasion of Europe by combined Anglo-American forces at the earliest possible date, and in any case not later than
September 1943. The operation was given the somewhat bombastic
title of ROUND-UP. Forty-eight divisions, of which the British contribution was to be eighteen, and 5,800 combat aircraft, of which the

British contribution was to be 2,550, were to be employed. In principle, though certainly not in timing, this proposal was in line with our own thinking. There may have been a few enthusiasts in England who thought that the war could be won by air bombardment alone, but the vast majority were sure that ultimately we would have to make a frontal assault on the enemy in France, liberate the captive countries, and advance into the heart of Germany itself.

In addition, the Americans proposed that a plan should be prepared for much earlier action on a smaller scale. This was to be called SLEDGEHAMMER. The idea was to capture an area, such as the Cotentin or Brittany Peninsula, and maintain a bridgehead until ROUND-UP could be got ready. The Americans described it as an 'emergency measure,' which would be launched if Russia seemed on the point of collapse, or alternatively if Germany suddenly looked like disintegrating. They recognised that it could not take place before the autumn of 1942, and that not more than five divisions could be established and maintained on the Continent. They recognised too that the British would have to provide not only half of these divisions, but also all the naval forces, and not less than 5,000 combat aircraft.

About a week after their arrival, Marshall and Hopkins were invited to discuss their proposals with the Defence Committee. Everyone at the meeting was enthusiastic about the prospect of the despatch of a mighty American army to Europe, and of the English-speaking peoples 'marching ahead together in a noble brotherhood of arms' as Churchill put it. Everyone agreed that the death-blow to Germany must be delivered across the Channel. In fact everyone seemed to agree with the American proposals in their entirety. No doubts were expressed; no discordant note struck. It is easy to be wise after the event, but perhaps it would have obviated future misunderstandings if the British had expressed their views more frankly. This is the sort of thing which might have been said: 'We have not yet had time to study your proposals in detail, but you will doubtless wish to hear our first reactions. We agree in principle with ROUND-UP, but would not as yet like to commit ourselves to so early a date as September 1943. On the other hand, we regard SLEDGEHAMMER as an extremely doubtful proposition, and wonder whether you have given sufficient weight to its immense difficulties and embarrassing implications. The landing would be very hazardous; and if it failed, the result would be catastrophic. Even if it were successful, the maintenance of a bridge-head would be a terrible strain on our resources, and might cripple all other future enterprises, including ROUND-UP itself. Nor is it at all certain that it would draw off a single division from the Russian front. However we will immediately examine all the possibilities, and if there is a reasonable prospect of success, we will do our share faithfully.' But nothing of the kind was said, and the upshot of the meeting was that the Defence Committee accepted the proposals *in principle,* with the single, and not very relevant, reservation that sufficient strength must be maintained in the East to prevent a junction between the Japanese and the Germans.

The Prime Minister undertook to report this result to President Roosevelt, and our American friends went happily homewards under the mistaken impression that we had committed ourselves to both ROUND-UP and SLEDGEHAMMER. This misunderstanding was destined to have unfortunate results. For, when we had to tell them, after the most thorough study of SLEDGEHAMMER, that we were absolutely opposed to it, they felt that we had broken faith with them. Worse still, they got it into their heads that our opposition to SLEDGE-HAMMER would later extend to ROUND-UP as well. They suspected that we were haunted by memories of the carnage of Passchendaele and the Somme and that we would always shrink from undertaking an assault on Fortress Europe. This suspicion persisted for a very long time, and lay at the root of many future misunderstandings.

The crux of the matter was that we felt sure that there were much more promising possibilities of bringing British and American forces into action against the Axis in 1942, elsewhere than in France. The Prime Minister, supported by the Chiefs of Staff, favoured a descent upon French North-West Africa; and he wished, in addition, to seize northern Norway. He would have liked to do both; but if that was beyond our means, French North-West Africa was his first love, and he was anxious to sell the idea to the President and his advisers as quickly as possible. Accordingly, in spite of bad news from Cairo — this story will be told later — he left for Washington on 17 June, taking the CIGS and me with him.

This was my first flight across the Atlantic, and I enjoyed it immensely. Our Boeing flying-boat was the acme of comfort — plenty of room, full-length bunks, easy chairs, and delicious food. On some of my subsequent war-time journeys I had to lie in a bomb rack or sit on a bucket seat, and I used to think longingly of the comforts of my first long trip abroad. We were in the air for over twenty-six hours at a stretch, but the time passed quickly and pleasantly. When we were about four hours from Washington, the Prime Minister looked at his watch. 'It is nearly eight o'clock, Tommy.[1] Where's dinner?' Tommy explained that he was engaged to dine at the British Embassy, and that it was only about 4:30 P.M. according to sun time. The Prime Minister retorted that he didn't go by sun time. 'I go by tummy time, and I want my dinner.' He had it — and so did we all — and a very good dinner it was! We landed on the Potomac River three or four hours later, and assembled at the British Embassy in time for a second meal.

The next morning the Prime Minister went to Hyde Park to stay with the President, and the CIGS and I had a meeting with the American Chiefs of Staff and our Joint Staff Mission. This was the first time that I had seen the American Chiefs in action. They had not yet acquired the cohesion of their British counterparts, but individually they were formidable. General Marshall, in particular, greatly impressed me. He was a big man in every sense of the word, and utterly selfless. It was impossible to imagine his doing anything petty or mean, or shrinking from any duty, however distasteful. He carried himself with great dignity. At first he seemed somewhat cold and aloof; he never used nicknames or Christian names. Eisenhower was never Ike; Dill was never Jack. But he had a warm heart. He once admitted to me that the most painful part of his job was to have to tell officers, some of them his close friends, that they could expect no further employment. His integrity was unshakable, and anything in the nature of intrigue or special pleading was anathema. To a senator, who rang up to suggest that a certain officer should be promoted, his reply was ruthless. 'Mr Senator, the best service that you can do for your friend is to avoid any mention of his name to me.' Marshall will go down to history as one of the great military organisers of all time. Under his guiding hand, the pre-war army of a few hundred thousand men was expanded into a mighty force of several millions. As a picker of men he was remarkably successful. His selection of Eisenhower, a recently-promoted brigadier-general, to com-

[1] Commander Thompson, RN, Equerry to the Prime Minister.

mand all the American troops in Europe, was a stroke of genius; and nearly all his appointments to high command were vindicated by results.

In the First World War, he had served on General Pershing's staff on the Western Front. Like almost everyone, both American and British, who fought in the main theatre, he regarded our failure at the Dardanelles as well-deserved retribution for an unjustifiable strategic gamble; and he condemned the expeditions to Salonika and Palestine, etc., as diversionary debauches. In the Second World War, he used all his influence to prevent the slightest deviation from the principle of concentration of all available force at the decisive point. His supreme object was to attack across the Channel as soon as possible, and in as great strength as possible; and he vigorously opposed any enterprises elsewhere as wasteful and dangerous dissipations of force. He failed to prevent the expedition to French North-West Africa in November 1942; but it may well be that his consistency and single-mindedness prevented the postponement of our assault on Europe beyond June 1944.

He was modest, simple and very human. One morning, General Leslie Groves, who was in charge of expenditure on atomic research, asked to see him at a very early hour. After a short delay he was shown into Marshall's room, and reported that a further half-billion[1] dollars were immediately required. Marshall signed the authorisation without a moment's hesitation, and then said: 'I owe you an explanation for having kept you waiting. I was busy making out an order for seeds for my garden. The bill amounts to $3.50.' His loyalty and devotion to duty were absolute. In September 1945, I dined with him in his official house at Fort Myer a few days before he was due to retire. He told me how much he longed for his cottage in Leesburg, Virginia, and brushed aside my suggestion that he was unlikely to remain there undisturbed for very long. Within a fortnight, he was in Chungking. He told me the story three years later. He was hanging pictures in his cottage, when President Truman rang up on the telephone and asked him to go to China at once to try to bring together the Chinese Communist and Nationalist leaders. Marshall, without further parley, replied 'Yes.' After eight weary months of fruitless endeavour, he once more went into retirement, only to be

[1] The total cost of producing the bomb was estimated at two billion dollars.

recalled again early in 1947 to become Secretary of State. At that time, Europe was disunited, disarmed and almost bankrupt. It was the Marshall Plan which saved the situation, and laid the foundations on which the North Atlantic Alliance was built. Marshall retired from the State Department in 1949, but in the following year he was yet again recalled to public service — this time as Secretary of Defence. Churchill once described him as 'perhaps the greatest Roman of them all.' History may well endorse that verdict.

Admiral Ernest King, the naval member of the Joint Chiefs of Staff, was a very different character. He was as tough as nails and carried himself as stiffly as a poker. He was blunt and stand-offish, almost to the point of rudeness. At the start, he was intolerant and suspicious of all things British, especially the Royal Navy; but he was almost equally intolerant and suspicious of the American Army. War against Japan was the problem to which he had devoted the study of a lifetime, and he resented the idea of American resources being used for any other purpose than to destroy Japanese. He mistrusted Churchill's powers of advocacy, and was apprehensive that he would wheedle President Roosevelt into neglecting the war in the Pacific. Like Marshall, King was a great organiser. Under his leadership, the United States Navy expanded with unprecedented speed into the most powerful in the world. The story goes that when an American fleet entered the Mediterranean some three or four years after the end of the war, the Admiral in command signalled to his British counterpart: 'Greetings to the second largest Navy in the world.' To which the British Admiral replied: 'Welcome to the second best Navy in the world.' As we all got to know each other better, King mellowed and became much more friendly. The last time I saw him was at a big official dinner in Potsdam in July 1945 when, to my amazement, he proposed my health in very flattering terms. I was as proud as a subaltern getting his first mention in despatches.

The third member of the Joint Chiefs of Staff, General Arnold, was a veteran airman, with an unlimited belief in air power. He was in a difficult position. He was a member of the American Joint Chiefs of Staff; but, since there was no independent Air Force in the United States, he was under Marshall's command. Consequently, he spoke very little at Combined Chiefs of Staff meetings. But he did splendid work behind the scenes, and the friendship and confidence between him and Portal enabled many difficulties to be ironed out. He was always cheerful and smiling. His nickname 'Hap' was a natural. But he could be tough when occasion required, notably when he fought, and won, his battle for the day bomber. The farewell message which the British Chiefs sent to him on his retirement expressed what we all felt about him. 'From the first visit to England in the days of our loneliness and adversity right up to the hour of victory, you have proved a staunch and generous friend.' Hap died shortly after the war ended. If any man had worked himself to death, it was he.

The Joint Chiefs of Staff remained together until the end of the war, except for the addition of Admiral Leahy as Chairman in December 1942. When one recalls the number of changes which Lincoln had to make before he found General Grant, President Roosevelt must be accounted fortunate in his original choice of military advisers.

The President and the Prime Minister returned to Washington on the early morning of 21 June. It was my fifty-fifth birthday. I reported to the Prime Minister at the White House shortly after his arrival, and he told me that he had reached a very satisfactory agreement with the President about TUBE ALLOYS (the code name for the atom bomb). He also said that he had had a few words with the President about GYMNAST[1] and had given him a note on the subject. He hoped that the problem would be discussed in the course of the day. I had never met the President, and was taken to his study to pay my respects. Scarcely had we entered the room, when a secretary came in with a telegram. Roosevelt read it quickly and passed it without a word to Churchill. It announced the fate of Tobruk. This was a hideous and totally unexpected shock, and for the first time in my life, I saw the Prime Minister wince. On his instructions, I left the room and made for his office at the other end of the building, to find out whether there was any confirmation of the news. On the way, it crossed my mind that it was Auchinleck's birthday as well as my own. Poor Claude! What a horrible anniversary! I wondered what he would do. Would he take command of the Eighth Army himself? I hoped so. Would he stand at Mersa Matruh, or go back to the Alamein position? I uttered a silent prayer that he might be given a right judgment. His courage and fighting spirit I took for granted. My

[1] The original code name for operations against North-West Africa.

thoughts were interrupted by a secretary emerging from the Prime Minister's office with a telegram from Admiral Harwood, now Commander-in-Chief of the Mediterranean Fleet. He confirmed that Tobruk had surrendered, and added that, in view of the deterioration of the situation, he was sending the Eastern Fleet south of the Suez Canal. I returned to the President's study and handed the telegram to the Prime Minister. For a moment or two no one spoke. The silence was broken by President Roosevelt. In six monosyllables he epitomised his sympathy with Churchill, his determination to do his utmost to sustain him, and his recognition that we were all in the same boat. 'What can we do to help?' Churchill asked for some Sherman tanks to be sent to the Middle East at once. Marshall was summoned. He could easily have made difficulties. The only Sherman tanks immediately available had just been issued to the 1st US Armoured Division. But he did not hesitate. 'The British must have them.' Three hundred Sherman tanks and a hundred 105 mm. guns were at once despatched to the Middle East in six of America's fastest ships. They arrived in time to play a big part in the victory of Alamein.

It was at moments like this that one realised what a priceless asset the Allies possessed in the intimate friendship and mutual understanding between Roosevelt and Churchill. Any mistrust which there may have been in those early days between the British and American Chiefs of Staff did not extend to their political masters. 'No one could have a better or sturdier ally than that old Tory,' said the President to Eisenhower.[1] 'I have formed the very highest regard and admiration for the President,' wrote Churchill during their first meeting in Washington. 'His breadth of view, resolution and his loyalty to the common cause are beyond all praise.' [2] It is interesting to consider what might have happened if the business which they put through in a matter of minutes in the White House had been handled through normal official channels. A desperate appeal for tanks might have come from General Auchinleck to the CIGS. The General Staff would have said to themselves: 'There are none available here, but there is just a chance that Washington might be able to help.' A telegram would have gone to the Pentagon, and the probable reaction

[1] Eisenhower: *Crusade in Europe.*
[2] Telegram of 3 January 1942 to Lord Privy Seal.

would have been, 'We are sorry that we cannot do anything at the moment. The only available Shermans have just been issued to our own troops, and it would be impossible to take them away. But we will do our best to send you a consignment as soon as they come off the production line.' The same sort of argument would have gone on about the provision of the necessary shipping. No doubt the Americans would have ultimately let us have some Sherman tanks, and the American Shipping Administration would have ultimately provided the necessary shipping. But the chances of this vital equipment arriving in time would have been remote.

It had been intensely interesting to see Roosevelt and Churchill together at close quarters. There was something so intimate in their friendship. They used to stroll in and out of each other's rooms in the White House, as two subalterns occupying adjacent quarters might have done. Both of them had the spirit of eternal youth. Both were the spokesmen of democracy. Both had superlative courage. But Churchill never allowed himself to forget that Roosevelt was the head of a State as well as head of a Government, and never failed to pay him the deference that was due to his position.

In the course of the next twenty-four hours, three conferences were held in the President's room; but everyone's thoughts were on the disaster in the Egyptian Desert, and the discussions centred round the steps which should be taken to restore the situation. The problem of a Second Front in North-West Africa, which the Prime Minister had come to Washington to settle, was scarcely mentioned.

The British and American newspapers were filled with stories of our crushing defeat, and criticisms of the Prime Minister. The American papers carried banner headlines. 'CHURCHILL FACES STORMY SESSION WHEN HOUSE CONVENES.' 'BRITISH IRE IS HIGH. CHURCHILL UNDER FIRE.' Many organs of the British Press were equally critical. It is hard for a leader who is representing his country abroad on a mission of vital importance to be pilloried by his own countrymen, and Churchill was not altogether joking when he said that he was the unhappiest Englishman in America since General Burgoyne on the day of his surrender at Saratoga. But he refused to be stampeded into rushing home at once, and insisted on carrying out his visit to Fort Jackson in South Carolina.

It was an interesting and instructive day. In the morning we saw a battalion do a parachute drop. This was a competent, professional performance. In the afternoon, we were shown a brigade of young soldiers doing a field firing exercise with ball ammunition. The troops were obviously very green; and in reply to a question by the Prime Minister, I ventured the opinion that it would be murder to pit them against continental soldiery. Churchill agreed that they were still immature, but added that they were magnificent material who would soon train on. The battles which they fought in Europe two years later showed how right he was.

The next night we took off from Baltimore in the Boeing Clipper. Churchill was in splendid form. 'Now for England, home, and — a beautiful row,' was his farewell remark to Hopkins. His last act before leaving the White House had been to send Auchinleck a message of encouragement. 'You have my entire confidence, and I share your responsibilities to the full.' Would many Prime Ministers facing a Vote of Censure have been so considerate, loyal and generous to the commander whose defeat had caused this political storm?

Five days later Churchill faced a restive and critical House of Commons. For close on three years there had been an almost unbroken record of defeat all over the world. The recent disaster in the Desert was the last straw. The Debate lasted two days and brought little credit to those who took part in the attack on the Government. Nearly all of them seemed unable to recognise that our misfortunes were largely the result of our unpreparedness for war. Nearly all of them put the blame on the one man who had been primarily responsible for our survival and was shortly to lead us out of the valley of the shadow. Nearly all of them appeared to have elementary ideas about the conduct of total war. None of the proposals which they put forward were of any great value. But there was one that had at least the merit of originality. It was that British generals should be removed from their commands, and that Czechs, Poles and Frenchmen should be put in charge of British troops until we could produce trained commanders of our own.

The Prime Minister's winding up speech was remarkable for its restraint; but he was insistent that there should be a division. The Vote of Censure had been given world-wide publicity, and it was essential that the whole world should be left in no doubt of the extent to which it represented the opinion of Parliament. The motion was defeated by 475 to 25. 'Good for you,' wired President Roosevelt. 'More power to you,' added Hopkins.

Shortly after our return from Washington, General Eisenhower arrived in London as Commanding General of the European Theatre of Operations, United States Army. He was a recently promoted major-general, and unknown, even in America, outside his own profession. Little did we foresee what peerless services he was destined to render to the cause of freedom. I was surprised that so junior an officer had been appointed to such an important command, but directly I set eyes on him, I understood some of the reasons. He was tremendously alert, and seemed completely sure of himself; at the same time there was no trace of conceit or pomposity. Frankness, sincerity and friendliness were written all over him. But, with it all, he was master in his own house, and he could be firm to the point of ruthlessness if the occasion demanded.

One of his first questions to me was a revelation. Whom should he see about making arrangements to ensure that good relations were established between his troops and the civil population in England? His soldiers were apt to regard themselves as crusaders who had come over to Europe to help us out of a mess, and to think that they should be treated with the utmost generosity and consideration. The British people, on the other hand, who had been fighting alone for the best part of two years, would tend to resent the discomforts and deprivations which the arrival of these self-styled crusaders would inevitably involve. Unless something were done to enable both sides to understand each other, there was bound to be irritation and bad feeling. He would like to make an immediate call on the Briton who could help to solve this sort of problem. I told him that Brendan Bracken was the man to see, and he went straight to his office. It struck me as remarkable that one whose previous experience had been almost exclusively confined to the military field should have so broad an outlook and such thoughtfulness for the civilian population.

From the outset he regarded Anglo-American friendship almost as a religion. Shortly after his arrival it was brought to my notice that a certain senior American officer was apt, under the influence of alcohol, to boast that his troops would show the British how to fight. He was a first-class soldier and popular with everyone, but his unguarded talk was beginning to give rise to a good deal of indignation. It seemed only fair to Eisenhower to bring the matter to his notice in the strictest privacy. When I had finished my story, he went white with rage, summoned one of his aides, and told him to arrange for the officer in question to report at his office at seven the next morning. 'I'll make the son of a bitch swim back to America,' he hissed, as the aide left the room. I begged him to do no such thing. I told him that, in reporting this very delicate matter, I had hoped that he would do no more than rebuke the offender, and that, if I had known that he was going to take such extreme measures, I would have remained silent. After a pause he promised to heed my intercession. But he then turned his wrath on me. 'If we are not going to be frank with each other, however delicate the topic, we will never win this war.'

The Prime Minister at once proceeded to establish close relations with the new American commander. Luncheon on Tuesdays and dinner on Fridays became standing engagements. The two men took to each other from the start, and their mutual esteem and affection grew with the passage of time. They had many arguments, and Eisenhower always stood up sturdily for his own point of view; but however heated the discussion, he never failed to pay Churchill the deference due to his age, experience and position. Nor did Churchill ever fail to appreciate Eisenhower's special position as the senior American commander in Europe.

Meanwhile no decisions had as yet been reached about the operations which were to be carried out in 1942. The British would have nothing to do with SLEDGEHAMMER; the Americans would have nothing to do with anything else. In mid-July, therefore, President Roosevelt despatched the American Chiefs of Staff and Mr Hopkins to London, with orders to clinch matters one way or the other, and a series of discussions took place at Chiefs of Staff level. The Americans argued that a landing in Europe in 1942 was essential; they had understood that we had agreed to this in April, but had now apparently weakened on it. They said that there was a danger of Russia collapsing or making a separate peace, and that public opinion in America was getting impatient. Unless the vast American army was very soon engaged in Europe, there would be a demand for all

American resources to be concentrated in the Pacific. They insisted that the only way of knocking out Germany was to attack across the English Channel, and that all operations elsewhere were irrelevant. Marshall admitted the dangers and difficulties, but argued that, if a great business man were faced with the choice between pulling off a big coup like this and going bankrupt, he would certainly have a go — and would probably succeed.

The British Chiefs of Staff contended that a considerable landing in France was out of the question unless the Germans were completely demoralised, and of this there was not yet the slightest sign. They pointed out that, even if they had overestimated the difficulties of getting ashore, all our energies and the bulk of our resources would be involved in maintaining the bridge-head throughout the winter. The bombing of Germany would have to be much curtailed, and we were bound to lose so much shipping, particularly landing craft, that the chances of a successful mass invasion in 1943 would be ruined. They asserted that the Germans already had sufficient forces in France to deal with anything that we could send across, and that nothing that we could do in the way of a Second Front in Europe would compel them to bring back a single division from the east. They dismissed the possibility of Russia making a separate peace. As Churchill once said: 'The hatreds between the two races have become a sanitary cordon in themselves.' Stalin's only alternative to fighting on was slavery. Even if there were a risk of his giving in, we would not help matters by committing suicide. Arguments raged back and forth. Neither side would give way. Finally the American Chiefs of Staff telegraphed to the President that a dead-lock had been reached. Roosevelt took the news philosophically. Perhaps he had always had a warm corner in his heart for North Africa. Anyway, he at once sent instructions to his advisers that, since they were unable to persuade the British to undertake SLEDGEHAMMER, they must reach a decision on some operation in another part of the world, which would involve considerable American forces being engaged with the enemy in 1942. In the face of this order from their Commander-in-Chief, Marshall and King agreed that French North-West Africa was the best solution, and before they left our shores, the decision had been taken that GYMNAST, re-christened TORCH, should be launched at the end of October, and that the Commander-in-Chief should be General Eisenhower. This decision was one of the turning-points in the war.

Before detailed planning could be started, a number of basic decisions were necessary. Where were the landings to be made? What forces were to be employed? Where were these forces to come from? There was considerable disputation on all these questions. The Americans argued on the following lines: 'We think that there is a good chance that American troops will be welcomed by Vichy forces, whereas we are sure that British troops would be fiercely resisted. Initially therefore, the invasion must be exclusively American. We have sufficient combat troops and craft for only two landings. One of these must be at Casablanca; the second should be at Oran. We insist on taking Casablanca, because it is essential to have a shore base on the north-west coast of Africa outside the Mediterranean, as an insurance against the danger of the Straits of Gibraltar being closed to us by the Germans.' The Americans seemed to regard the Mediterranean as a trap which might be sprung at any moment. With us, familiarity had bred contempt. We scarcely gave it a thought.

The British views were very different: 'We look on the capture of the Tunis and Bizerta area as the primary objective of TORCH, and it is therefore essential that one of the initial landings must be made at least as far east as Algiers. Otherwise we would be making a present of Tunis, and possibly Algiers itself, to the Germans. We agree that the troops of 'perfidious Albion' would be fiercely resisted, but we are not at all sure that Uncle Sam will be given the friendly welcome which you imagine. Nevertheless we entirely agree that initially at any rate the expedition must as far as possible look like an American enterprise. On the other hand, the French are bound to know very soon that the British are taking part, since we will be providing a large number of naval and air units. Why not go one step further, and allow us to provide the balance of resources that would permit three simultaneous landings to be made? We do not share your apprehensions about the possibility of the Straits of Gibraltar being closed. In any case, the possession of remote Casablanca, with its ramshackle single-line railway to Oran, would not provide a very effective insurance. Surf conditions at Casablanca may make a landing impossible, and we ourselves would prefer not to go there; but if you insist on doing so, we, for our part, must insist on a landing at

Algiers. We suggest that this might be entrusted to British troops, with an American contingent in the van to give the operation an American flavour.'

The Combined Chiefs of Staff might have continued their arguments until Domesday had it not been for the personal intervention of the President and the Prime Minister. As a result of their exchange of telegrams, it was decided that there were to be three landings — at Casablanca, Oran and Algiers — and that D-Day for TORCH should be at the end of October or early November. Eisenhower and his Staff could now go full steam ahead with detailed planning. There was not a moment to be lost.

It was about this time that Major-General Bedell Smith arrived in London as Eisenhower's Chief of Staff. He and Vivian Dykes had been the original Joint Secretaries of the Combined Chiefs of Staff in Washington. They had got along famously and had given the new organisation a splendid start. Bedell Smith had a face like a bulldog and many of the characteristics of that attractive breed. He was a master of his profession — business-like, decisive and self-confident; and in spite of a not too strong constitution, his hours of work were prodigious. He was the perfect complement to Eisenhower, to whom he was the soul of loyalty and devotion. He had a direct manner and a quick temper, which he was wont to vent on friend and foe alike. But the storm generally blew over quickly and left not a vestige of ill-feeling. Many years after the war, Eisenhower told me that in one respect he had been the luckiest commander in history. He had had the two best Staff officers that any nation could produce — Bedell Smith throughout the Second World War, and Al Gruenther throughout his period of service with NATO. Having served with both officers, I do not find myself in disagreement with that verdict.

Norfolk House, St James's Square, where TORCH Headquarters was located, became the scene of a remarkably successful experiment in inter-Allied co-operation. When Foch was appointed Supreme Commander on the Western Front in 1918, he was served by a mere handful of French officers — his *'famille militaire'* as he called them — and there were no foreigners on his staff. In 1939-40, General Gamelin, Commander-in-Chief of the Allied armies in France, and later General Weygand, had much the same arrangement. But now Eisenhower was served — and TORCH was being planned — by a completely integrated Anglo-American staff, in which officers of all three Services of both countries were closely intermingled in every branch. The prophets of gloom protested that an organisation composed of such diverse elements could never be efficient, and they might have proved right if it had not been for Eisenhower. He made it clear from the outset that his Staff had to be a closely-knit team, and that any quarrelling between the nationals of the two countries was a cardinal sin which would be mercilessly punished. By way of strengthening his hand, he was told that, if any British officer serving under him proved unsatisfactory, he was at liberty to get rid of him without reference to the British authorities. On the first occasion that a serious fracas between an American and a British officer was reported to him, he came to the conclusion, after a careful consideration of all the evidence, that it was the American who was in the wrong. He ordered him to be dismissed from the Staff and sent back to the United States. The British officer who had been embroiled pleaded for him. 'He only called me the son-of-a-bitch, sir, and all of us have now learnt that this is a colloquial expression which is sometimes used almost as a term of endearment, and should not be taken too seriously.' To which Eisenhower replied, 'I am informed that he called you a British son-of-a-bitch. That is quite different. My ruling stands.' It did. Before very long, the nationals of both countries of his Staff worked together as harmoniously as though they had always served under the same flag. There may have been other American or British generals who could have wrought this miracle of co-operation, but I cannot name them.

Originally Eisenhower's principal British subordinates were Admiral Sir Andrew Cunningham, who was to be the naval commander of the expedition, and General Alexander, who was to command the task force which was to land at Algiers and drive on Tunis. Directly he met Alexander, Eisenhower said how grateful he was to the British for having given him a man of such great fighting experience and natural charm. A few days later, it was decided that Alexander was to replace Auchinleck as Commander-in-Chief, Middle East, and I was instructed to explain to Eisenhower what had happened, and to say that General Montgomery had been selected to be his new task force commander. In passing on this information, I laid emphasis on

Montgomery's great qualities both as a trainer of men and as a commander in the field. Scarcely had Montgomery arrived in London to take over his new appointment, when General Gott, the commander designate of the Eighth Army, was killed in the Western Desert, and the Prime Minister, who was in Cairo at the time, telegraphed for Montgomery to take his place. Once more I had to break the news to Eisenhower and tell him, with suitable regrets for yet another change of plan, that General Kenneth Anderson, who had now been selected for TORCH, had proved himself a fine commander in the retreat to Dunkirk. Eisenhower remarked, rather sadly, 'You seem to have a lot of Wellingtons in your Army. Tell me, frankly, are the British serious about TORCH?'

As an illustration of the extent to which Eisenhower had already gained the confidence of the British Government, the directive issued to General Anderson was markedly different from those which were issued to Lord Haig in 1918 and to Lord Gort in 1939. The latter were instructed to carry out any order given by the French Commander-in-Chief, subject to the proviso that if any such order appeared to imperil the British Expeditionary Force, they were at liberty to appeal to the British Government *before executing it*. The instructions issued to General Anderson were couched in a very different tone. He was told that in the unlikely event of receiving an order which would give rise to a dangerous situation to his force, he was authorised to appeal to the War Office, *provided that, by doing so, no opportunity was lost and no part of the Allied force endangered*. In addition, he was enjoined to inform the Allied Commander-in-Chief before making such an appeal, and to give him his reason for doing so.

The task force for the Casablanca landing was to come direct from America, and all planning was carried out in that country. The naval commander was to be Admiral Hewitt, and the army commander was to be that colourful personality, General Patton. Since the Americans had not as yet had any practical experience of amphibious operations, they asked us to lend them a couple of planning experts. Our officers found, on arrival, that the Admiral's and General's headquarters were miles apart, and suggested that everyone working on plans which had to be so closely interlocked should be under the same roof. On this General Patton exploded. 'Go anywhere near that bunch of rattlesnakes? Not I!'

The success of Torch largely depended on achieving complete surprise. Considering the magnitude of the preparations not only in the United States and the United Kingdom, but also at Gibraltar — within a stone's throw of spy-infested La Linea — it is a sorry reflection on the German Intelligence Service that they had no suspicion of what was afoot until the landings actually started. We ourselves had many anxious moments. First, there was the case of an aircraft which was shot down *en route* to Gibraltar. A naval officer who was killed in the crash was carrying a letter from General Bedell Smith to the Governor of Gibraltar which would have given the show away if it had fallen into enemy hands. His body was washed ashore near Cadiz, and handed over to us by the Spaniards. The pocket containing the compromising letter was still buttoned up, and the envelope was still sealed: but who was to know that the Spaniards had not allowed the Germans to extract and photograph it? The security experts were confident that the presence of sand in the buttonhole of the pocket was conclusive proof that the document had not been tampered with. We breathed again.

Shortly afterwards, a confidential secretary, contrary to all regulations and elementary common sense, took home with him a copy of a particularly top-secret Minute from the Prime Minister to the Chiefs of Staff, suggesting that an additional landing should be made at Bône, 200 miles or so east of Algiers. This document, of all others, fell out of his pocket as he boarded his bus, and was picked up by a charwoman. She took it at once to an airman who was lodging with her, who was sensible enough to go to the Air Ministry and demand to see the Chief of the Air Staff. Again there arose the question whether the document had been seen by alien eyes; and again the security authorities were reassuring. The fact that it had started to rain just as the secretary had boarded the bus, and that the paper was quite dry when recovered, was taken as proof that it had only been on the ground for a matter of seconds and that no leakage could have taken place. Once again we breathed.

Lastly, there was an incident which might have been not only dangerous but also extremely embarrassing. The maps of North Africa which were to be issued to the troops were printed in a country town and distributed by lorry to the various military headquarters. The covering of one of the packages broke loose, and the contents were scattered all over the road. The local police, seeing that they were maps of French North Africa, rang up Free French Head-quarters in London to find out whether they were theirs. Inasmuch as the French had been deliberately kept in ignorance of the impending operations, it would have been very awkward if the officer to whom the inquiry was addressed had asked to see a copy of the map. Fortunately he suspected nothing, and answered in the negative. Once again we breathed a sigh of relief. Our guardian angel had been looking after us — perhaps better than we deserved.

Apart from the haunting fear of leakages, there were many other grounds for anxiety in the weeks of waiting. Would everything be ready in time? Would the surf at Casablanca permit a landing? Would the paratroops flying all the way from England be able to secure the vital airfield at Algiers? Would the Vichy French resist the invasion *à l'outrance*? As to this, our hopes were raised in an unexpected way. Some senior French officers in North Africa had told Mr Murphy, the United States' political officer in that part of the world, that American troops would be welcomed, and asked for an American general to be sent to Algiers to discuss plans. General Mark Clark was deputed for the duty by Eisenhower, and was smuggled ashore from a submarine. The story of his hair-raising adventures has been told in his own book.[1] He returned with the good news that certain highly-placed French officers would do their best to ensure that our entry into Algiers would not be resisted.

Meanwhile our affairs were prospering elsewhere in Africa. Rommel's thrust for Cairo had been decisively repulsed. The initiative in the Western Desert was now in our hands, and a massive offensive by the Eighth Army under General Montgomery was timed to start about a fortnight before the TORCH landings. If this were successful, the whole situation in the Middle East would be transformed. The Afrika Korps would be destroyed; the Mediterranean would be cleared; Malta would be saved. A wonderful fortnight lay ahead. On 23 October Montgomery struck. The next day, the TORCH Armada

[1] General Mark Clark: *Calculated Risk.*

sailed from England. A week later we learned that Montgomery's victory was decisive and that Rommel, who had returned posthaste from sick leave in Germany, was on the run. On 4 November I said goodbye to Eisenhower in London, and on the following day he set off for Gibraltar. Three days later, the landings at Algiers, Casablanca and Oran were successful though stubbornly opposed by orders of the Vichy authorities. Our local friends — notably Generals Mast and Bethouart — did their best for us, but each side suffered some 3,000 casualties before hostilities ceased on 11 November. The tide had turned, and ultimate victory now seemed certain.

CHAPTER XX

Auchinleck and After

1941–1942

I N M Y desire to tell the story of TORCH consecutively from the moment of its conception to the initial landings, I have gone far ahead of the war in other theatres. I must now return to the Western Desert.

On 30 June 1941 General Sir Claude Auchinleck arrived in Cairo to assume command in the Middle East. Our last offensive in the Western Desert — BATTLEAXE — had been unsuccessful, and except for Tobruk, which was besieged, the enemy held all Cyrenaica. But the Syrian affair, which was the only remaining extraneous commitment, was on the point of being successfully concluded; and with the surrender of the remnants of the Italian forces in East Africa, the Red Sea was no longer an operational area, and therefore open to American shipping. Thus the supply problem was much simplified. On the whole, therefore, Auchinleck was confronted by a less complicated task than his predecessor, General Wavell.

'The Auk,' as he was generally known, had been a marked man for many years. Following a fine record in the First World War, he had been an unqualified success, both in command and on the Staff. Yet practically the whole of his service had been spent in the East; and it speaks volumes for the universal esteem in which he was held that the appointment of a sepoy general to the all-important Middle

East command was not resented by his British Service colleagues. Auchinleck was a most impressive figure: dignified, commanding, and apparently completely self-confident. Only those who knew him well realised that he was shy and sensitive. He was as much an introvert as his political chief was an extrovert, and there were likely to be misunderstandings between them unless they got to understand each other. It would have helped matters if Auchinleck had been able to pay a visit to England before taking up his new appointment, but apparently his immediate presence was required in Cairo. It was not long before he found himself involved in a number of arguments with the Prime Minister. The main bone of contention was the date of the next offensive in the desert. Churchill, smarting under the failure of BATTLEAXE, was impatient to 'try the game again' at the earliest possible date, and he was sharply disappointed by Auchinleck's protest that he could not be ready to undertake a major operation for at least four or five months. There were soon other divergencies between them, and relations became so strained that Churchill thought it essential that they should get together in London and have a talk. Auchinleck flew home at once, and his visit went off extremely well. He succeeded in persuading the Chiefs of Staff that it would be inadvisable to mount his attack until 1 November: and although Churchill himself was unconvinced, he was favourably impressed by the strength of character, professional competence and freshness of mind of the new Commander-in-Chief.

One week-end, Auchinleck and I were together at Chequers. We had known and kept touch with each other for close on twenty years, and I thought that the best service that I could render to an old friend, for whom I had both admiration and affection, was to try to give him a close up picture of the remarkable phenomenon who was now his political chief. Here is the gist of what I said. Churchill could not be judged by ordinary standards; he was different from anyone we had ever met before, or were ever likely to meet again. As a war leader, he was head and shoulders above anyone that the British or any other nation could produce. He was indispensable and completely irreplaceable. The idea that he was rude, arrogant and self-seeking was entirely wrong. He was none of these things. He was certainly frank in speech and writing, but he expected others to be equally frank with him. To a young brigadier from Middle East

Headquarters, who had asked if he might speak freely, he replied, 'Of course. We are not here to pay each other compliments.' He was a child of nature. He venerated tradition, but ridiculed convention. When the occasion demanded, he could be the personification of dignity; when the spirit moved him, he could be a *gamin*. His courage, enthusiasm and industry were boundless, and his loyalty was absolute. No commander who engaged the enemy need ever fear that he would not be supported. His knowledge of military history was encyclopaedic, and his grasp of the broad sweep of strategy unrivalled. At the same time, he did not fully realise the extent to which mechanisation had complicated administrative arrangements, and revolutionised the problems of time and space; and he never ceased to cry out against the inordinate 'tail' which modern armies required. 'When I was a soldier,' he would say, 'infantry used to walk and cavalry used to ride. But now the infantry require motor-cars, and even the tanks have to have horse boxes to take them to battle.' He had a considerable respect for the trained military mind, but refused to subscribe to the idea that generals were infallible or had any monopoly of the military art. He was not a gambler, but never shrank from taking a calculated risk if the situation so demanded. His whole heart and soul were in the battle, and he was an apostle of the offensive. Time and again he would quote from Nelson's Trafalgar memorandum:[1] 'No captain can do very wrong if he places his ship alongside that of an enemy.' He made a practice of bombarding commanders with telegrams on every kind of topic, many of which might seem irrelevant and superfluous. I begged Auchinleck not to allow himself to be irritated by these never-ending messages, but to remember that Churchill, as Prime Minister and Minister of Defence, bore the primary responsibility for ensuring that all available resources in shipping, man-power, equipment, oil, and the rest, were apportioned between the Home Front and the various theatres of war, in the best interests of the war effort as a whole. Was it not reasonable that he should wish to know exactly how all these resources were being used before deciding on the allotment to be given to this or that theatre? He was not prone to harbouring grievances, and it was a mistake to take lasting umbrage if his criticisms were sometimes unduly harsh or even unjust. If I had done so, I should

[1] Written on board HMS *Victory* on 9 October 1805.

never have had a moment's happiness. There was much comfort to be derived from the words of St Paul: 'Whom the Lord loveth, he chasteneth.' One must remember that the way of life of the politician was very different from that of the soldier. One politician could accuse another on the floor of the House of Commons of every crime under the sun and then be seen a few minutes later having a drink with his adversary in the bar. If a soldier used similar language to another soldier, he would probably make an enemy for life.

On his return to Cairo, in August, Auchinleck went full speed ahead with plans and preparations for his attack on Rommel. The operations were to be undertaken in two distinct phases: first, the capture of Cyrenaica (Operation CRUSADER); and secondly, the capture of Tripoli (Operation ACROBAT). Now and then he used to unburden himself in long letters to me, and the last one that he wrote before the battle included a passage which revealed an aspect of modern war that I had not fully realised. 'I am not nervous about CRUSADER, but I wonder if you and those others who sit at the council table with you realise what a peculiar battle it is to be, and how everything hangs on the tactical issue of one day's fighting, and on one man's tactical ability on that one day. It is something quite different to battles as we knew them. All these months of labour and thought can be set at nought in one afternoon; rather a terrifying thought?' [1]

CRUSADER started on 17 November 1941. To begin with all went well, but after five days' fighting, it was clear that something had gone very wrong and that our armour had suffered a resounding defeat. Auchinleck went to the front himself, and found that General Sir Alan Cunningham, who had done so brilliantly in East Africa, and whom he had personally selected for the command of the Eighth Army, seemed on the verge of a nervous breakdown. He had been deeply affected by his losses in armour, and was inclined to break off the battle. Auchinleck would have none of it. He returned to Cairo at once and discussed the problem with Captain Oliver Lyttelton. What a godsend it was for the military Commander-in-Chief to have such wise and authoritative political experience at his immediate disposal. Lyttelton entirely agreed that there must be an immediate

[1] Personal letter from Auchinleck to Ismay of 6 November 1941.

change in the command of the Eighth Army, and Auchinleck acted at once. His decision was endorsed by the Prime Minister and Chiefs of Staff. I was desperately sorry for Alan Cunningham, a fine soldier and an old friend who had worked himself to a standstill; and I felt deep sympathy for Auchinleck for having to make such a hateful decision. As the great Duke of Marlborough once said: 'To relieve a general in the midst of a campaign, that is the mortal stroke.'

In London it was expected and hoped that Auchinleck would take personal control of the battle; but to the general astonishment, he appointed Major-General Ritchie, his Deputy Chief of Staff, to the command of the Eighth Army. Ritchie was a Staff Officer of the highest calibre, but he had had little or no experience of command. In addition he was junior in rank to both the corps commanders. On both these counts, it did not seem a very happy arrangement. But Auchinleck explained that Ritchie knew exactly how his mind worked: and all at home felt that he should be given a free hand. Auchinleck himself returned to the front and stayed there for ten days. He threw everything into the battle, and turned defeat into victory. Tobruk, after a siege of ten months, was relieved, and Cyrenaica was once again ours.

But Rommel was never a man to allow an opponent to exploit his gains, or even to enjoy them in peace. On 21 January 1942 he counterattacked with all the strength he could muster; and before the end of the month, the port of Benghazi, which was in process of being developed with a view to the advance on Tripoli, had to be evacuated, and most of western Cyrenaica was again in enemy hands. However, we still held Tobruk.

In reporting these operations to the House of Commons, the Prime Minister caused a good deal of surprise by paying a handsome tribute to Rommel's leadership. This was in keeping with his impulsive and chivalrous nature. Had he not shocked the Tory Front Bench in his maiden speech forty years previously by his favourable reference to the enemy fighting in South Africa? 'If I were a Boer fighting in the field, and if I were a Boer I hope I should be fighting in the field . . .' Nevertheless it was scarcely wise to lead the Army of the Nile to believe that the enemy were commanded by a superman.

It almost goes without saying that the Prime Minister was feverishly impatient for Auchinleck to take the offensive again at the earliest possible moment. He could not bear the thought of our vast army in the Middle East standing idle at a time when the Soviet forces were locked in a titanic struggle along their whole front, and we ourselves were suffering disaster in the Far East. He thought that every week's delay would be in favour of Rommel. Above all, there was Malta.

'Malta, my dear sir, is in my thoughts sleeping and waking.' Thus wrote Nelson in 1799 to the Russian Minister in Palermo; and there were many who might have echoed his words in 1942. Ever since the Napoleonic Wars, the fortunes of Malta had been indissolubly bound up with our own. On a wall in Admiralty House — originally called the House of the General of the Galleys — there are engraved the names of all the great British sailors who have lived there: 1793 — Vice-Admiral Lord Hood; 1795 — Admiral Sir John Jervis; 1803 — Vice-Admiral Horatio Viscount Nelson; 1805 — Vice-Admiral Cuthbert Collingwood. Reading the list is like turning over the pages of British naval history. The loss of our great base at Singapore had been a bitter blow; but she was far away and, historically speaking, a comparative upstart. Malta was near at hand, and almost one of our kith and kin. To lose her would be almost as painful as to lose a part of England itself.

Quite apart from sentiment, Malta was a pivot of immense strategic value. Provided that we held the island, we could, and often did, fight our way through the Mediterranean, thus saving fifteen thousand miles and forty-five days on the journey round the Cape. With Malta in enemy hands, the Mediterranean route would be completely closed to us. In addition, the island provided a staging base for aircraft reinforcements *en route* for Egypt; and more important still, it constituted the only base from which our light naval forces, submarines, and aircraft could exercise continuous pressure on the Axis supply lines from Italy to North Africa. With Malta in enemy hands, or even effectively neutralised, Rommel could be reinforced far quicker than Auchinleck. Thus, this tiny island was a vital feature in the defence of our Middle East position.

At the outset of the war, Malta had been more or less defenceless against air attack, but advantage was taken of the interval before Italy came into the struggle, to increase the A-A gun defences to a considerable extent. Fighter aircraft could not however be spared at that time, and when the Italians delivered their first air attacks, the solitary defenders were three Gladiators — Faith, Hope and Charity — which chanced to be in Malta as spares for the aircraft-carrier HMS *Eagle*. They did heroic service, but could not prevent the island from being roughly buffeted. As time went on, fighter reinforcements were flown in from the aircraft-carriers *Ark Royal* and *Eagle,* and latterly the USS *Wasp*. With this constant accession to her strength, Malta was able not only to defend herself, but also to continue to serve as a base for the naval and air forces which inflicted such serious losses on the Axis supply line to Africa. But early in 1942, the Luftwaffe moved to Sicily in considerable strength and made a supreme effort to paralyse the island. Convoy after convoy paid terrible forfeits, and by the end of April, the supply position was so critical that the intrepid Dobbie, Governor of the island, had to report that if his vital needs of food and oil could not be replenished, the 'very worst might happen very soon.' Shortly afterwards, Dobbie broke down under the strain. He had built up a special position for himself in the hearts of the Maltese, and was not an easy man to follow. But Lord Gort proved an ideal successor. He was fearless, indefatigable and tough. In order to save precious petrol, his means of conveyance was a bicycle instead of a motor-car, and the sight of His Excellency the Governor pedalling furiously along the bomb-raddled streets showed the islanders that he was determined to take his full share of hardship.

At this period the inter-dependence of the struggle for Malta and the fight in the Western Desert placed the British High Command in a most awkward dilemma. Unless supplies of oil and food could reach the island in time, it was bound to fall. There would then be no base in the central Mediterranean from which naval forces and bomber aircraft could operate against the Axis supply lines between Italy and North Africa, and the difficulties of reinforcing Rommel would be so substantially reduced that it would be only a matter of time before he was strong enough to render our whole position in Egypt untenable. On the other hand, the chances of getting a convoy into Malta were remote unless it could be given air cover from the landing grounds in Cyrenaica, which were at present in enemy hands. It was therefore imperative for Auchinleck to recapture them by the middle of June. This he regarded as hopelessly premature. The British High Command were thus confronted with a choice of evils. Either they must order Auchinleck to attack before he thought that he could be ready, and risk a bloody repulse: or alternatively they must supinely accept the loss of Malta and the ultimate destruction of our whole position in the Middle East. They decided on the former course of action, and issued orders to Auchinleck accordingly. He protested vigorously, but eventually agreed to have a try.

In the event, the timing of the operation was taken out of his hands. On 26 May, Rommel lunged forward at lightning speed. This time there was no question in his mind of a limited advance or of a spoiling attack. His objective was nothing less than the destruction of the Eighth Army and the capture of the Nile Valley. His action was not unexpected by Auchinleck, and Ritchie was well-placed to defend himself. In the bitter fighting of the first few days, we held our own, and Rommel's plans seemed to have gone awry. But on 10 June he renewed his attacks and it was apparent, even before Churchill left for Washington, that we were getting much the worst of it. Nevertheless we all hoped that Tobruk would be held as a sally-point, while the rest of the army fell back as far as was necessary. Our hopes were not fulfilled. Tobruk surrendered, and the Eighth Army streamed back eastwards. It looked as though Egypt might soon be lost.

It was not until 25 June that General Auchinleck took personal command of the battle. How we all wished that he had done so earlier! Now that he had no armour to guard his southern flank, he decided that Mersa Matruh was not defensible, and continued the retreat to El Alamein, where his flanks were protected on the one side by the Qattara Depression, and on the other by the Mediterranean Sea. Rommel pressed the pursuit relentlessly, but thanks largely to the magnificent work of the Royal Air Force, Auchinleck was able to concentrate his whole force at Alamein by the end of the month. He handled this critical situation with the utmost skill and courage. Rommel's every attack was bloodily repulsed. His German troops were exhausted, and many of his Italian troops were demoralised. Mussolini, who had flown over to North Africa at the end of June with a view to taking part in a triumphal entry into Cairo, abandoned hope and returned to Rome.

*   *

Towards the end of July the Prime Minister told me that he had decided to go to Egypt to see for himself what was happening in the Middle East, and that thereafter he proposed to pay a visit to Moscow to explain to Stalin that we were going to do TORCH at the end of the year, instead of attempting to form a Second Front in Europe. I did not envy him his mission, but was disappointed when he said that he wished me to stay at home.

Shortly after his arrival in Cairo, the Prime Minister notified the War Cabinet that an immediate change in the High Command in the Middle East was imperative, and proposed that Auchinleck should be replaced by Alexander. I was very sad to think how keenly the Auk would feel his dismissal. His whole life had been dedicated to the profession of arms, and he had proved himself a courageous, robust and highly-competent commander. He had retrieved the battle of Sidi Rezegh when all seemed lost, and more recently he had saved Cairo. On both occasions he had shown resolution and tactical skill of an exceptional order. But some of his decisions were not easy to understand. He may have been perfectly right to put Ritchie in temporary command of the Eighth Army when Cunningham broke down, but was it wise to keep him there as a permanency? If no one on the spot seemed the right man, there was nothing to prevent his asking for a replacement from England; and there is little doubt that even so senior a man as Alexander would have jumped at the opportunity. Again, was he not unwise to refuse to fall in with the suggestion from London that he should take personal command of the June battle as soon as it became apparent that things were going wrong? There was surely no need at that moment for him to be so apprehensive about the dangers from his northern flank. But whether he was right or wrong in these matters, Auchinleck had not enjoyed the element of luck which is essential for success, and there was an undercurrent of feeling both at home and in the Middle East that a change was advisable.

Alexander flew to Cairo at a moment's notice and took command of the Middle East on 15 August. With his generous spirit and personal admiration for Auchinleck, he would be the first to admit that the inheritance upon which he entered was an easier one than had fallen to his predecessor. Admittedly, the enemy was now at the gates of the Nile Delta, but his on-rush had been brought to a halt, and the Eighth Army was concentrated in a position of great natural strength. Reinforcements of men and equipment, including tanks of the highest quality, were pouring in from America as well as the United Kingdom. The Afrika Korps had had the stuffing knocked out of them and were almost at the end of their tether. 'It cannot go on like this for long,' wrote Rommel to his wife on 18 July. 'Otherwise the front will crack.' [1] He himself was not the Rommel of old. He was a sick man, thinking more of a hospital in Berlin than of a victorious entry into Cairo. In point of fact, he left for Germany at the end of September, and did not return until after the Alamein battle had started. Alexander was more fortunate than Auchinleck in three other respects. In the first place, he was spared any anxiety about his northern flank by the Prime Minister's Directive[2] to the effect that his prime and main duty was the destruction of Rommel. Secondly, Malta now had sufficient oil and food to carry her on for a few months, and there was no question of his being pressed to undertake a premature attack. Thirdly, and most important of all, he was given a lieutenant in the person of General Montgomery, who was the ideal commander, not only to revitalise an army which was more bewildered than defeated, but also to fight the battles which were to hurl the enemy out of Egypt once and for all. One could wish that the victor of Alamein had acknowledged that his immediate predecessor in command of the Eighth Army had paved the way for his triumph by the punishment which he had meted out to Rommel and the Afrika Korps.

The story of Malta must be continued. It has a happy ending. Despite the disasters in the desert, a supreme effort to bring succour to the island at almost any cost could not be delayed. On 11 June, two convoys set out from either end of the Mediterranean. The eastern convoy, consisting of nine merchant ships, had an escort of cruisers

---

[1] Edited by Liddell Hart: *The Rommel Papers.*

[2] Directive of 10 August:

'1. Your prime and main duty will be to take or destroy at the earliest opportunity the German and Italian Army commanded by Field Marshal Rommel together with its supplies and establishments in Egypt and Libya.

'2. You will discharge or cause to be discharged such other duties as pertain to your command without prejudice to the task described in paragraph 1, which must be considered paramount in His Majesty's interests.'

and destroyers but no battleship or aircraft-carrier, and was under the command of Admiral Vian. Three days out of Alexandria, the convoy was heavily attacked from the air, and that night Vian received information that a powerful enemy fleet, which included two modern battleships, was on its way to intercept him. Malta could not re-fuel his fighting ships, and there was not the remotest chance of a single merchant-man slipping through to Malta. He therefore had no option but to return to Alexandria. His losses had been one cruiser, three destroyers and two merchant ships.

The Gibraltar convoy consisted of eight merchant ships under escort of the A-A cruiser *Cairo,* and nine destroyers, with a supporting force which included a battleship and the carriers *Eagle* and *Argus.* Three days out of Gibraltar, they were heavily attacked by German and Italian Air Forces and suffered losses. That night the supporting force withdrew according to plan, and the next day the enemy resumed the attack by naval forces, which out-ranged our ships, and swarms of aircraft. In all, six merchant ships were sunk, but two, carrying fifteen thousand tons of precious cargo, arrived safely in Malta. For the moment, but only for the moment, the island was saved from starvation.

By the end of July, the position had again become critical, and even that happy warrior Gort could not conceal his forebodings. A letter written to me at the time gives the picture as he saw it. 'As you know we live a hand-to-mouth existence and our future, indeed our fate, depends on the success of the next convoy. Aviation spirit remains our Achilles' Heel and the Middle East Defence Committee consider it *vital* that aircraft operating from Malta should attack ships crossing the Mediterranean, despite the fact that we are regularly overspending the weekly amounts we can afford if we are to hold out to the utmost limit . . . If we run out of aviation spirit and can no longer operate fighters, the chances of getting another convoy into Malta will be very doubtful. From another angle, if the Luftwaffe again gets the upper hand, it will be very difficult indeed to get the population to withstand another phase of intensive bombing on their present short rations. I do not mean to imply that morale is bad, because I think it still remains surprisingly good, but I would be misleading you if I did not say that it is brittle.'

A desperate effort was demanded, and in mid-August, fourteen fast merchant ships, with a very powerful escort, which included two battleships, three large carriers, seven cruisers and thirty-two destroyers, left Gibraltar. It was difficult to keep out of the Map Room in the days that followed, and the news which greeted one was almost invariably bleak. Three days out of Gibraltar, enemy air forces attacked continuously and furiously. The carrier *Eagle* was sunk, and the carrier *Indomitable* damaged. Once in the Narrows, there was little danger of attack by capital ships, and our battleships withdrew, leaving the cruisers and destroyers to shepherd the flock. Thereafter the enemy assaults by aircraft, U-boat and E-boat increased in intensity. At one time we who followed the struggle in the Map Room almost gave up all hope. The cruisers *Manchester* and *Cairo* were reported sunk, two other cruisers damaged, and practically all the merchant ships seemed either to have been sent to the bottom of the sea or crippled. But at last the thrilling news arrived that three survivors had reached the Grand Harbour and were already being unloaded; and on the next day a fourth, the *Brisbane Star,* which was thought to have been lost, limped in on her own. On the following day there was the best news of all. The American tanker *Ohio* had arrived in the tow of a destroyer. She was scarcely afloat, but her precious cargo was intact. Her captain and crew had upheld the glorious traditions of the American merchant marine. Never again was Malta in grave danger, or even in serious want. Once more, she became a thorn in the side of our enemies.

1942 was a year of extraordinary contrasts. It opened on a scene of hideous calamity. The American Fleet had been crippled at Pearl Harbor. The *Prince of Wales* and *Repulse* were at the bottom of the China Sea. The *Ark Royal* and *Barham* had been sunk in the Mediterranean. The *Valiant* and *Queen Elizabeth* had been put out of action for several months by one-man submarines in Alexandria harbour. The light forces based on Malta had been practically annihilated in a minefield. The German armies were on the outskirts of Leningrad, and only twenty miles from Moscow. Hong Kong had fallen. Even worse was to follow in the early months of the New Year. Singapore, the Dutch East Indies, Burma and the Philippines, all passed into Japanese hands. India, Ceylon, Australia and New Zealand were wide open to invasion. Nearly all that was left of the

Allied naval forces in the Far East, including the Dutch cruisers *De Ruyter* and *Java,* was destroyed in the Battle of the Java Sea. The news arrived when the Pacific War Council[1] was in session at 10, Downing Street. For the Dutch, the destruction of almost the last remnant of their naval power was a particularly bitter blow, and on hearing the report Field Marshal Smuts left his seat and moved into the chair next to Dr Gerbrandy, Prime Minister of Holland. 'At times like these, we Dutchmen stick together,' he said.

The German armies continued their advance into Russia. Sebastopol had fallen and the Caucasus and Stalingrad were threatened. The Arctic convoys had been costing us dear, and convoy PQ 17 had twenty-three ships sunk out of thirty-four. In the first six months of the year, shipping losses in the Atlantic alone amounted to over three million tons. Nearer home, the escape of the battle-cruisers *Scharnhorst* and *Gneisenau* from Brest to Germany, aroused a storm of criticism. The position at Malta was becoming daily more desperate, and Rommel was at the gates of Cairo. So much for the first months of 1942.

But there was to be a complete reversal of fortune. On 23 October, Montgomery routed Rommel at the Battle of Alamein, and by Christmas the Eighth Army had got safely round the fatal Agheila corner, and were not far off Tripoli. The TORCH landings were successful, and although Eisenhower's advance on Tunis had been held up by bad weather and was later to be checked at the Kasserine Pass, it could only be a matter of time before Tunis was captured, and the whole of North Africa cleared. Malta had been re-injected with life and could not only live but fight. The Japanese had been forestalled in Madagascar. Thanks to the American victory at the Battle of Midway early in June, Australia, New Zealand, India and Ceylon were secure. The German thrust on Stalingrad had bogged down and was destined to end in appalling disaster. Bomber Command were now

[1] In order to ensure that those countries which were concerned with events in the Far East, but not represented on the Combined Chiefs of Staff, were kept continuously informed and consulted about all that was happening in that area, two Pacific War Councils had been set up — the one in Washington under President Roosevelt, and the other in London under the Prime Minister. The Netherlands, Australia, New Zealand, India and Burma were represented on both bodies. Neither Council had any responsibility for the executive conduct of the war. This remained the business of the Combined Chiefs of Staff.

strong enough to launch a thousand aircraft against Germany on a single night, and the US Air Force was almost ready to join in the massive destruction by daylight bombing.

As we look back on that period, we can never be sufficiently thankful that the three Axis powers had from the start pursued their own narrow, selfish ends, and that they had no integrated Plan, and no machinery corresponding to the Combined Chiefs of Staff for the supreme direction of their war efforts. Had they consulted together before the infamy of Pearl Harbor, it would surely have been decided that Japan should first drive westwards against the British, leaving the United States to be dealt with later, and that the Germans and Italians should attack the British in the Middle East from the west and north simultaneously, and leave Russia alone for the time being.

Mr Churchill has called the volume of his memoirs which deals with this period of contrasts, *The Hinge of Fate*. The part which he himself played in turning that hinge should not be forgotten. Directly Hitler attacked Russia, he unhesitatingly proclaimed a policy of all help to the Soviet, and lost no time in concerting with President Roosevelt the measures by which immediate effect should be given to that policy. Had it not been for this prompt intervention the campaign in Russia might have taken a different course. Directly after Pearl Harbor, he dashed off to Washington, accompanied by his military advisers. His visit resulted in the confirmation of the policy that Germany should be treated as Enemy No. 1, and Japan contained until Germany had been defeated; and also in the setting up of the Combined Chiefs of Staff, which was to prove the most effective machinery for the co-ordination of Allied war effort which history has ever seen. The speech which he made to Congress at that time gave the American people a closer understanding of the British case than they had had before, and did much to cement a partnership which, in spite of occasional differences, was to endure to the end. In his anxiety not to lose a moment in grappling with the problems which faced him in England, he undertook the hazards of the direct flight from Bermuda to the United Kingdom.

Then came TORCH. Churchill not only conceived the idea, but pressed it so persistently that President Roosevelt overruled his advisers and agreed to its adoption. Even then, there was still opposition at the lower levels in Washington, and the British and American

Chiefs of Staff were at loggerheads on the question of the ports of entry. The expedition might never have taken place, and would almost certainly have been dangerously delayed, if Churchill had not again intervened with President Roosevelt and convinced him that one of the initial landings must be at least as far east as Algiers. He rallied Parliament and the people in the face of a succession of disasters which would have brought down any other administration. At the end of July, he dashed out to the Middle East. He saw for himself that drastic changes were required, and had them immediately enforced. Finally, he bearded Stalin in his den and convinced him, so far as it was ever possible to convince that obstinate man, that Alamein and TORCH were a pretty good substitute for a premature Second Front in Europe.

History may acclaim the year 1940, in which Churchill came to the leadership of the country and rallied his countrymen, as Churchill's finest hour. But many people will always regard the fourteen months which elapsed between the German attack on Russia and the Battle of Alamein as the period of his greatest achievement. In the one case, he steeled a nation to defy defeat; in the other, he laid the foundation of Allied victory.

CHAPTER XXI

The Casablanca Conference

1943

NINETEEN FORTY-THREE was Conference Year. In January, Casablanca; in May, Washington; in August, Quebec; in October, Moscow (Conference of Foreign Ministers); in November, Cairo (Conference with the Turks); in November and December, Cairo and Teheran. I had the good fortune to attend all of them, with the result that I spent no less than twenty-four weeks out of England, and travelled over forty thousand miles.

At the end of 1942, the President felt that it was high time for the three major Allies to decide on their future strategy, and suggested that military representatives of Russia, the United States and the United Kingdom should be assembled to review the situation, and make recommendations. The Prime Minister demurred. He said that a purely military conference would be a waste of time. The Russian generals would not have authority to engage in free discussions, and their contribution would be limited to demands for an immediate Second Front in Europe, and for more frequent and larger convoys of supplies to Russia. But he was very much in favour of a meeting of the three Heads of Government, accompanied by their military advisers, and was prepared to accept any rendez-vous which was acceptable to the other two. Roosevelt agreed, but Stalin regretted that the military situation did not permit him to leave Moscow. Accordingly, Roosevelt and Churchill decided to go ahead without him, and to hold an Anglo-American Plenary Conference as soon as possible. Casablanca was selected as the venue, and the date was fixed for 15 January.

The more junior members of the British delegation, together with cipher and secretarial staffs, left England for Casablanca early in the month on HMS *Bulolo*. This was a liner which had been specially fitted up as a headquarters ship for amphibious operations. She lay at Casablanca throughout the Conference, and provided us with all essential communications.

The remainder of the British delegation left by air on the night of 12 January, and the security authorities insisted upon extraordinary precautions. They feared that the exodus of a large party of very senior officers from a London railway terminus would give rise to speculation, and all that we were told was that we were to leave London individually by car and rendez-vous at 11 P.M. at a small village in Wiltshire, where we would get further instructions. After an early dinner at White's, I sneaked away like a thief in the night. It was a horrid journey in pitch darkness and pouring rain. On arrival at the rendez-vous I found the narrow village street cluttered up with powerful motor-cars, and the solitary policeman looked bewildered. Eventually we were marshalled into some sort of order, and set off for the airfield which, as we all suspected, turned out to be Lyneham. We were hospitably received in the officers mess, but our troubles soon started. First, we were briefed as to what we should do in the case of various unpleasant emergencies, such as forced landings and the like. Next, we were strapped into parachute harnesses and clothed in Mae Wests. Next, we were supplied with the currency of every country over which we might have to fly, together with a note in Arabic to any tribal cut-throat who might find us, promising a reward in return for our safe conduct to the nearest town. Our parting present was a gadget which was supposed to catch the night dew. It would, we were assured, save us from dying of thirst in the desert, if we were clever enough to use it properly. Hitherto I had never regarded an air journey as a dangerous excursion. This was evidently going to be an exception.

After I had been fully clothed and accoutred, there was still some time before we were due to start, and I was laid out on a sofa in front of a roasting fire. Just as heat apoplexy seemed inevitable, I was bundled into a bus and taken to a bitterly cold aircraft. It turned out to be a crudely converted Liberator, but Lord Leathers and I, as the senior passengers, were to have the comparative luxury of sleeping in the bomb racks. Before the war, Leathers had been a big figure in the business world, and I could not resist a silent chuckle at the contrast between the conditions in which he was accustomed to travel, and those of his prospective journey. Sleep was out of the question, and the next ten hours were acute discomfort. Never in my life have I been so glad to feel the wheels touch down. As I climbed down the steps backwards, I bumped into the Prime Minister. He had just arrived in another Liberator which was only slightly more comfortable than mine, and went by the name of The Commando.[1] He was walking about in high spirits and showed no trace of fatigue. Meanwhile, a harassed security officer was trying in vain to entice him into a closed car, and take him to the hermetically sealed enclave which was to be our home for the next ten days. He reminded me of an anxious nanny at the seaside trying to induce an unruly charge to come out of the water. The American Chiefs of Staff arrived the same day. Having travelled in luxuriously appointed Skymasters, they were a good deal fresher than their British opposite numbers.

The Anfa area, some four miles south of the city of Casablanca, was an ideal site for the Conference. The hotel itself and the adjacent villas had more than ample accommodation for both delegations, and two of the best-appointed villas were set apart for the President and the Prime Minister. The climate was delightful, the prospect pleasing — especially at dawn and sunset — and there was a profusion of fruit and flowers. These creature-comforts were particularly welcome after the austerity of an English winter in wartime.

The Combined Chiefs of Staff had their first meeting on the afternoon after our arrival, and thereafter continued to meet daily, and sometimes twice a day. At the outset, there seemed to be an atmosphere of veiled antipathy and mistrust. Both sides gave the impres-

---

[1] This machine was used by Mr Churchill on subsequent journeys. It was lost without trace in March 1945.

sion that they would cling obstinately to their own preconceived ideas, and there seemed little hope of reaching agreement. The British had the great advantage of knowing exactly what they wanted. First, to clear North Africa and open the Mediterranean. Secondly, to capture Sicily. Thirdly, to invade the Italian mainland and knock Italy out of the war. Fourthly, and simultaneously with the above, to intensify the bombardment of Germany and press on with preparations for the cross-Channel assault.

The Americans felt at a disadvantage in not having agreed plans to put forward. They were at sixes and sevens among themselves. Marshall wanted to get away as quickly as possible from all 'wasteful diversions,' whether in North Africa, Italy, the Greek Islands, the Balkans, or anywhere else, and to concentrate exclusively on preparations for the earliest possible cross-Channel assault. King would have been much happier if a greater proportion of American resources had been devoted to the Far East, but, as a sailor, he saw the advantages of the Mediterranean strategy proposed by the British. Arnold's paramount interest was to bomb Germany by day as well as by night every day of the week and every week of the month from all points of the compass. He was therefore inclined to favour a strategy which would provide him with more bases from which to attack. All of them were united in suspecting that the underlying motive of the British proposals to continue operations in the Mediterranean was to postpone the cross-Channel assault for as long as possible, if not to prevent it altogether. They were conscious of the fact that they themselves were not as yet a closely-knit team, and that the British were served by a more efficient machine than they as yet had had time to establish. They were nervous that they would be 'outsmarted.' It looked as though the Conference was going to provide an occasion for a battle of wits, rather than a golden opportunity for reaching agreement on the vitally urgent question of the strategy which the Alliance ought to adopt. The outlook was not promising. But Dill, who enjoyed the complete confidence of both sides, soon proved himself an invaluable intermediary and gradually a spirit of tolerance and readiness to give and take manifested itself.

The Combined Chiefs of Staff held fifteen meetings, in addition to three meetings under the Chairmanship of the President and the Prime Minister. On some of the main issues agreement was reached without difficulty. The defeat of the U-boat was to have first priority. The build-up of American forces in the United Kingdom was to continue as fast as possible. The German homeland was to be intensively bombarded by day as well as by night as soon as the American Fortress bombers were ready. Efforts were to be made to bring Turkey into the war on our side. Immediate attention was to be directed to the planning of cross-Channel operations in 1943. For this purpose a British Chief of Staff, together with an integrated US-British staff, was to be appointed and to begin work at once. It was this conclusion which led to the nomination of General F. E. Morgan as COSSAC[1] and to the preparation of the original plan for OVERLORD.

Accommodation was also reached on the more controversial issues. As regards the continuance of operations in the Mediterranean, the Americans were persuaded that the capture of Sicily would help to take the weight off Russia, in that it would intensify the threat to the Italian mainland and compel the Germans to maintain significant forces for its defence. They were also satisfied that the operation would be a valuable prelude to the cross-Channel assault. They therefore agreed that the invasion of Sicily should be undertaken as soon as possible after Tunisia had been cleared of Axis troops. But they were not as yet prepared to fall in with the British proposal that the next step should be an immediate attack on the Italian mainland.

The British Chiefs of Staff, for their part, gained a clearer understanding of American anxieties over the position in the Far East, and realised that the priority given to the defeat of Germany could not be absolute. They agreed that sufficient Allied forces should be allotted to the Far East and the Pacific theatre to maintain pressure on Japan, sustain China, and achieve a position from which a full-scale offensive could be launched against the Japanese immediately Germany was defeated. They also agreed that 15 November 1943 should be the provisional date for the start of operations to recapture Burma and reopen the Burma Road. As regards cross-Channel operations, they agreed under pressure from the Prime Minister that plans should be made to seize and hold a bridge-head on the Cotentin Peninsula, the target date being 1 August 1943, with whatever resources were available for the purpose at that time.

Scarcely had the Americans agreed to the invasion of Sicily when

[1] Chief of Staff to the Supreme Allied Commander.

the British Joint Planning Committee again pressed their original proposal that Sardinia should be the first objective. The Chiefs of Staff would have none of it, and even if they had been persuaded to alter their opinion, the Prime Minister would not have approved. 'I absolutely refuse to be fobbed off with a sardine,' he had declared when the suggestion was first mooted. He was insistent that the period of inaction after Tunisia had been cleared of the enemy must be the irreducible minimum, and that operations against Sicily should be launched with the least possible delay. North Africa was 'a springboard, not a sofa.' The Joint Planners reported that the earliest possible date for attack was 30 August. Mr Churchill declined to accept this estimate, and spent the best part of an afternoon with the planners checking the calculations on which it was based. As a result, he formed the conclusion that the invasion could start towards the end of June, or at the beginning of July at the latest; and with the approval of the President an order to that effect was issued to the Combined Chiefs of Staff. In the event, the landings in Sicily commenced at dawn on 10 July, over seven weeks earlier than the Joint Planning Committee had estimated, and they were completely successful. Those who criticise Churchill for his impatience to attack and his tendency to meddle in details, must admit that on this occasion at any rate the combination of these tiresome traits saved a delay of seven precious weeks.

Apart from the future strategy of the war, there was an immediate question of command to be settled. Eisenhower's troops advancing eastwards, and Alexander's troops advancing westwards, were now directed on the same objective — Tunisia. The time was therefore approaching when unity of command would be esential in order to ensure that their operations were closely co-ordinated. Accordingly, the Prime Minister, after consultation with the Chiefs of Staff, proposed that the Eighth Army should come under Eisenhower's command from the moment that it crossed the Tunisian border, and that Alexander should be his Deputy and exercise executive command of all Allied forces on the Tunisian front. The Americans readily agreed to this arrangement. Some people thought that since about three-quarters of the Combined Forces would be British, the Prime Minister had been too generous. Others thought that, since Alexander was to conduct the land battle, and Admiral Cunningham and Air Marshal Tedder were to command the combined naval and air forces, he had been very astute in grasping the substance and letting go the shadow.

Our only recreation at Casablanca was an occasional walk to the seashore. There was invariably a tremendous surf, and there was scarcely a single day on which a landing in small craft would have been possible. It was extremely fortunate that the day of our initial attack, 8 November, was the only one in that week on which conditions were not prohibitive. Even as it was, a number of boats were overturned. In the fighting which ensued, an American colonel of the name of William H. Wilbur won the first Congressional Medal of Honor to be awarded in the Second World War. At the small presentation ceremony in the President's villa, I found myself standing next to Wilbur's task force commander, General Patton, and I congratulated him that one of his officers had distinguished himself so conspicuously. There were tears in his eyes and a burning conviction in his voice, as he said: 'I'd love to get that medal posthumously.' Patton was emotional and impulsive by nature, and took a delight in playing to the gallery. But I have not the slightest doubt that he meant what he said, and that it was his greatest ambition to die on the field of battle. It is ironical that a man of his superlative courage should have survived the hazards of war, only to meet his end in a motor accident.

Several weeks before we left England for Casablanca, the Prime Minister had drawn the attention of the Chiefs of Staff to the great advantages to be derived by bringing Turkey into the war on our side at an early date. This was discussed and formally agreed by the Combined Chiefs of Staff, and it seemed likely that the negotiations with the Turks would be handled through the normal official channels. But a few days before the Conference ended, the Prime Minister told me that he had decided to go to Adana, and deal with the matter himself. He added that he wished me to return to London at once. I thought that the proposed trip to Turkey was somewhat dangerous, and would impose a great strain on him after all his recent exertions. But knowing that nothing I could say would turn him from his purpose, I confined myself to asking permission to look in at Algiers on my way to London, in order to talk over several problems with Eisenhower and Bedell Smith. He approved, but said that I was not to 'loll about' in Algiers for too long. I assured him that, since my association with him, I had lost the habit of 'lolling about' anywhere.

The first Plenary Conference was held on 23 January. The President and the Prime Minister approved the recommendations of the Combined Chiefs of Staff, and warmly congratulated them on the results of their labours. The military experts might truthfully have returned the compliment by saying that the results were largely due to the guidance and support which they had received from their political masters.

The next morning the President, supported by the Prime Minister, held his first and only press conference at Casablanca. It was then that he proclaimed the formula of Unconditional Surrender, which was to lead to so much criticism. His purpose has been the subject of a good deal of argument. Some people say that he wished to reassure Russia that we were with her to the death; others, that he thought that the British and American people needed a warning against any wishful thinking that peace was just round the corner; others again, that he was determined that Germany should not again be able to claim that she had not been defeated in the field. It is my personal belief that if Roosevelt had had any deep-laid scheme in mind, he would have had the implications of the formula examined by his advisers. Churchill, with whom he had discussed the idea in private conversation, would have done likewise. As it was, neither of them attached sufficient importance to it to include it in the communiqué. It might therefore be inferred that they had forgotten all about it until Roosevelt found himself facing an army of news-hungry reporters, and that the phrase then recurred to his mind and was released fortuitously. Everyone will agree that it is unwise for great men to give vent to public announcements without having their implications examined with scrupulous care. Everyone will agree that the quickest and cheapest way of winning a war is to make your enemy realise that nothing is to be gained by further fighting, and that his only sensible course is to sue for peace. A man robbed of hope will fight it out to the bitter end, and it is defeating your own object to let him think that the terms of surrender will be utterly merciless. This being so, no one will claim that the use of the formula of Unconditional Surrender at Casablanca served any good purpose. But I belong to the minority who doubt whether it made any material difference to the length of hostilities. It certainly did not prevent the Italians from suing for peace at the first opportunity. Nor would it have prevented the Germans from doing likewise, if it had not been that Hitler was all-powerful, and would neither surrender himself nor allow anyone else to do so. If the plot against his life in July 1944 had been successful, it seems certain that whoever had assumed the leadership of the German nation would have at once thrown himself on the mercy of the Allies, irrespective of what had or had not been said at Casablanca. But I admit that I have not attempted to set out the whole of the argument on this highly controversial issue.

The day after the Conference ended, I flew to Algiers and went straight from the airfield to Eisenhower's office. I had not seen the morning's telegrams before starting, and asked if there was any important news. Eisenhower rang for his Intelligence Officer, and I enquired whether he was British or American. The reply was typical. 'I can't remember, but he is very good at his job.'

Mindful of my instructions not to 'loll about,' I completed my business as quickly as possible and left for Gibraltar. There I found a big Casablanca party, and we were all entertained by General Mason Macfarlane that evening. At about midnight we set off for the airfield, where two Liberators were standing by to take us home. Admiral Pound, Mountbatten and I set off in one, and Brigadier Dykes and Brigadier Stewart in the other. Our machine arrived at Lyneham first, and I decided to wait for Dykes. I wanted him to return to Washington the next day in order to give our Mission there a firsthand account of all that had transpired at Casablanca, and hoped to give him parting instructions on the drive to London. Half an hour passed, and as there was no sign of the second machine, Mountbatten and I set off for London alone. On arrival at my flat, a message awaited me that the second aircraft had crashed and that Dykes and Stewart had both been killed. Both of them were officers of exceptional promise, and I felt Dykes' death particularly keenly on personal grounds. He had been with me at the Committee of Imperial Defence from 1936 to 1938, and had left to be an instructor at the Staff College, Camberley. When war broke out, I managed to get him back, and he had been a tower of strength first in London, and then in Washington, as Joint Secretary with Bedell Smith to the

Combined Chiefs of Staff. The President's award to him of a post-humous Distinguished Service Medal is evidence of the high esteem in which he was held in America.

The only other officer whom I could spare to go to Washington to tell our Mission the Casablanca story was Lieutenant Colonel Groves, who had recently joined my Staff and accompanied me to the Conference. He left by air the following night. His machine crashed at Gander, and all the occupants were killed. This, our second casualty within three days, hit my small office very hard.

With the attack on Sicily less than six months ahead, the Deception Planners had little enough time to mystify the enemy and mislead him as to our intentions. But they proved equal to the task. The ruse which they adopted, with the approval of the Prime Minister and Chiefs of Staff, was as astonishing and macabre as it was successful. The story has been told in detail,[1] and my account will deal only with its salient features. They procured the body of a man who had just died of pneumonia, dressed him up as an officer of the Royal Marines, and attached a brief-case containing ingeniously faked documents which gave the impression that our next objective would be the Peloponnese or Sardinia. The body was floated out of a submarine, opposite Huelva, a hundred miles north of Gibraltar, was washed ashore in exactly the right place, and was discovered by the Spaniards, who passed it over to the Germans for a preview. After the Germans had photographed the documents and made a thorough examination of the body, it was delivered by the Spaniards to the British Vice-Consul and buried with full military honours in the cemetery at Huelva. The German Intelligence Service were completely deceived, and their General Staff not only sent troops right across Europe to meet our imaginary incursion into Greece, but also ordered a number of MTBs to proceed from Sicily to the Aegean. Truth is sometimes stranger than fiction.

---

[1] Ewan Montagu: *The Man Who Never Was.*

CHAPTER XXII

The Washington Conference

1943

I T W A S generally realised at Casablanca that another Plenary Conference would be necessary within six months at the most, and we
had not been long in London before it became apparent that there
were a number of problems which called for even earlier consideration and decision. Foremost among these was the question of what
should be done after Sicily had been captured. The British had no
doubt as to the next step, but the Americans were known to have different views. The longer the delay in getting round the council table
together, the more would each side harden on its own ideas and the
more difficult it would be to reach agreement. Another problem
which called for urgent consideration was the question of future operations in the Burma-China theatres of war. The Americans suspected,
perhaps with reason, that we were not putting sufficient energy and
drive into the prosecution of the campaign in Burma; and they were
apprehensive of an internal collapse in China unless Chiang Kai-Shek
was given more positive support.

Accordingly, towards the end of April, the President and the Prime
Minister decided to get together as soon as possible, and Washington
was chosen as the venue. The Conference was to be called TRIDENT.
In view of the wide range of questions to be considered, a large staff

was required, and the transport problem looked like presenting serious difficulty. But Lord Leathers came to the rescue with the suggestion that the whole delegation should travel in the *Queen Mary*, which was due to sail for New York early in May to bring over a further batch of American troops. When all seemed satisfactorily settled, there was a last minute complication. The *Queen Mary*'s cargo on a recent voyage from the Middle East to Australia had included a number of kit-bags which had been stored for several months in warehouses at Suez and become infested with vermin. She was now bug-ridden, and there had not yet been time to delouse her. It looked like being an uncomfortable journey. But the shipping authorities managed by supreme efforts to disinfect that portion of the ship which was to be reserved for the British delegation, and we were unmolested. Some of the passengers who were not travelling in 'the holy of holies' were less fortunate, and I regret to say that Sir William[1] and Lady Beveridge soon bore unmistakable signs of ravage.

The delegation left London for the Clyde by special train on 4 May, and went aboard the *Queen Mary* the following evening. It consisted of the Prime Minister and his personal staff, Lord Leathers and some of his senior advisers, the Chiefs of Staff with their planning and intelligence experts, Field Marshal Wavell, Commander-in-Chief in India, and his naval and air colleagues, Admiral Somerville and Air Marshal Peirse, a large quota from my office, a dozen or more Wrens for cypher duties, and a posse of Marines for security and general purposes.

The *Queen Mary* was a most convenient and comfortable workshop. We were all under one roof, and each had our own offices. There were ample conference rooms, and the reproduction and circulation of papers went forward with the same methodical precision as in London. We received the usual stream of telegrams, and the Prime Minister's Map Room, in charge of the indefatigable Pim,[2] was kept as up to date as its counterpart in Great George Street. The *Queen Mary* had of course to observe wireless silence, but there were special arrangements for the transmission of outgoing messages. These were signalled by visual means to attendant destroyers which, after placing

---

[1] Later Lord Beveridge.
[2] Capt. R. Pim, RNVR, later Sir Richard Pim.

sufficient distance between themselves and us to avoid giving away our position, passed them on to London.

The Chiefs of Staff met morning and evening and thrashed out all the questions which were likely to arise at TRIDENT. Their recommendations, after being approved by the Prime Minister, were embodied in a series of memoranda for circulation to the Combined Chiefs of Staff on arrival at Washington.

There was never a dull moment, and my only appearance on deck throughout the voyage was to attend a lifeboat drill. The Prime Minister insisted on having a machine-gun mounted in the boat to which he was allotted. He was determined to resist capture if we were torpedoed, and it was a mercy that the occasion for such a strange duel was unlikely to arise. Apparently the chances of a U-boat being able to get into the correct position to score a hit on a zig-zigging ship of the speed of the *Queen Mary* was infinitesimal; and in any event, we were assured that she could take half a dozen torpedoes and still swim.

We disembarked at Staten Island instead of New York harbour, and were taken to Washington by special train. 'Small steak' figured on the luncheon menu, and was chosen by a hundred per cent of the delegation. When it appeared, it resembled a whole week's meat ration, and even the greediest failed to finish their portion. We were out of practice.

On arrival at Washington the Prime Minister was taken off to the White House by President Roosevelt, and the rest of us lived in the Statler Hotel. The arrangements were well-nigh perfect, and work was conducted on a routine which was to set the pattern for all future conferences. Each morning at, say, 9:30 A.M., the British Chiefs of Staff and the American Joint Chiefs of Staff met independently. At 11 A.M. the two teams joined together for a Combined Chiefs of Staff meeting, accompanied by such advisers as the questions under discussion required. As a general rule we all lunched together and often there was a second combined meeting in the afternoon. Periodically there were plenary conferences at the White House, presided over by the President and the Prime Minister. At these the Combined Chiefs of Staff reported progress, sought approval for the recommendations on which agreement had been reached, and were given directions for their future work. Thanks to the admirable Combined Chiefs of Staff Secretariat, the programme of work went surprisingly smoothly. The traditions of methodical efficiency and unfailing helpfulness which had been laid by those two remarkable Staff officers, Bedell Smith and Dykes, were evidently safe in the hands of their successors, Brigadier Redman and Brigadier-General Deane.

A new figure at this Conference was Admiral Leahy. He had been American Ambassador to the Vichy Government from early 1941 to July 1942, and had then been appointed Chief of Staff to the President in his capacity as Commander-in-Chief of the United States Army and Navy, and Chairman of the Joint Chiefs of Staff Committee. He was shrewd and dependable, and his loyalty and devotion to the President and Churchill may be gauged from the inscription which he wrote in my copy of his book *I Was There.* 'Memories of our happy association with the two greatest war leaders of the English-speaking world persist always.' When the Combined Chiefs of Staff assembled for their first session, Leahy was voted into the chair, and the formalities were punctiliously observed. But there was an unmistakable atmosphere of tension, and as soon as the controversial question of future operations after the capture of Sicily came under discussion, it was clear that there was going to be a battle royal. Let me try to assemble the arguments which would have been used by either side, if at that time they had been able to speak together with the freedom and frankness permitted to old friends.

The American case was something like this. 'Over a year ago we told you in London of our proposals for SLEDGEHAMMER in 1942 and ROUND-UP in 1943, and we were under the impression that you agreed to them in principle. But scarcely had we returned to Washington, when you said that SLEDGEHAMMER was out of the question, and started pressing for TORCH. We returned to London in July to try to resolve the dead-lock, but this proved impossible. The President then ruled that the Combined Chiefs of Staff *must* reach agreement on some theatre in which American troops could engage the Germans and Italians in 1942. We therefore agreed to TORCH, on the understanding that the operations would be concluded in time not to interfere with the attack across the Channel in 1943. We are not yet masters of Tunisia, and there is no hope of a cross-Channel attack this year. You now propose that the next step after the capture of Sicily should be to the Italian mainland, and you claim that this would knock Italy out of the war. You may be right, but this would not be a significant contribution towards the defeat of Germany. We believe that the German reaction will be to clear out of the country and leave your proposed expedition in a vacuum. We foresee that you will then start pressing for other diversions in southern Europe. We cannot escape the suspicion that you intensely dislike the idea of landing in France, and that your principal object is to postpone it as long as possible, or even prevent it altogether.'

The British counter-arguments may be summarised with equal candour. 'You are quite wrong in thinking that we are opposed to the idea of a cross-Channel attack. On the contrary, we agree with you that in no other way can the final knock-out be delivered. The only difference between us is one of timing. You appear to imagine that OVERLORD is like a great business enterprise which can be pulled off if one is prepared to devote sufficient resources to it. We on the other hand belong to a generation which suffered sixty thousand casualties in a single day on the Somme, and which had practical experience of the hazards of opposed landings in the First World War. The defences of Gallipoli had been improvised at the last moment, and the Turks were few in number and poorly-armed. Even so, an airman who witnessed our assault on Cape Helles reported that the sea was "absolutely red with blood for a full fifty yards from the shore." You cannot therefore expect us not to resist the idea of a premature attack on a coast which has been elaborately fortified and is defended by the finest soldiery in Europe. Nor is the landing the only difficulty. We have got to be prepared to maintain ourselves against whatever reinforcements can be brought against us. In all these circumstances, it would be the height of folly to risk an assault on the French coast unless a number of conditions are fulfilled. In the first place, the German forces must have been so dispersed before the attempt is made, that their strength in France is reduced to an extent which will give us a reasonable chance, not only of effecting our landings, but also of building up our bridge-head. Secondly, we must have virtually complete command of the air. Thirdly, we must have disrupted the communications running east to west in Europe, in order to prevent the Germans being able to bring reinforcements rapidly to France from their eastern front. Fourthly, a reasonable proportion of the troops to be employed must be battle-tried. Fifthly, there must be a sufficiency of landing-craft and all the other technical paraphernalia which are required for opposed landings. As for TORCH, you must surely be glad that we insisted upon it. Just look at the priceless gains that have been achieved, and the tremendous losses inflicted on the Germans and Italians. It is true that it has taken longer to finish than we had hoped, but you will forgive us if we point out that this is partly due to your refusal to agree to the initial landings being made farther east than Algiers. We agree with you that an attack across the Channel is out of question until next summer, but that is all the more reason for our insistence that the million and a half troops now in North Africa should engage the enemy, and not be sent to England to wait in idleness. We do not agree that the knocking out of Italy would be an insignificant contribution to winning the war. It was the surrender of a junior partner, Bulgaria, which started the German collapse in 1918. Apart from the moral effect of an Italian surrender, the Germans would be hard pressed to find troops to replace the Italian divisions which are at present holding down Yugoslavia, Albania and Greece; and the opening of the Adriatic Sea would enable us to nourish the patriot guerrillas in those countries. We emphatically disagree that the Germans will leave a vacuum in Italy. Hitler's inveterate obstinacy at Stalingrad, and more recently in Tunisia, convinces us that he will fight for every inch of ground.'

The arguments went back and forth, and occasionally got so acrimonious that the junior Staffs were bidden to leave the principals to continue the battle in secret session. But do what we could, the Americans would not commit themselves definitely. The most that we could achieve was a resolution that the Allied Commander-in-Chief, North Africa, should be instructed as a matter of urgency, 'to plan such operations in exploitation of HUSKY[1] as are best calculated to eliminate Italy from the war, and to contain the maximum number of German forces.' Which of the various alternatives should be adopted was a decision which would be reserved to the Combined Chiefs of Staff.

Operations in the Burma-Chinese theatres were also the subject of prolonged discussions. They were attended by the officers who would be responsible for giving effect to whatever decisions might be reached. On the British side, Wavell, Somerville and Peirse, and on the American, General Stilwell, commanding the American and Chi-

---

[1] Code name for capture of Sicily.

nese forces in Burma, and Major-General Chennault, who had for some time been doing heroic work in command of the American Volunteer Air Force serving under Chiang Kai-Shek. Joseph Stilwell, nicknamed 'Vinegar Joe,' was as tough as whipcord, immensely brave and resourceful, and spoke Chinese fluently. But he was essentially an individualist who was incapable of co-operating with anybody. He hated the British, and despised Chiang Kai-Shek, to whom he used to refer openly as 'Peanut.' But his pet aversion was his own countryman, General Chennault. They fought like cat and dog from the beginning to the end, until finally the irrepressible Stilwell had to be recalled.

It had been settled at Casablanca that the British should attack Akyab in the spring and press forward with plans for the ultimate invasion of Burma. The attack on Akyab had failed, and could not be renewed until after the monsoon, and the prospect of starting a serious campaign in Burma was remote. In the end the only firm conclusion which emerged from TRIDENT was that Chennault's air force was to be reinforced.

The Combined Chiefs of Staff had no difficulty in reaching agreement on a number of other points, such as the prosecution of the U-boat war, the bombing of Germany, and the occupation of the Azores. The last named was a delicate problem. Both the Americans and ourselves were anxious to have a base on that island for operating the long-range aircraft which were employed in giving cover to our convoys and dealing with the U-boats, but there seemed little hope that Portugal would grant this concession of her own free will. It was therefore agreed that the British should mount a small expedition to capture the islands at an early date, it being understood that this must be done without the use of violence. It is for high authority to make that sort of stipulation, but the unfortunate commander may easily find that his attempts at seduction are unavailing and be compelled to have recourse to rape. Fortunately the British Foreign Office, who were horrified at the idea, managed to extract the necessary concession from our oldest ally, Portugal, by diplomatic methods.

However acrimonious official discussions may have been, personal relationships between the British and Americans were all that could be desired. The short week-end which the Combined Chiefs of Staff spent together at Williamsburg, on General Marshall's invitation, was a memorable interlude in a fortnight of hard slogging, and enabled us all to get to know each other much better. The war was never mentioned until we returned to our offices in Washington.

Although agreement had been reached over a wider field than had at first seemed probable, Churchill was bitterly disappointed that there was still no firm decision about the post-HUSKY operations. He considered the recorded resolution[1] far too vague, and was not prepared to let the matter rest without a further personal effort. Accordingly he conceived the idea of returning to the United Kingdom via North Africa. This would give him a chance of visiting the scenes of victory in Tunisia, and of having a talk about the future with Eisenhower, Alexander, Cunningham and Tedder. But he felt that he might be criticised for trying to exert undue influence upon an American commander, unless a representative of the United States High Command were present, and he suggested that General Marshall might accompany him. The President and Marshall himself readily agreed, and Churchill decided that Brooke and I should complete the party.

We left Washington by Clipper on the morning of 26 May. Having kept very late hours during the Conference I was tired out, and dozed most of the way to Botwood, Newfoundland. After refuelling and an early dinner, we took off for Gibraltar, a distance of over three thousand miles. Before the Clipper had left the water, I fell asleep and did not regain consciousness until seventeen hours later, with the Rock of Gibraltar already in sight. Apparently the Prime Minister thought I ought to be awakened for a meal, but my companions persuaded him that I needed sleep more than food. Never have I felt more hale and hearty than when I stepped ashore at Gibraltar. Sleep is a wonderful restorative.

The following morning we flew to Algiers, and the next few days were thoroughly enjoyable. We drove round some of the battlefields in Tunisia, and heard about all the prisoners and booty that had been taken. Even General Marshall admitted that he viewed TORCH with a less jaundiced eye. We paid a visit to Carthage and had some delightful swims in the sea. Everyone was happy. But the primary purpose of the Prime Minister's visit was to settle the question of the sequel to Sicily, and this was thrashed out at three meetings held in General

[1] See page 298.

Eisenhower's villa at Algiers. The British delegation included in addition to the Prime Minister, Mr Eden, General Brooke, Admiral Cunningham, General Alexander, Air Chief Marshal Tedder, and, for the last meeting, General Montgomery. The United States delegation consisted of General Marshall, General Eisenhower, General Handy and General Bedell Smith. The discussions made it clear that, although the Americans were not prepared to bind themselves to any hard and fast post-HUSKY plan in advance of the event, they were ready to agree that we should cross to the Italian mainland, if the enemy collapsed fairly quickly in Sicily. It was therefore decided that General Eisenhower should designate two separate headquarters, each with its own Staff, the one to make a plan for an operation against Sardinia, and the other to make plans for crossing the Straits of Messina and landing in Italy; it being understood that he would determine which of the two should be adopted in the light of the progress of HUSKY, and submit his proposals to the Combined Chiefs of Staff. In the knowledge that Eisenhower would almost certainly opt for Italy, the Prime Minister was well content. But he left no one in any doubt that, in his own view, Sardinia would be a mere convenience, while Italy would yield immense prizes.

On the afternoon of 4 June, we assembled at Maison Blanche airfield for the return journey to London. Just as the Prime Minister was entering his plane, he told General Alexander, who had come to see him off, that he had some more things to talk about and would be glad of his company to Gibraltar. Alexander agreed at once, and climbed into the machine. I followed them in, only to be told by the Prime Minister that I was very heavy and would overload the aeroplane, and that I had better follow in another one. It never occurrred to me to protest. Looking back on that incident, it is remarkable that neither Alexander nor I felt in the least aggrieved at Churchill's deliciously ingenuous lack of consideration for our personal convenience. We knew that he would treat himself in exactly the same way — and worse — if he thought that it would help the war.

I managed to extricate my suitcase from the Prime Minister's plane, and waited disconsolately for rescue. Within the hour, I found myself sitting in a bucket-seat in an American transport plane, bound for Gibraltar. Half way across the Mediterranean, our port engine went on fire, and the pilot started sending out the SOS message. The sea looked smooth and warm, and I was confident of being able to remain afloat almost indefinitely; but the crew managed to put the fire out, and we proceeded on our way. The *contretemps* may have upset the navigator. In any case, he steered a course which took us over a corner of Spain, and we were dutifully but harmlessly saluted by some Spanish anti-aircraft artillery. Their shells exploded more than half a mile behind us.

On arrival at Gibraltar, I found that the Prime Minister had already left for London in a Liberator, but was comforted to be told that his Clipper was still in the harbour, and that I could take passage in her that night. Early next morning I was awakened by the pilot, who asked me whether I was expecting an escort, as there were two fighters coming up on our tail. He looked slightly anxious, and we were relieved when they turned out to be our own Spitfires. Presumably they had not been warned that the Prime Minister had already arrived and that the Clipper did not carry anyone of sufficient importance to be provided with an escort.

CHAPTER XXIII

The First Quebec Conference

1943

WITHIN six weeks of our return from Washington, it was clear that yet another full-dress conference would have to be held very soon. Things were moving fast. The landings in Sicily on 10 July had been successful, in spite of rough seas and a serious mishap to our airborne troops. The enemy were putting up a stout resistance but were being pressed steadily back, and it looked as though the island would be ours in a matter of weeks. If, as seemed most probable, Eisenhower then decided to cross to the mainland, the Italians might immediately sue for peace. The position would be seriously complicated by the presence of large German forces in Italy, which had no intention of surrendering and would do their utmost to prevent the Italian troops from doing so. It was important that President Roosevelt and Mr Churchill, supported by their Foreign Ministers, should get together at an early date and decide from day to day how the business was to be handled.

The situation in Italy was not the only topic which called for urgent consideration. The outline plan for OVERLORD, which COSSAC had been ordered to prepare, was now ready for examination by the Combined Chiefs of Staff. The target date, the beginning of May, was only ten months ahead, and the immense preparations which would be necessary could not be started until the plan had been approved. At the other end of the world, the operations in the Burma-Chinese theatre were lagging, and it was essential to make arrangements for a more positive direction and closer co-ordination between the British, American and Chinese forces.

President Roosevelt was as eager for an early conference as Churchill, and his suggestion that Quebec should be the venue was warmly welcomed, especially by Mr Mackenzie King, the Prime Minister of Canada. The conference was to be called QUADRANT. Considering that the previous meeting at Washington had been called TRIDENT, this code name was not likely to deceive anybody. Perhaps it was not intended to.

We sailed in the *Queen Mary* for Halifax on 5 August. Our party was much the same as on our previous voyage except that the Prime Minister was accompanied by his wife, and daughter Mary, and that General Wavell and his brother Commanders-in-Chief in India were not with us. Mrs Churchill's presence was a great comfort. If the Prime Minister got ill, or was too naughty, she could look after him as no one else could. Junior Officer Mary Churchill, ATS, was worth her weight in gold as her father's aide-de-camp. What other member of his Staff could march into the Prime Minister's bedroom and make him get up in time for his appointments?

The other additions to our party were Brigadier A. W. S. Mallaby, Director of Military Operations in India, Brigadier Orde Wingate, Wing-Commander Guy Gibson and three representatives of COSSAC. Mallaby was the brother of George Mallaby of my Staff, and had been specially flown from India to represent his Commander-in-Chief in discussions about the Burma-Chinese theatre. He survived the war, only to be murdered in Java in October 1945. Orde Wingate was an extraordinary character who had done splendidly with the patriot forces in Abyssinia. On his return to England, he had come to see me, on Randolph Churchill's introduction, and expounded a plan for raising a large guerrilla force to be based on the Tibesti Mountains[1] for operations against Libya. When I asked whether he had made an approximate estimate of the resources that he would require in the shape of manpower, equipment, and shipping, his reply was the acme of arrogance. He said that he must insist on being given *carte*

[1] The Tibesti Mountains are in the Sahara Desert, just south of the Libyan border.

blanche on these matters, and that he could brook no interference from higher authority, whether political or military. I wonder if there has ever been a man who went so far out of his way to be intolerable to the very people who wished to help him. But he was a brilliant individualist, with a remarkable gift of leadership, and was destined to become a legend in his lifetime. Shortly after our talk, he was summoned to India by Wavell to undertake the organisation, training and command of the first Long-Range Penetration Group. In February 1943 the Group penetrated far behind the Japanese lines, and was maintained by air support. Churchill once said that going into the jungle to fight the Japanese was like going into the water to fight a shark. That is what Wingate and his 'Chindits,' as they came to be called, set out to do. From the military point of view, the expedition was almost disastrous. Out of the three thousand men who had started, eight hundred were killed or missing; and of those who returned, only six hundred were ever fit for active service again. But from the psychological point of view it was invaluable. It proved to all the troops in South-East Asia Command that the Japanese could be beaten at their own game of jungle fighting.

It was thought that the experiment might be repeated on a larger scale, and Wingate was sent to London to report to the Chiefs of Staff. He arrived on the very day that we were leaving for QUADRANT, and was immediately invited to dine with the Prime Minister. The man and his ideas made an instant appeal to Churchill; and before the meal was over, the Prime Minister decided to take him to Quebec in order to tell the Americans the story of his experiences. It was typical of Churchill's human understanding that he gave immediate orders that Mrs Wingate, who was in Scotland, should be woken up by the local police, invited to pack a suitcase at once, and taken to Edinburgh Station. Imagine her surprise when her husband stepped out of a train which arrived there in the early hours of the morning, and gave her the glad tidings that she was to accompany him to Quebec. Wingate had nothing but the somewhat disreputable thin khaki in which he stood, and was fitted out in naval battle dress as soon as we boarded the *Queen Mary*. He made a very favourable impression on the American Chiefs of Staff at Quebec; and it was forthwith decided that the Long-Range Penetration Force should be increased threefold, and that Wingate should command it. Six months later his two leading brigades were successfully flown in to areas a hundred miles behind the Japanese lines, and the future looked rosy. But Wingate himself was killed in an air accident almost at once.

Guy Gibson was a most remarkable young man. His technical skill, leadership and courage were superlative, even judged by the standards of Bomber Command, and he had just been awarded the Victoria Cross for his successful attack on the Möhne and Eder Dams. Having dropped his own bombs, he had remained in the inferno over the target watching and encouraging those who followed him. One would have thought that with a VC, a DSO and bar, and a DFC and bar to his credit, he might have welcomed a tour of duty on the Staff. But his one thought was to go on fighting, and Air Chief Marshal Harris appealed to Mr Churchill to take the young man with him to Quebec, and thereby ensure him an enforced rest. Churchill agreed at once, and Gibson was bidden to lecture at various American and Canadian air bases. On returning to England, he was posted to the Staff of a Bomber Group, but he never ceased to beg to be allowed to fly on operations again. Finally Harris gave way, and Gibson flew as 'Master Bomber' in one of the raids on München-Gladbach. He was last heard of circling the target, at about two thousand feet and congratulating the crews on the success of their mission. Perhaps it was wrong of Bert Harris to have yielded to his importuning? Perhaps he should have been preserved, as a living inspiration to his countrymen? I only know that when I heard that he had 'failed to return,' I felt a sense of national, as well as personal, loss.

It has always seemed to me that there has never been adequate recognition of the services rendered by Bomber Command in carrying the war into the enemy camp. There are those who argue that the immense resources in terms of manpower and material which were devoted to the bombing of Germany were not justified by the results achieved. There are others who argue that area-bombing was indiscriminate and indefensible on ethical grounds. But whatever the arguments about the policy which Bomber Command were ordered by the War Cabinet to pursue, no-one can question the valour, efficiency and teamwork which they brought to their task, or deny that the ordeals which they faced night after night, week after week, month after month, seemed too frightful for flesh and blood to endure. Let the story of a typical sortie by a single air crew speak for the many thousands of their comrades who took part in similar adventures. It is based on information given to me by the captain of a Lancaster bomber who survived many sorties of this kind.

On a cold morning in March 1943, the squadron was warned for a night attack on Krupps' Works in the Ruhr. It was not a popular area. Those who had been there before had vivid memories of heavy concentrations of flak batteries and night fighters, and of many good friends who had 'failed to return.' The sixteen captains and crews who were named in the Battle Order were fully briefed at 3:30 P.M. on such matters as the defences, the targets to be attacked, signals, weather to be expected, and bombing procedures. The captains then gathered their crews round them and discussed their several duties. Out on the dispersal points the Lancasters were made ready: bombs loaded; wireless and radar tested; guns and turrets checked; cameras installed; engines run up to full power; oxygen cylinders filled; and every single item in the complicated system of the aeroplane thoroughly examined by devoted ground crews. Meanwhile the air crews had supper and perhaps a short rest. One would imagine that even the most hardened warriors could not help giving more than an occasional thought to what the night might hold for them.

At 6:40 P.M. the Lancaster was airborne and climbed away into a dark sky towards the Dutch coast. The utmost vigilance had to be exercised almost from the outset, since night fighter attacks were to be expected from mid-Channel onwards. From the Dutch coast the crew could see the first faint beams of the massed searchlight defences already in action, and it was not long before they were on the outskirts of the Ruhr and attracting attention from the heavy flak on the perimeter. As they drew nearer searchlights tried to hold them whilst the A-A gunners below poured shells into the apex of the many 'cones' thus formed. For a moment or two they were held, but evasive action by the captain, diving, climbing and changing course, shook off the beams, and they were clear. With five minutes to go, the target was seen to be already ablaze; there were many explosions, and the smoke billowed up to great heights. The bomb-aimer lying in the nose of the aircraft and looking directly into the inferno, gave the first early corrections to his captain to bring the bomber on to its correct course. 'Left — left — hold her' came his voice: and then 'Bomb doors open, sir.' From this point the Lancaster was committed to the attack, and no avoiding action could be taken. Straight and level the captain had to fly — complete concentration on the instrument panel, and utter disregard of all else. The bomber immediately in front was blown to pieces. (How tempting to take evasive action! But it must not be done.) Straight and level — the supreme moment was almost at hand — only a small correction was needed — 'Right — right a shade — steady skipper — steady — hold her there — hold her — BOMBS GONE.' With a mighty rumble the four thousand pounder and twelve thousand pounds of incendiaries left the aircraft. The feeling of relief was overpowering, but the danger was still as great as ever. Presently there was a loud bang directly underneath. The Lancaster shuddered violently; a near miss had blown off the bomb doors. The captain swung the machine up and up and up until she was almost standing on her tail, but the bursts still followed. Then down with the nose, a ninety-degrees change of course. For the moment they were clear — or so they thought. But almost at once they were attacked by fighters who had seen the flames from the burning bomb-bay and cabin. A burst of cannon shell crashed into the rear turret, and tracer bullets ripped through the fuselage. The captain called his rear gunner but there was no answer: the flight engineer coped with the fire in the cabin and got it under control, and the fight continued. Twisting and turning, the captain worked his way down to cloud cover, and the fighters, baulked of their prey, sought other victims.

The rear gunner, a veteran of many sorties over Germany, was still alive; but the turret doors were jammed and he could not be extricated. His heated suit was too thick for the hypodermic needle to penetrate, and the injection had to be made in his hand. The mid-upper gunner held it by way of comfort, but after a little there was no answering pressure. The captain landed at the first available airfield, but the gunner was already dead; his legs had been almost completely severed.

Two nights later the same air crew, with a new rear gunner, set forth in another Lancaster on yet another sortie. Three nights later they repeated the performance.

Throughout the voyage to Halifax we worked unceasingly. It was the first opportunity that the Prime Minister had had of learning the full details of the OVERLORD plan, and COSSAC's representatives explained all its ramifications. Needless to say, he took the greatest interest in the various ingenious devices for building and protecting the synthetic harbours which were to enable our forces to be maintained across open beaches. If a stranger had visited his bathroom, he might have seen a stocky figure in a dressing-gown of many colours, sitting on a stool and surrounded by a number of what our American friends call 'Top Brass,' while an admiral flapped his hand in the water at one end of the bath in order to simulate a choppy sea, a brigadier stretched a lilo across the middle to show how it broke up the waves. The stranger would have found it hard to believe that this was the British High Command studying the most stupendous and spectacular amphibious operation in the history of war.

South-east Asia was also the subject of prolonged discussion on board ship. After hearing Wingate's story, there was general agreement that Long-Range Penetration Groups should operate on a considerably extended scale in northern Burma, but no agreement was reached in regard to other operations in that theatre. The Prime Minister was strongly opposed to any idea of trying to retake Akyab, and wanted an amphibious operation to be mounted against the tip of Sumatra (Operation CULVERIN). The Chiefs of Staff were not enamoured of the project, and felt in any case that our resources were inadequate. Consequently the proposal was not put to the Americans at Quebec.

It was during this voyage that a decision was made which was destined to revolutionise the system of command in south-east Asia. The Prime Minister suggested, and the Chiefs of Staff agreed, that the responsibility for the direction of operations in that area should be taken away from the Commander-in-Chief, India, and assigned to a separate Commander-in-Chief with his own Staff. It is surprising that this decision was not taken much earlier. The Commander-in-Chief in India had an immense load to carry. He was responsible for the command, organisation and training of vast British and Indian forces, for the internal security of a sub-continent with a population of over three hundred and fifty millions, and for preserving peace on the turbulent North-West Frontier. In addition, as Military Member of the Viceroy's Executive Council, he shouldered the responsibilities of a

Secretary of State for War. It was manifestly wrong to expect him to bear the added burden of directing a considerable campaign on India's eastern flank. I was ashamed of myself for not having remembered the ruling given by the Committee of Imperial Defence in 1929, that in the event of an expedition beyond the borders of India, a special Commander-in-Chief should be appointed. I had drafted their report myself.[1]

Of the many names canvassed on board ship for the new appointment, none commanded more general confidence than that of Admiral Lord Louis Mountbatten, and his selection proved entirely agreeable to President Roosevelt and Generalissimo Chiang Kai-Shek. Mountbatten himself knew nothing about it until we reached Quebec. He came into my office after being told the secret by the Prime Minister and said that he felt as though he had been pole-axed. He asked what I thought about it. My reply was non-committal. I said that I knew of no one who could be guaranteed to command success in a job of such magnitude and complexity, but that, by general consent, he had a better chance of doing so than anyone else.

On arrival at Quebec, we found that the Canadian Government had made admirable arrangements. The whole of the Château Frontenac was reserved for the exclusive use of the American and British delegations. All the residents had been moved elsewhere, except for one old lady who was not expected to live a fortnight. It is pleasant to record that she was reported to be still alive, and in occupation of the same room, when we returned for the Second Quebec Conference a year later. It was a great convenience to have both delegations living under the same roof. Problems which had not been fully resolved at committee meetings could be thrashed out at the luncheon or dinner table, and on the whole, the work went forward more smoothly than at any previous gathering.

OVERLORD was the most important item on the agenda. After full consideration, COSSAC's plan was formally approved, and he was given authority to proceed with detailed planning and preparation. The target date of 1 May was confirmed, and the Combined Chiefs of Staff reached agreement on to the conditions which would have to be fulfilled before the operation was launched. They are sufficiently important to be quoted *in extenso*.

[1] See page 62.

1. There must be a substantial reduction in the strength of the German fighter aircraft in north-west Europe before the assault takes place.

2. There should be not more than twelve mobile German divisions in northern France at the time the operation is launched, and it must not be possible for the Germans to build up more than fifteen divisions in the succeeding two months.

3. The problem of beach maintenance of large forces in the tidal waters of the English Channel over a prolonged period must be overcome. To ensure this it is essential that we should be able to construct at least two effective synthetic harbours.

The British Chiefs had never had any doubts about the necessity for these reservations, but were afraid that the Americans would suspect that they might be used as a loophole which would enable us to evade our responsibilities when the time came. It was a relief when they recorded their agreement.

The question of the Supreme Command of OVERLORD was not officially discussed at Quebec, but the President and Prime Minister had some private talks on the subject. It was not until five months later that a decision was reached, but the reasons for that decision may conveniently be considered at this point.

The Prime Minister had originally thought that General Brooke should have the supreme command, and had so informed him. But when he realised that after the initial landings the Americans would have a large and ever increasing preponderance of the forces engaged, he felt bound to tell Roosevelt that the Americans were entitled to the appointment. Those of us who knew what was afoot felt sure that General Marshall would be selected; and this was undoubtedly Roosevelt's original idea. Various reasons have been put forward for his subsequent change of mind. Robert Sherwood, in his authoritative study, *Roosevelt and Hopkins,* suggests that the President selected Eisenhower because he felt that he could not sleep at night if Marshall were out of the country. There is another suggestion that Admiral Leahy, Admiral King and General Arnold protested to the President that to break up the Joint Chiefs of Staff team, which was functioning so smoothly, by allowing Marshall to leave it, would be a terrible mistake. There is yet another suggestion that the American Press would have been highly critical if Marshall were moved from the most important job in his profession to the command of a single expedition. In my view, none of these reasons provides the whole answer to the puzzle.

Just before leaving for the Conferences at Cairo and Teheran, we were astonished to receive a memorandum from the United States Chiefs of Staff suggesting that 'a Supreme Commander should be designated at once to command all United Nations operations against Germany from the Mediterranean and the Atlantic.' We reacted immediately and violently. We pointed out that total war was not an affair of military forces alone, and that there were political, economic, industrial and domestic implications in almost every big war problem. If there were a single Supreme Commander, responsible not only for OVERLORD and the Italian Front, but also the Balkan Front and the Turkish Front (if one were opened), he would have to consult both the United States and the British Governments on almost every important question. The delays involved would be endless. In addition, the proposal of the United States Chiefs of Staff that the decisions of the Supreme Commander should be 'subject to reversal by the Combined Chiefs of Staff' would inevitably lead to deplorable consequences. There might be cases, for instance, in which the Supreme Commander had issued orders, and the troops had marched, only to be followed by a reversal of the order by the Combined Chiefs of Staff. Or again, it might happen that the British Chiefs of Staff would agree with the Supreme Commander on this point or that, while the United States Chiefs of Staff entirely disagreed. What happened then? In short, we made it absolutely clear that we could in no circumstances agree to the proposal, and the Prime Minister backed us up with an even stronger rejoinder to the President. The American Chiefs of Staff may or may not have been convinced by our arguments, but in any case they never raised the matter again. Nor did the President ever mention it to the Prime Minister. It is my personal belief that had we agreed to the proposal that there should be a single Supreme Commander in charge of all operations against Germany, President Roosevelt would have nominated Marshall. As it was, he felt that the OVERLORD command by itself was not a sufficiently big plum for his leading soldier.

Whatever arguments there may be about the motives which influenced the President, there is no doubt that his decision yielded the happiest results. Marshall continued to be a tower of strength in the Supreme Council of the Allies, and Eisenhower proved an ideal Supreme Commander of OVERLORD. Coming to the task fresh from his victory in North Africa, he already enjoyed the confidence of the British and American forces from the highest to the lowest. He had proved himself to be fair-minded and generous to a degree. There are some commanders who seem to fear that credit given to subordinates may detract from the merit of their own performances. Eisenhower was exactly the reverse. He was so determined to do justice to all who had served him well, that he was apt to give the impression to those who did not know all the facts, that his own role had been merely supervisory. It was indeed suggested that although he had great charm and a remarkable flair for co-ordination, he was an amateur in the field of strategy and military command. This criticism is as unfair as it is unjustifiable. Eisenhower had devoted his whole life to the study and practice of his profession, and it was due to his conspicuous military ability that he was summoned to Washington almost directly after Pearl Harbor to take up the appointment of Head of the War Plans Division, and subsequently promoted to command all the American forces in Europe. His critics argued that he had never seen active service. Anyone will admit that it is a valuable experience for a soldier to hear the crack and whine of bullets, but it is ridiculous to suggest that a man who has not had this particular experience is unfit for High Command. Several great men have managed very well without it, notably Oliver Cromwell and Stonewall Jackson. Nor does any amount of active service necessarily qualify a man to lead great armies. Frederick the Great's mules went through many campaigns, but were mules at the end of them.

One might have expected that after Eisenhower had gained one of the most complete victories in the annals of war, the attempts to belittle his military capacity would have ceased. But not a bit of it. 'If only Eisenhower had adopted this or that strategy,' say one set of critics, 'the war would have been won six months earlier.' 'If only he had been content to be a co-ordinator,' say another set of critics, 'and left the direction of the campaign to others, countless lives would have been saved.' Since the conduct of war is an art, and not a science, these dogmatic calculations must be accepted with reserve. What might have happened is in the realm of speculation. What did happen was singular and precise — overwhelming victory. Those who seek to detract from Eisenhower's name and fame would do well to ponder a story which went the rounds in the early days of the First World War. There was much argument as to who won the battle of the Marne, and Marshal Joffre, the Commander-in-Chief of the French armies, was asked for his views. 'I cannot say who won the battle,' he replied, 'but there is no doubt as to who would have lost it if it had been lost.'

Two special appointments decided upon by the Prime Minister at this time must be mentioned. His insatiable thirst for information about the war extended to every corner of the globe. A complete conspectus of all that was happening everywhere was essential, he said, for a proper perspective. Accordingly he decided, with the agreement of all concerned, to have a personal representative with Generalissimo Chiang Kai-Shek and another with General MacArthur; and he selected Major-General Carton de Wiart and Lieutenant-General Herbert Lumsden respectively for these appointments. Both of them were warriors after his own heart.

Carton de Wiart has already figured several times in my story. After his return from the ill-fated Namsos expedition, he was retired from the Army on account of age. But apparently he was still thought sufficiently youthful and active to be sent on a dangerous mission to Yugoslavia at the time of the *coup d'état* in Belgrade in the spring of 1941. His aircraft crash-landed in the sea off Bardia, which was in Italian hands, and he had no option but to swim ashore and be taken prisoner. He made repeated attempts to escape, and in company with his friend, General O'Connor, he once managed to get a hundred miles before recapture. One would have thought that, with the patch over his eye, and the hook which served for a left hand, he could not have escaped detection for a hundred yards. In the end he gained his freedom in a very unexpected way. While the Quebec Conference was in progress, the Italians sent a certain General Zanussi to Lisbon to discuss peace terms with the Allied representatives, and Carton de Wiart was released from captivity in order to accompany him as intermediary. When the negotiations broke down, Carton de Wiart volunteered to return to Italy as a prisoner of war, but General Zanussi, to his credit, would have none of it, and told him that he was entitled to return to England. He was eating out his heart in unemployment when Churchill gave him the chance of going to Chungking. Never have I seen a man more overjoyed. He very quickly gained Chiang Kai-Shek's esteem and confidence; so much so, that he was requested to remain with him after the war was over.

General Lumsden was another admirable choice. The outbreak of war found him in command of the Twelfth Lancers, and he earned great distinction for himself and his regiment in the retreat to Dunkirk. He received rapid promotion and commanded the Tenth Armoured Corps at the Battle of Alamein. But his handling of armour did not meet with the approval of General Montgomery, and he was sent back to England. He, too, was overjoyed when Churchill gave him the chance of further service; and he was an instant success with General MacArthur. He came home periodically to bring the Prime Minister up to date with MacArthur's situation and plans and to be briefed, for MacArthur's information, on all that we were doing and proposed to do. I was instructed to tell him everything that it was necessary for him to know. In my zeal to be of the utmost help, I unwittingly let drop a secret of a domestic character which ought not to have been mentioned to anybody outside the innermost circle. Realising my slip of the tongue, I begged Lumsden to forget it. He had been a well-known steeplechase rider in his younger days, and his reply was characteristic. 'I have not raced for twenty years for nothing.' Those were almost the last words that I ever heard from his lips. Shortly after his return, he was killed on the bridge of the American battleship *New Mexico* by a Japanese suicide bomber.

The news that reached Quebec from the Italian front was consistently good. On 17 August, Alexander reported that the last German had been flung out of Sicily, and as we expected Eisenhower recommended that the next move should be an assault on the Italian mainland. The Combined Chiefs of Staff approved, and it was decided that his forces should cross the Straits of Messina on 3 September as a prelude to attacking Salerno on the 8th of that month.

At Quebec, as at all other conferences, the final task was to make certain that shipping could be found for all the operations that had been approved. This problem was handled by the American and British shipping authorities, headed by Mr Lewis Douglas and Lord Leathers respectively. It was their responsibility to estimate the nature and extent of the shipping involved, and to ascertain whether, and how, it could be provided. Requirements usually seemed so astronomical that one feared that this or that operation would have to be cancelled or curtailed. But Leathers and Douglas worked hand in glove, and never failed to produce what was needed. The only occasion on which they offered indignant resistance to the proposals of the Combined Chiefs of Staff was when they were asked to select some of their precious ships to be *sunk,* in order to provide break-waters for the synthetic harbours for OVERLORD. It took a lot of persuasion to get them to agree to what they regarded as an act of infanticide.

After the conclusion of QUADRANT practically the whole of the British delegation left for England, but the Prime Minister remained at Quebec for nearly a week. He was committed to delivering a broadcast to Canada at the end of the month, and then wished to pay a visit to Washington, to settle a number of odds and ends. He kept me with him. Pound also remained behind, in order to accompany the Prime Minister on his homeward journey in HMS *Renown*. Pound was the keenest of fishermen, and I, noticing that he had not availed himself of the superb trout fishing that was to be had locally, paid a visit to his room one morning to find out what was the matter. He seemed a changed man, and it was some time before he even recognised me. I went straight to the Prime Minister and told him that the First Sea Lord had had a breakdown. That same afternoon we were invited to attend a meeting of the Canadian Cabinet, and Pound put in an appearance looking, to my amazement, more or less normal. The Prime Minister upbraided me for having been an alarmist. But a week or so later the crash came and Pound told the Prime Minister that he must resign. On the way home in the *Renown,* he never left his cabin; on other voyages, he had scarcely ever left the bridge. He died on 21 October, the anniversary of Trafalgar. He was a master of his profession, a sailor to the very depths of his being. There seemed to be nothing that he did not know about the Navy and the Seven Seas. There had been a good deal of chaff, and even criticism, about his habit of apparently sleeping through important meetings. But on the mention of the word 'destroyers' or of any harbour in any part of the world, he was wide-awake at once, and showed that he had been following the discussion more closely with his eyes shut than many of those who had had their eyes wide open. He was a brave, generous character, and a willing horse, if ever there was one.

Pound's successor as First Sea Lord was Admiral of the Fleet Sir Andrew Cunningham, who was once described by General Eisenhower as a 'Nelsonian type of admiral.' He rendered incomparable services in the Mediterranean almost from the outbreak of war, and irrespective of the strength at his disposal, imposed his will unmercifully on the Italian Fleet. It was fitting that the last signal which he sent before leaving his beloved ships to take up his new appointment in Whitehall should have informed their Lordships of the Board of Admiralty that 'the Italian Fleet now lies at anchor under the guns of the fortress of Malta.'

From now onwards until the end of the war, the triumvirate of Chiefs of Staff remained unchanged. The CIGS, Brooke, had succeeded Field Marshal Dill in the dark days of December 1941, and had become Chairman of the Committee six months later. Field Marshal Lord Milne had been the only soldier of the seven occupants of the chair since the Committee had been brought into being. So it was the Army's turn. Brooke was by general consent the best all-rounder in his Service. He had been an unqualified success in all the Staff appointments which he had held in peace and war, and had made a great reputation as a fighting commander in the retreat to Dunkirk. In council he was so quick in the uptake that he was sometimes impatient with those who were slower witted; and his habit of expressing his opinions in positive terms led those who did not know him well to regard him as unnecessarily abrupt. He was apt to speak so fast that the Americans found difficulty in following his arguments, and were at first inclined to think that he was trying to bounce them. They never gave him the confidence and affection which they gave Dill, but when they got to know him better and became accustomed to his mannerisms, they formed a respect for his competence as a soldier, and a liking for his character as a man. It is a thousand pities that copious extracts from his private diaries have been published[1] verbatim. They were intended for the eyes of his wife alone; many of the entries were made when he was exhausted, irritated or despondent, and a number of minor errors on questions of contemporary fact,

[1] Arthur Bryant: *The Turn of the Tide* and *Triumph in the West*.

thought unimportant in themselves, bear witness to the lack of fore-thought with which the diary was compiled. In these circumstances, the dogmatic, sometimes wounding, and often unjustifiable comments which he makes from time to time on his war comrades, cannot be regarded as considered judgments. There is however a danger that posterity, not knowing the circumstances, will take at their face value the assertions and criticisms in the diaries, and will get the idea that Brooke was self-satisfied, self-pitying, ungenerous and disloyal. He was none of these things. On the contrary, his selflessness, integrity and mastery of his profession earned him the complete confidence, not only of his political chiefs and his colleagues in Whitehall, but also of all our commanders in the field. On that count alone, he was worth his weight in gold. In the course of my eighteen years' service in Whitehall, I saw the work of eight different Chiefs of the Imperial General Staff at close quarters, and I would unhesitatingly say that Brooke was the best of them all.

The Chief of the Air Staff, Air Chief Marshal Portal, was the youngest of the trio by at least ten years, but his selection over the heads of many older and more senior officers was universally acclaimed by his Service. Academically and scientifically he was probably the best educated of the Chiefs of Staff, and there was no aspect of Royal Air Force work in which he was not thoroughly versed. He was held in particularly high regard by the Americans, and was instrumental in smoothing over many difficulties.

The triumvirate was a well-balanced team, and it was characteristic of their sense of unity that for the Victory Parade at the end of the war they insisted on being provided with a motor-car which was wide enough to enable them to sit three abreast in their drive through London. The services which they rendered to their country, both individually and collectively, were incomparably greater than the public ever knew. But there can be no doubt that they owed a great deal of their success to the unrivalled knowledge of the broad sweep of war, the fertile imagination, the inspired leadership and the unswerving loyalty of their political chief.

The Prime Minister duly delivered his broadcast to Canada on 31 August. He had been complaining for some time that original composition was a terrible strain, but his speech certainly gave no indication that his powers were on the decline. It was magnificent in form, substance and delivery. On the same night, we left by train for Washington, and the next few days were spent in discussions at the White House on a variety of problems arising out of the downfall of Italy. These included the disposition not only of the Italian Fleet but of the British Fleet, which had hitherto been maintained in the Mediterranean to look after it; the exploitation of the situation in Italy itself; the support of the patriot forces in the Balkan countries; the occupation of Sardinia and Corsica; and the possibility of operations against Rhodes and the other islands in the Dodecanese. A good deal of consideration, much of it highly technical, was also given to the feasibility of building floating platforms which could either be used by fighters to support opposed landings until such time as airfields ashore were available, or act as staging points for ferrying aircraft over long distances. The idea as originally conceived by a member of Combined Operations staff, and vehemently supported by Mountbatten, was that these floating platforms should be constructed out of icebergs. They would be provided with engines which would enable them to steam at slow speed, and with refrigeration plants to prevent them melting. They would be unsinkable. The whole thing seemed completely fantastic, but the idea was not abandoned without a great deal of investigation. Various alternative methods of construction were then considered by the United States naval authorities, but in the end there was general agreement that carriers and auxiliary carriers would serve the same purpose more effectively.

Towards the end of our stay in Washington there was a remarkable episode. The President had to go to Hyde Park before Churchill had finished all that he wanted to do. On leaving, he said, in so many words, 'Winston, please treat the White House as your home. Invite anyone you like to any meals, and do not hesitate to summon any of my advisers with whom you wish to confer at any time you wish. Please break your journey to Halifax at Hyde Park and tell me all about it.' Churchill took advantage of this offer, and presided over a top level meeting on 11 September. The Americans were represented by Admiral Leahy, General Marshall, Admiral King, General Arnold, Mr Harry Hopkins, Mr Averell Harriman and Mr Lewis Douglas. On the British side there were Field Marshal Dill, Admiral Noble, Air Marshal Sir William Welsh, Lieutenant-General Macready and myself. It was like a family gathering, and every sort of problem was discussed with complete frankness. I wonder if, in all history, there has ever existed between the war leaders of two allied nations, a relationship so intimate as that revealed by this episode. The affection and trust which Churchill had inspired in Roosevelt was not the least of his services to the Allied cause.

That night we left for Halifax, breaking the journey at Hyde Park for a final talk with the President. The attack on Salerno had already started, and the news was none too good. It looked as though no headway was being made, and the Prime Minister was most upset. It reminded him of the Suvla landing in the Gallipoli campaign, when the troops got ashore successfully but failed to move inland for two or three days, thus giving the enemy time to concentrate against them. At one moment he threatened to fly to Salerno himself, instead of going home in the *Renown;* but he thought better of it and contented himself by sending a telegram to General Alexander suggesting, in tactful terms, that he might go and see for himself what was happening. Alexander had already anticipated his wishes.

The voyage in the *Renown* was a peaceful interlude, except that Mary Churchill nearly got swept overboard. The Commander and I both saw her disappear with the young naval officer with whom she was walking, under an enormous wave which swept over the quarterdeck. Our relief was unbounded when it receded and we saw Mary clinging for dear life to a stanchion. We had had visions of plunging overboard in an attempt to rescue her rather than face the Prime Minister. The poor girl looked like a drowned rat and we had not the heart to scold her. But her escort probably suffered suitable retribution at the hands of his brother officers.

CHAPTER XXIV

With Eden to Moscow

1943

W HILE at Quebec, President Roosevelt and the Prime Minister had done their best to persuade Marshal Stalin to agree to an early conference of the Big Three, but he had said that the war situation made it impossible for him to leave Moscow before November or December. It had therefore been arranged that, as a prelude to a meeting of the three heads of Government, the Foreign Ministers should meet together early in October. The Soviet pressed for Moscow as the venue, in spite of the fact that Mr Hull, the United States Secretary of State, was very aged and had never flown before, and, as usual, they got their way.

Scarcely had I set foot in England when Mr Eden told me that he would like me to accompany him to Moscow. At first I was not too pleased. It would mean that I had less than three weeks at home before setting out on my travels again, and I could not imagine what contribution I could make to a political conference. Eden explained that the one and only item which Molotov insisted on including in the agenda was 'the consideration of measures to shorten the duration of the war against Germany and her allies in Europe,' and that I would be required to expatiate on the QUADRANT decisions about OVERLORD. The prospect was not attractive. To judge from my only previous experience of negotiating with the Russians, they would assure us that fighting Germans was not really too bad if one plucked up the courage to try it, and taunt us for not attacking across the Channel before Christmas 1943, instead of after Easter 1944. All the same it would be fun to be on the move again and to see my friends in Algiers and Cairo *en route* to Russia.

There were a number of urgent problems to be discussed at both places. For some time past the Prime Minister had foreseen that an Italian collapse would give us a wonderful chance of seizing Rhodes and the other islands in the Dodecanese. Only relatively small forces would be required, and the fruits of success would be of considerable consequence. With the Aegean in our hands, Turkey would probably come into the war, and convoys could then be sent to Russia via the Dardanelles and the Black Sea, instead of through the hazardous Arctic Ocean. Churchill's underlying object was in fact much the same as that which had inspired him to press for the Gallipoli campaign in 1915. Perhaps it was for that very reason that there was opposition to it not only in Washington, but also, to a lesser degree, in Whitehall, on the part of those who still clung to the belief that Gallipoli had been a strategic heresy, and its champion an arch-gambler. If only Alan Moorehead's admirable study of the campaign had been available in those days, I would gladly have given presentation copies to those of my American and British friends who had not yet seen the light.

Field Marshal Sir Maitland Wilson, the Commander-in-Chief, Middle East, was as eager to lay hands on the Dodecanese as his political chief, and had prepared a detailed plan for an assault on Rhodes, with a target date of 1 September. But towards the end of August the assault shipping which was to have been used was sent to India for amphibious operations in the Burma theatre, while the 8th Indian Division, which had been specially trained for the operation, was despatched to the central Mediterranean. Consequently, when the Italian surrender took place Wilson's cupboard was bare and the Germans were able to overpower their late allies in Rhodes and take a firm grip of the island. The opportunity had been lost. Wilson, faithful to the Prime Minister's advice 'to improvise and dare,' occupied Castelrosso, Kos, Samos and Leros, with the odds and ends which had been left to him. But Rhodes was the key to the whole situation, and he asked for the relatively small resources which would enable him to capture it before the end of October. The Prime Minister backed him up by vigorous appeals both to General Eisenhower and the President himself, emphasizing that much was to be gained at very little cost. But Washington was hostile. The very word 'Balkans' was anathema to them, and they may have suspected that Churchill's enthusiasm for operations in the Aegean would lead to our getting seriously involved in that part of the world, and to a further postponement of OVERLORD. The final decision was, however, left to General Eisenhower. The Prime Minister thought that there was still a chance that he might change his mind, and instructed us to do all in our power to persuade him to do so.

It was a small party that left Northolt after dinner on 9 October. Eden's principal Foreign Office advisers were Mr Strang, Mr Harvey, and Mr Pierson Dixon; and my staff consisted of Colonels Price and Capel-Dunn. We arrived at Algiers at daybreak and spent the whole morning in discussion with Admiral Cunningham and General Whiteley. They told us the results of a conference of Commanders-in-Chief which Eisenhower had held in Tunis on the previous day. There had been an important change in the situation in Italy within the last forty-eight hours. The Germans had sent strong reinforcements to the south of Rome, and there was a prospect of heavy fighting for the city. The conference had therefore been unanimous that nothing could be spared from Italy for the Dodecanese. Eisenhower himself was still in Tunis, and Eden had intended to break his journey there and discuss matters with him. But we were told that weather conditions made landing in Tunis impossible for at least the next twenty-four hours, and that Eisenhower and Tedder were champing at the bit to start for the Italian front. In view of what we had heard in Algiers, there did not seem the ghost of a chance of inducing Eisenhower to change his mind, and Eden therefore decided to fly direct to Cairo. I hated to think of Churchill's disappointment, but there was nothing further to be done.

We arrived at Cairo on 11 October and spent the next few days in conferences with Field Marshal Wilson, Admiral Cunningham, Air Marshal Linnel and General Scobie. The Aegean Islands were the main topic of discussion. Kos had already fallen, but it was decided not to abandon Leros and Samos. Alas, these two islands were also destined to pass into enemy hands.

A pleasant interlude during our stay at Cairo was a visit to the troops stationed in the desert. The camps were an abomination, but the men looked surprisingly fit and well and gave Eden a warm welcome. The few friends whom I met were grumbling because they had arrived in the Middle East too late to see any fighting. I assured them that they would probably have all the fighting they wanted before the war was over.

We left Cairo on the morning of 16 October, lunched at Habbaniya and reached Teheran that evening. Eden found awaiting him a copy of a more than usually offensive telegram from Stalin to the Prime Minister on the subject of a variety of matters connected with the Arctic convoys, together with a request from Churchill to handle the business in Moscow as he thought best. It looked as though the Moscow Conference was going to start badly. The next day we had a useful talk with Mr Hull, the American Secretary of State, who had just arrived from America, and Harriman, who was now United States Ambassador in Moscow. Hull looked old and frail. It was shockingly inconsiderate of the Soviet to have made him fly half across the world.

Flying at a great height for most of the journey, we arrived at Moscow on 18 October. Molotov, Litvinov and Golikov gave us a genial welcome at the airport, and the whole atmosphere was very different from that of my first visit two years earlier. Eden and some of his advisers went straight to the British Embassy, and the rest of us made our way to the Hotel Nationale. The Manager himself was on the door-step to greet me with an assurance that he would do his utmost to make my party comfortable, while the elderly waiters, who had more or less put us in Coventry on our previous visit, were now all smiles. Evidently the edict had gone forth that we were to have special treatment.

The first Plenary Conference was held on the next afternoon. Molotov was voted into the chair, to the obvious delight of his compatriots, and the subsequent discussion was confined to settling the agenda. The Russians had only one proposal: 'That the Governments of Great Britian and the United States take in 1943 such urgent measures as will ensure the invasion of northern France by Anglo-

American armies, and, coupled with powerful blows of Soviet troops on the main German forces on the Soviet-German front, will radically undermine the military-strategical situation of Germany and bring about a decisive shortening of the duration of the war. In this connection the Soviet Government deem it necessary to ascertain whether the statement made in early June 1943 by Mr Churchill and Mr Roosevelt to the effect that Anglo-American forces will undertake the invasion of northern France in the spring of 1944 remains valid.'

It was agreed that this item should be taken at a restricted meeting on the following afternoon, and Eden told me that I was to open the ball. Fortified, or perhaps handicapped, by a stupendous lunch given by Molotov, I duly said my piece when the Conference assembled. I disclosed the proposed date of OVERLORD, the general area of the assault, the approximate strength of the initial landings, the rate of build-up, and the construction of artificial harbours; and I ended up by quoting verbatim the conditions which must be fulfilled if the operation was to take place.[1] My speech took over an hour, and I was followed by Major-General J. R. Deane,[2] who amplified the points which particularly concerned the Americans. The Russians, represented by Molotov, Voroshilov, Litvinov and Vishinsky, listened attentively but gave no indication of their feelings one way or the other. Molotov said that they would study the statements after they had been put on paper, and arrange a meeting for their discussion in four or five days' time. I had little hope of getting off so lightly again. The same evening Eden saw Stalin, and discussed the points raised in the offensive telegram about the Arctic convoys. To our immense relief, the meeting passed off extraordinarily well.

Thereafter the Plenary Meetings on most afternoons were devoted to political problems. The atmosphere throughout was noticeably friendly, and Molotov actually gave way on one or two points to which he had originally raised objections. He agreed, for example, to the American proposal that a Declaration should be signed pledging Russia, The United States, the United Kingdom, *and China* to a united conduct of the war 'against those Axis powers with which they are re-

[1] See page 311.
[2] Formerly Joint Secretary to the Combined Chiefs of Staff, and now Head of the U.S. Military Mission in Moscow.

spectively at war.' For a long time he had resisted the inclusion of China. Another important point on which agreement was reached was the establishment in London of a European Advisory Commission[1] to consider the problems which would be raised by the surrender of Germany, and to make plans for the post-war period. This was the body which was responsible *inter alia* for the plan that the American, British and Soviet forces should each occupy a separate zone of Germany, and for defining the boundaries of those zones. There will be more to say about this when we come to the Yalta Conference. But perhaps the most valuable result of the Foreign Ministers Conference was that it laid the foundations for an early meeting of the Big Three.

The splendid progress of the Red Army at this time no doubt contributed to the good temper of our hosts, and Molotov seemed to have a new victory to report every time that we met. His stutter often made it difficult to identify the places to which he referred, and Dnepropetrovsk and Dneprodzerzhinsk, which were captured on the 25th October, stumped us altogether. On most nights there were firework displays and lots of gun-fire in the Red Square by way of celebration, but there were very few Muscovites to witness them.

Just when we were congratulating ourselves that everything was going splendidly, we got a rude shock. The Prime Minister sent Eden an appreciation of the situation in Italy from General Alexander, which showed that his campaign had been almost too successful in drawing large German forces to that theatre of war. As a result their build-up was now more rapid than our own, and he would be faced with a grave situation if the bulk of his landing-craft and some of his best divisions were withdrawn to the United Kingdom on the dates laid down. Alexander's appreciation was accompanied by a telegram from the Prime Minister, saying that he was absolutely determined that 'Eisenhower and Alexander must have what they need to win the battle, no matter what effect is produced on subsequent operations. . . . It is no use planning for defeat in the field in order to give temporary political satisfaction.' [2] He asked Eden to explain the position to Stalin with complete frankness, and to warn him that

---

[1] This consisted of the US and Soviet Ambassadors in London and Mr Strang.
[2] Churchill: *The Second World War*: Vol. V.

OVERLORD might have to be postponed until early June, or even July.

Faced with this unpleasant assignment, Eden, accompanied by Sir Archibald Clark Kerr and myself, set out for the Kremlin after dinner on 27 October. He had had Alexander's appreciation translated into Russian, and started the proceedings by handing a copy to Stalin. Stalin read it out aloud to Molotov — and we waited for the explosion. To our surprise and relief it never came. On the contrary, there were no recriminations or veiled threats. Stalin appeared to comprehend our difficulties, and even went so far as to acknowledge, for the first time in his life, that the very threat of OVERLORD had been instrumental in pinning forty German divisions in the West. Once he had received Eden's assurance that his communication meant a short postponement and not a cancellation, he appeared perfectly happy.

Eden's handling of the interview was masterly, as indeed was his performance throughout the Conference. I had always liked and admired him, but I had hitherto been inclined to think that he was one of fortune's darlings, who had 'gained the palm without the dust,' and that his meteoric success had been primarily due to charm of manner and a lucky flair for diplomacy. I now saw how wrong I had been. His hours of work were phenomenal, and he was extremely thorough. Nothing was too much trouble and he never went to a meeting without making sure that he had every aspect of the problem at his finger tips. He could be tough when necessary, but he could also give way gracefully if the situation demanded it. He had a pretty wit, and transparent integrity. His physical courage, which had been fully proved in much front-line fighting in the First World War, was matched by his moral courage. It gave me immense confidence to have his support when I had to be a spokesman for the delegation, and so far from resenting having had to go half across the world to attend yet another conference under a new chief, I thanked my lucky stars that I had been given the chance.

On the day after our tricky interview at the Kremlin, there was a special secret session to discuss my statement on OVERLORD. I was closely questioned, as I expected to be, about the limiting conditions which I had quoted. Molotov wanted to know what would happen if, when the time came, there were thirteen or fourteen German divisions in northern France, instead of the twelve which we had stipulated; or if it were estimated that the Germans could bring over, say, twenty divisions from the East in two months, instead of fifteen. I explained that our figures were merely a yardstick, and that divisions varied greatly in size and fighting power. I was sure that the presence of even double the number of under-strength or poor-calibre divisions in northern France would not prevent us from carrying out the assault. The Russians were apparently satisfied. Indeed they must have been quite pleased, because next morning I received an invitation from Marshal Vassilievsky to accompany him on a tour of inspection of the Russian front line. This would have taken at least a week, and I had had orders from the Prime Minister to return to London in time to start with him for the Cairo and Teheran Conferences. I telegraphed for instructions, in case he might change his mind; but alas, he replied that, although he was sorry for my disappointment, I must come back as arranged. It would have been an interesting experience, but I doubt whether I should have been allowed to see very much.

The men of the Kremlin rarely accepted dinner invitations, and it was a mark of special favour when a large number of them, including Molotov, Mikoyan, Gryslov and Litvinov, consented to dine at the British Embassy on 28 October. Maisky, who had just concluded a long term of office as Russian Ambassador at the Court of St James, was also present. He had not as yet appeared on any official occasion, and to judge from his place at the dinner table, as arranged by the Russians themselves, he had somewhat come down in the world. He was a good deal more cordial than he had been in London, and presented me with a nicely inscribed English version of Tolstoy's *War and Peace*. Two days later the first snow fell in Moscow, and that night Stalin gave a banquet to the American and British delegations at the Kremlin. It was unduly lengthy, but seemed less artificial than my previous experience of that particular form of treat. We were glad that they were limited to one per visit.

I find from copies of letters which I wrote after the Moscow Conference that for the first time I was optimistic about our post-war relations with Russia. Their behaviour had been so friendly and apparently frank that I came to the conclusion that they now trusted our word and appreciated that we had made, and were making, a very substantial contribution to the war. This spirit of optimism remained with me through the Teheran Conference, and my visit to Moscow with the Prime Minister in October 1944. It even survived Yalta in the following February, but it had completely evaporated before we got to Potsdam in July.

We had planned to leave Moscow on 2 November, but there was a maddening hitch at the eleventh hour. On our last night in Moscow we were enjoying a farewell party at the Bolshoi Theatre, when the British Air Attaché arrived. He said that the two pilots of our York aircraft thought that the weather, although none too good, was quite possible for flying, but the Russian General in charge of aviation at Moscow thought the reverse and had refused us permission to start. I asked to see him at once, but the Air attaché told me that a meeting would take several days to arrange. I appealed to Molotov, who was with us in the box, and he telephoned to his General to give me an immediate interview.

Having heard a forecast of the meteorological conditions from both the General and our own pilots, I said that I was sure that the Foreign Secretary would wish to stick to his plans. But the General had a trump up his sleeve. He said that the anti-aircraft artillery stationed round Moscow had not been warned of the flight, and that there might be an accident. I would like to have retorted that, to judge from the accuracy of the Russian artillery which shot at me two years ago when flying at 500 feet, the risk at 15,000 feet would not be appreciable. But I thought it best to surrender with good grace. At the same time, I said that Mr Eden would insist on starting the following day, provided that weather conditions were not prohibitive, and asked the General to issue the necessary orders to his anti-aircraft artillery at once. I added that I would come to his office the next morning to make sure that there was no further misunderstanding. I have told this story in order to show how obstructive Soviet officialdom could be at the lower levels, and how easily this obstruction could be overcome if one had friends in high places. Perhaps these habits are not unique to Russia, or even to war-time!

Molotov and many others were at the airport to see us off in the early hours of 3 November, and we departed for Habbaniya in a cloud of goodwill. We went out of our way to have a look at Stalingrad, and circled it twice at a very low altitude. From a distance it looked as though it was still habitable, but as one came nearer one realised that all the buildings were roofless skeletons. Practically every one of them had served as a fortress to be defended to the death. I asked the Russian officer with us what had been done about the evacuation of women and children, and he replied that everyone strong enough to bear arms of any kind, whether male or female, had taken their share of the fighting.

We spent that night with Air Vice-Marshal Willock, the commander at Habbaniya, and Eden woke me up at dawn the next day to read a telegram of congratulations on the success of the Moscow visit which he had just received from the King. It was a great thrill. After an early breakfast, we had an hour's talk with the British Ambassador to Iraq, Sir Kinahan Cornwallis, and the Iraqi Prime Minister, Nuri Pasha. I had known the latter in pre-war days, and I felt that we had lost a staunch friend and a brave patriot when he was murdered in the *coup d'état* in Baghdad in 1958.

We arrived in Cairo before tea and had an immediate meeting with the Commanders-in-Chief on the subject of our military requirements in Turkey and the situation at Leros. The talks continued throughout dinner at the Embassy and late into the night. Eden bore a close resemblance to Churchill in methods and hours of work. The next day we met a Turkish delegation, headed by Menemencioglu, the Foreign Minister. They spoke fluent French, and it was a relief, after our experiences in Moscow, where proceedings had been much slowed down by translations, to be able to conduct business without the necessity for an interpreter. Eden's task of trying to persaude them to enter the war was not an easy one. It was perfectly clear that we stood to gain a good deal by their doing so. We would be able to use the Dardanelles for convoys to Russia; we would have air bases in south-west Anatolia for the support of Leros and Samos, and later for the capture of Rhodes; and it would be a discouragement to the Germans to have yet another enemy ranged against them. The advantages that the Turks would gain were not so obvious, beyond the fact that it is always nice to finish up on the winning side. But Eden was most persuasive. So far as I remember, he said that an Allied victory was now certain — it was only a matter of time. The sooner it was achieved the better for the whole world. He then proceeded to enlarge upon the great opportunity which Turkey now had of rendering immense service to the cause of freedom. The Turkish spokesman protested that the Germans would be quick to retaliate. The Luftwaffe would attack Istanbul, which would burn like matchwood, and German divisions now in reserve would at once invade their country. On Eden's invitation, I pointed out that the Germans were stretched to the limit, had no reserves, and could not spare a single brigade for an attack on Turkey. As for the Luftwaffe, the most that need be feared was an occasional sneak-raid, and we would gladly supply them with adequate fighter and A-A gun protection. The Turks argued that the information given to them by their own Chiefs of Staff was very different and I volunteered to arrange for one of our intelligence officers to visit Ankara and show them the error of their judgment. The argument continued at a second meeting in the afternoon and at a third meeting the next morning. But the Turks were still unconvinced, and the most that we could get out of them was a promise to report all that had been said to their Government. Recent events in the Aegean had evidently done nothing to decrease their fears of the German power to take reprisals, or increase their confidence in our ability to protect them.

On 7 November, I flew direct to England. By lunch time the next day I was back in my office, and by 2:30 P.M. I was reporting at 10, Downing Street.

CHAPTER XXV

The Cairo and Teheran
Conferences

1943

I HAD only four days in England before setting off again with the Prime Minister to the Cairo and Teheran Conferences (code names SEXTANT and EUREKA respectively). We sailed from Plymouth in HMS *Renown,* and the party included Mr J. G. Winant, the United States Ambassador in London. I had always thought him a very interesting character and was delighted to have this chance of getting to know him better. In appearance he bore a marked resemblance to President Lincoln; he had the same look of dedication. He was extremely shy, and public speaking seemed to give him almost physical pain. Nevertheless he generally struck the right note. I recall that in his opening words after a particularly rough week of the Blitz, he aptly quoted Kipling:

> 'I have eaten your bread and salt.
> I have drunk your water and wine.
> The deaths ye died I have watched beside,
> And the lives ye led were mine.'

On arrival at Malta on the night of the seventeenth, the Prime Minister went straight to Lord Gort's palace, but I asked permission to remain on board where I had my office and personal Staff. When I

332

reported to him early next morning, he was in bed with a feverish cold and evidently finding Gort's spartan régime a trifle unsatisfying. His first words were pathetic. 'Do you think you could bring me a little bit of butter from that nice ship?' Apparently he had also experienced a shortage of hot water for his bath. 'I only want a cupful of hot water,' he complained, 'but I can't get it.' Knowing how much he enjoyed wallowing in a bath full to overflowing, I suggested that he had made a mistake in leaving the *Renown*. He ignored my observation, and went on to say that Alexander, Tedder and John Cunningham were all in the island and that he would like to have a meeting with them and the three Chiefs of Staff as soon as they could be collected. Even if he had been at death's door, he would not have forgone the chance of a talk with the commanders in the Mediterranean. We all managed to squeeze into his none too large bedroom, and the topics discussed included the progress and prospects of the campaign in Italy, plans for the capture of Rhodes, and guerrilla operations in Yugoslavia. Before we dispersed, the Prime Minister was handed a telegram from the President, expressing anxiety about the danger of German air and airborne attacks on Cairo, and suggesting that the location of the Conference should be changed to Khartoum. None of us had any doubts that Cairo, heavily protected as it would be against all forms of attack, was perfectly safe, that Khartoum was out of the question owing to lack of accommodation, and that in any event it would be disastrous to change our plans at the eleventh hour. We hoped that the Prime Minister would reply in that sense without further ado, but before doing so, he wanted to make quite sure that Malta would not serve our purpose. Hollis and Burgis duly surveyed the local facilities and were able to report within a couple of hours that they were primitive and inadequate. The majority of both delegations would have to be housed in bomb-battered barrack rooms without any modern conveniences, and subsist almost exclusively on army rations. This might be a salutary change after the lush comforts of the Anfa Hotel at Casablanca, the Statler at Washington and the Château Frontenac at Quebec, but would not be conducive to good work or good tempers. The Prime Minister telegraphed explaining the position and strongly advising that we should stick to original plans. The President agreed. We were all fairly certain that the objections to Cairo had been made without his knowledge. He was the last man to allow any thought of his personal safety to stand in the way of his public duty.

We continued our journey in the *Renown* to Alexandria and flew to Cairo on 21 November. The arrangements were all that could be desired from every point of view. Mena House Hotel provided a convenient headquarters for the Conference, and accommodated the majority of the more junior Staffs. The President was to stay at the villa of the US Minister, Mr Kirk, and the Prime Minister at Mr Casey's[1] villa, while the British and US Chiefs of Staff were allotted villas of their own. The area was guarded by a brigade of infantry and a good number of anti-aircraft guns, and the British fighter squadrons at Alexandria were admirably placed to deal with any German attempt to molest us.

To our dismay we found that the Chinese delegation, under Generalissimo Chiang Kai-Shek, was already on the spot. We had understood that the primary object of meeting the American Chiefs of Staff at Cairo was to settle a number of outstanding questions connected with OVERLORD before meeting the Russians at Teheran. It was necessary to decide, for example, whether any operations should be undertaken in support of OVERLORD, and if so, where, when and on what scale. Until all this was settled it was impossible to say what resources, particularly landing-craft, would be necessary for OVERLORD and its subsidiaries, or to determine how much would be available for the residuary legatees, such as the Burma-Chinese theatre. We had therefore hoped that our talks with the Chinese would follow, rather than precede, the Teheran Conference. We were now faced with the necessity of putting the cart before the horse.

The President and his principal advisers arrived in Cairo early on 22 November. The American Chiefs of Staff, so far from being upset by the premature arrival of the Chinese delegation, seemed positively pleased to have a chaperone. They had been averse to meeting us in Cairo before going on to Teheran on the grounds that the Russians would accuse us of 'ganging up' against them. It is easy to understand the Russians floating this idea with the object of making mischief; it is less easy to understand how anyone could take it seriously. The rejoinder was so simple. 'We are planning a colossal operation of war in which British and American forces will be completely inte-

[1] The Right Honourable R. G. Casey, Minister of State in the Middle East.

grated under unified command. The more closely we "gang up," the better for everybody, especially our Russian allies.' And it might have been added, 'If we had not always made a practice of "ganging up" in arranging the Arctic convoys, you would have been very short of supplies.' It must be added in fairness that we ourselves were equally guilty on very many occasions of not being as blunt as we ought to have been with the trumped-up grievances of the Kremlin.

That the Americans were uneasy about Soviet and Chinese susceptibilities is evident from a paper which they circulated shortly after their arrival, proposing that there should be set up an organisation known as the 'United Chiefs of Staff,' which for the time being, would consist of Russia and China, in addition to England and the United States. The British were strongly opposed to any standing machinery of this kind, and suggested that it would be sufficient if the Russians and Chinese were invited to send representatives to any CCOS meetings at which problems of particular interest to them were to be discussed. We had intended, if the Americans had persisted with their proposal, to deploy some powerful arguments against its adoption. In the first place, the Russians would have never agreed to sit at the same table as the Chinese, with whom they had no common warproblems. They were not fighting Japan, and China was fighting no one else. Secondly, no Russian military experts would have been given any latitude by the Kremlin. Thirdly, some of our other allies, such for example as Canada, who were making an enormous contribution to our common effort, would have justifiably demanded that they should be included in the new organisation. The Americans, however, did not press their proposal.

The first Plenary Meeting was held at the President's villa on the morning after his arrival, and there was a record attendance. In addition to all the 'regulars,' there were the Generalissimo, Madame Chiang Kai-Shek, three Chinese Generals, Admiral Mountbatten, Lieutenant-General Carton de Wiart, Lieutenant-General Stilwell and Major-General Chennault. The meeting was devoted exclusively to affairs in south-east Asia, and Madame Chiang Kai-Shek, attired in her national costume, made a charming interpreter. She gave the impression of having decided opinions, and there is no knowing that she did not inject some of them into her translations of what her husband had said.

Mountbatten gave an outline of his plans (which had not yet been approved by the Combined Chiefs of Staff) for land operations in Burma the following spring, while the Generalissimo set his sights high and pressed for the immediate capture of Rangoon by an amphibious operation. The discussion was continued that afternoon at a Combined Chiefs of Staff meeting which was attended by the Chinese Chiefs of Staff; but they made no comments on Mountbatten's plan, beyond insisting that the Japanese must be thrown out of Burma and the supply lines to China reopened as soon as possible. Subsequently we learned that the President, in the course of a private conversation with Chiang Kai-Shek, had given him a promise of a considerable operation across the Bay of Bengal in the coming spring — namely the capture of the Andaman Islands (BUCCANEER). He had been warned that it might be difficult to provide the necessary resources, but great men have a tendency to brush aside any practical objections which they find inconvenient, and to make concessions to expediency. This often leads to difficulties. It certainly did so in this case.

There was a second Plenary Meeting in the President's villa the next day — this time without the contingent from the Far East. The Prime Minister pleaded, among other things, that Alexander should be authorised to retain until 15 January, the sixty-eight LSTs which were under orders to return to the United Kingdom for OVERLORD on 15 December. Our United States friends were at first opposed to any measure which might delay the launching of OVERLORD, but eventually agreed. The Prime Minister also pleaded that Wilson should be given the very, very little that he needed to capture Rhodes, within the next two months. But the Americans were up in arms at once. They were still haunted by the ghost of Gallipoli and suspected Churchill, in spite of his protests that we were with them in OVERLORD 'up to the hilt,' of an attempt to get a footing in what they regarded as his favourite hunting-ground, the Balkans. The most to which they would agree was that operations in the Aegean might be carried out, provided that they could be fitted in without the slightest detriment to OVERLORD or its supporting operations. That stipulation ruled them out altogether.

The Combined Chiefs of Staff continued to meet daily until the time came to leave for Teheran, but discussions were confined almost exclusively to south-east Asian affairs, and to hearing reports from General Eisenhower and General Wilson about the situation in their respective commands. As a result, there was no time left to reach agreement as to the exact line which should be taken with the Russians about a Second Front in Europe.

On 27 November we flew to Teheran. The Prime Minister and most of our party stayed at the British Legation, a ramshackle house built by the Indian Public Works Department in the days when our Minister required a small escort of Indian cavalry for his personal protection. There was now a whole brigade to guard us. The Legation gardens adjoined those of the Soviet Embassy, which housed Stalin and which was even more heavily guarded, and it was possible to go from one to the other without leaving the protected area. The United States Legation was a mile or so away by road, and it was to this that President Roosevelt went on his arrival at Teheran. But the Russians were determined that he should not stay there. I was just settling down to some work when one of their officials came to me with the story that there were a number of Axis agents in Teheran, and that a plot had been unearthed to assassinate one or more of the Big Three when they were on their way to meetings. He said that there was a building in the grounds of the Soviet Embassy which could be made available for President Roosevelt. If he would consent to use it, conference meetings could be held without anyone having to take the risks involved in journeys through the streets of the city. Our own security people could neither corroborate nor discount the Russian story, and I went at once to the United States Legation to see Hopkins and Harriman. They had already heard about the supposed plot from another Soviet official and were actually discussing the problem when I joined them. We were all agreed that it was probably a Russian trick, but that we could not afford to take any risks. They therefore advised the President to accept the Soviet offer of accommodation, and he moved to his new quarters with the most elaborate precautions on the following day. The Soviet had once more got what they wanted. I wonder if microphones had already been installed in anticipation!

The first Plenary Meeting was held at the Soviet Embassy on the following afternoon. It was a thrilling experience to see the Big Three sitting round the same table at long last. They represented, as the Prime Minister said, the greatest concentration of worldly power that had ever been seen in the history of mankind. Roosevelt, as head of his State, as well as the head of his Government, was the obvious chairman, and he filled the part most effectively. He looked the picture of health and was at his best throughout the Conference — wise, conciliatory and paternal. The Prime Minister was suffering from a feverish cold and loss of voice; but, as always, mind triumphed over matter, and he did his full share of talking. Stalin would have made a fine poker player. His expression was inscrutable as the Sphinx and it was impossible to know what he was thinking about. He did not speak much, but his interventions, made in a quiet voice and without any gestures, were direct and decided. Sometimes they were so abrupt as to be rude. He left no doubt in anyone's mind that he was master in his own house. He saw no point, for example, in the proposal that the military experts of the three countries should meet next morning and consider the statements which had been made at the meeting. 'The decisions are our business,' he said. 'That is what we have come here for.' In the end he agreed to a military meeting, but added that he had brought no military experts with him. Voroshilov however would do his best. Voroshilov, who invariably wore the uniform of a Marshal of the Red Army, might have been expected to resent this reflection on his military competence; but he did not show it. Nor did his performance the next morning belie Stalin's estimate of his limitations. One of his contributions to the discussion was that the Red Army had experienced little difficulty in crossing wide rivers and that we ought not to make such a fuss about crossing the English Channel. My outstanding impression of Stalin was that he was completely ruthless and devoid of the milk of human kindness. I was thankful that I was neither his enemy nor dependent upon his friendship.

The proceedings of this first meeting and of the two which followed it have already been fully recorded by Churchill and many others. My account can therefore be very brief. There was unanimous agreement from the outset that Operation OVERLORD provided the best means of taking the greatest weight off the Soviet forces and bringing Germany to her knees, and that it should be launched as soon as possible after 1 May. There was however considerable argument about the operation, or operations, which should be undertaken in support of OVERLORD. The Prime Minister said that the first essential was to decide what should be done with the considerable Anglo-American forces which were to remain in the Mediterranean area during the six months before OVERLORD started. Clearly they must not stand idle. Their first objective might be the capture of Rome and the airfields to the northward. Thereafter they could advance to the Pisa-Rimini Line and hold it with the minimum forces required. This would leave a considerable surplus which could be used either to land in the South of France and advance up the Rhône valley, or alternatively could move to the northern Adriatic and thence north-east to the Danube. The decision as to which of these alternatives should be undertaken could be left open for the moment. Our second immediate objective should be to persuade Turkey to enter the war, seize the islands in the Aegean and open the Dardanelles route for the passage of convoys to Russia.

Stalin took a very different line. He was sure that the Turks would not come into the war and did not much mind if they did not do so. He had no objection to seizing the islands in the Aegean if they could be picked up for a song, but the opening of the Dardanelles was not a necessity. The last Arctic convoy had got through unscathed. The capture of Rome and of the airfields to the northward was desirable but not of great importance. As for OVERLORD it was vital that it should be undertaken at the earliest possible moment and that it should be supported by as large an operation as resources permitted against the South of France. If this could be launched before OVERLORD, so much the better; but if not, it could be launched simultaneously with, or even after OVERLORD. The area of the attack was far more important than the timing. It must be the *South of France*. The capture of Rome was a mere diversion in comparison. It is doubtful if many of those who listened to the discussion grasped the significance of Stalin's determination to keep Anglo-American forces as far as possible away from the Balkans. It was not until later that we realised that his ambitions were just as imperialistic as those of the Czars, whose power and property he now enjoyed, but that he was capable of looking much further ahead than they had ever been.

On our last morning at Teheran, the American Chiefs of Staff came to the British delegation to discuss a paper on operations against the South of France which had been prepared at Cairo by the United States Planners, in the hope of reaching agreement as to the line that should be taken on this matter at the final Plenary conference that afternoon. It was impossible at that late hour to estimate either the date or the scale on which the operation could be undertaken, but it was agreed to recommend to the President and the Prime Minister that they should approve it. As a result Roosevelt, Churchill and Stalin all put their signatures to the conclusion that OVERLORD would be launched in May 'in conjunction with an operation against the South of France on the largest scale that is permitted by the landing craft available at the time.'

The Russians had got exactly what they wanted. We, for our part, were in the position of a man who has signed a formal agreement to purchase a property at some future date without knowing how much it is going to cost, or whether he will have the money to pay for it when the time comes, or whether a more desirable property will not be in the market before the purchase is completed. An agreement which seemed so innocent at the time was destined to sow discord between the Americans and ourselves before many months had passed, and perhaps be one of the links in the chain of events which ultimately placed Europe, and indeed the Free World, in mortal jeopardy.

The communiqués issued at the end of previous conferences had usually been a mixture of platitudes and generalities. The EUREKA communiqué was an exception. It sounded, as the Prime Minister had suggested, a note of mystery and a foretaste of impending doom to Germany. 'The Military Staffs of the three Powers concerted their plans for the final destruction of the German forces. They reached complete agreement as to the scope and timing of the operations which will be undertaken from east, west and south, and arrangements were made to ensure intimate and continuous co-operation.'

Our last day at Teheran, 30 November, was the Prime Minister's sixty-ninth birthday, and he celebrated the occasion by giving a large dinner party in the British Legation, at which the President and Marshal Stalin were the principal guests. The whole of that afternoon the house was full of American and Russian security personnel with bulging pockets, and movement from one room to another was fraught with danger. Fortunately there were no casualties. The dinner went off extremely well and the Big Three seemed in high spirits. The speeches started directly we sat down and continued almost without interruption until we got up. It is a great advantage on these occasions to be too unimportant to be required to get to one's feet. The highlight of the dinner was the pudding. It went by the name of 'Persian Lantern,' and consisted of an enormous ice-cream perched on a large block of ice in which there burned a candle. The waiter responsible for passing this *chef d'oeuvre* paid more attention to the speech which Stalin was making than his own business. As a result, instead of holding the dish straight he allowed it to tilt more and more dangerously, and by the time he reached Pavlov, the Russian interpreter, the laws of gravity could be denied no longer and the pudding descended like an avalanche on his unfortunate head. In a moment, ice-cream was oozing out of his hair, his ears, his shirt and even his shoes. But his translation never checked. 'Mr Stalin says that the Red Army is worthy of the Soviet people. . . .' Pavlov's devotion to duty, perhaps sharpened by his fear of the consequences, was subsequently recognised by the award of a CBE, but perhaps not for this incident alone.

The British and American Chiefs of Staff had now attended at least two meetings a day for nine days on end, and there was plenty of work awaiting them on their return to Cairo. Everyone felt in need of a break, and it was decided to invite the United States Chiefs of Staff, none of whom had ever visited Jerusalem, to spend twenty-four hours there on their return journey, as our guests. We were made extremely comfortable at the King David Hotel, which was later to be blown up by terrorists, and shown round the Holy City by a Franciscan monk, the most expert of guides. As we tramped up the Via Dolorosa, I dared to think that our pilgrimage was symbolic of the Crusade which had been the principal topic of discussion at Teheran.

On our return to Cairo the Combined Chiefs of Staff resumed their daily meetings, and a number of odds and ends were satisfactorily cleared up. Not so the question of BUCCANEER. The British felt strongly that OVERLORD or ANVIL (original code name for the operation in the South of France) or both, were bound to suffer for lack of landing craft that would be required for BUCCANEER; and they pressed hard for its cancellation or at least curtailment. The United States Chiefs of Staff, whatever they may themselves have thought, were not prepared even to discuss the question, on the grounds that their Commander-in-Chief, the President, had made his decision. Our only hope, therefore, was that the Prime Minister, who felt even more strongly on the subject than the Chiefs of Staff, would be able to persuade Mr Roosevelt to change his mind. He tried hard, but failed in the first instance. On the afternoon of 5 November, with the end of the Conference in sight, I was sitting alone in my office feeling very unhappy at the thought that for the first time in the war the Americans and ourselves were separating in an atmosphere of discord. Suddenly the telephone bell rang. It was the Prime Minister. 'He that ruleth his spirit is greater than he that taketh a city.' [1] I had no idea what he meant, but after a pause, he explained that the President had given way over BUCCANEER. He then rang off. If I had given a thought to the bitter disappointment which Dickie Mountbatten would feel at yet another postponement of his offensive against the Japanese, I would have capped his quotation with another quotation from Proverbs. 'Hope deferred maketh the heart sick.' But Mountbatten and the Far East were a long way off, and my relief that OVERLORD was not going to be weakened was so great that if anyone had said a harsh, or even a kind, word to me at that moment, I should have burst into tears. My only excuse for this passing hysteria is that I was sickening for an acute attack of bronchitis. Within a few hours, I was put to bed with a high temperature, and there I remained until the good ship *London,* which had carried me safely through the Arctic and back in 1941, gave me passage to England. When we reached Gibraltar, we learned that the Prime Minister was seriously ill with pneumonia at Carthage; and two days later Mrs Churchill passed through on her way to nurse her husband. It was not until late in January that he was able to return to London. He had been away for more than two months and had been unwell the whole time. But temperature or no temperature, he had got through more work than most men could do in two years.

[1] Proverbs XVI: 32. 'He that is slow to anger is better than the mighty; and he that ruleth his spirit than he that taketh a city.'

CHAPTER XXVI

France Redeemed

1944

NINETEEN FORTY-FOUR will always live in my memory as the year of destiny. Our fate, nay the fate of the whole free world, depended upon the outcome of OVERLORD, and for the first six months of the year, thoughts of that supreme adventure dominated all our minds. Momentous events, such as the landing at Anzio, the prolonged and bitter fighting for Cassino, and the stupendous, and at times immensely costly, bombing of Germany, were dwarfed by comparison. I do not believe that any responsible person in England or America ever gave serious consideration to what should be done if OVERLORD failed. It did not bear thinking about. On the other hand, surely Hitler would be thinking of little else, for in the defeat of OVERLORD lay his only chance of survival. Surely he would withdraw all his best troops from Italy, the Balkans, the Aegean Islands, Scandinavia, and the rest, in order to form a mass of manoeuvre to strike at our landings. Surely the almost unlimited labour at his disposal would enable him to make the Atlantic Wall impregnable. Surely he would be ready to transfer the greatest possible strength from his eastern to his western front immediately we set foot in France. Surely he would make superhuman efforts to bring his secret weapons — the V1 and V2 — into operation against our invasion forces as they concentrated for embarkation. Surely he would try to conserve his air forces for *Der Tag,* and accept punishment elsewhere in the meanwhile. But, as the weeks passed, he did not appear to be attaching undue importance to OVERLORD. He continued to refuse to give up an inch of ground anywhere. Indeed the already slender reserve in the hands of the OKW was depleted in a fruitless attempt to stem the tide in Italy. It seemed almost too good to be true. Meanwhile our own plans and preparations went forward unceasingly. The problems to be resolved were of almost infinite variety and complexity, and time was short.

The plan which had been prepared by COSSAC and approved at Quebec envisaged that the assault should be delivered by three divisions on a corps front of about twenty-five miles, and that three corps should be landed immediately behind the initial lodgement. Churchill's view that this weight of attack was inadequate was shared by many others, including General Morgan himself. On the other hand, it was the most that could be done with the landing-craft and other naval resources which had been provisionally allotted to the operation; and it was recognised that final decisions could not be made until a Supreme Commander had been selected and had had time to study the problem for himself.

General Montgomery, who was in command of the whole of the initial assault on the coast of France until the time came for Eisenhower to establish his headquarters overseas, arrived in England early in January. He at once insisted that a bridge-head of adequate depth and strength could not be built up sufficiently quickly, unless the frontage of the attack was doubled from twenty-five to fifty miles. He proposed that the operation should open with an assault from the sky by at least two, or preferably three, airborne divisions (instead of the two brigades which had been provisionally contemplated), and that it should be followed by an assault from the sea which would be delivered by five, instead of three, divisions, and supported by a further two divisions pre-loaded in landing-craft. General Eisenhower arrived in England on 21 January, and warmly endorsed these proposals. But where were the landing-craft, mine-sweepers and other naval resources to come from? And would there be time for the intensive training of the considerable number of additional personnel now required for the initial landings? If only the decision to appoint Eisenhower as Supreme Commander had been taken at Quebec, he could have given up his command in the Mediterranean and returned to England in October, accompanied by his principal subordinates, Tedder, Montgomery and Ramsay. There would have been three more precious months in which to prepare for the supreme adventure. How right Stalin had been at Teheran when he said that it was essential that a man should be appointed at once to be responsible not only for the planning, but also for the execution of OVERLORD.

Eisenhower estimated that the revised plan required at least another thousand landing-craft, over and above the three thousand odd originally contemplated — double the number of mine-sweepers, and an increase of almost fifty per cent in the number of ships of war which would be necessary for escorts and bombardment. He proposed that these requirements should be met by postponing OVER-LORD from early May to early June, reducing the landing in the South of France (ANVIL) to a threat, and drawing upon the United States Navy for the additional ships of war.

The Combined Chiefs of Staff found no difficulty in approving a delay of one month in launching OVERLORD; but the Americans at first strongly protested against any interference with the scale or timing of ANVIL, and it was some time before they were prevailed upon to agree to its postponement until mid-July. It was not until even later that Admiral King was persuaded to provide the additional war-ships which were now required. At long last ample resources appeared to be in sight, and the plan was definite and clear-cut. It remained to fit all the pieces of this gigantic jig-saw puzzle into their proper places.

The Prime Minister, as soon as he returned from Marrakesh, decided that he would preside over a weekly conference on OVERLORD preparations. There was no limit to the range of problems which had to be settled. On one day it might be a shortage of tugs; on another, it might be the bombing policy to be followed in the pre-OVERLORD period; on yet another the construction of the various component parts of the artificial harbours. But whatever the problem the Chairman's fiery energy and undisputed authority dominated the proceedings. Everything had to be done at once, if not sooner; the seemingly slothful or obstructive were tongue-lashed; competing differences were reconciled; priorities were settled; difficulties which at first appeared insuperable were overcome; and decisions were translated into immediate action.

Along the whole stretch of coast selected for the assault there was not even a sheltered anchorage, much less a fully-equipped port. The story of the artificial harbours which were created to fill the gap has often been told, but there is some uncertainty about the origin of this amazing conception. General Morgan, in his *Prelude to Overlord,* gives Commodore Hughes-Hallett the credit for originating the idea, but there can be no doubt that Churchill's own contribution was significant. It was he who had proposed, as far back as 1917,[1] the construction of flat-bottomed caissons made of concrete, which could be towed to a selected site and there sunk. 'By this means a torpedo-proof and weather-proof harbour would be created.' It was he who, in 1942, had given directions to Admiral Mountbatten that floating piers, which would go up and down with the tide, should be designed. These directives were given in the minute which ended with the oft-quoted injunction: 'Don't argue the matter. The difficulties will argue for themselves.' Nor was his contribution limited to the fruits of his imagination. If it had not been for his drive and authority, the diverse paraphernalia required for the project would not have been ready in time.

The selection of D-Day, i.e. the day on which the initial landings were to take place, and of H-Hour, i.e. the hour at which the leading assault craft should 'touch down,' were intricate problems. The airborne troops must have darkness to conceal their approach, but sufficient moonlight to enable them to identify their dropping zones. They therefore needed a late-rising moon. There had to be a sufficient interval after dawn to enable the sea-borne assault to identify their beaches, and the war-ships to identify the target for bombardment; but this interval must not be so long as to enable the enemy to recover from his surprise before the infantry assault started. The tide had to be sufficiently low for the underwater obstacles to be exposed, but not so low as to involve the attacking troops in an unduly long advance across the beaches. These considerations led to the decision that

[1] Churchill's memorandum to Mr Lloyd George of 17 July 1917 on plans for the capture of Borkum.

H-Hour should be three hours before high water. So far as D-Day was concerned there were only three days in the month of June on which all the necessary conditions were likely to occur, namely the fifth, sixth and seventh.

At a very late hour one night the question of timing was being discussed by the Defence Committee, and I regret to admit that I was half-asleep when I heard the Prime Minister ask when William the Conqueror had landed. Hitherto I had made no contribution to the debate. Here was my chance. '1066,' I exclaimed. To my surprise this was greeted with a roar of laughter, and the Prime Minister said pityingly: 'Pug, you should have been in your basket ages ago.'

There was no possibility of concealing the fact that OVERLORD was going to be launched in the summer of 1944. All that we could hope to do was to mystify and mislead the Germans as to how, when and where the landings would be made. It was necessary, not only to conceal the truth from them, but also to 'educate' them to believe what was false. So far as concealment was concerned, it was essential to ensure that the German and Japanese Embassies in Dublin were isolated in good time. From February onwards, all civilian traffic between the United Kingdom and Eire was forbidden. In March, the whole coast from the Wash to Land's End, to a depth of ten miles, was declared a prohibited area. Shortly afterwards all embassies in London were forbidden to communicate in cypher, and their diplomatic bags were deliberately delayed. These high-handed and unprecedented restrictions may have aroused resentment at the time, but a man who is fighting for his life cannot afford to be squeamish. A week before D-Day, all the troops destined for the initial assault were hermetically sealed in their camps, and fully briefed.

As for planting false information, the story had been deliberately put abroad for the past year or more that although a landing on a considerable scale might be made across open beaches, it would be impossible to establish a defensible bridge-head without the use of a fully equipped harbour. It was hoped in this way to create the impression that OVERLORD, when it took place, was merely a diversion that need not be taken too seriously. And to lend colour to this story, and lead to the belief that the Pas de Calais was our true objective, a 'notional' army was created in South-East England. It was 'notionally' to consist of the Canadian First Army and American Third Army, and to be commanded by that apostle of the offensive à *l'outrance,* General George Patton. Masses of dummy ships and aircraft were installed, and incessant wireless activity, most of it bogus, was maintained. Meanwhile the existence of large forces in the south-west of England and of preparations for their embarkation was kept a deadly secret.

There was very little that could be done to mislead the enemy about the timing of OVERLORD, but the 'cover-planners' thought out a ruse which was put into operation when D-Day was imminent. Their object was to induce the Germans to believe that Montgomery, who was known by them to be the commander of the initial assault, had left the country, and to assume that the invasion could not take place until his return. Accordingly, they looked for, and found, a lieutenant in the Army Education Corps who bore a distinct resemblance to the General. His name was Clifton James, and he was an actor by profession. After a week's study of Montgomery's mannerisms, he was to be dressed in a suit of his uniform — the well-known beret and all — and despatched to Gibraltar, with what looked like an appropriate staff, and in an imposingly large aircraft to look as though he were on his way to Algiers. Meanwhile I wrote to General Eastwood, the Governor, telling him the plot, and asking him to play his part as he thought best. On the appointed day, Clifton James arrived at Gibraltar in the Prime Minister's aeroplane, and was met with due deference by the Governor's ADC. On his way to The Convent (which was the name of the Governor's residence) he guardedly poked his head out of the window and was greeted by the local soldiery with cries of 'Good old "Monty." ' Meanwhile the Governor had arranged that a Spaniard, who was known to be a 'double agent,' should be asked on some trumped-up pretext to be in the vicinity when 'Monty's' car drew up at The Convent. The timing was perfect. Our double-crossing friend spotted what he was meant to spot, returned to Spanish territory at top speed and telephoned to Madrid that he had just seen Montgomery with his own eyes. The information was passed to Berlin at once. Clifton James was given breakfast, and taken back to the airfield by Air Vice Marshal Elliot, AOC Gibraltar. Good-byes were said in full view of spy-infested La Linea; the Air Marshal gave the subaltern an exaggeratedly smart salute, and the great four-engined plane soared off to Algiers. The play was over, and Clifton James reverted to his own humble status. *Sic transit gloria mundi.*

The part to be played in the pre-OVERLORD period by Bomber Command under Air Chief Marshal Harris and the US Strategic Air Force, under General Spaatz, was the subject of prolonged and anxious argument. Eisenhower, supported by Tedder and Leigh-Mallory, insisted that they should concentrate on the destruction of the railway system of France, the Low Countries and Western Germany, in order to isolate Normandy and prevent the Germans opposing our landings from being rapidly reinforced. Harris and Spaatz protested. The former said that his crews were trained to bombard industrial areas and could not, at short notice, achieve the pin-point accuracy which would be necessary to destroy targets such as bridges and key points on railways. Spaatz claimed that more decisive results on the German war effort as a whole would be obtained if he were permitted to pursue his plans of destroying the synthetic oil plants, and postpone switching to railway communication until just before D-Day. The Combined Chiefs of Staff considered that, from the military point of view, OVERLORD should have absolute priority, and recommended that from April onwards, all the heavy bombers in the United Kingdom should operate under Eisenhower's orders against whatever targets he thought advisable. But there were serious political objections to be taken into consideration before this policy could be approved by the Governments concerned. It was estimated that French civilian casualties would amount to not less than eighty thousand, and Churchill and the War Cabinet were aghast at the prospect of inflicting such grievous losses on our allies. It would be almost as repugnant and painful as it had been to attack the French Fleet at Oran in 1940. The latter had been a case of life or death, whereas even professional opinion was divided as to the necessity for the desperate measures now contemplated. After much argument, it was decided that the Prime Minister should put the whole problem to the President. Roosevelt replied in a telegram to Churchill that, much as he deplored the idea of inflicting heavy casualties on the French civilian population, he was 'not prepared to impose any restriction on the military action by the responsible commanders which, in their opinion, might militate against the success of OVERLORD.' That settled it. The Eisenhower-

Tedder plan was approved and put into immediate effect. Thanks to the elaborate precautions which were taken, and to the accuracy of our bombing, French casualties were mercifully much fewer than had been anticipated; and subsequent enquiries showed that our long-suffering friends, so far from resenting what was done, were ready, nay anxious, to make any sacrifices which were deemed necessary to destroy their oppressors and hasten the day of liberation.

The whole of the south of England became an armed camp, the south-east being allotted to British forces, and the south-west to the Americans. The steps which Eisenhower and the British authorities concerned had taken to ensure good relations between the American troops and the civil population were now to bear fruit. In those stirring anxious times, many friendships were formed which persist to this day; and as a general rule, the American forces identified themselves whole-heartedly with local interest. In one village they subscribed most generously to funds for rebuilding a church which had been heavily bombed. The work was completed some years after the end of the war, and the Re-dedication Service was broadcast and relayed to America. The general who had commanded the troops in that area was an interested listener, but he blew up in fury when he heard the bishop observe, in the course of his address, how fortunate they had been in having the '*succour* from America.' He switched off abruptly, vowing that never again would he do anything for such so-and-sos.

The British Isles had already proved a gigantic — and unsinkable — aircraft-carrier. They now had to fulfil the additional role of a gigantic ordnance depot. War stores of every kind continued to pour in from America and our own factories, and their storage was an acute problem. Every suitable pit, quarry, and cave was filled to overflowing; but even so, there was an enormous surplus to be accommodated. Recourse was therefore had to a novel expedient, which went by the name of Roadside Storage. Miles and miles of country roads were studded on either side with small hutments every fifty yards or so; and each of these dumps contained ammunition or some other form of ordnance stores. Permanent guards would have been too costly in man-power, and the only protection was provided by an occasional patrol. But so far as I know there was not a single case of sabotage.

Shortly before D-Day my wife and I had occasion to drive along one of these roads in the middle of a terrific thunderstorm, and she asked what would happen if a hutment was struck by lightning. I replied that I was not in a position to answer her question, as such a thing had never happened, nor was I likely to be in any better position to do so if it did. I learned afterwards that I had been unduly alarmist. Apparently the road-side hutments were used only for those types of ammunition which had a very low explosive risk. If one of them were struck, the only result would be that some of the boxes might be charred or, at the worst, catch fire.

As the appointed time approached, the days passed too slowly and yet too fast. Too slowly because of our impatience to start: too fast because of the haunting fear that all would not be ready in time. About three weeks before D-Day, a large and extremely distinguished gathering assembled at St Paul's School to hear a final exposition of the arrangements for OVERLORD — the King, the Prime Minister, Field Marshal Smuts, the British Chiefs of Staff, General Eisenhower and his principal subordinates, and all senior officers in any way connected with the operation. The explanations were admirably done, and Montgomery in particular was at his best. I have no clear recollection of his actual words, but the impression left on my mind is still vivid. Plans and preparations were now complete in every detail. All difficulties had been foreseen and provided against. Nothing had been left to chance, the troops had been intensively trained. Every man knew exactly what he had to do. They were full of ardour and confidence. Their equipment left nothing to be desired, and the various ingenious devices which had been invented had revolutionised the problems of seaborne landings and of maintenance across open beaches. OVERLORD was in fact a perfectly normal operation of war which was bound to succeed. If there was anyone who had doubts, he would prefer his room to his company. It reminded me of King Henry's speech before Agincourt in Shakespeare's *Henry V:*

> '. . . he which hath no stomach to this fight,
> Let him depart; his passport shall be made,
> And crowns for convoy put into his purse.'

The administrative arrangements were explained in considerable detail by General Humfrey Gale, the Chief Administrative Officer. In his desire to give an idea of the magnitude of the undertaking, he revealed that the number of vehicles to be landed within the first twenty days was not far off two hundred thousand. The Prime Minister winced. He had been amused, but shocked, by the tale — probably apocryphal — that in the TORCH operation, twenty dental chairs had been landed with the first flight at Algiers. I had never had the courage to tell him of another tale — probably equally aprocryphal — that the first crates to be unpacked on the beaches at Anzio were found to contain harmoniums and hymn books. He was of course aware that there could not be any substantial changes in the loading tables at this late hour, but the first instruction which he gave me as we drove away from St Paul's was to write to Montgomery and tell him that the Prime Minister was concerned about the large number of non-combatants and non-fighting vehicles which were to be shipped across the Channel in the early stages of OVERLORD. He did not press the matter any further.

Shortly afterwards I happened to find the Prime Minister closeted with Admiral Ramsay. He confided in me that he had decided to accompany the invasion in one of the bombarding cruisers, and that the Admiral was going to make a plan. I was horrified, not so much at the risk involved, but at the prospect of the Prime Minister being cut off from communication with the outside world at a time when critical and immediate decisions might have to be taken. But my objections were abruptly silenced by the whispered promise that, if I kept my mouth shut, he would take me with him.

A day or two later I learned that arrangements had been completed for him to sail in HMS *Belfast* and perhaps go ashore after the beaches had been captured. Eisenhower's protest had been brushed aside, and I was wondering whether I ought to suggest to the Chiefs of Staff that they should intervene. But fortunately the King himself took a hand. His Majesty's first reaction had not been altogether unfavourable to the Prime Minister's idea; indeed, he had said that he would like to go himself. Later however he came to the conclusion that it would be wrong for either of them to go, and he sent for me to ask my views. I felt guilty at opposing the wishes of my Chief, but I made no attempt to conceal my anxiety at the prospect of his being out of touch at such a critical moment. That afternoon His Majesty wrote and asked him to give up the idea. The next day they had a talk, and

I got the impression that the Prime Minister, though persisting in his plan, had been slightly shaken. I rang up Sir Alan Lascelles and suggested that one more shot from the King might do the trick. The letter which His Majesty wrote that evening settled it. Churchill deferred to his Sovereign's wishes; but he was bitterly disappointed, and scolded me for having opposed him. How could he do his job as Minister of Defence, he asked, if he was not allowed to see things for himself? He protested that he was always most careful about his personal safety. It reminded me of a conversation I had had with Carton de Wiart after the First World War. Having admitted that he had been wounded four times as a brigadier-general, he asserted that he had never taken any unnecessary risks, and that it had been sheer bad luck. The men whom he led told a different story.

With D-Day only three days off, the Prime Minister left by train for Southampton, taking Field Marshal Smuts, Mr Bevin, and myself with him. He wanted to be close to General Eisenhower at this momentous time. Our train was parked in a siding and connected by a single telephone line with the local exchange. The next morning everybody seemed to be on edge, and there was chaos. The Prime Minister wanted to talk to all and sundry at one and the same moment — to the President in the White House, to Eden at the Foreign Office, and to the Chiefs of Staff in Whitehall. When the inevitable delays occurred, he was full of complaints. When I suggested in desperation that it might be better to get back to civilisation, my head was bitten off. Were we not next-door to Eisenhower and at the very centre of affairs?

In the afternoon we went down to the harbour and watched the embarkation. Everything seemed to be going according to plan, and the bearing of the troops was most impressive. I had never before seen British soldiers in that mood. There was no joking about the 'picnic' on which they were starting, and no singing about hanging up their washing on the Siegfried Line. They seemed to have no illusions about the hazards of the enterprise to which they were committed, but to be relieved that the long suspense had ended and that the time for action had come. Above all, they appeared to have absolute confidence in themselves and their leaders. Paget had forged a magnificent weapon, and Montgomery had imparted the final polish. The men cheered the Prime Minister with gusto, and Bevin's eyes filled with tears when several of them called to him, 'You'll look after the missus and kids, won't you, Ernie?'

When we visited the Headquarters Ship of the 50th Division, my friend Admiral Douglas-Pennant[1] — we had hunted the fox together in more peaceful days — suggested that I should play truant and remain on board. He promised to find me a job of work, and told me that Harold Campbell [2] was already stowed away. I replied that it was as much as my life was worth, and dutifully disembarked with the rest of our party. When I mentioned the invitation to the Prime Minister the next day, he said, 'Why didn't you go? I wouldn't have been a dog in the manger.' I wonder.

After calling at Eisenhower's camp and wishing him good-bye and godspeed, we set off for the train. I travelled in the same car as Mr Bevin, and we had a heart-to-heart talk. Anxiety seemed to draw us closer together, and he told me about the struggles of his early life. Hitherto I had regarded him with great admiration: from now onwards, I regarded him with great affection. He was intensely human, warm-hearted, simple and brave, and his common sense was as massive as his shoulders. He threw his whole heart and soul into the war, and no Englishman of any political party had a deeper love for his country, a greater pride in her past, or a surer faith in her future. At the same time he loved his fellow men the world over, and was very internationally minded. As Foreign Secretary in the years of Soviet expansion westwards he was one of the principal architects of the North Atlantic Alliance. At almost the last meeting of the Council before his death, he was overjoyed by the decision of the twelve Governments concerned to establish and maintain an integrated international force, under unified command,[3] for the defence of Western Europe. 'It is given to few men to see their dreams fulfilled,' he said to Marshal of the Royal Air Force, Sir John Slessor, when the meeting was over. 'Three times in the last year I have nearly died, but I kept myself alive because I wanted to see this North Atlantic Alliance properly launched. This has been done today.'

We did not sit down to dinner until a late hour, and half way

---

[1] Admiral Hon. Sir C. E. Douglas-Pennant.
[2] Captain Sir Harold Campbell, RN, Equerry to the King.
[3] General Eisenhower was appointed the first Supreme Commander.

through I was called to the telephone by Bedell Smith. He said that the weather was most unpromising and that it would probably be necessary to postpone the landing for twenty-four hours. The decision would be taken at a conference to be held at four the next morning. I repeated this grim message to the assembled company, and no one made any comment. All had learned in the hard school of experience that what cannot be cured must be endured. Smuts reacted magnificently. Usually it was Churchill who did most of the talking and Smuts most of the listening, but on this occasion it was the reverse. The Field Marshal's account of the two most critical moments in his life made us forget our immediate troubles. The first was at the end of the South African war, when, as a young man, he had insisted that there was nothing to be gained by further fighting, and that the only course open to the Boers was to throw themselves on the mercy of the British. He had been vilified as a coward; but he had won his point, and the signature of peace at Vereeniging was the result. The second occasion was on the outbreak of the Second World War, when he had had to oppose his Prime Minister, Mr Hertzog, who wished South Africa to be neutral. It was by only a handful of votes that he had won the day.

It was well after midnight before the party retired to bed. I told the Prime Minister that I had a good deal of work to do, and that I would wait up to hear the result of the conference. Did he want to be awakened? 'Of course not,' he replied. 'What can I do about it?' It was getting on for 5 A.M. when the telephone bell rang, and Bedell Smith told me that OVERLORD had been postponed for twenty-four hours. He added that he would like to see me as soon as possible. Could I get round to his camp? I promised to be with him as soon as I had had a couple of hours sleep. But just as I had dropped off, a heavy-footed marine banged on the door of my compartment. The Prime Minister wanted me. I went along and told him what had been decided. In his memoirs he quotes me as saying that he made no comment, but to be truthful he said a good deal. 'I suppose it never occurred to you to let me know at once. I suppose you think you are running this war? I would have you know that I too have some small responsibility.' I was obviously not expected to take this reflection on my modesty too seriously; but by that time it was too late to try to go to sleep again. I made for Eisenhower's camp and had a full hour's nap on the bed in Bedell Smith's caravan. He saw to it that no one disturbed me; and I did the same for him for the following hour.

Shortly after I had left the train, General de Gaulle and Eden arrived. The General had just flown from Algiers, and was in his most uncompromising mood. He had been furious at the restrictions placed on cypher communications between the Free French in London and those in North Africa: and he was outraged by the idea that authority in liberated France should be exercised in the first instance by General Eisenhower, and not the French Committee of National Liberation. His recent discovery that the so-called French currency which had been printed by the Allies was to be recognised as the lawful currency of France, had added fuel to the flames. The talks which he had with the Prime Minister that morning in the train were chilly, but he was somewhat mollified when he was taken to Eisenhower's camp and given a full briefing on OVERLORD. Nevertheless, he acidly refused the Prime Minister's invitation to return to London in his train that evening.

De Gaulle's greatest admirers could not deny that he was sometimes very difficult, but even those who suffered most from his tantrums would admit that he was in a hideously difficult position. The Army to which he had devoted his life had collapsed; his beloved France had been enslaved; he had been condemned to death as a traitor by the government of his own country; he was a stranger in a strange land; his proud spirit revolted at his dependence for practically everything that the Free French required on the generosity of the British and American governments; and he seemed to be at pains to disguise any gratitude that he may have felt for favours received. Refusing to recognise that France was, for the time being, somewhat in eclipse, he continued to insist that, by virtue of her past greatness, she should have an equal voice with the two major partners in the conduct of the war. Nevertheless, when all is said and done, we should be very thankful on many counts. First, that when France was tottering, de Gaulle had been recalled from the fighting front by M. Reynaud, and appointed Assistant Secretary for National Defence; secondly, that when the collapse came, he realised that only from the British Isles could the spirit of French resistance be kept alive, and so flew to London carrying with him the honour of France; thirdly, that

he had the vision, inspiration and personality to be the almost unchal-
lenged leader of the Free French Movement from the day of its birth
to the day when Frenchmen were once more reunited; and finally,
that he proved himself a completely dedicated patriot, who sought
nothing for himself, and never flinched from any word or deed that
might be of service to his country.

We returned to London in an agony of uncertainty. If the bad
weather persisted for another two days, OVERLORD would have to be
postponed for at least a fortnight. The troops had already been
briefed. What was to be done with them? They could not remain
cooped-up in small landing-craft, but there was a terrible danger that
information would leak out if they were brought ashore again. The
sense of relief was inexpressible when we heard the next morning that
the meteorological experts had forecast a short period of relatively
fine weather and that Eisenhower had decided that D-Day would be 6
June. It had been a terrible decision for Eisenhower. What if the experts were wrong? With characteristic courage, he gave the order to
go; and having done so, he wrote a note in his own hand emphasising
that the responsibility for the decision was his, and his alone, and that
no blame should be attached to anyone else. There was the audacity
of a great commander, and the selflessness of a great patriot.

I had a long day's work on 5 June, and did not get back to my flat
until a very late hour. Just as I was on the point of falling asleep,
there was the drone of aircraft heading southward, and the whole
building seemed to shake. I thought that perhaps Richard Gale, the
Commander of the 6th Airborne Division, might be in the sky above
me at that very moment. I had first met him when he was a Staff
Captain in India, and incidentally Master of the Delhi Foxhounds. In
the early days of the war he used to attend occasional meetings of the
Chiefs of Staff as one of the advisers of the CIGS, but he had managed to escape from an office stool in London and become a pioneer
in the training and organisation of airborne troops. He was now setting out on a mission after his own heart, and, as he climbed into his
glider that night, he is said to have muttered:

'And gentlemen in England now a-bed,
Shall think themselves accurs'd they were not here.'

As one of the gentlemen in question, all that I could do was to wish him 'good hunting' and try to compose myself for sleep.

The first reports that reached London were encouraging. Surprise had been achieved, and except at the American beach OMAHA, where heavy fighting was still in progress, all the landings had been successful and not unduly costly. OMAHA beach was stormed the next day, and all now depended on our ability to extend and consolidate the beach-head. Would Marshal Rundstedt, who had the best part of twenty divisions in the Calais-Boulogne area, size up the situation correctly and order strong reinforcements to Normandy at once? Or would he persist in the belief that our landings were a diversion and that our main assault would be delivered against the Pas de Calais? Thanks to the overwhelming superiority of the Allied air forces, and the ingenuity of our deceptive measures, he guessed wrong, and by 10 June, we had secured a lodgment area which was about sixty miles in length and about twelve miles in depth. The foundations of success had been well and truly laid. Meanwhile Marshall, King and Arnold had arrived in London in case there should be any hitch which required the immediate consideration of the Combined Chiefs of Staff. But all had gone so well that on 12 June, less than a week after D-Day, the position was such that the Prime Minister, Smuts, Brooke, and the American Chiefs were able to visit their respective sectors of the front. They brought back glad tidings. The commanders were full of confidence; the troops were in fine fettle; and everything was proceeding according to plan.

Three days later the King decided to visit his Army in the field, and graciously invited Cunningham, Portal, Laycock and me to accompany him. We travelled to Portsmouth in the royal train and crossed the Channel in HMS *Arethusa*. His Majesty was the kindest and most considerate of hosts. He was so obviously happy to get away from his papers in London, and so completely in his element on the bridge of the cruiser. If 'Action Stations' had been ordered, he would have been happier still. When we got to the other side, the King went ashore at Courcelles Beach, attended by Sir Alan Lascelles, and spent the day at Montgomery's tactical headquarters. The rest of us, after lunching on Admiral Vian's flagship, went ashore at Ouistreham in that remarkable army amphibious craft, a *Dukw*. Admirals are not accustomed to travelling in vessels manned by army personnel, but they refrained from commenting on the seamanship, and we all enjoyed our outing immensely.

On our return to London at about midnight, we learned that the V1 pilotless aeroplane attack had started in earnest, and that over two hundred of them had fallen in Greater London in twenty-four hours. This new form of horror continued for rather more than eight weeks, but the intensive bombing to which the launching-sites had been subjected for many months appreciably reduced the weight of the attack. Even so, it caused immense material destruction and seemed to have a greater effect on public morale than the authentic blitz had done. Is it to be wondered at? The British people were getting war-weary. In the early days they had been bombed night after night for months on end, and had borne it with amazing fortitude and cheerfulness. Ultimately the RAF had got the better of the Luftwaffe, and the Londoners thought that their ordeal by fire was over. Now they were once again faced with the prospect of days and nights of intense strain, and of all the physical discomforts, such as sleeping in crowded underground shelters, which the duty of self-preservation imposed upon them. To make matters worse, the 'doodle-bug' — as Hitler's V1 came to be called — was in some ways more frightening than manned aircraft. It engendered a feeling of helplessness. Its accuracy was not affected by darkness or fog; and, if it were shot down anywhere but over the sea or in a completely open space, it did just as much damage as if it had come down of its own volition. The constant air-raid alarms which were sounded throughout the twenty-four hours got on people's nerves, and there was something uncanny about a weapon that was harmless so long as it emitted a noise but deadly dangerous as soon as the noise stopped.

There was a certain amount of absenteeism from work and a fall in war production; and reports were received that our men in France had begun to worry about the safety of their families. No one imagined that the V1 could be decisive, but it would not have been unnatural if there had been a demand on political grounds that, for the sake of public morale, the armies in France should be diverted to the destruction of the launching sites. In that event, it would have been the duty of the Chiefs of Staff to argue that this would be military heresy. But our political leaders, most of whom had had practical war experience in 1914-18, were so alive to realities and so sure that London could 'take it' as it had done before, that the question never arose. To quote General Eisenhower, 'We in the field wanted to capture the areas from which these weapons were fired against southern England. However, it must be said to the credit of the British leaders that never once did one of them urge me to vary any detail of my planned operations merely for the purpose of eliminating this scourge.'[1] When Germany surrendered, Mr Churchill designed a commemorative medallion to present to his war-time colleagues of all political parties. It bore the inscription: 'Salute the Great Coalition.' Let us do so with thankfulness in our hearts that, in the days of our trial, the Ministers of the Crown were worthy of the people whom they represented.

Our whole anti-aircraft defence organisation was skilfully adapted to meet the new menace, and gradually got its measure. In the latter part of August only about fifteen per cent of the bombs launched succeeded in reaching Greater London, and on 7 September the Government announced, a little too optimistically, that the battle was over. On the very next day, the first example of Hitler's second secret weapon, the V2, fell in London. This new form of devilry continued until our armies captured The Hague, from which most of the rockets were launched, seven months later. The Londoners did not like 'the new-fashioned sort,' as they called them, any more than the old; but they 'took it.'

On 25 June the Americans broke into Cherbourg: a fortnight later Montgomery, after very heavy fighting, and a tremendous air bombardment, completed the capture of Caen, and the Prime Minister decided that the time had come to pay another visit to the Front. On 20 July — the day of the abortive attempt on Hitler's life in Berlin — we flew to Cherbourg and inspected the harbour. It had been smashed to pieces and was still full of mines. We were also shown a flying-bomb pit. It was very elaborate and most artfully concealed. That we were able to knock out so many of them speaks volumes for the excellence of our intelligence and the accuracy of our bombing. From Cherbourg we went by road in a blinding rain-storm to UTAH, the most westerly of the American beaches, and thence by *Dukw* and MTB in a very rough sea to the MULBERRY at Arramanche. The hospitality of Captain Alan Peachy of HMS *Enterprise* was extremely

[1] Eisenhower: *Crusade in Europe.*

welcome at the end of an arduous journey, and the Prime Minister made the ship his headquarters for the next three days.

The MULBERRY was working like the proverbial piece of clockwork. Stores were being landed at the rate of ten thousand tons a day, and the fleet of *Dukws* which carried them from lighters to dumps on the high ground above the harbour looked, from a distance, like a never-ending procession of beetles. On the second day of the tour, I paid a visit to Caen and beyond. The city was a shambles, and there was scarcely a street which was fit for traffic. But one of the main churches — a fine example of Romanesque and Gothic architecture — was untouched, except for one small shell-hole in the roof. It was a curious sensation to walk out of the welter of destruction into that peaceful house of prayer. It seemed a portent of the triumph of good over evil. The troops looked tough, battle-wise and confident. The youths who had been seen slopping about in England in 1940 had become veterans. It had been an interesting and enjoyable interlude, and I returned to London refreshed in mind and body. Two days later, General Omar Bradley, under cover of a tremendous air bombardment, struck southward. The long drawn-out bitter fighting in the bridge-head was over. The hour for the break-out had arrived.

The reader will recall that it was decided at Teheran that a supporting operation against the South of France on the largest scale permitted by the landing craft available should be launched in May in conjunction with OVERLORD. Considering that the Prime Minister had repeatedly emphasised, in the course of the discussion, that better options might be open to us when the time came, it would have been better if the British had insisted on a qualification that the problem be examined nearer the date in the light of the then existing circumstances.

As it turned out, there were three events of capital importance in the period which elapsed between the Teheran Conference and the OVERLORD landing. In the first place, ANVIL had had to be postponed until mid-August at earliest and therefore could not be a supporting operation for OVERLORD. Secondly, the heavy fighting at Anzio and Cassino had, to a large extent, accomplished the very purpose for which ANVIL had been designed, by drawing off some of the best German divisions from France. Thirdly, and perhaps most important of all, Alexander had gained an overwhelming victory in Italy. Rome had fallen on 4 June and Kesselring's army was in full retreat. Now was the moment to press the pursuit relentlessly, and reap the fruits of victory.

The alternatives were clear-cut. Should three American and four French divisions be withdrawn from Alexander's command to enable ANVIL to be mounted in mid-August? Or should ANVIL be either cancelled or undertaken on a much smaller scale, and Alexander allowed to retain the necessary strength to exploit his recent victory?

From the military point of view, General Eisenhower not unnaturally pressed hard for ANVIL. He argued that OVERLORD was the supreme operation of the war in Europe, and that the greater the concentration of troops that could be deployed between the North Sea and Switzerland, the more quickly would the German armies be destroyed. Marseilles was likely to fall into his hands more or less undamaged, and a fully-equipped port in the Riviera would be of immense assistance in maintaining the armies on the southern flank of his line, and save the long haul from Brittany. He estimated that the ANVIL forces, in combination with the Maquis, would be able to advance up the Rhône Valley at great speed and give their left hand to the right hand of the US forces already in France in a matter of weeks. Eisenhower was at pains to make it clear to Churchill that he was looking at the problem from the purely military angle, and that the political issues involved were a matter for superior authority. His proposals were warmly endorsed by the American Chiefs of Staff. Perhaps their pet aversion, the Balkan bogey, loomed large in their minds. In any case they were adamant that in no circumstances would US troops be permitted to take part in any adventures in that direction.

The British Chiefs of Staff had a very different view. They argued that Alexander, provided that he was not required to give up any of his troops, or at least the three American divisions,[1] for ANVIL, could maintain the momentum of his advance and tear Kesselring's army to pieces. He could press on to the Po Valley, and swing right-handed through the Ljubljana Gap into the plains of Hungary and beyond.

---

[1] De Gaulle was insistent that the four French divisions under General Juin should take part in the liberation of France.

This threat to the upper Danube would draw away from OVERLORD many more German forces than ANVIL.

Both sides refused to give way, and the decision was left to the Heads of Governments. Churchill argued the British case vehemently and persistently. On military grounds, it would be folly not to seize the golden opportunities which Alexander's resounding victory in Italy had opened up; on political grounds, it was of the first importance that the Allies should reach Prague and Vienna before the Russians. But Roosevelt refused to budge an inch. He thought that, on military grounds, the direct reinforcement of OVERLORD by at least ten American and French divisions should have priority; and that, on political grounds, we could not go back on the promise that had been given to Stalin at Teheran. He may also have felt that there was no lasting advantage to be gained by forestalling the Russians in Prague and Vienna, since the Anglo-American forces were committed to withdrawing to their respective zones of occupation as soon as Germany surrendered. Churchill was grieved, but felt unable to press the matter any further. In the early days of OVERLORD, the British and American armies in France had been practically equal in numbers. But the British strength had now practically reached its peak, whereas the American strength was continually increasing. Churchill, always the fairest-minded of men, felt that the Americans, as the biggest share-holders, were entitled to the final say in the matter; and it was de-decided that ANVIL, re-christened DRAGOON for security reasons, should take place on 15 August. Much as the British High Command disliked the project, they put their whole heart and soul into it once the decision had been taken. The Americans had done exactly the same in the case of TORCH, which they had vehemently opposed for many months. This spirit of give-and-take was the very foundation of our partnership. Mr Churchill himself watched the Riviera landings from the deck of a British destroyer. He said that his purpose was to 'do the civil' to DRAGOON, much as he disliked it. But the instinct of an old war-horse scenting battle may have had something to do with his presence on that occasion.

The landings were carried out with very few casualties; the port of Marseilles was captured intact, and General Devers' Franco-American Army drove up the Rhône Valley at great speed, co-operating with the Maquis, and gathering thousands of German prisoners on the way. In less than a month DRAGOON and OVERLORD joined hands. It may therefore be claimed that, from the military point of view, DRA-GOON was fully justified: its political wisdom is not so easy to assess. On the credit side, it provided the French Army with an opportunity to take part in the rescue of their own soil, and regain the prestige which they had lost in 1940. On the debit side, it enabled the Russians to have the honour and glory of capturing Prague and Vienna before the Anglo-American forces could get there.

CHAPTER XXVII

Warsaw and Athens

1944

WHILE all was going so well in France, terrible things were happening in Poland. We had to suffer the grief of seeing our friends in Warsaw tortured beyond endurance, the humiliation of being powerless to help them, and the stigma of being bound by an alliance with the nation primarily responsible for the tragic episode. When the fortunes of the millions of men fighting in a world-wide struggle are at stake, 'terrible and even humbling submissions must at times, be made to the general aim.' [1] Nevertheless I cannot escape a feeling of nausea as I tell the tale.

Towards the end of July, the people of Warsaw heard the Moscow radio announcing that the Russian Armies would soon be with them, that the hour of their deliverance was at hand, and that they must be ready to play their part. The roar of the guns could already be heard, and the Soviet Air Force had started bombing the city. On the afternoon of 1 August, General Bor-Komorowski ordered his underground forces, about forty thousand strong, into action. They rose as one man. For the next sixty days there ensued a most desperate, fantastic and bestial battle. It 'raged literally underground. The only means of communication between the different sectors held by the Poles lay

[1] Churchill: *The Second World War*: Vol. VI.

through the sewers. The Germans threw hand grenades and gas bombs down the manholes. Battles developed in pitch-darkness between men, waist-deep in excrement, fighting hand to hand, at times with knives, or drowning their opponents in the slime.' [1]

The Soviet Army, which was already at the gates of the city, halted where it stood. The Soviet Air Force ceased all activity. Heartbreaking appeals poured into London and Washington. Could we not drop anti-tank guns, machine-guns and ammunition on the insurgents? Could we not bombard the Germans from the air? Could we not send Polish fighter squadrons to land in Warsaw and to take part in the fight? And why should not the Polish Parachute Brigade be sent as well? Air Chief Marshal Slessor, the commander of the Royal Air Force in the Mediterranean, was ordered to do what he could with bombers based on Italy. He did his best, but the distance was too great and the difficulty of distinguishing between the German and Polish sectors of the city almost insuperable. His squadrons suffered heavy casualties, and most of the supplies dropped fell into German hands. More could have been done if American and British bombers had been permitted to land on Russian airfields east of Warsaw for refuelling and repair; but this was not allowed by Stalin on the grounds 'that he did not wish to associate himself either directly or indirectly with what he called "the criminal adventure in Warsaw." ' He was determined that all who were guilty of the crime of preferring a free Poland to a Poland under the Communist yoke should be exterminated.

The Poles in London paid almost daily visits to everyone who they thought might have any influence in bringing relief to their brothers in Warsaw; and General Kukiel, the Minister of Defence, sent me a letter by the hands of a Polish officer, in which he asserted in the most bitter terms that, unless we sent immediate and effective aid, we should be guilty of a gross breach of faith. I glanced through it in the officer's presence and said that I could not accept it. Would he kindly take it back to his Minister and ask him to reconsider its terms? If after so doing he decided to send it back to me, I would, with the greatest regret, place it before the British High Command. Poor Kukiel wrote at once apologising for his outburst and excusing himself on the grounds of his agony of mind.

[1] Churchill: *The Second World War*: Vol. VI.

After six long weeks, Stalin was presumably satisfied that the spirit of free Poland had been crushed. The Red Army continued its advance, and the Red Air Force resumed its bombardment of Warsaw. By now the population was starving; and, although the Americans sent over a hundred bombers to drop supplies on 18 September, it was too late. On 2 October the fighting, but not the agony of Warsaw came to an end. The future of Poland, as a whole, had yet to be settled. But the writing was on the wall.

I did not realise until the war in Europe was drawing to its close, how deep or long standing were Mr Churchill's anxieties about Communist expansion. As far back as September 1943, he addressed a minute to the Chiefs of Staff drawing attention to the possibility of a Communist *coup d'état* in Greece in the event of a German withdrawal, and asking that preparations should be made to meet that eventuality by sending 'five thousand troops with armoured cars and Bren gun carriers into Athens . . . Their duty would be to give support at the centre to the restored lawful Greek Government.' His foresight was once more to be amply vindicated.

In the spring of the following year, the whole question of Soviet expansion was discussed by the Imperial Conference assembled in London, and the Prime Minister asked the Foreign Office for a paper setting forth 'the brute issues between us and the Soviet Government which are developing in Italy, in Roumania, in Bulgaria, in Yugoslavia and, above all, in Greece.' He evidently expected our diplomats to spread themselves on this essay, as he added characteristically, but perhaps optimistically: 'it ought to be possible to get this on one page.' On the same day, he minuted to the Foreign Secretary: 'we are approaching a showdown with the Russians about their Communist intrigues in Italy, Yugoslavia and Greece. Their attitude becomes more difficult every day.'

On 31 May 1944, Churchill told the President that he had suggested to the Soviet Government that there should be an arrangement under which Roumania should fall within the sphere of the Russian armies and Greece within the sphere of the Allied command in the Mediterranean, and that Stalin had approved the idea subject to American endorsement. The State Department were slightly sanctimonious and very lukewarm, and it was only after considerable argument that they eventually agreed, on condition that it was made clear that we were not 'establishing any post-war spheres of influence.' This no doubt admirable idealism revealed a profound ignorance of Soviet mentality and purpose. Did they imagine for a moment that Russia would not insist on completely absorbing all the Baltic States, or that she would be content with 'a sphere of influence' in Roumania, Bulgaria, Poland, Hungary and the rest? If so, they were soon to be disillusioned.

By August 1944 the Germans were being hammered in Russia, France and Italy, and it looked as though they would soon have to evacuate Greece and other Balkan countries. The Prime Minister therefore decided that the time had come for the force earmarked for Greece to be held at instant readiness to embark. He emphasised that the operation was to be 'regarded as one of reinforced diplomacy and policy rather than an actual campaign.'

As it turned out, the Germans hung on longer than was expected, and it was not until 12 October that they withdrew from Athens. Two days later a British force of some five thousand men, under General Scobie, moved into the capital. They found the country war-ravaged, starving and torn by dissensions. It seemed clear that the former resistance groups, who went by the initials EAM and ELAS, were now Communist-controlled and likely to try to seize power and proclaim themselves the lawful Government of Greece. On 3 December they defied constitutional authority and attacked the police, and Scobie found himself involved in the twin horrors of street fighting and civil war. Street fighting is an operation which is particularly repugnant to the regular soldier. His enemies generally know every nook and cranny, are seldom in recognisable uniform, and have no regard for the laws of war. Civil war is even more distasteful to the military commander. If he does not use sufficient violence he fails in his mission, and suffers undue casualties. If, on the other hand, he uses all the violence which the situation demands, he is apt to be arraigned as a murderer. On this occasion Scobie, in a telegram of 5 December, was given the most explicit instructions as to what was expected of him by the Prime Minister himself. 'We have to hold and dominate Athens. It would be a great thing for you to succeed in this without bloodshed if possible, but also with bloodshed if necessary.' The fighting was fierce, and Scobie could make little headway. To make matters worse, our intervention in Greece was vehemently criticised as a negation of the causes for which we were fighting, not only by the State Department and most of the press in America, but also by some of the leading organs at home, and a small section of the House of Commons. It should be placed on record that, in the midst of all this hullabaloo, no word of protest came from the Kremlin or the newspaper *Pravda*. Stalin had given his word and kept it.

Churchill faced his critics in the Commons on 8 December. 'Democracy is not based on violence or terrorism,' he said, 'but on reason, on fair play, on freedom, on respecting the rights of other people. Democracy is no harlot to be picked up in the street by a man with a tommygun. I trust the people, the mass of the people, in almost any country, but I like to make sure that it is the people and not a gang of bandits who think that, by violence, they can overturn the constituted authority.' He won his Vote of Confidence by an overwhelming majority.

Meanwhile our troops continued to have a very rough time and were almost besieged in the centre of Athens. Substantial reinforcements improved the position, but Field Marshal Alexander, who was the last man in the world to take counsel of his fears, reported to the Prime Minister that, with his present strength, he could not possibly do more than clear and hold the Athens-Piraeus area. He added that the situation in Italy did not permit the despatch of futher reinforcements to Greece, and recommended that a solution of the Greek problem should be sought in the political field.

Churchill decided to go to Athens at once. He had already passed the age of three score years and ten, and was much looking forward to a family Christmas party at Chequers. But, as always, personal convenience was sacrificed on the altar of public duty. Eden, the most loyal of lieutenants, and as eager as his chief for adventure, went with him. They landed at Athens airfield at about noon on Christmas Day and had a long discussion with Field Marshal Alexander, Mr Macmillan[1] and the British Ambassador, Mr Leeper. That night the Prime Minister slept in HMS *Ajax* which was lying at anchor off the Piraeus, and the next morning he made his way to the British Embassy in an armoured car. The old warrior must have felt in his ele-

[1] Mr Macmillan's official designation was Minister Resident at Allied Force Headquarters, Mediterranean Command.

ment again. In the evening there was a long conference, at which the United States Ambassador, the French Minister and a Russian representative were present, in addition to the British party. The Greek factions were represented by Archbishop Damaskinos and three leaders of the Greek Communists respectively. The Prime Minister opened the meeting by explaining that the problem facing Greece was one for the Greeks themselves. All that the British and their allies desired was to restore order in the country and make sure that it was controlled by a freely elected Greek Government. He and all the other non-Greeks then withdrew, and an acrimonious and lengthy discussion took place between the rival parties. The upshot was that the King of Greece should be requested to appoint Archbishop Damaskinos Regent, and instruct him to form a Government without any Communist members. By the end of the month, Churchill was back in England and persuaded King George II of the Hellenes to make the necessary announcement. The British troops in Greece gradually gained the upper hand; and on 11 January, the Communists accepted a truce. The troubles were at an end. Greece continued to be a free country.

The fighting had been insignificant compared with the gigantic struggles which were raging in other parts of the world, but the result had a profound effect on the shape and structure of post-war Europe. I have thought it right to describe the sequence of events in some detail in order to show the dominating part which was played by Mr Churchill in this episode. It was he who foresaw the possibility of trouble in Greece a year before it occurred, and asked that preparations should be made to meet the eventuality of a Communist *coup d'état* when the Germans withdrew. It was he who, in August 1944, gave instructions for the necessary force to be held in instant readiness to embark. It was he who was primarily responsible for their timely arrival in Greece, and for the subsequent despatch of reinforcements which could ill be spared. It was he who took full responsibility for ordering the military commander to use whatever force he thought necessary to achieve our object. It was he who was bitterly criticised both at home and in America for his 'reactionary' policy, though he managed to persuade sensible opinion in both countries that our intervention was wholly unselfish and in accordance with the best traditions of democracy. It was he who went to

Athens on Christmas Eve at great personal sacrifice and brought the contending parties round the same table. Finally it was he who had the delicate task of persuading the King of the Hellenes to promise not to return to his country unless summoned by a free expression of the national will, and in the meantime to appoint Archbishop Damaskinos as Regent. All in all, it can be claimed that had it not been for Churchill's foresight, courage and drive, Greece would now be a Russian satellite, and Turkey isolated from her friends in Western Europe. I wonder how many people remembered this at the meeting of the North Atlantic Council at Lisbon in February 1952 at which Greece and Turkey became members of the North Atlantic Alliance. Nor should it be forgotten that military opinion both in London and Washington condemned our intervention in Greece as bad strategy, and trotted out all the well-worn arguments about the folly of side-shows. No one would dispute that, from the purely military point of view, the despatch to Greece of troops who were sorely needed in other theatres of war was unsound. But no one comprehending all the issues on which strategy must be based would deny that, on political grounds, it was absolutely essential.

CHAPTER XXVIII

The Second Quebec Conference

1944

SHORTLY after his return from watching the Riviera landings, Churchill thought that the time had arrived for a plenary conference to review the operations in progress and in prospect, and in particular to decide upon plans for the overthrow of Japan. The President was agreeable, and after both Scotland and Bermuda had been canvassed as meeting places, the choice again fell upon Quebec. The Conference was given the somewhat obvious code name, OCTAGON, and it was agreed that the size of both delegations should be kept to the minimum. This was easier said than done. Protests poured in that this or that expert adviser was absolutely essential, and the expert advisers, in their turn, demanded a generous quota of staff. I was somewhat uneasy at the prospect of having to report to the Prime Minister that instead of the twenty-five persons originally contemplated, we were going to be over two hundred strong but I felt more comfortable when I learned from our people in Washington that the Americans were bringing about two hundred and fifty. On 5 September we set off once again in the *Queen Mary* for Halifax, and once again my days were spent either at the conference table or in the Prime Minister's cabin. Mr Churchill had not yet recovered from his illness, but instead of having a rest, he insisted on working harder than ever.

Large doses of M and B had wrought miracles with his pneumonia but had not improved his temper; and although the sea was calm, some of us had a rough passage.

When our train drew into Quebec, it was a pleasant surprise to find the President and Mrs Roosevelt and all the American Chiefs of Staff on the platform. The Roosevelts' train had arrived a few minutes earlier than ours, and they had decided to wait at the station to welcome the Churchills. The scene that ensued was more like the reunion of a happy family starting on a holiday than the gathering of sedate Allied war leaders for an important conference. It was evident that the mutual suspicion of the early days of the partnership had been replaced by mutual esteem, and that the spirit of friendship which had from the outset animated the two great political chiefs had extended to their military advisers. We were sad to hear that Harry Hopkins had been prevented by illness from coming to Quebec. He sent a message to say that better men than he had been killed on the Plains of Abraham and that he was taking no risks.

The President and the Prime Minister again stayed at the Citadel, while both delegations once more took possession of the Château Frontenac. The arrangements of the Canadian Government were admirable, as always, and their hospitality princely.

The first plenary meeting was held on 13 September, and I was shocked to see the great change that had taken place in the President's appearance since the Cairo Conference. He seemed to have shrunk: his coat sagged over his broad shoulders, and his collar looked several sizes too big. What a difference from the first time that I had set eyes on him less than two and a half years ago! Seated at the desk of his study, on what I shall always remember as 'Tobruk morning,' he had looked the picture of health and vitality. His instinctive and instantaneous reaction to the shattering telegram had won my heart for ever. No formal expression of sympathy, no useless regrets: only transparent friendship, and an unshakable determination to stand by his allies. 'Winston, what can we do to help?' Thereafter I had seen him in action in many different parts of the world, and had never ceased to marvel at the fortitude which enabled him not merely to defy, but to ignore, his physical affliction. He had much in common with my beloved chief. Both were unspoiled by success; both had the exuberance of youth; both were incurable optimists. To see them together, whether at work or play, was a joy; and to read their telegrams to each other was a revelation of their mutual understanding and friendship. Above all, the President had proved, by all that he had done for us in the days when we seemed alone, that he was a friend who would never fail. It was grievous to think that the shadows were closing in. There had been a marked change, too, in Field Marshal Dill. He looked frail and almost at the end of his tether. He would work till he dropped, but it was only too clear that his days were numbered. Within seven weeks he was dead: and the President within seven months.

Churchill, despite his recent illness, was in splendid form. After a masterly review of the world situation, he turned to what he regarded as the most important problem which called for decision. He said that the British had not only the duty, but the right, to play a full part in the overthrow of Japan. It would be fatal for Anglo-American post-war relations if it could be said that America had made a great contribution to the defeat of Germany, whereas the British effort against Japan had been limited to the pursuit of her own selfish interests in Burma, Malaya and Hong Kong. Admittedly it would not be possible to move British armies or air forces to the Far East until Germany surrendered; but now that the German Navy had practically ceased to exist, a British Fleet, which would include the newest battleships and an ample fleet train, could be sent to the Central Pacific at once and operate under United States command. He asked point blank whether this proposal was approved. It was common knowledge that Admiral King was opposed to it, partly because he did not want anyone else to intervene in his own pet war, and partly because he thought that the British war-ships, relying as they did on bases all over the world, were constructed for short hauls and would need considerable conversion before they could be used in the vast expanses of the Pacific. A paper setting out his arguments had in fact already been circulated to the Combined Chiefs of Staff. It was therefore a surprise to everyone when the President unhesitatingly accepted the Prime Minister's offer. The British delegation heaved a sigh of relief, and the story went the rounds that Admiral King went into a swoon and had to be carried out. But this was an exaggeration. The Prime Minister followed up his success with the further request that the Royal Air Force should be allowed to take part in the bombing of the Japanese mainland, but this involved considerable technical difficulties, and it was agreed that experts should study the proposition before a final decision was taken.

The meetings of the Combined Chiefs of Staff were primarily devoted to reviewing the reports of the commanders in the field and approving their proposals for further action. They reminded me of a body of specialists who were very satisfied with the progress of their various patients, and were agreed that the prescribed treatments should be continued. They decided, among other things, that the target date for the end of the war against Japan should be eighteen months after the collapse of Germany; it being understood that this estimate would be reviewed from time to time. Personally I had a feeling that it was either too short or too long. The Japanese were already on their last legs; but if they were given to think that a rigid interpretation would be placed on the term 'Unconditional Surrender,' and that their Emperor — to them the Son of Heaven — would be treated as a war criminal, every man, woman and child would fight on till Domesday. If, on the other hand, the terms of surrender were phrased in such a way as to appear to preserve the right of their Emperor to order them to lay down their arms, they would do so without a moment's hesitation.

OCTAGON ended on 16 September. It had been the shortest conference of the series; as Churchill said, it had started 'in a blaze of friendship': it ended on the same note. The principal difficulty had been to find 'room and opportunity for marshalling against Japan the massive forces which both nations were ardent to engage against the enemy.' [1] We had come a long way from the days when every cupboard had to be scraped bare in order to find the wherewithal to attack, or even to defend ourselves.

Our return in the *Queen Mary* was a delightful relaxation. It was the first voyage throughout the war on which I had been able to find time for a daily promenade on deck.

[1] Roosevelt's press conference. See Sherwood: *Roosevelt and Hopkins.*

CHAPTER XXIX

Visits to Moscow and Paris

1944

N O S O O N E R had we returned to England than the Prime Minister decided to pay a visit to Moscow. His main purpose was to discuss political matters, particularly the problem of Poland; but he also wanted to find out when the Russians would enter the war against Japan and what form their intervention would take. The President welcomed the idea of the meeting and would like to have joined them himself, but this was impossible owing to the impending Presidential election in the United States. He therefore authorised Mr Harriman to represent him as such meetings as Churchill and Stalin desired, and to explain, with the help of Major-General John R. Deane, the American plans for the overthrow of Japan.

I left London with the Prime Minister on 5 October. It was a joy to be able to fly direct over France with a free air above, and a free land below, instead of having to go half way to America in order to avoid the attentions of the Luftwaffe. At Naples we were joined by Eden and the CIGS, and a conference was held with Wilson, Alexander, Macmillan and John Cunningham. They left us in no doubt that the withdrawals from the armies in Italy for the Riviera landings had emasculated their campaign.

That night we dined in Cairo, and took off again shortly after midnight. By noon we were in Moscow. Our welcome at the airfield was more cordial than it had been in the previous year, and the atmosphere of goodwill continued throughout the visit. On the social side it was an unqualified success. Stalin broke his self-imposed rule of never dining outside the Kremlin and attended a dinner given in his honour at the British Embassy. He spent most of that evening cheek by jowl with Mr Churchill, now in serious discussion, now in chaff, and the party did not break up until the early hours of the morning.

Two days later the Prime Minister and Eden were booked for political discussion at the Kremlin, and the Russians invited the rest of the delegation to the ballet. Our party numbered fourteen, and we were given a box to hold twelve and two seats in the front row of the stalls. We gave the tickets for the latter to our two young sergeant clerks, thinking that they would be happier alone, but they came to us before the curtain went up with the news that other ranks were not allowed in the stalls. The solution was simple. Two brigadiers took the stall tickets, and the two sergeants had seats in the front row of our box. It was puzzling that there should be so wide a gulf between the commissioned and non-commissioned ranks in a classless state, but it was in keeping with the meticulous attention which the Soviet Army paid to saluting. When the ballet was over, Mr Harriman invited a few of us to the American Embassy to meet Semyonova, the Moscow ballerina. Although a very favoured person in the Soviet hierarchy, she was unassuming, simple and charming. And when I told her that she would get a great welcome if she came to London, she said that she dared not face an audience who had seen the great Pavlova.

On 14 October Stalin attended a special command performance which had been arranged in our honour in the Bolshoi Theatre. He sat in the centre of the royal box, with Churchill on his right hand and Harriman on his left. During the first interval he asked Churchill to stand up at the front of the box alone in full view of the audience, and the cheering was tumultuous. Many of us were astonished that such a ruthless man of steel as Stalin should be capable of such old-world courtesy. When he moved forward and stood by Churchill's side, the uproar was deafening.

After the performance we assembled at the Kremlin for military discussions. The Soviet delegation consisted of Stalin, Molotov and General Antonov. The United States were represented by Harriman and Deane, and the British by the Prime Minister, Eden, Brooke, Burrows[1] and myself. Stalin was in a good mood, and very much on the ball, and the Soviet delegation were unusually frank and co-operative. Brooke started off with an admirable exposition of the situation in France, Italy and Burma, and Deane described the operations in the Pacific. He also outlined the American plans for the defeat of Japan, and indicated the facilities which they hoped to get from the Russians. They were followed by General Antonov, the Soviet Chief of Staff, who explained the Russian military situation in Europe and their plans for participation in the war against Japan. Stalin left us in no doubt that he would fight the Japanese after the collapse of Germany, but gave no indication of the precise period which would elapse before he did so. On the other hand, he surprised us by agreeing to the American proposal that they should at once start stockpiling in the Russian maritime provinces, and by allowing the immediate use of a number of airfields in that part of the world. On the next day there was another equally successful meeting on military matters, but the Prime Minister had a temperature and could not attend.

If only the meetings on Polish affairs had been equally successful, we could have returned to London in triumph. But alas, they were a complete failure. Neither Brooke nor I was present, but we learned that in the bilateral conversations which the Prime Minister and Eden had with the Russians, the latter would not budge an inch, and that the meetings were equally fruitless in which Mikolajczyk, head of the Polish Government in Exile in London, took part together with the Lublin Poles, the self-styled Polish Government in Warsaw. The latter were obviously nothing but Communist stooges, and their qualifications to represent Poland may be judged by their assertion that Lvov should belong to Russia. Lvov was, in Polish eyes, a sacred shrine, for which ninety-nine out of every hundred Poles would have gladly gone to the stake. A Polish friend once told me that to ask them to cede Lvov would be like asking the British to deliver Canterbury into the hands of unbelievers. No wonder that the Lublin Poles were regarded as Quislings. Nevertheless neither Churchill nor Eden was altogether without hope that a settlement might soon be reached.

[1] Lieutenant-General M. B. Burrows, Head of British Military Mission to USSR, 1944.

Our send-off from Moscow airfield, headed by Marshal Stalin himself, was even more cordial than our welcome had been, and when we saw two large crates of vodka and caviare being loaded into our aircraft without a word of explanation, we assumed that Russian hospitality had excelled itself. On arrival in London the delicacies were divided up in appropriate proportions between all the members of the delegation, from the Prime Minister downwards. My own share was a whole pound of caviare, and I distributed it in small jars to several of my friends who had not tasted it for many years. Their gratitude was profuse, and I remember in particular a note from Colonel Oliver Stanley thanking me 'for the lovely black diamonds.' A few days later we had an unpleasant surprise. An agitated Foreign Office official telephoned to say that the Soviet Ambassador in London was anxious about the non-arrival of a consignment of a caviare and vodka which had been loaded in our plane at Moscow and was intended for the forthcoming celebration of Russia's National Day — the anniversary of the Bolshevik revolution — at the Soviet Embassy. The unfortunate diplomat was aghast when we explained what had happened. What was he to say to the Russians? We could only suggest that he should tell them the truth, the whole truth, and nothing but the truth, and at the same time offer to make up for our unintentional, and deeply regretted, act of robbery by a handsome present of Scotch whisky. That was the last we heard of the matter.

CHAPTER XXX

Armistice Day in Paris

1944

ABOUT a fortnight after our return from Moscow, I was overjoyed to be told by the Prime Minister that he had accepted General de Gaulle's invitation to go to Paris for the anniversary celebration of the first Armistice Day, and that he wished me to accompany him. It would be like waking up out of a nightmare to see Paris her own lovely self again, and I knew how much the visit would mean to Churchill. He had been deeply grieved and humiliated by our inability to help his beloved France in her agony, but, as he had promised four years ago, the dawn had now come. I was glad that I, who had been a witness of his distress, was going to be with him when he received the rapturous homage which Paris would surely pay him.

At the last moment the security authorities advised that the visit should be postponed, owing to the danger of an attempt on the Prime Minister's life by German agents who were believed to be still at large in the city. But Mr Churchill would not hear of any change of plan, and on the afternoon of 10 November we landed at Orly airfield, which I was destined to use so frequently in later years, when I was Secretary-General of NATO. A general who had been on Gamelin's staff in the early days of the war and with whom I had worked very closely met me and accompanied me to my hotel. As soon as we were

380

alone he asked whether we had forgiven France for quitting the fight. I begged him to put any such thoughts out of his mind. Who were we to cast stones? We had been so powerless to help our friends and had owed our own salvation, not for the first time in our history, to twenty miles of salt water. His comment was revealing. 'There will be Frenchmen who will not forgive you for two generations. You made our shame so great by fighting on.' Mr and Mrs Churchill and Mary were the guests of the French Government at the Quai D'Orsay, and General Brooke and I were installed at the Continental Hotel. It was at that time dilapidated, as cold as a mausoleum, and there was practically no hot water.

The next morning General Koenig, the hero of Bir Hakeim and now Governor of Paris, drove me to the Arc de Triomphe, where we awaited the arrival of the Prime Minister and General de Gaulle. Never have I heard such a sustained roar of cheering as heralded their approach. After the two leaders had laid wreaths upon the tomb of the Unknown Warrior, we all proceeded on foot down the Champs Elysées to a dais about half a mile distant. Again the pent-up emotion of perhaps half a million Parisians broke loose like a flood. Some were cheering: some were laughing: some were sobbing: all were delirious. *'Vive Churchill. Vive de Gaulle. Vive l'Angleterre. Vive la France.'* There followed a march past of French and British troops, with a detachment of Guards bringing up the rear. They looked very young, but they bore themselves like veterans and seemed to take it for granted that they should be treading the famous highway which so many conquerors had trod before them. Their forefathers, who had died fighting in the same cause and were buried in war cemeteries not far distant, would have been proud of them. It was a bitterly cold day, and the tears froze on our cheeks.

While the Prime Minister and Mr. Eden were busy with political discussions, Brooke and I had talks with General Juin and General Koenig. Juin begged the CIGS to support his request to the Americans for equipment for eight new French divisions. With the hard fighting in progress and in prospect, it was clearly necessary for military reasons that the equipment of fully trained troops should have first priority, but for political and psychological reasons, it seemed most important that the French Army should be given an opportunity to play as large a part as possible in the overthrow of Germany, and a chance to regain the prestige which they had always enjoyed until the scythe of German armour ripped them to pieces in 1940.

On the next night the Prime Minister and Brooke left Paris with General de Gaulle to visit the First French Army under General de Lattre de Tassigny, in the region of Besançon, near the Swiss frontier. I saw them off at the Gare de Lyon, and flew home the next morning.

We had become so accustomed to an almost unbroken run of victories that it was rude shock to learn in mid-December that Rundstedt had launched a powerful and completely unexpected attack through the Ardennes — the same route that the Panzers had used with such tremendous results in 1940. At first it was difficult to take the news too tragically. The Luftwaffe had been fought out of the skies, and most of Rundstedt's divisions were likely to be not too well-equipped, and short of oil. The break-through was said to be on a front of about fifty miles; and it seemed unlikely that Runstedt would get very far before the weather cleared sufficiently to allow the Allied air forces to rain destruction upon his columns from the skies, and the Allied armies to strike at the flanks of his salient.

Surveying the operations from London, one could not but recall that in March 1918 Ludendorff's last desperate gamble had created havoc for a few days, and then petered out. It seemed that Rundstedt's chances of success were far more slender, and that the ultimate result of his gamble would be to hasten the final collapse of Germany. And so it eventually proved. Thanks to the magnificent fighting of the American troops, his advance was brought to a standstill before the year was out. He never managed to cross the Meuse, much less take Liége; and his Panzer armies suffered crippling casualties.

CHAPTER XXXI

The Yalta Conference

1944–1945

I T IS a truism that war is a continuation of policy by other means; and history shows that civilised sovereign states do not as a rule resort to arms until it is clear beyond any shadow of doubt that their essential purposes cannot be achieved in any other way. Once the die is cast, contacts between the Foreign Offices are broken off and the subtleties of diplomacy give way to the brutalities of naked force. Military considerations become overriding, and continue to be overriding, until such time as the ultimate result of the conflict appears certain. When that moment approaches, both sides must give increasingly greater weight to political considerations — the potential loser, in order to save what he can out of the wreck: the potential victor, in order to ensure that the purposes for which he took up arms will be realised in the post-war world.

By the end of 1944, Rundstedt's last desperate fling had failed. The German armies had, with one or two minor exceptions, been flung out of all the countries which they had enslaved. They were now hemmed within their own borders, fighting against hopeless odds on both their eastern and western fronts. The cities and factories of Germany were being pulverised by round-the-clock bombardment; her transportation system was being shattered; and her stocks of oil and other essentials were already dangerously low. Doom stared her in the face. If anyone but a megalomaniac like Hitler had been in control, she would at once have thrown herself on the mercy of the Allies.

The time had therefore come for a conference of the leaders of the three Powers which, by their exertions and sacrifices, had earned the right, and incurred the duty, to settle the shape and structure of post-war Europe. In a letter to Churchill of 30 August 1944, Smuts wrote that this was 'the crucial issue on which the future of the world for generations will depend.'

From the British point of view, the future of Poland was of out-standing importance. We had drawn the sword when she was assailed in September 1939, and were pledged to restore her full independ-ence as a Sovereign Power. The hated Germans had been driven out of the country; but the Russians, who had in the past been even more cordially detested, were now in occupation, and seemingly de-termined that Poland should remain under the Communist yoke. Vic-tory was near at hand, but the purpose for which we had taken up arms was as yet far from having been achieved.

President Roosevelt, Mr Churchill and Marshal Stalin were all agreed that an early meeting was essential, and it only remained to decide upon the place at which it should be held. Stalin, character-istically, gave no consideration either to Roosevelt's physical infirm-ity, or to Churchill's recent severe illnesses; nor did he make any al-lowance for the fact that both of them had travelled half way across the world to meet him little more than a year ago. He insisted that he could not leave Russia owing to the military situation, and that air travel did not suit him. Having learned that it was only neces-sary to say *Nyet* often enough in order to get his way, he said that he was willing to go as far as the Crimea, but not an inch further. The President and the Prime Minister were agreeable, and it was decided without further ado, that the conference should be held at Yalta. It would have been difficult to find a more unget-at-able, inconvenient or unsuitable meeting place. The President said that he would arrive at Malta by battleship on 2 February and fly direct to the Crimea that night. Churchill proposed that they should have preliminary talks at Malta before meeting the Russians, but the President replied that he could not spare the time. He acceded however to Churchill's further suggestion that the Combined Chiefs of Staff should meet in Malta two or three days earlier to discuss a number of urgent technical problems, including in particular the plans for the final assault on Germany from the West. The plan proposed by Eisenhower was in three phases: first, to close the Rhine along its whole length; secondly, to cross the river at several points and establish bridge-heads; and thirdly, to advance on a wide front into Germany. The British, on the other hand, argued that the Germans were already beaten, and that the methodical plan proposed by Eisenhower was too cautious. It would not only unduly prolong the war, but also result in the Russians getting to Berlin first. They therefore supported Montgomery's proposal for an immediate advance on Berlin via the Ruhr by a force of some thirty-five to forty divisions, who would be given all the logistic resources which they required, while the rest of Eisenhower's armies did their best with what was left over.

The Combined Chiefs of Staff duly met on 29 January, and General Bedell Smith was in attendance. He said that the Supreme Commander totally disagreed with what he described as 'a pencil line thrust on Berlin,' and the altercation which ensued was vehement and at times acrimonious. It may be thought that honest differences of opinion should not have been allowed to generate so much heat, but there is a good deal to be said for Churchill's advice that there should be no 'smoothings or smirchings' to disguise one's true feelings. The closer one's personal relations, the more brutally frank one can be. General Marshall stood four-square behind Eisenhower, and the British had no option but to give way. The merits and demerits of the rival plans are likely to be argued for many a long day, but it cannot be gainsaid that, from the military point of view, Eisenhower's plan was completely successful. It is less easy to determine whether it unduly prolonged the war or whether it was wise, from the political point of view, not to forestall the Russians in capturing Berlin.

The Prime Minister reached Malta just before dawn on 30 January. He had a high temperature and did not move from his aircraft to HMS *Orion,* in which he was to live, until the following afternoon. Two days later the President arrived in the USS *Quincy;* and that afternoon there was a plenary meeting on board, at which the Combined Chiefs of Staff were able to report that they had reached agreement on all the points at issue. Roosevelt looked a very sick man.

That night both delegations started on their journey to Yalta. It involved a flight of one thousand four hundred miles to Saki airfield, on which a large advance party of RAF technicians had been at work for several weeks. From there it was eight hours by car to Yalta itself. A mighty force of Russian soldiery had done wonders in improving the road through the mountains, with its rough surface and innumerable hair-pin bends; but even so, it was a boneshaking and extremely cold drive. Nearly all the houses at Yalta had been much knocked about by the Germans before they evacuated; and except for the VIPs, the accommodation was inadequate and primitive. The climate was unexpectedly bleak, and the only redeeming feature was the scenery.

The Prime Minister and senior members of our delegation were housed in Vorontzov Villa. The site was lovely. On one side the Black Sea a few hundred feet below us and less than five minutes' walk, and on the other a buttress of mountains rising steeply to a height of several thousand feet. The Villa was a fantastic mixture of bogus Scottish castle and Moorish palace; but the rooms were well enough proportioned, and, thanks to enormous log fires, warm and comfortable. It had been the headquarters of General Manstein during the German occupation of the Crimea, and been left a shambles when they were driven out. But shortage of manpower was never a weakness of our Russian allies, and we were told that over a thousand men had been employed for a full month in putting it to rights. Every stick of furniture, every piece of cutlery, glass and china, every bottle of wine, and practically every bite of food, had been imported from Moscow, as had the domestic staff. Two of the waiters who had looked after me at the Hotel Nationale were standing in the entrance hall when I arrived, and I felt hurt that they gave me no sign of recognition. But they made amends as soon as they were out of sight of their masters. They conducted me to my bedroom, dropped on their knees, kissed my hand and went out without a word.

There were over thirty of us living at Vorontzov, including Eden, Leathers, three Field Marshals, one or two Admirals of the Fleet, a Marshal of the Royal Air Force, a posse of generals and a number of high civilian officials, including Sir Edward Bridges, Secretary of the Cabinet. His attendance for the first time at an international conference was indicative of the increasing importance of civilian and political questions. Except for an acute shortage of bathrooms, we had nothing to complain about, but the rest of our delegation were less fortunate. They had to sleep six or eight in a room in ramshackle buildings which were called Sanatoria, but which were almost entirely innocent of sanitary arrangements.

Russian hospitality was as lavish as usual, and nothing was too much trouble for them. Sarah Oliver, who was acting as ADC to her father, happened to mention one evening that caviare was improved by lemon juice. Three days later a large lemon tree covered with fruit had been planted in the orangery next door to the dining-room. It proved more than sufficient for our needs.

The Conference lasted about a week. From the gastronomical point of view, it was enjoyable: from the social point of view, successful: from the military point of view, unnecessary: and from the political point of view, depressing. The general atmosphere was extremely friendly, and at the customary round of banquets, the speeches were more than usually fulsome. Churchill said that he walked through the world 'with greater courage and hope' when he found himself in 'a relationship of friendship and intimacy' with Stalin. Stalin, not to be out-done, toasted Churchill as 'the man who is born once in a hundred years.' President Roosevelt likened the relations between the three countries to those of a happy family. This seemed to be going a little too far, but I believe that he meant what he said.

On the military side, I cannot recall that anything was achieved which could not have been equally well settled by the Combined Chiefs of Staff machinery in Washington, and the British and American Missions in Moscow. At all previous conferences, the military element had been the *prima donna,* occupying the centre of the stage. At Yalta we hung about in the wings waiting for calls which never came. Hitherto my difficulty at conferences had been to find time to do all the work which fell to my lot. At Yalta, my difficulty was to find sufficient work to occupy my time.

The civilian element of the delegation, on the other hand, were very hard-pressed. Political problems of infinite variety and great complexity were under discussion all day and every day — now at plenary meetings, now at meetings of the Foreign Secretaries, now at small lunches or dinners. A number of knotty points were resolved. The recommendations of the European Advisory Commission in regard to the Zones to be occupied by Great Britain, the United States and Russia were approved; and it was further agreed that France should also have a Zone of Occupation in Germany, and be a member of the Control Commission. There was a measure of agreement on certain matters connected with the World Organisation. Stalin undertook to participate in the war against Japan within two or three months after Germany had been liquidated; and Russia's post-war requirements in the Far East were embodied in a personal agreement between 'the Big Three.' The rewards that she claimed in return for a contribution which was bound to be belated, and proved to be insignificant, were on the very generous side. The *status quo* in Outer Mongolia was to be preserved, and all the Russian rights which had been lost in the Russo-Japanese War of 1904 were to be restored.

But the deadlock over Polish-Soviet affairs continued. In particular the vital problems of holding free elections in Poland, and of setting up a single Government on a broader democratic basis, were no nearer settlement at the end of the Conference than they had been at the beginning. All that emerged was an agreement that these matters should be studied by a committee consisting of M. Molotov, Mr Harriman and Sir Archibald Clark Kerr. Churchill was anxious that the Conference should not break up until more definite arrangements had been made, but the President said that he could not spare the time. In any case, he and his delegation were exultant at the results already achieved. 'We really believed in our hearts,' said Hopkins to Sherwood, 'that this was the dawn of the new day we had all been praying for and talking about for many years. The Russians had proved that they could be reasonable and far-seeing and there was not any doubt in the minds of the President or any of us that we could live with them and get along with them peacefully for as far into the future as any of us could imagine.' [1] Nor were the Americans alone in their optimism. I believe that I was voicing the general opinion of the British delegation, with the exception of the Prime Minister who had been disillusioned by the failure to settle the Polish problem, when I wrote to Admiral Mountbatten, that the Conference had 'been a great success not so much because of the formal conclusions that were reached, but because of the spirit of frank cooperation which characterised all the discussions.'

Looking back on those days, I suppose that we ought to have

[1] Robert Sherwood: *Roosevelt and Hopkins.*

seen the red light when Stalin insisted that for Russia, Poland was a question not only of honour but of security, or, in other words, that it was thought to be a matter of life and death for the Soviet that Poland should be under the Communist yoke. But perhaps we were all deceived by the spirit of exuberant *bonhomie* which had prevailed throughout the Conference; or perhaps we preferred not to look unpleasant facts in the face.

It was a weary party which left Vorontzov in a snow-storm and boarded the SS *Franconia* in Sebastopol harbour. This vessel had acted as our communications ship, and we were greatly looking forward to returning in her as far as Malta. A peaceful voyage through the Black Sea and the Dardanelles was just what the Prime Minister needed after his illness and hard work at the Conference, and I was horrified when he announced that he had decided to fly to Athens at once to see how things were going. It was yet another example of his readiness to subordinate his personal convenience to his sense of public duty, and to subject himself to strains from which much younger men would have shrunk. It made me ashamed to think of the occasions on which I had been resentful at being deprived of leisure to attend to my own petty affairs.

I was determined not to leave the Crimea without visiting Balaclava. Had I not learned Tennyson's *Charge of the Light Brigade* by heart in my early youth and declaimed it to myself times beyond number in odd corners of the world? Fortunately Mr Churchill, whose regiment, the 4th Hussars, had taken part in the charge, had the same idea, and directly he came on board he announced his intention of paying a visit to the battlefield. He was particularly anxious that we should be a small party, and I was embarrassed when the Russian Admiral commanding the Black Sea Fleet paid me a visit and asked whether the Prime Minister proposed to go ashore, and if so, when. I started by prevaricating, but he left me in no doubt that it was as much as his life was worth not to be in continuous attendance on Mr Churchill from the moment that he set foot on Russian soil to the moment that he returned to the ship. I therefore told him the programme and begged him not to bring more than one Staff officer with him. Needless to say, protocol required him to bring at least four.

It was a great thrill to look upon the scene of one of the most glorious blunders of the British Army. The valley down which the Light Brigade attacked the Russian guns was as flat as a pancake. 'Any self-respecting cavalry would want to charge on ground like this,' commented the First Sea Lord. Brigadier Peake, the DDMI, who had learned up all the details, proceeded to explain the battle to the assembled company. 'There,' he said, pointing with his stick, 'is the line on which the Light Brigade were drawn up.' 'And there,' chimed in the Russian Admiral, pointing in another direction, 'is where the German tanks came through.' Peake, nothing daunted, continued his story. When he pointed to the ridges on either flank of the valley, through which the Light Brigade had run the gauntlet of fire, the Admiral again chipped in with the observation that a Russian battery of artillery had died there to the last man. Mr Churchill thought it right at this point to explain that Peake was not talking about a 'war of peoples', but about 'a long-past war of dynasties.' I doubt whether the interpreter was capable of translating this gem; but whatever he said evidently satisfied the Admiral, and there were no further interruptions.

Early the next morning the Prime Minister did the long tiring drive to Saki and flew to Athens. Thanks to his own foresight and courage and to the sturdy behaviour of the British soldier, the city was at last at peace. By way of showing that he was as fresh as ever, he flew to Alexandria next morning and lunched with Roosevelt on board the American cruiser *Quincy*. He afterwards wrote: 'The President seemed placid and frail. I felt that he had a slender contact with life. I was not to see him again.' Two days later Churchill had talks with King Ibn Saud at Fayoum Oasis, and it was not until the 19th that he returned to England. All this time I was living in clover on the *Franconia*. I had been moved into the suite which had been specially prepared for Mr Churchill. The sea was calm; the weather was lovely; and I had no work to do. I was sorry to leave the ship at Malta and fly to London.

CHAPTER XXXII

The End of the Road

1945–1946

T H E Prime Minister's first task on his return to London was to give the House of Commons an account of the Yalta Conference. Most of it was plain sailing, but it was no easy matter to account for the failure to reach agreement about the future of Poland. The most that he could say was that negotiations were to be continued in Moscow by Molotov and the British and American Ambassadors to Russia, and that Stalin and his Government had solemnly declared that Poland's sovereign independence would be maintained. He may have been going a little too far when he added that the word of the Russian Government was their bond, but as he put it, he 'felt bound to proclaim his confidence in Soviet good faith in the hope of securing it.' The Prime Minister won his Vote of Confidence by a very large majority. But there were a good many people, both inside and outside Parliament, who were far from reassured. We had drawn the sword in defence of the integrity of Poland, and we were bound in honour not to sheathe it while Poland was still under foreign domination.

This is not the place to set out all the representations which Churchill made to President Roosevelt and Marshal Stalin in his desire to get a fair deal for Poland. The United States Government were at first a good deal more optimistic about Soviet intentions than we were, but they too lost hope in the end. The final episode in the story was a journey to Moscow by Hopkins after the war in Europe had ended, to try to persuade Stalin to right the wrong. But he made very little impression. The stark truth is that, from the very start, the Soviet Government were determined that Poland should never throw off the Communist yoke and that they were completely successful in their aim. From that day to this Poland has been a Soviet satellite.

It is easy, and perhaps natural, to blame President Roosevelt and, in a lesser degree, Mr Churchill for not having taken a tougher line with Marshal Stalin. Nobody can deny that the failure to secure freedom and independence for Poland has brought shame on the Western democracies. At the same time, those who now aspire to prescribe what ought to have been done, must in fairness bear in mind the circumstances of those days. For over three years, public opinion in America and Britain had been led to believe that Russia was a brave and faithful ally who had done the lion's share of the fighting, and endured untold suffering. If their Governments had now proclaimed that the Russians were untrustworthy and unprincipled tyrants, whose ambitions must be held in check, the effect on national unity in both countries would have been catastrophic. And if the British and American Governments had pushed the matter to extremes, and threatened to oppose the Soviet by force, what was to be done about the two to three hundred German divisions which the Germans still maintained in the field? Should Britain and America have continued to fight the Wehrmacht with one hand and the Red Army with the other? Or should they have forgotten all that they had said about their determination to destroy Nazism, taken the Germans into their fold, and proceeded, with their help, to crush their recent allies? One is forced to the conclusion that such a reversal of policy, which dictators could have taken in their stride, was absolutely impossible for the leaders of democratic countries even to contemplate.

On the very day that Churchill was defending the agreements at Yalta in Parliament, there was a *coup d'état* in Bucharest of the kind with which the world was soon to become so painfully familiar. Vyshinsky forced himself on the King of Roumania and demanded the dismissal of his Government, and simultaneously Soviet troops occu-

pied the capital. A week later a Communist government was set up.
Roumania has been behind the Iron Curtain ever since. Mr Churchill
suggested to the President that they should send a joint remonstrance
in the strongest terms to Stalin, but Roosevelt, who was already a sick
man, was not prepared to agree. Matters went from bad to worse.

While there was so much that was so ominous and unsatisfactory
in the political field, our armies were enjoying almost unbroken success. By the end of February, they had broken through the Siegfried
Line, and on 2 March the Prime Minister, accompanied by Brooke
and myself, left London for Montgomery's headquarters at Geldrop
in Holland. We lived in General Eisenhower's very comfortable train,
and spent the next two days visiting various sectors of the Front. It
was very agreeable to set foot on German soil again, to cross the
vaunted Siegfried Line and to see villages bedecked with white flags.
The troops were in high spirits, and the advance was going splendidly.

On our last night in Holland Montgomery and his Chief of Staff, de
Guingand, dined in the train. Montgomery, as usual, left at a very
early hour, and shortly afterwards the conversation turned to the
crossing of the Rhine, which was to be carried out within the next
three weeks. Churchill announced that of course he intended to be
present, and that he expected to have a front seat in the stalls. Freddy
de Guingand, not knowing how his Chief would feel about it, tried to
temporise, but it was useless. Churchill was absolutely determined to
be there, and there was no valid reason why he should not be. The
risks would be little greater than those to which he had been exposed
in the Blitz or when flying all over the world in all sorts of weather.
When the time came, he stayed in Montgomery's camp at Venlo, and
not only watched the battle for two days, but also crossed to the far
bank of the Rhine and got as near as he could to being under the fire
of the enemy. He enjoyed every minute of it.

From now onwards the Germans were incapable of offering effective resistance. The tempo quickened and the Anglo-American and
Russian armies drew closer and closer together. But before the bells
rang out for victory, we were destined to suffer a grievous loss. In the
early hours of 13 April, I was awakened and told the news that President Roosevelt had suddenly collapsed and died on the previous eve-

ning. It had been obvious at Yalta that the end could not be far off, but we were all shocked by its suddenness, and deeply grieved at the loss of so staunch a friend and so powerful a champion of our cause. He had, as Churchill said in the House of Commons, 'brought his country through the worst of its perils, and the heaviest of its toils.' But how one could have wished that he had lived to see the victory which he had done so much to win! It was very near at hand.

Before the month was out, Himmler had offered unconditional surrender to the Western Allies. His offer was refused. Very shortly afterwards Mussolini was murdered, and on 30 April Hitler committed suicide in his bunker at Berlin. It was a relief that he did not fall into our hands alive. What on earth could have been done with him? On 2 May, the German army in Italy capitulated, and on the same day Berlin surrendered to the Russians. On the 4th, the German forces in Holland, Denmark and north-west Germany surrendered to Field Marshal Montgomery on Lüneburg Heath, and in the very early hours of the 7th, the unconditional surrender of Germany was signed at Rheims.

At about 3 A.M. that morning, I was awakened by my telephone bell, and told that the Supreme Commander was on the line. These nocturnal calls had never brought good news and I was afraid that something had gone wrong. But my mind was soon put at rest. 'Is that you, Pug?' 'Yes, Ike. What has happened?' 'They have signed on the dotted line. It's all over.' My wife heard what had been said, and her eyes filled with tears. I too felt a lump in my throat, and could scarcely voice my congratulations. I had got back into bed before it occurred to me that Eisenhower may have intended me to pass the news to the Prime Minister. To be on the safe side, I rang No. 10, but the operators had evidently failed to disconnect me from Rheims and my telephone was dead. There was nothing for it but to collect some coppers, put on a dressing gown, and go to the public call-box a hundred yards down the road. I had no difficulty in making contact with No. 10, only to be told by the best switchboard in London that Mr Churchill had already heard the glad news and gone to bed.

Throughout the war I had seldom failed to drop off to sleep the moment my head touched the pillow, but that night I lay awake for some little time. Our most powerful enemy had been laid low, but it was impossible to be completely happy about the future. Japan was still unconquered; and apart from that, there was no certainty that we would not again have to fight for our lives in Europe before many years had passed. When I eventually got to sleep, I may have had dreams about grappling with an enormous bear.

We expected that the Prime Minister would broadcast the announcement of the German surrender almost at once, but Stalin asked that it should not be made public for twenty-four hours, and as usual he had his way. Thus, 7 May was somewhat of an anti-climax redeemed only by the Prime Minister's thoughtfulness in giving a small lunch to the Chiefs of Staff, Hollis and myself. Before we went into the garden of No. 10, Downing Street to have a group photograph taken, Churchill toasted the triumvirate as 'the architects of victory.' I hoped that they would raise their glasses to the chief who had been the master planner; but perhaps they were too moved to trust their voices.

VE day, 8 May, did not open too well from my point of view. It was past noon before I received the script of the Prime Minister's victory broadcast, and found that he required a good deal of supplementary information, which could only be obtained from Rheims. But by dint of a long telephone conversation with Bedell Smith, all was ready by the time that he returned from his weekly lunch with the King, and punctually at 3 P.M. he went on the air. Even in that moment of rejoicing he did not shrink from uttering a sombre warning. 'On the continent of Europe we have yet to make sure that the simple and honourable purposes for which we entered the war are not thrust aside or overlooked . . .' There would be little use, he said, in punishing the Hitlerites for their crimes if law and justice did not rule, and if totalitarian or police Governments were to take the place of the German invaders. It is very doubtful if one in ten thousand people in our island realised the significance of his words.

In the afternoon the War Cabinet, accompanied by the Chiefs of Staff, drove to Buckingham Palace to offer their humble duty to the King and congratulate him on having vanquished his enemies in Europe. The Mall and Birdcage Walk were packed with cheering crowds, and our cars had to proceed at snail's pace. After several group photographs had been taken, His Majesty remarked that he and Bridges and I ought to be taken together as the only three who had kept their jobs throughout the war. But, alas, the proposal was not pressed! Later in the afternoon the Prime Minister, the War Cabinet and Chiefs of Staff assembled at the Home Office, and stood on the balcony overlooking the Cenotaph. Whitehall was a seething mass of humanity, and Churchill's appearance was greeted with a roar of cheering which continued for several minutes. In that sublime moment, he could little have thought that in less than two months very many of those who now acclaimed him would vote against his continued leadership.

In the evening we had a large and curiously assorted supper-party at our flat. There was Mr Lewis Douglas, who had recently arrived in London as United States Ambassador to the Court of St James in succession to Mr Averell Harriman; there was the Dowager Lady Reading, who had done such magnificent work as head of the Women's Voluntary Services: there was the whole of my personal staff: there was the head porter of our block of flats, who had become an officer of some eminence in Civil Defence: and there was my Belgian factotum, Felicien Glaudot, who had been with my family for thirty-four years and had looked after me in the flat throughout the war. He had been entirely unmoved by the Blitz or Hitler's secret weapons; but on the black day in May 1940 on which the Belgian Army capitulated I found him in great distress. 'Has Belgium done anything disgraceful?' he asked. I was glad to be able to tell him in all truth that, on the contrary, the Belgian Army had fought very gallantly against overwhelming odds, and to assure him that his country would be liberated again as it had been in 1918.

After supper the whole party walked arm-in-arm to Buckingham Palace and mingled with the crowds. There was none of the unrestrained enthusiasm which had broken all bounds on 11 November 1918: the general mood seemed to be one of immense relief and infinite gratitude, tempered by the realisation that Japan was still unconquered, and the feeling that all our troubles might not yet be over. But, like the Londoners of the First World War, they were united in their loyalty and devotion to the King and Queen who had shared their hardships and dangers. Each time that Their Majesties appeared on the balcony, the cheers were deafening; and each time that they returned to their rooms, their subjects clamoured for yet another appearance; each time I found myself saying: 'I do hope they will come back just once more.'

Amidst all this rejoicing the Prime Minister was filled with forebodings about the future. He thought it vital that there should be a meeting of the Big Three in order to try to reach a comprehensive and lasting settlement with Soviet Russia while America and Great Britain still had mighty forces on the continent of Europe. He put this suggestion to President Truman only three days after the German war had ended and followed it up the next day with the now famous 'iron curtain' telegram, in which he described with unerring vision the ugly possibilities which confronted the free world.

'I am profoundly concerned about the European situation. I learn that half the American Air Force in Europe has already begun to move to the Pacific theatre. The newspapers are full of the great movements of the American armies out of Europe. Our armies also are, under previous arrangements, likely to undergo a marked reduction. The Canadian Army will certainly leave . . . Meanwhile what is to happen about Russia? I have always worked for friendship with Russia, but, like you, I feel deep anxiety because of their misinterpretation of the Yalta decisions, their attitude towards Poland, their overwhelming influence in the Balkans, excepting Greece, the difficulties they make about Vienna, the combination of Russian power and the territories under their control or occupied, coupled with the Communist technique in so many other countries, and above all their power to maintain very large armies in the field for a long time. What will be the position in a year or two when the British and American Armies have melted and the French has not yet been formed on any major scale, when we may have a handful of divisions, mostly French, and when Russia may choose to keep two or three hundred on active service? An iron curtain is drawn down upon their front. We do not know what is going on behind . . . Surely it is vital now to come to an understanding with Russia, or see where we are with her, before we weaken our armies mortally or retire to the zones of occupation. This can only be done by a personal meeting.'

It was eventually decided that the Big Three should assemble for a conference at Potsdam on 15 July. This was a good deal later than Churchill had hoped, but it was better than nothing. Meanwhile he did his utmost to persuade Truman to delay the withdrawal of the American forces from the forward positions which they had reached in the fighting to their own zone of occupation, until the Conference had taken place. But the President would not hear of it. He said that the boundaries of the Zones had been approved at Yalta, and that it would be a breach of faith with the Soviet to depart from that agreement. There was nothing more to be said. The American forces began their withdrawal on 1 July, and the British conformed. Thus within a few days Soviet Russia was established in the heart of Europe. To quote Churchill: 'This was a fateful milestone for mankind.'

At home the Coalition Government which had been in office for five years came to an end at the end of May and was succeeded by a Caretaker Government under Mr Churchill. It was sad to think that the well-tried team which had brought us through so many vicissitudes was to be changed before the surrender of Japan, and that the unity which had been our strength in the dark days would now be marred by party strife.

Polling Day was fixed for 5 July, but in order to allow time for the votes of the Forces to be brought home, the counting of the votes was not to take place until 26 July. This meant that the Prime Minister and Mr Attlee, who was accompanying him to Berlin, would have to return to London before the Conference ended.

Now that the war in Europe was over and the Prime Minister had electioneering problems added to his other business, I had more time to myself; and I took the opportunity to spend a week-end with Bedell Smith in a charming villa a few miles from Frankfurt. I was surprised to find that the woodwork of the villa had recently been given a double coat of paint of a quality which no private individual in Great Britain had seen for years; that the garden was beautifully kept; that there were yards and yards of new rubber hose-pipes, and that even the swimming-pool had been freshly painted. Well-to-do Germans who dwelt in rural districts had evidently not been required to suffer the austerities which the British people had accepted so patiently for so many years.

On the day after my arrival Marshal Zhukov flew in from Berlin to present the Russian Order of Victory to General Eisenhower and Field Marshal Montgomery. It was a magnificent, if somewhat flamboyant, decoration and its intrinsic value was obviously considerable. At the luncheon party which followed, Zhukov made an admirable speech and Eisenhower, speaking off-the-cuff, an even better one. If only the men of the Kremlin had acted in accordance with the sentiments expressed at that luncheon table, the world would be a happier and better place.

Eisenhower was to receive the Freedom of the City of London two days later. He told me that he had already written and memorised his speech, and asked whether I would be sitting near him. I replied that I might be lucky enough to have a seat on the platform, but would be too far away to prompt him if he forgot his words. He admitted that this might be difficult, but suggested that I would surely be able to raise a cry of fire and distract everyone's attention. When the time came, he made one of the best speeches that has ever been heard in the Mansion House.

On 14 July I flew to Gatow Airfield for what was to be the last plenary conference of the war. I looked forward to seeing Berlin and meeting our American colleagues again, but after the experience of Yalta the prospect of spending a fortnight in Potsdam did not appeal to me. On the political side the pressure of work would be immense, but on the military side there would be little to discuss except the measures for knocking Japan out of the ring.

It was a mercy that the conflict between the Prime Minister and his military advisers on the question of our long-term strategy in the Far East was now past history. It had been protracted and vehement, and the story must be told. Early in 1944 the Chiefs of Staff produced their plans for British participation in the final overthrow of Japan. They recommended that as and when naval, land and air forces became available from Europe, they should be based on Australia, and operate across the Pacific under American command. They were also insistent that the preparation of the necessary base installations in Australia should start at once. The Prime Minister would have none of it. He pressed for his 'old favourite,' an operation across the Bay of Bengal against Sumatra; and from there he proposed to strike at Malaya and the Japanese line of communications with Burma. Doubtless there lay at the back of his mind the desire that we should recover by our own efforts, not only the territories, but also the prestige, which we had lost in south-east Asia. In addition he may have been appalled by the prospect of the long haul which the plan of the Chiefs of Staff involved. He foresaw that shipping requirements would be astronomical, that base installations would spring up like mushrooms all over Australia, and that the length of the 'tail' would leave little over for the 'teeth.'

The conflict became more and more heated. Neither side would budge an inch, and there was a possibility of resignations in high places. This, with OVERLORD only three months off, would have been disastrous. I therefore conceived it my duty to try to mediate in a manner which I had never done before and never did again. 'The Chiefs of Staff,' I wrote to the Prime Minister, 'are extremely unlikely to retract the military opinions that they have expressed . . . nor can we exclude the possibility of resignations . . . A breach of this kind would be little short of catastrophic at this juncture . . . Would it not be possible and right for you to take the line that the issue cannot be decided on military grounds alone and that . . . political considerations must be overriding? I cannot but think that the Chiefs of Staff would accept this decision with complete loyalty.'

The suggestion did not appeal to the Prime Minister, and about a fortnight later he issued a ruling on the subject to each Chief of Staff individually, instead of to the Chiefs of Staff as a corporate body. This made no reference to political considerations, but laid it down that the Bay of Bengal strategy had the approval of the War Cabinet, and must be taken as mandatory. The Chiefs of Staff returned to the charge, but very soon we all became so immersed in OVERLORD that long-term policies elsewhere were forgotten for the moment. They were subsequently rendered purely academic by the swiftness with which the struggles both in Burma and in the Pacific drew to their climax. By June 1944 the Japanese attack on Imphal and Kohima had been decisively repulsed by General Slim's XIVth Army. This was the beginning of the end in that part of the world. Later in the year the Prime Minister had agreed with the Chiefs of Staff that a strong British fleet should be sent to the Pacific as soon as possible to operate under American command, and the President had accepted the offer. In October Admiral Halsey practically annihilated the Japanese Navy in the stupendous battle of Leyte Gulf. This was as decisive as Trafalgar had been. In March 1945 General MacArthur cleared the last Japanese soldier out of the Philippines, and by the end of the month a British fleet, which included two of our latest battleships and four aircraft-carriers, was operating off Formosa. In

May 1945 Rangoon fell to General Slim's XIVth Army. Thus by the time the Potsdam Conference assembled, the bone of contention between the Prime Minister and his military advisers had disappeared.

The three delegations lived in separate enclaves, the British being allotted a number of villas in Babelsberg, a suburb of Potsdam. It had suffered no bomb damage, and our living-quarters were comfortable and in an excellent state of repair.

For the first four days there was a Chiefs of Staff meeting each morning and a Combined Chiefs of Staff meeting each afternoon. At one of these, the American Chiefs of Staff gave us the approximate dates of their final assaults on the Japanese homeland, where they expected the most bitter opposition. For some time past it had been firmly fixed in my mind that the Japanese were tottering, and I whispered to General Arnold that they would collapse long before this desperate and costly venture had to be undertaken. 'I bet you two bucks they do not fold up this year,' he said. 'Taken,' said I. In the event, the Japanese surrendered within a month of that conversation, and shortly afterwards I received a novel form of paper-weight — two silver dollars mounted in a block of polished walnut wood. It was inscribed: *'To Pug Ismay from Hap Arnold. Thank God I can pay this now.'* It is one of my most cherished mementoes of the war.

Only one other meeting with our American colleagues lives in my memory. We were discussing some unexciting topic when a telegram was brought into the room by an ADC and handed to General Marshall. He read it without emotion and placed it face downward on the table. A little later he proposed that the meeting should go into secret session; and as soon as we were alone he announced in a matter-of-fact tone of voice that the atom bomb experiment in New Mexico had been completely successful. My first reaction was one of revulsion. I had always had a sneaking hope that the scientists would be unable to find a key to this particular chamber of horrors. But first thoughts were soon erased by a surge of thankfulness that the secret had eluded our enemies.

A party of us visited Berlin one afternoon. It was a depressing experience. The only Germans to be seen were a few old men and women pushing wheelbarrows, perambulators and hand-carts piled up with their pathetic possessions aimlessly about the streets. The part of Berlin that we visited was a shambles with scarcely a house that was habitable. There was a smell of death and decay, and one wondered how many corpses still lay in the ruins. The only building that I entered was the Chancellery. It was smashed to smithereens and the Russians had made no attempt to clear up the mess. Perhaps they had left it on purpose, as an awful warning. In Hitler's study a huge marble-topped table had been blasted into a thousand pieces. I had the feeling of being in the presence of evil. How shameful it was to think that the devil incarnate, whose malignant spirit still haunted the room, had come so near to dominating the whole world. And how tragic it was that the civilised nations of Christendom had been compelled to use such terrible and indiscriminate agencies of destruction in order to preserve their freedom.

I hurried out of the study in disgust, but an adjacent room was almost equally obscene — Iron Crosses and medal ribbons strewn all over the floor in hopeless confusion. Decorations that would have brought pride to brave men seemed in that setting to be a symbol of utter degradation. I was sorry that I had gone sightseeing, and when, some months later, I was given an opportunity of visiting the Nuremberg Trials, I refused without a moment's hesitation. My first act on returning to Babelsberg was to plunge into a hot bath with a great deal of disinfectant in it: my second was to take a very strong drink to try to get the taste out of my mouth.

On 23 July we had a tripartite military meeting — the Americans, the Russians and ourselves. The Russian team included Marshal Zhukov and General Antonov, and the latter was authorised to say that the Soviet would enter the war against Japan in August. They were leaving it rather late.

That evening Mr Churchill gave a large dinner-party with President Truman and Marshal Stalin as the chief guests. The new President gave the impression of being decisive, intensely human, and full of common sense, but he had as yet had little time to get into the whole picture. Stalin was in the best of tempers and seemed to be on particularly friendly terms with Churchill. The latter, in his capacity as host, proposed a number of toasts, including one to 'the next leader of the Opposition in Britain, whoever that might be.' When he sat down Stalin's expression was as much as to say: 'It won't be you, anyone but you, you old fox.'

Two days later I flew back to London in the same aeroplane as the Prime Minister and Mr Attlee. They had probably put the Conference out of their minds for the moment, and were thinking of little else but what the morrow had in store for them. Early the next day they knew. For Churchill overwhelming defeat; for Attlee overwhelming victory. As the morning went on, the land-slide gathered momentum, and the afternoon was nearly spent before I could bring myself to go and see my chief.

That evening he tendered his resignation to the King, and that night he broadcast to the people, expressing his gratitude 'for the many expressions of kindness shown towards their servant.' Despite his dominating and masterful personality, that is exactly how he always regarded himself — a servant of his country. The British people the world over should thank God that in the hour of their trial their principal servant was the greatest Englishman of his time, perhaps of all time.

Two days later I flew back to Potsdam with Mr Attlee, and Mr Bevin arrived almost simultaneously. Mr Attlee had been a member of the Government since May 1940, and had been present at the previous meetings in Berlin. He knew all the ropes. Mr Bevin had not had the same advantages. He had been Foreign Secretary for only a few hours when he was thrown into the midst of the turmoil, but he was in no doubt about the line that he was going to take. 'I'm not going to have Britain barged about' were almost the first words that he said when I greeted him at the airport.

Five days later, the Conference ended and we returned to London. Things now began to move very fast in the Far East. On 6 August, the first atomic bomb was dropped on Hiroshima. Two days later Russia declared war on Japan. Her participation at that eleventh hour was worthless from the military point of view, but Stalin had been astute enough to climb on to the wagon in time to secure valuable prizes. On 8 August, a second atomic bomb was dropped on Nagasaki. The next day the Japanese Government announced their readiness to surrender, provided that it did not involve any demand which prejudiced the prerogatives of the Emperor as sovereign ruler. A face-saving formula was devised, and on 14 August it was all over. That night the Cabinet were summoned after dinner to hear the broadcast which Mr Attlee proposed to deliver. As we dispersed after the meeting, Mr J. Lawson, Secretary of State for War, endeared himself to me by saying how much he felt for me in my grief that the 'old chief' was not at the helm to see the completion of his handiwork. He had read my thoughts correctly. Mr Attlee had made an immense and self-effacing contribution to the victory which he was about to proclaim, and was a grand chief to serve. But, to me, Churchill always had been, and always would be, in a class entirely by himself.

So long as the winning-post lay ahead, the human frame could make light of strains and stresses which would have been intolerable in normal times. But once the winning-post had been reached, the incentive which had supplied my energy was gone, and a great weariness descended on me like a pall. I would have liked to retire at once; but the transition from war to peace is a protracted and complicated business, and nobody whose services were still required was entitled to release. Mr Attlee suggested that I should take a long holiday at once, and then continue in office for a further twelve months; and I was very ready to do so.

My wife and I thought that America would be a nice change, and early in September we set sail in the *Queen Mary*. The whole of the 35th US Division were on board. The organisation of the Cunard Line was beyond praise, but the men had to be packed like sardines. Nevertheless it was obvious that not one of the fifteen thousand objected to the crowding, or to having to take it in turns to sleep on a hard deck with a life-jacket for pillow, owing to the shortage of bunks. They were going home, and nothing else mattered. The welcome which they received from the moment that the *Queen Mary* passed the Statue of Liberty had to be seen, and heard, to be believed. It had been richly deserved.

We divided our six weeks in America between Chicago, Washington, South Carolina and New York, and were almost killed by kindness. It was fun to meet many of my war comrades again and to have carefree talks about past quarrels with each other as well as with the enemy. Our countrymen as a whole were in bad odour with the Americans for having been so ungrateful as to have thrown out the man who had saved the free world; and we, for our part, were hurt by the aspersions which we occasionally heard cast on President Roosevelt, who had been such a wonderful friend to Britain.

During my last year at the Cabinet offices, the main problem under consideration was the future organisation of Defence. The experiment of having a Minister whose powers were limited to co-ordination had proved unsatisfactory both in peace and war, and it was clearly impossible to perpetuate the war-time arrangements under which the Prime Minister, with the assistance of a small 'handling machine,' had performed the duties of Minister of Defence. The solution which emerged from prolonged discussions was announced in Parliament in October.[1] The Committee of Imperial Defence, as such, ceased to exist, but its parenthood of the new arrangements was unmistakable. The Prime Minister was to retain the supreme responsibility for defence; and the Defence Committee, under his chairmanship, was to perform the functions of the old Committee of Imperial Defence. But there was to be a Minister of Defence, who was to have *executive authority* in certain matters over the three Service Departments and the Ministry of Supply, and to be served by a full-blown Ministry. The individual and collective responsibilities of the Chiefs of Staff were to remain as they had always been. I was sad that the old title Committee of Imperial Defence had disappeared, and felt that perhaps the new organisation might lack the flexibility which had been one of its most valuable characteristics. But certainly the new scheme seemed to provide an admirable starting point for further progress and development in the light of experience.

It was now over forty years since I had received His Majesty's commission as Second Lieutenant in his Land Forces, and the changes that had taken place since then were so revolutionary as to be almost incredible. When I was about to join the Army, I was warned by an uncle never to trust my life to a bad sword. So I duly went to Wilkinson's in Pall Mall and saw a piece of tempered steel bent almost double before it was inscribed with my monogram and became a treasured possession. I never had occasion to use it for the purpose for which it was intended, but it came in handy for opening sardine tins. In those days machine-guns were a luxury, and nearly always jammed at the critical moment. There were no mechanical

[1] White Paper on the Central Organisation for Defence. Cmd. 6923.

transport, no wireless and of course no aeroplanes; and the South African War, which had ended three years previously, was still regarded as a major campaign. In the span which covered my service, there had been over nine years of total war in its most absolute form, and the culminating point had been the dropping of the atom bombs at Hiroshima and Nagasaki. In November 1946 I retired. I had had an eventful and very lucky innings.

PART THREE

ROLLING STONE

CHAPTER XXXIII

Last Days of the Raj

1947

I O N C E came across a prayer which greatly appealed to me. 'May God give me work while I live. May God give me life while there is work to do,' and I had no intention of spending the evening of my days in complete idleness. I was already committed to the Chairmanship of the National Institute for the Blind, and the Presidency of the Gloucestershire British Legion; I hoped to make occasional contributions to the debates on Defence in the House of Lords; my farm had been sorely neglected for the past fourteen years; and there were many other local activities to occupy my time. But before settling down in Gloucestershire, I was engaged to pay visits to Australia and New Zealand, on the invitations of the two Prime Ministers, Mr Chifley and Mr Fraser. They had to be cancelled at almost the last moment for a most unexpected reason.

A few weeks before we were due to embark, Admiral Mountbatten told me in the strictest confidence that the Cabinet had decided that power in India should be transferred to Indian hands by June 1948 at the latest, and that the Prime Minister had asked him to succeed Lord Wavell as Viceroy, in order to give effect to that policy. What did I think about it? My first reaction was that it was one of the most delicate and perhaps distasteful assignments imaginable, but that it was difficult to see how he could refuse. Might I think it over and give him a considered opinion the next day? Directly he left me I wondered whether I ought not at least offer to accompany him. The idea of emerging from my new-found retirement and getting involved in the last chapter of the story of British rule in India was singularly unattractive. On the other hand, I owed so much to India that it was my bounden duty to lend a hand, if I was wanted. My wife, whose sense of duty has always been more highly developed than my own, had no doubts whatsoever. I therefore told Mountbatten next morning that if he thought I could be of any help as a sort of Chief of Staff or general factotum, I was ready to accompany him. At the same time, I made no attempt to disguise my feelings about the prospects. We would be 'going out to the last chukka twelve goals down.' He was kind enough to accept my offer without a moment's hesitation, and suggested that Sir Eric Miéville might be persuaded to come too. Would I sound him? Eric's reaction was immediate. Of course he would come. His readiness to make the considerable sacrifice involved, and the prospect of his companionship in the grim days ahead, made me feel much happier. But I was sad that I could not confide my plans to Mr Churchill until the new policy was announced to Parliament. He would undoubtedly disapprove of what I was doing, and I should like to have been the first to explain to him why I was doing it.

Mountbatten lost no time in selecting the rest of his special staff. This included Captain (S.) R. V. Brockman, RN, as Personal Secretary, Lieutenant-Colonel V. F. Erskine-Crum as Conference Secretary, and Mr Alan Campbell-Johnson, who was later to be the author of the story of these days,[1] as Press Attaché. It was Mountbatten's intention that this special staff should be additional to the personal staff which was at present serving under Lord Wavell, and which he hoped would continue to serve under him. It would indeed have been scarcely possible to do without these experts with their up-to-date knowledge of the situation. They included Mr Abell,[2] who was one of those rare birds, a first at Oxford and a triple Blue. He was destined for the highest offices in the land, if the British raj had continued.

1 *Mission with Mountbatten.*
2 Later Sir George Abell.

There was a great deal for the special staff to do and not much time in which to do it, but until the plan became public property, our meetings had to be hole-and-corner affairs. However, the Prime Minister's announcement of the new policy and of Mountbatten's appointment as Viceroy in the House of Commons on 20 February, enabled us to come out into the open. We were at once allotted rooms at the India Office and given facilities for studying the problems which would confront us when we got to India. In particular it was necessary to bring ourselves up to date with the history of past efforts to devise a realistic and acceptable scheme for the transfer of power to Indian hands.

Ever since 1858, when India came under the direct rule of the Crown and Queen Victoria became Empress of India, it had been recognised that Indians would ultimately be given their independence. The British were, in fact, in the position of guardians; and they set themselves a twofold task. First, they had to bring together all the diverse elements of a vast sub-continent, which was inhabited by some 300 million people, speaking some 370 different languages, and having different race origins, religions and cultures, and which, in its many centuries of recorded history, had never been a unity. Secondly, they had to train Indians in the management of their own affairs. The British may have been inclined to be patronising; they may have tended to hold themselves aloof socially; they may have been over-cautious in their approach to Home Rule. But they were sympathetic teachers, whose professional competence, integrity and devotion to duty earned them the enduring trust and admiration of the peoples whom they served.

By the turn of the century great progress had been made. India had become a single entity. A first-class all-India administration had been established. Law and order prevailed throughout the land. Roads, railways, canals and harbours had been built, and vast areas of hitherto waterless desert had been brought under irrigation. Simultaneously, there had been an ever-increasing number of Indians in every branch of the Administration. They had proved themselves to be quick learners, and their immense contribution to the war effort of 1914-18, in particular the glorious services of the Indian Army, showed that they were already capable of taking a greater share in the management of their own affairs. Henceforward successive British

Governments addressed themselves unremittingly to the problem of how the reins of government could, in course of time, be handed over to a successor authority which would be acceptable to all the diverse creeds and classes, and ensure that all the peoples of the peninsula would continue to enjoy life, liberty and the pursuit of happiness. It would be beyond the scope of my narrative to do more than mention the milestones on the rough road that was ultimately to lead to their objective.

In 1917, there had been the Montagu Declaration, in which the promise of ultimate Dominion status was implicit. This was quickly followed by the Act of 1919, which introduced a significant measure of responsible self-government in the Provinces. This touched off a demand by Gandhi for full self-government immediately, and there was an increase in the rioting. The next step was the setting up of the Simon Commission in 1927. In its report it recommended that provincial autonomy should be strengthened by further devolution from the centre and the extension of responsible government over the whole field of administration. It also recommended that the Central Legislature should be reconstituted on a federal basis, with its members elected by the provincial legislatures. The proposals were rejected by Congress, the predominantly Hindu party of the Indian nationalist movement. There followed the round-table Conferences in London of 1930, 1931 and 1932, and the important Act of 1935. This Act established full responsible government, subject to safeguards, in all the Provinces, and made provision for a Federation of India comprising both Provinces and Indian States. At the centre, foreign affairs and defence were preserved in the control of the Governor-General, but all the other central subjects were transferred to Ministers, subject to the same safeguards as were laid down for the Provinces. It was formally declared that those provisions of the Act which precluded full self-government were to be regarded as transitional. It was also declared that that part of the Act which established the Federation was not to come into effect until a specified number of States had acceded. This hope was never realised, and the Federation was never set up. This was perhaps the last chance of a unified India surviving the withdrawal of British power, and the last chance of the Princes retaining a large measure of the power and authority which they enjoyed under the British. In 1942, when the Japanese were almost at the gates of India, Sir Stafford Cripps, who was then Lord Privy Seal and a member of the War Cabinet, went out with an offer from His Majesty's Government that, immediately after the war, full Dominion status would be granted to India if it was demanded by a constituent assembly elected by Indians themselves, and that it would be left to Indians to frame their own constitution. This offer was not accepted. In 1946, a mission of three Cabinet Ministers proceeded to Delhi to try to reach agreement on the setting up of a constituent assembly which would frame the constitution for a completely self-governing India, and the establishment of an Interim Coalition Government to take charge of the country while this was being done. In October 1946 an interim Government comprised exclusively of Indians was set up, but all the other proposals were rejected. Thus, when Mountbatten was appointed Viceroy, the problem of finding a suitable successor-authority to take over the reins of government was still unresolved. Perhaps, it was thought, the imposition of a time limit might enable him to succeed where all previous attempts had failed. Mr Attlee had taken a great risk, and his courage deserved its reward.

At this point I would like to offer a few general observations on some of the fallacies about India that were prevalent at this time, both in England and America. The most unreasonable of these was the idea that we were deliberately making difficulties about the successor-authority, in order to postpone the grant of self-government to India. When I was in America two years before the war, a friend of mine who was also the owner of two newspapers expressed surprise that the British, whom he much admired, should be so hard-hearted as to refuse India her freedom. When I said that, so far as I knew, we were prepared to quit the country the moment that the communal problem was settled, he obviously had no idea what I was talking about. In the middle of the war, President Roosevelt himself had suggested to Churchill that the communal difficulty was exaggerated. All that was needed, in his opinion, was that a temporary government should be set up in India, headed by a small representative group covering different castes, occupations, religions, and geographies, which would be recognised as a temporary Dominion Government.[1] Did he and

[1] Telegram of 11 March 1942 from Roosevelt to Churchill.

his advisers imagine that 'the representative group' which he suggested, could be induced to sit round the same table for five minutes, much less carry out the functions of government? Was it not understood that India was merely a geographical expression, and that its population of nearly four hundred million[1] included nearly one hundred million Moslems, who were not prepared to be ruled by an inevitably paramount Hindu majority? It is true that for many generations all creeds and classes in India had lived together side by side, but this had been rendered possible only by the impartial rule of the British raj. To remove that rule without making proper arrangements to replace it, would be to court measureless calamity. No one could accuse Lord Morley of being a reactionary. Yet this is what he had to say about a premature withdrawal from India: 'There is, I know, a school of thought which says that we might wisely walk out of India and that the Indians could manage their own affairs better than we can. Anybody who pictures to himself the anarchy, the bloody chaos that would follow from any such deplorable step might shrink from that sinister decision.'

Another widespread fallacy was that the Indian masses were writhing under our yoke and counting the days until their country was free. What rubbish! We could not have ruled for a single week without the consent of the vast majority of the population. How could a Commissioner of a district the size of Wales maintain law and order, preside over the Law Courts, collect taxes and carry out the multifarious duties that fell to his lot, with the aid of a handful of assistants and a few score of Indian policemen, unless he enjoyed the goodwill of the masses? To have attempted to stay in India for a moment longer than the majority of the population desired, would have broken us financially and militarily.

Of course the political classes were anxious to get rid of us as quickly as possible, but they carried little weight with the masses and even less with the rank and file of the magnificent Indian Army, whose trust in their British officers was unlimited. Several old Moslem friends told me that they were delighted that I had returned to India,

[1] According to the Census of 1941, the population of India (including the Indian States) was approximately 390 million. These numbers included 255 million Hindus; 92 million Moslems; 6 million Indian Christians; and $5\frac{1}{2}$ million Sikhs.

because they were sure that I would use all my influence against leaving them in the lurch. When I said that, on the contrary, I had come for the express purpose of doing all I could to ease the transition, they were dumbfounded. The words of a senior Indian officer, who had been a close friend for a quarter of a century, cut me to the quick: 'We soldiers have trusted you for forty years, and now you are going to betray us.' With that, he walked out of my room — and out of my life.

Mention must be made of another question of the first importance which had to be settled before Mountbatten left London. There were bound to be a large number of members of the Indian Services who would not wish, or might not be wanted, to continue to serve in India after our withdrawal, and it was necessary to determine what compensation should be paid to them. Towards the end of 1946, a scheme had been drawn up by a Committee in London, and sent to the Governor-General for the comments of the Interim Government. The latter had raised a host of objections, and made it clear that if His Majesty's Government insisted on the scales being adopted, they would have to foot the bill themselves. Thereupon a fresh scheme was worked out in London, which was not nearly so generous to the officers concerned. Lord Wavell, on seeing it, strongly advised Lord Mountbatten to get the question settled before he left England. Mountbatten, Miéville and I were unanimous in taking exception to the new scheme. The original proposals had evidently been considered equitable on their merits, and it was manifestly unjust to abandon them merely because the Government of India objected to the expenditure involved. Mountbatten prepared a paper for the India-Burma Committee of the Cabinet, advocating the adoption of the original scheme and strongly recommending that if the Government of India persisted in their attitude, the British Government should themselves accept full responsibility in the matter. His recommendations were approved lock, stock and barrel. It was a great encouragement to see this evidence of the determination of Mr Attlee and his colleagues to give their unstinted help to the last of the Viceroys, and to know that the men who had borne the heat and burden of the day in India, and were about to lose their means of livelihood, were at least assured of monetary compensation on a not ungenerous scale.

* *

Miéville and I and some of the staff started for India on 19 March, and the Mountbattens followed the next day with the rest of their entourage. The last two or three months in England had been particularly cheerless and uncomfortable. There had been an almost record snow-fall, followed by a prolonged frost; there was a grave shortage of coal, and electric power was drastically restricted; food and clothing rationing were still in force: and finally there had been a very rapid thaw, with much flooding. As our aeroplane headed southwards the country looked waterlogged and depressing, and I tried to persuade myself that I was lucky to be escaping to sunnier climes. But it was no use: I felt leaving England more deeply than I had ever done before. On 22 March we arrived at Delhi in the boiling heat of an Indian noon, and I was astonished and touched that the Commander-in-Chief, Field Marshal Sir Claude Auchinleck, had done the long drive to the airport to welcome us — the more so as he would have to repeat the journey in three or four hours in order to greet the Viceroy Designate. I was more than astonished to see that he was wearing a beret. Having been brought up in the belief that anyone who failed to wear a pith helmet while the Indian sun was still in the sky was a lunatic, I blurted out, 'Have you gone mad, Claude? Where is your topee?' He replied that, on the contrary, we had all been mad for a hundred years or more to wear such an uncomfortable and unnecessary form of head-gear.

Miéville and I drove to the houses on the Viceregal estate in which we had lived when we were members of Lord Willingdon's staff, and found nearly all our old servants drawn up in serried ranks on the veranda. Since we were going to share a house, the sensible course would have been to have selected the particular individuals we wanted; but we had not the heart to get rid of any of them, and decided to retain them all. In addition to the domestic staff, I found Pensioner Abdur Rahman Khan, who had joined the 21st Cavalry as a recruit about the same time as I had done. He had been my orderly on and off for about a quarter of a century, and for some years I had been paying him a small monthly allowance to supplement his meagre pension. Just before leaving home, my Bank Manager told me that Abdur Rahman Khan had not drawn his money for the last two months, and I feared that he was ill, or even dead. But his explanation was simple. He had heard on the radio several weeks previously that I was coming out to India, but no date had been mentioned. He had therefore taken a train for Delhi the next day, in order to make sure of being on the spot when I arrived; and he had been there ever since.

I had thought before I left England that a period of fifteen months was far too short a time in which to complete arrangements for the transfer of power. But I had not been three weeks in India before I was convinced that so far from being too short, it was too long. The principal reason for this change of mind was the realisation that communal bitterness had grown to incredible proportions since I was last in India. Within a week of my arrival, I attended a dinner-party, at which a Congress Minister was sitting on my right, and a Moslem League Minister on my left. Throughout the meal both of these cultured men, who normally had impeccable manners, spoke to me unceasingly and in loud voices about the iniquities of the opposing community. This spirit of bitter animosity had been rampant throughout the country for several months, and there had been a fearful record of massacres. Riots in Calcutta, where at least five thousand were killed, had been followed by holocausts in Eastern Bengal, Eastern Behar and the Rawalpindi area. At the time of our arrival, fighting was in progress in the Gurgaon district, a hundred miles from Delhi, and there was tension everywhere. There was no knowing when a new outbreak would start, or where it would start, or when and where it would end. Panic and a lust for revenge stalked the land. In the past there had been a splendid police force to deal with disturbances of this kind, but they had ceased to be fully reliable from the moment that our impending departure from India had been announced. Until then, the Indian policeman had seldom hesitated to act against his co-religionists. He knew that if he did his duty, he would be supported by higher authority, and that if he failed to do so, he would get into trouble. But soon the British would no longer have the power either to reward or to punish; and it was only natural that the policeman should not be willing to compromise himself with his new masters.

A second reason for my conviction that we could not continue to bear responsibility until June 1948 was that the administration of the country was going to the dogs. Up to 1946, the Viceroy had looked for advice to an Executive Countil of wise, experienced men, both British and Indian. But this had now ceased to exist, and in its place there had been set up the Interim Coalition Government,[1] over which the Viceroy presided, with Mr Nehru as Deputy Prime Minister. Nine of the members belonged to the Congress Party and five to the Moslem League. The latter were always referred to by Mr Jinnah, head of the Moslem League, as 'sentinels' looking after Moslem interests. I doubt whether there has ever been a coalition whose members were so determined not to co-operate with each other. The only point on which there was agreement was that the British should quit India as soon as possible. Every other problem was regarded exclusively from the communal angle. Whenever, for example, there was a vacancy for an appointment, the Minister in charge of the Department concerned unashamedly nominated one of his own co-religionists to fill it, irrespective of his qualifications for the post. Since the British members of the Service had no Minister to back them, they were generally thrown to the wolves without rhyme or reason. So much so, that by the time we arrived, there were only two British officers in the whole of the Secretariat of the Government of India — discounting the Army and Political Departments. Apart from this unfair discrimination, the British members of the Indian Civil Service had for years past been living under an almost intolerable strain. They were very short-handed. They had had practically no holiday since the war had started. They were blamed for everything that went wrong. Their integrity and impartiality were continually called in to question. Shortly after our arrival in Delhi, Congress pressed the Viceroy to dismiss a certain Governor — one of the ablest in the country — on account of his excessively pro-Moslem sympathies. A week later, the Moslem League demanded the expulsion of the same man on account of his transparent prejudice against them. To cap it all, nearly every member of the Administration was racked with anxiety about his future. This state of affairs could not be allowed to continue for much longer.

Finally, Nehru had complained that the Interim Government in its existing form was wholly unfitted to administer the country, and had threatened that he and his Congress colleagues would resign unless

[1] This was originally formed in August 1946. The Moslem League joined it in October of the same year.

other arrangements were made in the very near future. Mr. Gandhi's ingenuous suggestion that a Moslem League Government should be formed was clearly impracticable, and the only alternative would have been direct rule of the whole of India by Mountbatten himself. This was unthinkable.

There was no blinking the fact that successive British Governments had little by little divested themselves of power in India, and that the statement of 20 February that it was their definite intention to quit the counry not later than June 1948, had been the last straw in creating a situation in which they were no longer able to discharge their responsibilities. It was therefore vital that the Viceroy should reach a settlement with the interested parties on the problem of the successor-authority as quickly as possible. If agreement could be reached on a plan which would preserve the unity of India, so much the better. If not, other expedients must be tried. Speed was the essence of the problem.

The Viceroy at once started a non-stop series of discussions with Indians of all shades of opinion. Eric Miéville and I lent him what help we could. It was frustrating and exhausting work. The Indian leaders were for the most part able, upright and courageous men, but at this period some of them were so swayed by their passions as to be unreasonable and irresponsible. They were torn with suspicion of each other and of the British. They read sinister motives into the most innocent proposals. They worked themselves into ungovernable rages with anyone who disagreed with them. They did not hesitate to wreck any plan that was not in entire accord with their own desires, but admitted no responsibility for finding any practical alternative.

At the start, the Viceroy tried out every conceivable arrangement which could possibly preserve the unity of India, but it was not long before we were forced to realise that the Moslem League would not agree to any plan which did not provide for the creation of Pakistan as an independent sovereign State. Since Congress would have nothing to do with any solution which had the slightest tinge of Partition about it, the outlook was far from promising. Gradually however both sides began to succumb to Mountbatten's shock tactics, applied with friendliness, sincerity and the patience of Job; and within a matter of weeks it appeared that Congress might be willing to withdraw their objection to the Partition of India, subject to the logical proviso that, if India as a whole were partitioned, the Provinces of Bengal and the Punjab in which there were almost equally large numbers of both the main communities, should be treated likewise.[1] The Moslem League, while bitterly denouncing any idea of partitioning the two Provinces in question, seemed ready to acknowledge that 'a moth-eaten Pakistan' — to quote Mr Jinnah's own phrase — would be better than no Pakistan at all.

While various alternative plans embodying these principles were in the course of being worked out, the Viceroy invited all the Governors to Delhi in order to exchange views on the situation in their Provinces and, in particular, to discuss the problem of the transfer of power. They were all agreed on two points. First, that a quick decision was of great importance; and secondly, that a united India was now out of the question. No one liked the idea of Partition, but no one could suggest how it could be avoided. The leaders of the British business community were also called in for consultation. They were not unduly worried about the future, but were insistent that an early decision as to the arrangements for the transfer of power was imperative.

A new version of the plan was drafted almost daily, and at long last it took final shape. The Indian peninsula was to be partitioned into two independent sovereign states, one predominantly Hindu, to be called India, and the other predominantly Moslem, to be called Pakistan. The Provinces of the Punjab and Bengal were also to be partitioned. Eastern Bengal and the Western Punjab were to go to Pakistan, and Western Bengal (which was to include Calcutta) and the Eastern Punjab were to go to India. The frontiers would be demarcated by a Boundary Commission, which would have a British Chairman[2] and one Hindu and one Moslem as members.

Mountbatten instructed me to proceed to London to present these proposals to the Cabinet. I left Delhi on 2 May, accompanied by George Abell, and was summoned to a meeting of the India-Burma Committee of the Cabinet at 10 Downing Street immediately on my arrival. In explaining the principal features of the plan, and the considerations upon which it was based, I emphasised that it was a case

---

[1] According to the Census of 1941, the population of Bengal was 60 million of whom 33 million were Moslems; and the population of the Punjab was 28 million of whom 16 million were Moslems.

[2] Sir Cyril Radcliffe, now Lord Radcliffe, accepted the invitation to undertake this delicate and thankless task.

of 'Hobson's Choice.' No one in India thought that it was perfect. Yet nearly everyone agreed that it was the only solution which had any chance of being accepted by all political parties, and of ensuring a fairly equitable deal for all minorities. It was not a gamble. There was no other way. Mr Attlee and his colleagues were not unnaturally disturbed by the prospect of Partition, but felt that, in the circumstances, there was no option but to approve the proposals. At the same time, they thought that the presentation of the case was susceptible to improvement, and a revised version was prepared under their orders, and sent to the Viceroy for his comments. Since this was identical in essentials with the paper which I had brought home, I anticipated no further difficulty; and I was about to return to my post when a telegram arrived from Mountbatten with the disturbing and wholly unexpected news that Pandit Nehru, to whom Mountbatten had shown a copy of the Cabinet paper, had reacted violently. He alleged that it bore little relation to the proposals which I had taken to England, and that the Cabinet were double-crossing him. Perhaps we should have known that Nehru, with his inveterate distrust of Whitehall, was almost certain to object to any proposals emanating from that quarter. There was now nothing for it but for Mountbatten, assisted by Miéville and V. P. Menon,[1] to try his hand at producing yet another version in a form which would be acceptable to the three parties concerned — His Majesty's Government, Congress and the Moslem League. While all this was in progress, Mountbatten telegraphed that he had good reason to believe that both of the new States would be prepared to accept Dominion status in the first instance, if by so doing power could be transferred at a much earlier date than June 1948.

By this time I was bewildered, out of touch with the situation in India, and useless as an envoy. I therefore suggested either that I should return to Delhi for two or three days in order to be brought up to date, or that Miéville should be sent to replace me, or that Mountbatten should come home himself. The Prime Minister pressed for the last of these alternatives, and Mountbatten, having completed a new version of the plan, duly arrived in London on 19 May. We attended a meeting of the India-Burma Committee that same afternoon. The

---

[1] Reforms Commissioner 1942-1947; Secretary to Government of India in States Ministry, July 1947-October 1948.

Committee found no difficulty in approving the latest version of the plan without the alteration of a comma, and Mountbatten then turned to the question of Dominion status. He was confident that Congress would agree to it, and was fairly sure that the Moslem League would do likewise, provided that it would result in a considerably earlier transfer of power. The crux of the matter was the speed with which the necessary legislation could be drafted and passed through Parliament. Could this be done in a matter of weeks? The problem was referred to the Lord Chancellor, Lord Jowitt, and the Law Officers of the Crown. Lord Jowitt reported to the Committee the next day that an amending Bill to the 1935 Act could, by supreme efforts, be prepared within six or seven weeks once a final decision had been taken on exactly what was required, but that there would be no hope of getting it through Parliament during the current session without the support of all parties. The Prime Minister took the leaders of the Opposition into his confidence, and Mr Churchill stated on behalf of the Tories that if there were an effective acceptance of the plan by both Congress and the Moslem League, they would do all in their power to expedite the passage of the necessary legislation. Thanks to this whole-hearted support from all parties in England, Mountbatten got all that he needed, and he proposed that 15 August should be the appointed day for the transfer of power. The Cabinet agreed.

We returned to India at breakneck speed and arrived at about midnight on 31 May. A long flight with Mountbatten was an experience which I was careful not to repeat. The idea of a reasonable degree of comfort never entered his head. Speed was all that mattered.

I woke up on 2 June feeling rather as I had on the various D-Days during the war; but on this occasion I had less confidence in the result. Since our return from London, both sides had put in reservations which, if insisted upon, would wreck the scheme; and there was no certainty that Gandhi would not throw in a spanner at the last moment. By 10 A.M. we were all assembled in the Viceroy's study. Congress was represented by Pandit Nehru, Sardar V. Patel[1] and

---

[1] Member for Home Affairs, later Deputy Prime Minister of the Dominion of India.

Mr Kripalani,[1] the Moslem League by Mr Jinnah,[2] Mr Liaquat Ali Khan[3] and Sardar Abdur Rab Nishtar;[4] and the Sikhs by Sardar Baldev Singh.[5] It was a tense moment, but it was at least encouraging to see that they all greeted each other with unusual bonhomie.

Copies of the announcement of the plan, as proposed by His Majesty's Government, were handed round at once, and in the long discussion which ensued, the Viceroy did most of the talking. He handled the meeting faultlessly, mingling firmness with tact, dignity with humour, and realism with sentiment. He said that at the moment he was not asking for complete agreement to the plan, but only for its acceptance in principle. After a good deal of manoeuvering, this was accorded by all three parties, albeit in somewhat grudging terms. In any case, Mountbatten felt sufficiently confident to ask Nehru, Jinnah and Baldev Singh if they would broadcast on the Indian radio the next night, saying that they themselves approved the plan and appealing to their followers to keep the peace, and not to resort to bloodshed or violence. They raised no objection. Mountbatten closed the proceedings with the request that the leaders should let him know by midnight whether their respective communities were prepared to accept the plan. Kripalani and Baldev Singh undertook to do so in writing, but Jinnah said that he would sooner explain his position orally to the Viceroy after dinner that night.

So far, things had gone pretty well, but there was a formidable obstacle round the corner. Gandhi, who had bitterly denounced the whole idea of Partition, was at that very moment waiting in the Viceroy's study for an interview. As luck would have it, it was one of his days of silence, and Mountbatten was able to do all the talking. He succeeded in convincing the Mahatma that the plan was in fact a 'Gandhi conception,' and that it was impossible to devise any other arrangement which would command general acceptance. This was a triumph for Mountbatten's power of persuasion.

Dinner that night was a military occasion, the principal guests being the Commanders-in-Chief of the Army, Navy and Royal Air

[1] President of the Congress Party.
[2] President of the All India Moslem League.
[3] General Secretary of the All India Moslem League; afterwards first Prime Minister of Pakistan.
[4] Member for Communications in the Interim Government.
[5] Minister for Defence in the Interim Government.

Force, and the Army commanders. After dinner was over, Mountbatten let his guests into the secret. They showed obvious relief that the period of uncertainty would soon be at an end, and as far as I remember most, if not all, of them felt that Partition, with all its risks and disadvantages, was the only possible solution of the problem.

Mountbatten and I left the party before it broke up to go and wrestle with Jinnah. He was in one of his difficult moods. After describing the plan as scandalous, he said that he himself would support it and do his best to get the Moslem League Council to do likewise, but he could not commit them in advance. After a good deal of 'horse trading,' the most that the Viceroy could squeeze out of him was an admission that Mr Attlee might safely be advised that he could go ahead with his announcement about the plan to the House of Commons on the following day. Later that night, letters arrived from Kripalani and Baldev Singh. Both of them accepted the plan subject to a number of qualifications and reservations, which were so patently absurd that the authors could not have expected them to be taken seriously.

The next morning, the same party reassembled in the Viceroy's study. The tension was somewhat eased by an army of photographers, behaving in the way that photographers are apt to do on these occasions. Mountbatten opened the proceedings by saying that all three parties had notified their acceptance of the plan, but had, at the same time, suggested certain reservations. Since none of these stood any chance of acceptance by the other parties, there did not seem much use in discussing them. He therefore assumed that the plan was universally approved and could now be made public. The Conference appeared to be quite happy with this somewhat naïve reasoning. But in order to make sure that they did not indulge in second thoughts, Mountbatten distracted their attention by distributing a tome, which had been prepared by John Christie, Deputy Private Secretary to the Viceroy, with the help of the rest of us, entitled 'Administrative Consequences of Partition.' It ran to over thirty closely-typed pages, and came as an obvious shock to the assembled company. The Indian leaders had been living with their heads in the political clouds, and it was high time that they got their feet on the ground. Christie's *magnum opus* achieved this with a vengeance, and the meeting broke up without again getting on to dangerous topics.

In the afternoon Mr Attlee announced the plan in the House of Commons, and Mr Churchill, Leader of the Opposition, gave it his blessing. In the evening the All-India radio was given over to the momentous news. Mountbatten spoke first. He was brief and simple. 'For more than a hundred years, hundreds of millions of you have lived together, and this country has been administered as a single entity. . . . It has been impossible to obtain agreement . . . on any plan that would preserve the unity of India. But there can be no question of coercing any large areas in which one community has a majority to live against their will under a Government in which another community has a majority. The only alternative to coercion is Partition. . . . The whole plan may not be perfect; but, like all plans, its success will depend on the spirit of goodwill with which it is carried out.' When Mountbatten had finished, the plan was read out in detail: this was followed by speeches from Nehru, Jinnah and Baldev Singh. Who could have believed that such a degree of unanimity would be achieved in the space of seventy-five days? It was little short of a miracle.

The decision that power should be handed over on 15 August meant that there were just over ten weeks in which to create two entirely new administrative machines and to divide all the assets and liabilities of the old India between the two new Dominions. Christie's paper proved a godsend, and his recommendations for tackling the problem were accepted in their entirety. At the summit a committee (or council) of Ministers, was set up under the Viceroy's chairmanship, to deal with high-level policy and arbitrate in matters that could not be settled at the lower level. At the bottom, there was a wide range of technical sub-committees, each dealing with the hundred and one different assets which had to be apportioned. Between these two bodies, there was a steering committee, or 'clamping machine.' This consisted of two of the ablest civil servants that I have ever known — H. M. Patel of India and Mahomed Ali[1] of Pakistan. There was a tendency on the part of the Indian politician to regard all the British members of the Civil Service as bigoted, scheming bureaucrats, and the Indian members of the Service as mere stooges of their British colleagues. They were soon to learn that both the new Administra-

[1] Afterwards Prime Minister of Pakistan.

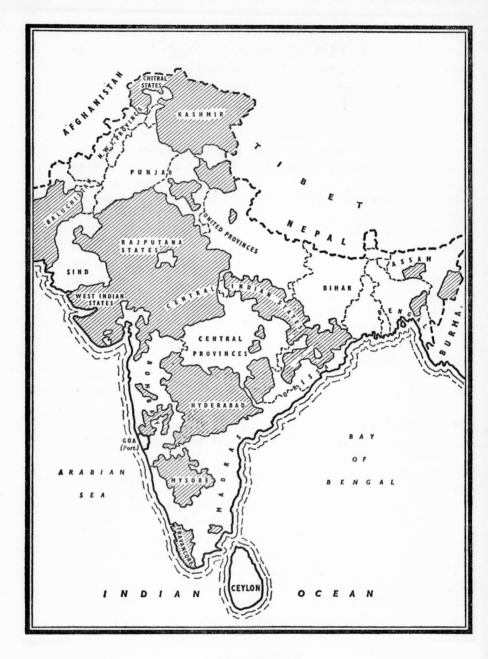

BEFORE PARTITION
BRITISH INDIA AND PRINCIPAL INDIAN STATES
(INDIAN STATES SHADED)

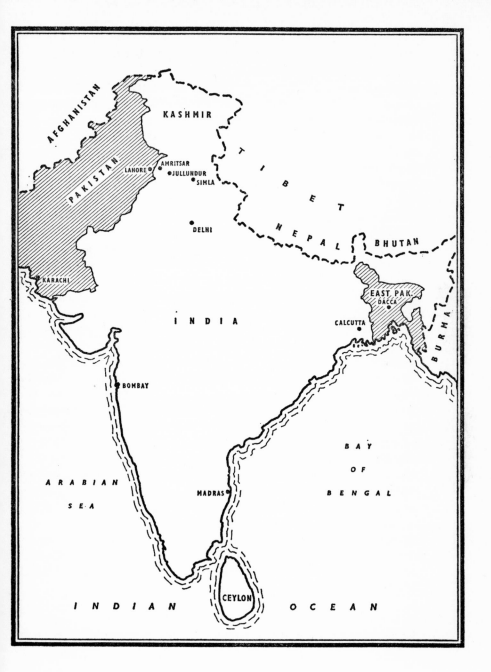

AFTER PARTITION
INDIA AND PAKISTAN

tions were going to be largely dependent on this handful of highly-trained, loyal and upright men.

The problem which caused many of us the greatest grief was the decision to divide the Indian Army on communal lines before Partition took place. Most of the regiments were of mixed composition, i.e. partly Mohammedan and partly Hindu, and no communal differences had hitherto disturbed their friendship or *esprit de corps*. Now these magnificent units were to be mutilated. I did my utmost to persuade Mr Jinnah to reconsider his decision. I suggested that both the new Governments would have special need of an instrument on which they could rely in the early days of their nationhood, and that the Indian Army as at present constituted was ideal for their purpose. I asked him to remember that an army was not merely a collection of men with rifles and bayonets and guns and tanks: it was a living entity, with one brain, one heart and one set of organs. The profession of arms was held in high honour, and the Indian soldier was, generally speaking, a dedicated man whose loyalty centred in his regiment. To break up these magnificent units before Partition was neither sensible nor necessary. Why not divide the Army on numerical lines in the first instance, India getting two-thirds, and Pakistan one-third? Later on, when things were more settled it might be found expedient to transfer the Hindu element in the Pakistan Army to India, and *vice versa*. But Jinnah was adamant. He said that he would refuse to take over power on 15 August unless he had an army of appropriate strength and predominantly Moslem composition under his control. There was nothing for it but to prepare a scheme for the immediate partition of the armed forces; and this was done in record time. Thanks to ingenious planning on the part of Auchinleck and his staff, and to the ingrained discipline and good comradeship of the soldiery of both sides, my fears of the harm that would result proved groundless. When the time came for the two new Governments of India and Pakistan to take over control, each of them already had at its disposal armed forces of which any country in the world would have been proud.

There was neither time nor need for all Partition arrangements to be completed in every detail by Independence Day. But it was essential that each of the two new Dominions should have a Governor-

General, a Cabinet, and at least the nucleus of an Administration, who would be ready to function from the moment that the clock struck twelve on the night of the 14th August. Nehru had already informed Mountbatten that Congress wished him to be the first Governor-General of India, and that they would not take it amiss if he were to accept the same office in Pakistan. Mountbatten had replied that, subject to the King's approval, he would be honoured to be Governor-General of India for a limited period. Jinnah was opposed to the idea of a joint Governor-General for both Dominions, and thought that a better solution would be for Mountbatten to be a super Governor-General or 'stakeholder.' Mountbatten had at once expressed grave doubts about the practicability of his remaining in any arbitral capacity, and there the matter rested for the moment.

Since time was getting short, Miéville and I made two or three attempts to persuade Jinnah to disclose his intentions. We failed to get a definite answer; but we got the impression that, in the end, he would invite Mountbatten to be Governor-General of Pakistan, and that he himself would be the Prime Minister. It was not until the end of June that we learned that our guess was wrong, and that Jinnah had decided to nominate himself as Governor-General, and to make Liaquat Ali Khan Prime Minister. In breaking the news to Mountbatten, Mr Jinnah expressed the hope that it would make no difference to his acceptance of office as the first Governor-General of India, or to his being Chairman of a Joint Defence Council of the two countries.

This unexpected turn of events was a blow. We had all felt that the best hope of an orderly transfer of power, an equitable partition of assets, and the establishment of friendly relations between the two new Dominions would be for them to start off with the same Governor-General. But since this was not to be, the question of Mountbatten's future became an urgent problem. Should he tell Congress that he could not now be Governor-General of India on the grounds that he might be accused of having deliberately favoured India in the Partition plan? Or should he allow his original acceptance to stand? Mountbatten himself was inclined to think that he ought to fade out of the picture; but nearly all his staff thought that the case for his remaining as Governor-General of India was overwhelmingly strong. In the first place, Congress would be affronted if the great honour which they had offered him were spurned. They would certainly not consider any other Englishman for the appointment, and the marked improvement in their relations with the British might receive a severe setback. Secondly, they would be furious with Mr Jinnah for having once again thwarted their plans, and the animosity between the two Dominions would be increased. Thirdly, the British element, from the Commander-in-Chief downwards, would probably refuse to continue to serve in India for a single moment after Mountbatten's departure. Finally, the Indian Princes would feel that they were losing their only chance of getting a square deal.

After prolonged discussions, Mountbatten said that he would be prepared to serve as Governor-General of the new India, provided that the King, His Majesty's Government and the Opposition desired him to do so. This was not a matter which lent itself to settlement by telegram, and it was decided that I should go to London at once, as Miéville was ill. I left Delhi on the afternoon of 5 July; and by the afternoon of the 7th, I was closeted with the Prime Minister. Mr Attlee was already convinced that Mountbatten should stay on, and the India-Burma Committee were of the same mind. Early the next morning the Prime Minister and some of his colleagues had a meeting with the leaders of the Opposition, and explained the situation that had arisen. Mr Churchill was convalescing at Chartwell, but Mr Harold Macmillan, Mr R. A. Butler, Sir John Anderson and Lord Salisbury were present. The Conservatives were disappointed at Mr Jinnah's eleventh hour bomb-shell, but agreed that, subject to Mr Churchill's concurrence, Mountbatten should be asked to remain as Governor-General of the new India. I was sent off to sound my old chief, and found that he was in no doubt at all about the answer. He said that the symmetry at the summit was of little consequence. What really mattered was that Mountbatten's guiding hand should be available during the difficult days that lay ahead, and he let me have a statement to that effect in his own inimitable phraseology. In the evening, the King received me and made it clear that he wished Mountbatten to stay on. That settled it, and I was happy to return to India with a feeling that my mission had achieved its object.

Nevertheless, I was worried at the prevalence of the idea that it was all now going to be plain sailing. I thought that there were still many fearful obstacles to be overcome, and I was particularly worried about the Sikhs. This warrior sect, which provided many thousands of splendid recruits for the Indian Army, had every cause to feel aggrieved. Out of their total population in India of some five and a half million, no less than four million were domiciled in the Punjab. It was therefore certain that, wherever the boundary line was drawn, roughly two million Sikhs would soon find themselves citizens of Pakistan, and that many of their holy places would be under the domination of men of an alien — and to them repugnant — faith. Miéville and I had had two or three talks with their leaders, Master Tara Singh and Giani Kartar Singh, before I left for England. They arrived carrying villainous-looking curved swords and many volumes of Hansard, from which they quoted interminably. They refused to budge an inch from their preconceived ideas, and occasionally used threatening language. We told them that if they resorted to violence, either before or after Partition, they would be very roughly handled; but we did not feel that our warnings had had the slightest effect.

I got back to Delhi on 22 July. Administrative preparations had proceeded apace, and it looked as though all could be completed in the three weeks which remained before the transfer of power. But the Sikhs had already started to give trouble, and from the beginning of August there had been spasmodic outbursts of rioting in Lahore and Amritsar. The giants of old, like the Lawrences and John Nicholson, would probably have clapped the Sikh leaders into gaol at once. But times had changed, and the three men who were unquestionably the best judges of the situation, namely Sir Evan Jenkins, the Governor of the Punjab, Mr Trivedi, Governor Designate of the Eastern Punjab, and Sir Francis Mudie, Governor Designate of the Western Punjab, unanimously advised that this should not be done.

At last Independence Day arrived, but a few hours before dawn I was prostrated by a severe attack of dysentery and unable to attend the celebration. This dispensation was painful, but not altogether unwelcome. I was convinced that the right thing had been done, but I was in no mood for unrestrained rejoicing. The India to which I owed so much had been artificially divided between two communities, who were at present consumed with suspicion and hatred of each other. Perhaps these animosities would die down in time, and the two new states would ultimately be brought together by their common allegiance to the Crown. But I had deep forebodings about the immediate future. The trouble which had already started in the Punjab looked as though it might spread through the country. Many of my Indian friends were likely to lose their lives, and many more were certain to lose their homes. But perhaps I was being unduly pessimistic? Both countries had able, resolute leaders, who were perfectly capable of governing, and could be counted upon to deal firmly with disturbances; both countries had a nucleus of highly-trained civil servants; both countries had magnificent soldiers. So far as the immediate future was concerned, a joint Indian-Pakistani force of some fifty-five thousand men, known as the Punjab Boundary Force, had been concentrated in the areas where trouble was most likely to occur. It was composed of units which were believed to be entirely trustworthy, and commanded by Major-General T. W. Rees, an Indian Army officer with a fine fighting record in both World Wars. Apart from this, excellent relations seemed likely to continue between the officers of the two new armies. Only a week previously, Auchinleck and I had been specially invited to a farewell party, which the Hindu officers at Army Headquarters had given to their Moslem colleagues who were leaving for Karachi; and the keynote of the speeches on both sides had been that though their countries might be divided, their blood-brotherhood would endure for ever.

Dysentery is a painful and depressing complaint, and I spent Independence Day in considerable discomfort; but my thoughts constantly turned to the Punjab which I knew so well and where I had been so happy. Everything seemed to depend upon what happened in that one Province. If the trouble were not suppressed, it might easily spread to other parts of the sub-continent and lead to a holocaust on a scale unparalleled in the history of the world. If, on the other hand, order could be restored, India and Pakistan would probably settle down together as good neighbours with a common defence policy and perhaps even a common foreign policy. In that event, Partition would have succeeded beyond my wildest dreams. But it was not to be. The situation, so far from getting better, became progressively worse, and the two Prime Ministers, Nehru and Liaquat Ali Khan, gave immediate proof of their courage and determination to co-operate with each other by travelling together in the same aeroplane to some of the principal danger spots. Their visits to Lahore in the West Punjab, and to Jullundur and Amritsar in the East Punjab resulted in a marked improvement in the situation: and it seemed that so long as the leaders continued to set such a fine example, the disturbances might be kept in bounds.

I was therefore easier in my mind when the doctors pronounced me well enough to escape from the shimmering heat of the Indian plains to the lovely Vale of Kashmir. My main purpose was to regain my health, but Mountbatten asked me to take the opportunity of seeing Maharaja Hari Singh and advising him to hold a referendum at once, on the question of whether his people wished to accede to India or Pakistan. His Highness himself was a Hindu, but ninety per cent of his subjects were Moslems, and there was little doubt as to which way the referendum would go. I was invited to the palace on two occasions, but each time that I tried to broach the question, the Maharaja changed the subject. Did I remember our polo match at Cheltenham in 1935? He had a colt which he thought might win the Indian Derby! Whenever I tried to talk serious business, he abruptly left me for one of his other guests. You may take a horse to the water, but you cannot make him drink, and it was useless to pursue the matter any further. The Maharaja had foiled Mountbatten a few weeks previously by a different technique. After arranging to have a serious talk on the last day of the visit, he pleaded a devastating attack of colic. His procrastination and refusal to face facts were to prove disastrous for himself, and to provide the principal cause of the estrangement between Pakistan and India, which persists to this day. His general behaviour at this time proved, if proof were necessary, that direct rule as practised by some of the Indian Princes was an anachronism, and that the inclusion of their States in an All-India Federation, such as had been proposed in the Act of 1935, would soon have wrecked the whole scheme. Nor can we ourselves be acquitted of all blame. We ought long ago to have used the paramount power which we possessed in order to reform the system of government in the more backward or reactionary States.

I soon felt well enough to pay a fleeting visit to Gulmarg, and Mr Nedou, kindliest of hotel proprietors, went out of his way to see that I had the same hut in which I had spent two blissful months as a subaltern in 1910. But it was a mistake to try to revive old memories. The beautiful polo ground looked like an untidy agricultural holding; the famous golf course was ill cared for and practically deserted; the public rooms in the hotel were strangely silent; and most of the private huts, which had been the holiday homes of many generations of British officers and their families, lay empty. It was all very depressing, and I was glad when the time came to ride down the hill to Srinagar. There I was met by alarming, though vague, reports of massacres in the Punjab, and it was a relief to find that the Governor-General's Dakota had arrived to take me back to Delhi two days earlier than originally arranged.

John Lascelles, who had travelled up in the plane, brought the news that Sarah, my second daughter, had had a horrible experience. She and her *fiancé*, Wenty Beaumont,[1] one of the Viceregal ADCs, had been on holiday with the Mountbattens in Simla and had returned to Delhi ahead of them. When they boarded the train, Wenty's Moslem servant showed signs of panic and was given permission to travel in their carriage. Nothing unusual happened until, at Sonepat station, about twenty miles from Delhi, a bomb was exploded on the platform. This was apparently the preconcerted signal for a general attack on all Moslem passengers. Men, women and children were pulled out of the train by their Hindu fellow-travellers and butchered in the most brutal manner. At this point, Wenty hid the servant under the seat and piled suitcases in front of him. A little later, two well-dressed and seemingly well-educated Hindus presented themselves at the door of his carriage and demanded the right to search for a Moslem who was believed to be with them. Wenty indignantly refused, and the intruders took themselves off. Maybe they were impressed by Wenty's ADC arm-band, or by the two revolvers which he and Sarah were flourishing. The servant, who had fainted from fright and kept a deathly silence, was the only Moslem to arrive alive at Delhi. The most significant feature of this incident was that a posse of Hindu armed police in the next carriage made no attempt to intervene. They were probably good men and true, but the frenzy of civil war had robbed them of their reason, and of all sense of duty or even decency.

The Moslem members of my domestic staff awaited me on the verandah of my house. They were frightened out of their wits, and many of them were in tears. Could I not arrange for them to be sent

[1] Later Viscount Allendale.

to Pakistan at once? I told my Hindu staff, who were lurking in the background, that I would hold them responsible for seeing that no harm came to their Moslem colleagues with whom they had worked for so long on friendly terms. They must take it in turns to act as sentries over the servants' quarters throughout the hours of darkness, and awaken me if there was any sign of trouble. I never had to be roused.

Later in the day came the first sign that the communal bitterness was spreading to the armed forces. Major Massey, Commandant of the Governor-General's Bodyguard, which consisted half of Sikhs and half of Punjabi Moslems, reported that many of his men of both classes had received news of horrible happenings in their homes and of the murders of their kith and kin. He thought that there was a real danger of their wreaking vengeance on each other. I told him to parade the Bodyguard at once and reason with them. He could remind them that they were members of the oldest and most famous unit in the Indian Army, with two hundred years of unblemished tradition behind it, and that they themselves were specially selected men, engaged on specially important and responsible duty. He could point out that many of the reports reaching Delhi were untrue or grossly exaggerated, and that, in any case, their comrades had no responsibility for the crimes. He could give them my promise that the Moslem element would be sent to Karachi to become the Bodyguard of the first Governor-General of Pakistan, as soon as the move could be arranged. Surely the two factions could live at peace and continue to do their duty for the few days that remained. I warned Massey that, unless he was satisfied that his talk had achieved its purpose, he should keep the men on parade and allow me to speak to them. Many of them had been my friends since the days when I was Military Secretary, and might have been ready to listen to me. I was immensely relieved when he reported an hour later that both sides had faithfully promised to refrain from violence. They would not speak to each other, but they did their duty to the bitter end.

It was at this juncture that Mountbatten was able to render services to India and Pakistan, and indeed to the whole British Commonwealth, which have never been fully realised. It was largely due to him that Delhi was saved from anarchy, and that the orgy of communal strife did not spread to the whole sub-continent. This is no reflection on the leaders of the two new Dominions. Nehru and Patel, Jinnah and Liaquat Ali Khan strove, with the utmost courage and resolution, to suppress the disorders, but none of them had the knowledge or experience to deal with a cataclysm of this kind.

Mountbatten, as a constitutional Governor-General, had no executive authority, but he had commanding influence, a flair for improvisation, dynamic energy, and a remarkable readiness to accept responsibility. Above all, he enjoyed the absolute confidence of the Indian Cabinet. His first step was to advise the immediate setting up of an Emergency Cabinet Committee to deal with the crisis on an hour-to-hour basis; and within a few hours the Committee was in action. At the request of Nehru, Mountbatten took the chair, and the permanent members were Nehru himself, Patel, the Home Minister, Baldev Singh, the Minister of Defence, and Mr Neogy, the newly-appointed Minister for Refugees. In addition, other Ministers and officials were co-opted as required, and the attendance generally numbered a score or more. My palatial office was turned into a Committee Room and Map Room combined, and became in effect an Operational Headquarters. Mountbatten was in his element. He was Captain of a Destroyer Flotilla, Chief of Combined Operations, Supreme Commander, and Governor-General, all rolled into one. The Emergency Committee was in practically permanent session; and questions which would have taken days, or even weeks, to settle by the normal procedure were decided in a matter of minutes.

Meanwhile, Lady Mountbatten, in her own sphere, made us all immensely proud of British womanhood. She was utterly dedicated, completely indefatigable and uniquely experienced. Undaunted by fatigue, danger, disease or stench, or the most gruesome scenes, her errands of mercy took her to hospitals and refugee camps all day and every day, and a good deal of the night. She had the missionary zeal of a Florence Nightingale, and the dedicated courage of a Joan of Arc.

At the start, the situation grew progressively worse. The Punjab Boundary Force did its best to keep order, but the control and protection of a frenzied, panic-stricken population of close on fifteen million people, distributed over nearly eighteen thousand towns and villages, proved beyond their powers. It got little or no support from the local civil authorities and little or no encouragement from either of the new Governments; and early in September it was dissolved. Delhi itself was on the verge of chaos. Moslems were being systematically hunted down and butchered. In some places, the dead lay rotting in the streets. The hospitals were choked with wounded. Arson and looting were widespread. Food supplies were disrupted. The Moslem policemen had deserted or been disarmed; many of the Hindu police were afraid to do their duty. There was only a handful of troops, and some of these were of doubtful reliability. Appeals for protection poured in from every side — public utility services, hospitals, refugee camps, and the Corps Diplomatique. The postal, telegram and telephone systems practically ceased to function. Public transport was largely suspended because the drivers were afraid to venture on the roads. Administration was hampered by the absence of clerical staffs, who could not get to their offices. The conditions in the refugee camps into which thousands of Moslems had been herded, defied description. Reports of horrors, sometimes true but more often false, inflamed men's passions and excited their fears. Nehru himself was on the prowl whenever he could escape from the Council table, and took appalling personal risks in his efforts to get the situation in hand. He looked infinitely sad. All that he had spent his life fighting for seemed to be crumbling.

To flee or not to flee. That was the question which Moslems domiciled in East Punjab and Delhi had to decide. It was not difficult to convince those who were serving on the Governor General's domestic staff that they would be safe and just as well treated as they had always been, and that it would be folly to throw up such good jobs, but those who did not enjoy the protection of the Governor General's enclave were a much more difficult problem. For the best part of a century, a number of villages in the Rohtak district, in the East Punjab, had supplied my regiment with recruits of the class known as Hindustani Mohammedans, and a deputation of pensioners came in to discuss the situation with me. I assured them that they had nothing to fear, and that Mr Trivedi, the Governor of the East Punjab, had given me an assurance that he would take special care to see that they were treated with evey consideration. They appeared more or less satisfied. But four days later they turned up again, with the complaint that the local Indian authorities were making things difficult for them, and that their people were becoming restive and wanted to see me. I could not spare the time to do the journey by road, but promised to fly low over their villages at a fixed time two days later. They were all on the roofs when my aeroplane appeared, waving improvised flags, and I hoped that all would be well. But I had scarcely returned to Delhi when they lost their nerve, and suddenly decided to abandon the homes that had been theirs for generations. Some of my particular cronies came to Delhi and billeted themselves on me until I could get them transported to Karachi. The remainder went off on foot to Pakistan.

Scarcely a day passed without some painful incident. One afternoon an old man in tattered clothing arrived at my house, and it was a shock to realise that this was my old friend Ali Sher Khan, who had won the Indian Distinguished Service Medal in France, and had finished up as senior Indian Officer in my regiment. He reported that his village had been attacked by a large number of Sikhs; that his family had been killed; and that he himself had escaped by the skin of his teeth. His house had been burnt down, and he had lost everything, including, he said, 'the watch which you gave me for helping you to train polo ponies, and your photograph.' He became my guest at once, and by the time he woke up next morning, a new suit of uniform was ready for him. Shortly after he had left for Pakistan, the Sikh Indian officer who had succeeded him as Rassaldar Major[1] of my regiment, called on me with the sad tale that his home in Pakistan had been burnt to the ground. He was thankful to say that his family had been in India when the riots started and were safe. After expressing my sympathy, I told him the story of Ali Sher Khan. His eyes filled with tears as he exclaimed, 'Where is he? Can I help him? He may be a Moslem, but he is dearer to me than a brother.'

The reports which reached Pakistan about the situation in Delhi were distorted and exaggerated. We learned that Mr Jinnah was under the impression that the Indian Government, so far from trying to check the orgy of bloodshed, were positively encouraging it. It was therefore thought advisable that I should pay him a visit, and tell him what was happening. In order to get a first-hand picture, I did a tour of the principal seats of trouble. The first refugee camp which I entered was crowded with men, women, children, bullocks, donkeys

[1] Senior Indian Officer.

and carts. A handful of scoundrels in houses overlooking the site were amusing themselves by firing occasional shots into the midst of them. A Moslem woman was killed by a stray bullet shortly after my arrival, and her husband and others rushed at me, screaming 'Sahib, help us.' I was wearing an old khaki shirt, and they had no idea who I was; but the habits of a lifetime are not easily forgotten. All that I could do was to advise patience and courage, and assure them that the Indian Government was doing its best. My next port of call, the Purana Qila (or old fort), was an appalling sight. Thousands of Moslems were herded within its walls. There was no shelter, no doctor, no sanitary arrangement, no means of communication. Once again I was surrounded, this time by a circle of men ten to twelve deep; and once more, the cry went up, 'Sahib, help us.' I told them that I happened to be in a position to know that the Government of India were doing their utmost to improve conditions in the camps at once, and to transfer them to Pakistan as quickly as possible. While I was speaking, there was a sudden storm of heavy rain, and the solitary umbrella available was passed without a word, from the outside of the ring surrounding me, until it rested over the head of the 'Sahib.' I was too moved to complete my homily.

On my return, I gave Mr Neogy, the Minister for Refugees, a full account of what I had seen. I said that I felt sure he would agree that there was a great deal that should, and could, be done within a matter of hours. One of the first essentials was the provision of loudspeakers, so that the inmates of the camp would have the comfort of hearing the human voice, preferably the voice of one of their own co-religionists, and of being given information on present arrangements and future plans. Doctors were an urgent necessity. Five Moslem women had had babies without any medical attention during the short time that I was in the camp. The provision of a proper water-supply and adequate sanitary arrangements should, it seemed, present no difficulty. Food supplies could easily be sent in bulk and distributed under supervision. I told Mr Neogy that I was flying to Karachi the next day to give Mr Jinnah an account of the situation in Delhi and of the efforts which the Indian Government were making to cope with it. It would strengthen my hand if I could give him a note, signed by the Minister, undertaking that steps such as I had mentioned were already being taken. I flew to Karachi the following afternoon, and Neogy's note reached me just as I was about to board my plane. This proved fortunate.

Mr Jinnah was standing at the top of the stairs when I entered Government House at Karachi. He looked very dignified and very sad, and he spoke as a man without hope. 'There is nothing for it but to fight it out.' We went to his study, and he let himself go. How could anyone believe that the Government of India were doing their utmost to restore law and order and to protect minorities? On the contrary, the events of the past three weeks went to prove that they were determined to strangle Pakistan at birth. The blood-baths taking place in the Punjab and in Delhi were the result of plans which had been prepared in the greatest detail. The whereabouts of all Moslems had been systematically reconnoitred; gangs of miscreants had been assembled and armed; their duties had been apportioned; and finally, at the appointed time, they had been loosed on their mission of murder. The conditions in the refugee camps were shameful beyond belief. How could any civilised Government permit such a state of affairs? Why were they not keeping their promise to evacuate Moslems to Pakistan as quickly as possible? They had more than ample resources to cope with all the difficulties, provided that they had the will to do so. Mr Jinnah must have spoken for twenty minutes, and it was then my turn. I assured him, with all the force at my command, that the Indian leaders ardently and sincerely desired to reassert law and order, to look after all the Moslems in their territory, and to evacuate them at the earliest possible moment. No one who had seen them at work during the last week, as I had done, could possibly doubt their good faith, or their courage, or their determination, or their readiness to adopt even the most unpopular measures in order to achieve their purpose. I had, with my own eyes, seen Pandit Nehru charge into a rioting Hindu mob and slap the faces of the ring-leaders. He seemed to have no thought whatsoever for his personal safety, and the Governor-General had given orders that an armed escort should accompany him wherever he went, whether he liked it or not. I went on to explain that the situation which had developed with such appalling suddenness would have shaken any Government in the world, however long-established and experienced. The Indian Government, which was neither, had been temporarily overwhelmed, and they were just as miserable about the tragedies as Mr Jinnah. But they were grappling with the situation to the very best of their ability. The necessary machinery had now been set up, and Ministers and officials were working day and night. They were determined to ride the storm and I was sure that they would succeed. On the question of the refugee camps, I agreed that conditions had been deplorable. They were however now being improved beyond recognition, and I handed him the note signed by the Minister for Refugees, setting out all that was being done. I begged Jinnah to realise that the reports reaching Pakistan were nearly always exaggerated and often completely untrue. The same sort of thing was happening in Delhi. For example, the move of a couple of score of policemen by lorry from Rawalpindi to Lahore had been reported by a so-called eye-witness as the massing of the Pakistan Army on the Indian frontier. The Indian Government had believed the story until I had obtained an absolute denial from General Meservy.[1] I ended up by describing the set-up and procedure of the Emergency Cabinet Committee, and said how glad I was to hear that he had set up a similar organisation in Karachi. It would be very helpful, I said, if there could be periodic meetings between the two bodies.

My talks with Mr Jinnah, either in his office or at meals in his house, extended over eleven hours, and I felt that I had done something towards convincing him of the true state of affairs. At all events, he pressed me on several occasions, and with great sincerity, to visit him again as soon and as often as I liked.

The situation in Delhi was gradually brought under control and there was considerable improvement in the Punjab. But until the enormous refugee columns moving from east to west and from west to east were safely inside their own boundaries, fighting was bound to continue. We flew over these columns in the Governor-General's Dakota towards the end of the month. It was pathetic to think of all these people being uprooted from the homes in which they had lived for many generations, and moving into the unknown. The contrast between the two columns was striking. The movement of the Sikhs had been carefully planned and was being executed with military precision. There was little or no interval between the bullock carts, in which the women and young children and goods and chattels were

[1] Commander-in-Chief of the Pakistan Army.

loaded, and all the men who were capable of bearing arms moved in front and on the flanks of the column. The Moslem migration had evidently been unpremeditated, and their column straggled hopelessly over fifty miles of road. From the air it looked like a pathetic stream of ants.

Ever since my return to India, the vernacular press had for the most part been consistently irresponsible, and, at this period, they were singularly unhelpful. Alarmist reports were published without any attempt at verification, and the most libellous aspersions were cast on all and sundry. Now that the British no longer bore any responsibility, and that such British individuals as remained in India and Pakistan were actuated solely by the desire to help, one would have thought that the continual attacks upon us would cease. But not a bit of it. Abuse continued to be our portion. For example, Sir Cyril Radcliffe had made great personal sacrifices to undertake the distasteful and thankless task of chairmanship of the Boundary Commission. He had refused to accept any remuneration for his services. But when his Boundary Awards were published, he was caricatured in both India and Pakistan carrying away enormous bribes from the other side. The climax came when a Liberal leader, Pandit Kunzru by name, made a statement to the press alleging that one of the worst massacres in the Boundary area had been deliberately inspired and encouraged by a British officer. With the Governor-General's permission I went to see Nehru, who happened to be with Gandhi at the Bhangi Colony, and begged him to issue an immediate denial in the name of his Government. He was ready to do so, but Gandhi intervened with the suggestion that it would be better if Kunzru himself withdrew his statement. I protested that this would not meet the case. The British officers concerned were the servants of the Government of India, and it was the duty of that Government to support them. In the end, Nehru agreed to take action.

Whenever one complained about outrageous reports of this kind, one was met with the rejoinder that India and Pakistan were democratic states, and that the Press was free to say what it liked. But the British Press was apparently expected to observe different standards, and we were bombarded with protests about the sometimes highly-coloured stories of the massacres which had been published in England. It was therefore decreed that I should go to London and try to put matters in the right perspective. I left Delhi on the 3rd October and spent a fortnight at home giving accounts of the position to the Cabinet and the press, and emphasizing that both Governments were doing their very utmost to deal with the trouble.

I found, as I rather expected, that many people, including some of the leading journals, were critical of Mountbatten on the grounds that his action had been precipitate, and that the bloodshed might have been avoided if the transfer had been done in a more orderly and leisurely manner. This misconception is still prevalent, but it is unnecessary to repeat the arguments that have already been put forward to show that if the transfer of power had been unduly delayed, there would have been no power to transfer; only chaos and anarchy.

In one respect at least my visit was worth while. Shortly after Jinnah announced that he proposed to be Governor-General of Pakistan, he said that he would like to have British Governors for all the Provinces. In particular, he was anxious to get Sir George Cunningham to take over the North-West Frontier Province. I told him that Sir George could not be expected to accept this invitation. He had already governed the Province for over eight years, and had now settled down in Scotland. I promised however to sound him at once. As I expected, the answer was in the negative, and the appointment was still vacant when I left for England. Scarcely had I reached London, when Cunningham came to see me. He said that perhaps he had allowed personal considerations to influence him unduly, and wanted to know the position in Pakistan. The picture that I painted was not a rosy one; whereupon, without further ado, he said, 'I'll go.' Within three weeks he was established in his old Government House at Peshawar, and from the moment he arrived, he ran the Province practically single-handed. Peace reigned throughout his territory, and when I paid him a visit, it was like entering an unruffled harbour after a long buffeting in stormy seas. George Cunningham, by his personality and the esteem and affection in which he was held by the Pathans, worked miracles. We all knew that he would.

I hoped to find on my return to Delhi that the movement of refugees had been completed, and that all was comparatively peaceful. But Erskine-Crum greeted me at the airfield in the early hours of the

28 October with news which was as disquieting as it was unexpected. On the 24 October a report had been received at Delhi that a large number of frontier tribesmen were moving on Kashmir. Thereupon Mr V. P. Menon had flown to Srinagar, and returned with the news that the Maharaja had signed a letter asking for accession to India, and had fled from the capital. Mountbatten, acting on the advice of his Government, had accepted the accession, but stipulated that a plebiscite to ascertain the will of the Kashmiris must be arranged as soon as possible. Thereupon, the Indian Government had flown a battalion to Srinagar to safeguard the lives of the British and Hindus living there. So far as was known, the Pakistan Government had sent none of their own troops to Kashmir, but had done nothing to prevent the raiders crossing their territory. Here was a pretty kettle of fish. I had feared for some time that Maharaja Hari Singh's vacillation and irresponsibility might lead to trouble, but I had never dreamed of anything as serious as this. At the worst, there would be war between India and Pakistan; at the best, their relations with each other would be poisoned until they could reach a friendly settlement of the problem. Tragic to relate, no such settlement is yet in sight.[1]

After a few hours' sleep I attended a meeting of the Indian Defence Committee, which had been summoned as a matter of urgency to discuss the imbroglio in Kashmir. Half way through, I left the room to take a telephone message from Auchinleck. He said that it had been touch and go, and that the danger of war was by no means past. Mr Jinnah, on hearing the news of the despatch of the Indian battalion to Srinagar, had flown into a rage and ordered General Gracey,[2] the acting C. in C. of the Pakistan Army, to send troops to Kashmir at once. Gracey had stalled on these orders and reported to Auchinleck just after midnight. He (Auchinleck) had flown to Lahore at dawn and called on Mr Jinnah, who fortunately happened to be staying at Government House at the time. He explained that any Pakistani troops entering Kashmir would be violating Indian territory and that the result was likely to be war with India. In any event, it would create a situation which would make it necessary for all British officers serving in the Pakistani and Indian forces to be withdrawn at once. Mr Jinnah had cancelled his orders for troop movements and

---

[1] Written in 1959.
[2] Acting for General Messervy, who was on leave.

had fallen in with Auchinleck's suggestion that he should invite Mountbatten and Nehru to come to Lahore as quickly as possible and discuss the Kashmir problem. I congratulated Auchinleck on having intervened in the nick of time, and made haste to extract Mountbatten and Nehru from the meeting and tell them the purport of Auchinleck's message. They agreed to fly to Lahore the next morning. But the other Indian Ministers were highly indignant at the idea of the Governor-General and Prime Minister going 'hat in hand' to Jinnah. Patel, who was particularly angry, said that it was reminiscent of Mr Chamberlain's visits to Germany to plead with Hitler. I thought it right to point out that President Roosevelt had, on two occasions, travelled half across the world to settle war business with Marshal Stalin, and had not lost face by so doing. Nehru stuck manfully to his promise: but unfortunately he had to go to bed with a high temperature that evening, and was unfit to travel. The chance of striking while the iron was hot was lost.

Subsequently there were several meetings of the leaders on both sides to discuss Kashmir, but only one need be mentioned. In November, Liaquat Ali Khan came to Delhi, and I was invited to take part in his talks with Nehru. I suggested that it would be better if they had it out alone, and sent for me later, if they thought I would be of any help. When they had been together for a full hour, they asked me to join them and proceeded to summarise the results of their talk. They seemed on the friendliest of terms, and Nehru jokingly observed that very little had been agreed. On the other hand, they both said that they were determined to settle the business once and for all, and would meet again after dinner. Meanwhile would I try my hand at drafting a basis of discussion? I co-opted V. P. Menon and Mahomed Ali, and we drafted and redrafted for a full three hours. In the end, we were rather proud of our handiwork, and I went so far as to write to my wife that evening that at long last I could see a light at the end of the tunnel. But my hopes were dashed the very next morning. Each side thought that our paper was too biased in favour of the other to merit discussion.

It had always been understood that I should be released within three or four months of Partition, and early in December I said my last farewells. There had been a saying that the best view of India was Bombay from the stern of a homeward bound P. and O. ship. But on that final departure, I could not bear to watch the shore fading out of view, and I went to my cabin to be alone with my memories. I thought of the two million British graves that dotted the land, and of the devoted service that many generations of my countrymen had given to it. 'There be of them, that have left a name behind them. . . . And some there be which have no memorial; who are perished as though they had never been. . . . But these were merciful men.' [1] Would these forefathers of ours think that all their work and sacrifice had been wasted, and their trust betrayed by those who came after them? Or would they regard the renunciation of power as a fitting ending to the story of British rule in India? Whatever might be the answers to those questions, no one could doubt that those faithful guardians of old would feel themselves richly rewarded, if India and Pakistan were to learn to live side by side in brotherly love, and become happy, prosperous and influential partners in the British family of nations.

[1] Ecclesiasticus XLIV: 8 et seq.

CHAPTER XXXIV

A Medley of Assignments

1947–1959

I ARRIVED home just before Christmas, but my hopes of resuming the retirement which had been so abruptly interrupted were short-lived. Before the year was out, the Prime Minister told me that the Government of India had referred the situation in Kashmir to the United Nations and asked if I would be a member of the British delegation under Mr Philip Noel-Baker, Secretary of State for Commonwealth Relations, which was leaving for New York almost at once. I jumped at the chance. If only this quarrel could be settled, India and Pakistan would become good friends instead of bitter enemies, and the unity of the subcontinent would be virtually restored.

The Indian and Pakistani delegations arrived at New York at almost the same time as we did, and my first meeting with them was discouraging. Ayyengar, the Head of the Indian Delegation, left me in no doubt that Delhi thought me pro-Pakistan in sentiment; while Zafrullah Khan, the Pakistani Foreign Minister, whom I had known fifteen years earlier, when he had been a member of the Viceroy's Council, said how pleased he was to meet an old friend but that Karachi strongly suspected me of being 'tarred with the Delhi brush.' Evidently my sphere of usefulness as a mediator was going to be very limited.

447

The proceedings at Lake Success opened with interminable speeches. There was no sign of any give and take by either Pakistan or India, and my fortnight in the United States looked like being wholly frustrating. But there was one redeeming feature — an invitation from General Marshall, now Secretary of State, to go to Washington and tell him about the transfer of power in India. He had a host of old friends to meet me at dinner and hear the story — Eisenhower, Spaatz, Collins, Wedemeyer, Stark, Averell Harriman, Jim Forrestal and Lew Douglas. It was a red letter evening.

A few weeks after my return to England, I was summoned to 10, Downing Street by the Prime Minister, and went in fear and trembling that I was going to be asked to undertake some sort of overseas appointment. Mr Attlee quickly dispelled my anxiety. He told me that it had been decided, with the concurrence of all political parties, to hold a Festival of Britain in 1951, in order to mark the centenary of the Great Exhibition in Hyde Park of 1851, and to display the British contribution to civilisation, past, present and future, in science, the arts, and industrial design. Unlike its predecessor, the Festival would not be confined to London but would be nationwide and all-embracing. A Council, composed of men and women eminent in various walks of public life and of representatives of all political parties, was in process of being set up in order to exercise a general supervision over the Festival arrangements. Would I undertake the chairmanship? Mr Herbert Morrison, who was present at the interview and was to be the Minister in charge of the Festival, went on to explain that the overall responsibility would rest with the Government, and that detailed plans and preparations would be in the hands of Mr Gerald Barry, the Director General, aided by 'The Festival Office,' which was being set up as a new Government Department. The Council of which I had been asked to be chairman would be honorary and advisory. It seemed a very unsuitable assignment for one who was a complete ignoramus about science and somewhat of a Philistine about the arts; but I was so relieved at not being asked to go abroad again, that I accepted at once.

The Council collected by Mr. Herbert Morrison was indeed highpowered. Party politics were represented by Miss Margaret Herbison, Mrs Jean Mann, the Rt Hon Lord Wilmot, the Rt Hon R. A. Butler,

the Rt Hon W. E. Eliot, the Rt Hon Lord Clydesmuir and Lady
Megan Lloyd George: the Church was represented by the Very Rev
A. C. Don, Dean of Westminster: Music by Sir Malcolm Sargent:
Science by Sir Robert Robinson: the Stage by John Gielgud and Noël
Coward: Letters by T. S. Eliot and Sir A. P. Herbert: the BBC by
the Director-General, Sir William Haley: the Arts by Sir Kenneth
Clark, the Earl of Crawford and Balcarres and Sir Ernest Pooley,
Chairman of the Arts Council: Scotland by the Rt Hon Thomas
Johnston: Wales by Sir Wynn Wheldon: Northern Ireland by the Rt
Hon Sir Roland Nugent; and there were many other eminent persons.

The Council held its first meeting on 31 May 1948, and was addressed by Princess Elizabeth in her capacity as President of the
Royal Society of Arts. After reminding us that the Great Exhibition
in Hyde Park had been planned under the inspiration of her great-
great-grandfather, the Prince Consort, Her Royal Highness expressed
the hope that the Festival of Britain, in emphasising our achievements
of the past, would stress no less sharply our responsibilities to the future. In that pioneering spirit the Festival was launched.

The first essential was to ensure that its character, scope and purpose were understood by the country as a whole, and the Lord Mayor
of London, Sir George Aylwen, nobly came to our assistance by in-
viting all Lord Mayors, Mayors and Chairmen of County and District Councils to meet him at the Guildhall on 8 June and allowing
Barry and me to address them. The burden of our story was that
the centre-piece of the Festival would be a combined exhibition
somewhere in London, which would be sponsored by the Government. There would also be two travelling exhibitions and a few
other projects similarly sponsored. But the Festival would depend for
its success on the spontaneous co-operation of civic authorities
throughout the British Isles. Clearly there could be no ordered pattern, but it was hoped that every town and village would, on their
own initiative, arrange activities appropriate to their individual cus-
toms, tastes and resources, and that, in addition, they would undertake some project or improvement of permanent value which would
serve as a reminder to future generations. We promised that the Festival Office would help them at all times and in every possible way,
except in the matter of finance.

That meeting in the Guildhall lit a flame which was to become a prairie fire. The Festival Office, the Scottish, Welsh and Northern Festival Committees, the civic authorities throughout the land, and a number of voluntary organisations went at their task with a will, and gradually the grand design took shape. The combined Exhibition was to be on the South Bank of the Thames between County Hall and Waterloo Bridge. London was also to have a Festival Pleasure Gardens in Battersea, an Exhibition of science in South Kensington and an Exhibition of architecture in Poplar. In Glasgow there was to be an Exhibition of industrial power; in Belfast a factories Exhibition. There were to be two Travelling Exhibitions, the one moving by sea in the aircraft carrier *Campania* to many of the principal ports, the other moving by land to some of our principal cities. There were to be twenty-two Arts Festivals organised by the Arts Council of Great Britain in various parts of the country. In addition, more than two thousand different places, ranging from large cities to tiny hamlets, had decided upon the forms that their celebrations would take. Some were to stage sporting displays or folk dances; some to hold Exhibitions of local crafts; some had decided to build a new village hall, or to add to an old one; some proposed to erect a bus-stop shelter, or seats on the village green; some were to provide a new recreation ground, or a memorial garden; some were to restore derelict buildings; some were to give their houses a new coat of paint.

As the opening day approached, there were the usual last-minute alarms and excursions, now a builders' strike: now a shortage of some essential construction material: now a spell of impossible weather. But all was ready in time, and on 3 May the King and Queen drove in State to St Paul's Cathedral. The congregation which included Queen Mary and many other members of the Royal Family, numbered over three thousand, and the Service was as beautiful as it was appropriate. Blake's 'Jerusalem' might have been written for the occasion. After the service was over, the King broadcast to his people from the West steps of the Cathedral. 'This Festival has been planned, like its great predecessor, as a visible sign of national achievement and confidence. Two world wars have brought us grievous loss of life and treasure; and though the nation has made a splendid effort towards recovery, new burdens have fallen upon it and dark clouds still overhang the whole world. Yet this is no time for despondency; for I see this Festival as a symbol of Britain's abiding courage and vitality.

. . . I declare the Festival of Britain open and wish it universal success.'

That same evening an inaugural concert was held in the Royal Festival Hall. The King and Queen were again present and, after the customary presentations, the Lord Mayor of London, Sir Denys Lowson, the Lady Mayoress, the Gerald Barrys, and my wife and I went as fast as we could to the lift allotted to us, in order to be in our boxes by the time that Their Majesties made their entry into the foyer. Our lift started according to plan, but when it came to a stop, the doors failed to open. We telephoned for help, but the switchboard either thought that we were playing a practical joke or were too intent on listening to the music to pay any attention. What had at first seemed rather comic began to look serious; and, when we had been incarcerated for forty minutes, the Lord Mayor, a burly man, took off a large shoe and hammered on the walls of the lift with sufficient violence to wake the dead. At last a rescue party arrived. The lift had stuck about six feet short of the next floor, and we had to be hauled up one by one. It was an undignified performance; and to add insult to injury, nobody had noticed that the boxes of the Lord Mayor of London, the Chairman of the Festival of Britain and the Director-General, had been empty throughout the whole of the first part of the programme.

The next morning, the King and Queen, accompanied by Queen Mary and all the members of the Royal Family in London, paid their first visit to the South Bank, and, in spite of the rain and cold, spent over two hours on the site. Among the many distinguished guests who received invitations for this opening day was Mr Churchill. He seemed fascinated by the escalator, and went up and down, and down and up half a dozen times before rejoining the VIP party. Perhaps he had never been on one before? At 2:30 P.M. the gates were opened to the general public, and in the next five months a total of eight and a half million people passed through the turnstiles.

During that summer my wife and I attended celebrations of various kinds all over the country: festivals of music at Canterbury, York and Swansea, a Regency Festival at Brighton: a Farm and Factory Exhibition on the outskirts of Belfast: a Festival of Ancient Traditions at Chipping Campden: an Industries Exhibition at Bristol: a Cotswold Craft Exhibition at Cheltenham. All the endearing and enduring things that had gone to make our history and fashion our way of life seemed to have sprung up anew — the folk-songs and the dances, the sports and the pageants and the carnivals, the local handicrafts, the dramas and the concerts, the noble church services, the glow of gardens. Everywhere glimpses and echoes of long ago. We felt in the presence of that unity which had been our most precious possession in the days of war, and were convinced that the British people were determined to take up their lives and move forward again.

On 30 September the Festival came to an end. The King's illness had cast a shadow over its closing days, and the final ceremonies were simple. In the morning there was a religious service organised by the Advisory Council of Christian Churches in the Royal Festival Hall, at which it fell to me to read the Lesson. In the evening the crowds at the Festival site were so dense that movement was scarcely possible. After a splendid address by the Archbishop of Canterbury, the massed bands of the Brigade of Guards beat 'Retreat' and 'Tattoo.' The lights of the Exhibition were dimmed and the Festival flag was hauled down for the last time. The vast company sang 'Abide with Me' with the greatest reverence, and the National Anthem with the greatest devotion. It was all over.

Throughout the Festival year, the Labour Party had held office with an infinitesimal majority in the House of Commons, and although they had managed to keep their heads above the water, the situation was thoroughly unsatisfactory. Early in October, the King granted Mr Attlee's request for a dissolution, and polling for the General Election took place on 25 October. By the next afternoon it was clear that the Conservatives would have a majority of sixteen or seventeen. Mr Attlee resigned, and Mr Churchill once again received the King's mandate to form a Government. I went to bed very early that night and was fast asleep when the telephone bell rang — the same bell which had awakened me to hear of the invasion of Norway, the asault on the Low Countries, the death of President Roosevelt, and the signature of the German surrender at Rheims. I was told that Mr Churchill wanted to speak to me. There were many people sitting by their telephones that night, hoping, and perhaps praying, that the new Prime Minister might have something to offer them, but these were problems which were no concern of mine. The conversation was brief. 'Is that you, Pug?' 'Yes, Prime Minister. It's grand to be able to call you Prime Minister again.' 'I want to see you at once. You aren't in bed, are you?' 'I've been asleep for over an hour.' 'Well, I only want to see you for five minutes.'

I put my head under a cold tap, dressed in record time, and was at 28, Hyde Park Gate, within a quarter of an hour of being wakened. Mr Churchill was alone in his drawing-room, and told me, without any preliminaries, that he wanted me to be Secretary of State for Commonwealth Relations. I thought that the cold tap had failed to do its work and that I was still dreaming; but Mr Churchill brushed aside my doubts and hustled me into the dining-room, where I found Mr Eden, Lord Salisbury, Sir Norman Brook, and a bevy of secretaries working away on a variety of drafts. The years rolled back. It was like old times. Officials do not usually make good Cabinet Ministers, and there was no reason why I should be an exception to the rule. But I was overjoyed at the prospect of serving under Churchill again.

On the next afternoon I received the Seals of Office from the hand of the King and carried them off in triumph to the Commonwealth Relations Office. My reception was markedly different from that which had been accorded me when, in the winter of 1916, I had entered this same building — which then housed the Colonial Office — in order to plead to be allowed to spend my leave in France. On this occasion the red carpet was out, but I was still uncertain whether I was standing on my head or my heels.

The work of my new post proved to be heavier, and the hours longer, than I had anticipated. I had to make myself familiar with the organisation of the office: I had to study a multitude of Commonwealth problems that were entirely new to me: I had to attend many debates in the House of Lords: and I had to make speeches at a large number of official functions. In addition I found myself more closely involved in defence matters than is usual for a Secretary of State for Commonwealth Relations. Field Marshal Lord Alexander, the Minister of Defence designate, was still in Canada completing his term of office as Governor-General, and the Prime Minister, who had assumed charge of the Defence Ministry pending his return, frequently summoned me 'after hours' for consultation. It was therefore necessary to bring myself abreast of all that had happened in the field of Defence since I had left Whitehall.

I found that the situation *vis-à-vis* Russia had developed very much on the lines foretold by Churchill in his 'iron curtain telegram.' Immediately the war had ended, the American and British forces began to melt away, and within twelve months there were less than 400,000 Americans and less than half a million British on the Continent of Europe. The Soviet, on the other hand, continued to maintain vast armies on a war footing, and to keep their armament industries working at full blast. As early as March 1946 Mr Churchill had sounded the alarm in a speech at Fulton, Missouri. 'If the Western Democracies stand together . . . no one is likely to molest them. If however they become divided or falter in their duty . . . catastrophe may well overcome us all.' But the Democracies were not yet ready for so far-reaching a step as a defensive alliance within the framework of the United Nations, and continued to persevere in their efforts to reach an accommodation with their late allies. It was all to no purpose. Conference after conference broke down in the face of Soviet intransigence. The work of the Security Council was paralysed by their abuse of the power of veto. By mid-summer 1947 the war-ravaged countries of Western Europe were on the verge of bankruptcy. At that critical moment America came to the rescue. On 5 June 1947, General Marshall, now Secretary of State, announced that the United States were prepared to give economic assistance on a considerable scale to all European nations who desired it. Stalin refused to avail himself of an offer which he described an 'an instrument of American imperialism' and ordered the Soviet satellites to do likewise. But to the democracies of Western Europe, the Marshall Plan brought hope, confidence, and a sense of comradeship.

So far so good. But the danger was not only economic. Soviet Russia had the best part of four and a half million men on a war footing, and the threat of overwhelming military strength, combined with political cunning, had enabled them to get control of one country after another without having recourse to arms. By the end of 1947, Bulgaria, Roumania, Hungary, Eastern Germany and Poland were all behind the iron curtain; and in February 1948 a Communist *coup d'état* in Prague resulted in the enslavement of Czechoslovakia. The mortal danger to the Western democracies was now only too obvious. Their armed forces were weak in numbers, ill-equipped and uncoordinated, and there was nothing, except perhaps America's possession of the atom bomb, to prevent the Soviet armies from advancing to the waters of the Atlantic and the North Sea. In March 1948, Belgium, France, Luxembourg, the Netherlands and the United Kingdom pledged themselves by the Treaty of Brussels to set up a joint defence system, and agreed that if one of the parties to the Treaty were attacked, the others would go to the rescue with all the aid in their power. Simultaneously President Truman told the American Congress that he was sure that 'the determination of the free countries of Europe to protect themselves will be matched by an equal determination on our part to help them.' Here at last was a beginning, but it was soon apparent that the combined resources of the Brussels Treaty Powers alone could never be a match for the Soviet, however much aid they received from across the Atlantic, and that if America were to stand aloof until after the aggressor had marched, there would be very little left to liberate. The United States themselves were under no illusions. They recognised that unless they were full members of the Alliance, the Soviet would have matters their own way. On the other hand, they were categorically debarred by their Constitution from entering into any foreign alliance in time of peace. The difficulties that then seemed insuperable were shortly to be overcome by the now famous Vandenberg Resolution which recommended 'the association of the United States, by constitutional process, with such regional and other collective arrangements as are based on continuous self-help and mutual aid, and as affect its national security.' The Resolution passed through the United States Senate on 11 June 1948. America had at long last abandoned her traditional policy of isolationism from the affairs of Europe, and the way was now open for the Brussels Treaty system to be superseded by a far larger grouping of like-minded peoples. The climax to much consultation came on 4 April 1949. On that date the North Atlantic Treaty was signed by no less than twelve sovereign States: Belgium, Canada, Denmark, France, Iceland, Italy, Luxembourg, the Netherlands, Norway, Portugal, the United Kingdom and the United States.

Perhaps the most important feature of the Treaty was the provision that an armed attack against one or more of the parties should be considered an attack against them all. Thus no future aggressor could hope to devour his victims one by one as Hitler had done. But a promise to stand together in the event of attack would be no deterrent to aggression unless it were backed by armed strength, and it was therefore provided that the parties should pledge themselves to maintain and develop their individual and *collective* capacity to resist attack.

Many Treaties are signed with pomp and ceremony and then filed away in the archives until they are time-expired or broken. But the North Atlantic Treaty was a very different sort of instrument. The parties had pledged themselves to immediate and continuous action in the military, political, economic and social fields, and it was therefore essential that some sort of collective organisation should be set up as quickly as possible. Beyond the fact that there must be a Supreme Council, and that this should normally consist of the Foreign Ministers of all the member countries, all else was uncertain; and it was wisely recognised that the structure of the North Atlantic Treaty Organisation — or NATO as it soon became — would have to be devised by a process of trial and error. As a first step a number of Committees or working groups were set up to deal with the manifold problems that called for consideration, and the Foreign and Defence Ministers of the member countries met at frequent intervals to discuss their reports and give directions for future action.

In December 1950 there was an all important step forward. It was decided at a meeting of the North Atlantic Council in Brussels that an integrated force, consisting of contingents from all the member countries, should be built up in Europe and placed under a single Commander. The willingness of proud sovereign States to entrust their precious armed forces to the command of a foreigner in time of peace was a measure of their readiness to subordinate their national interests to the common weal. Fortunately for the Alliance, General Eisenhower, with his unique prestige, qualifications, and experience was available to undertake the appointment in question, and he assumed operational control of the allied forces in Europe in April 1951. I spent a week-end with him in Paris shortly after his arrival, and was impressed by the team spirit which already animated the members of his international staff. He also showed me round the 'flats' which were being built for the officers and other ranks working at his Headquarters. It was characteristic of the man that one of his first thoughts was to do all that he could to ensure that the soldiers of the more poorly paid armies should be able to enjoy the same living conditions as those whose countries grant them much larger salaries. Little did I imagine on that first visit to SHAPE that I too would be a worker in the same vineyard.

But while the military arrangements were now getting on to the right lines, there seemed to be a lack of central direction in the political, economic and production fields, and I was glad to be told a few weeks after taking office that proposals for streamlining the existing agencies would be considered by the North Atlantic Council at the meeting which was to be held in Lisbon towards the end of February. I was less glad to hear that the Prime Minister wished me to go to the meeting as Acting Minister of Defence. It is very much easier to tell others how to hold a difficult baby than to hold it oneself. But before the time came for me to leave for Lisbon, the whole nation was to be plunged in gloom.

On the departure of Princess Elizabeth and the Duke of Edinburgh to East Africa, Australia and New Zealand on the morning of 31 January, I was one of the ministers in attendance at London airport. The King and Queen were there to bid them farewell; and, although it was a bitterly cold and windy morning, His Majesty walked out to inspect the aeroplane and then climbed to the roof of the Royal waiting-room to wave good-bye. On his return he suggested to his Prime Minister that in view of the intense cold, a little whisky might be permissible. Mr Churchill said that he had already taken precautions. 'Already?' asked the King. 'Yes, sir,' the Prime Minister replied. 'When I was younger I made it a rule never to take strong drink before lunch. It is now my rule never to do so before breakfast.'

Five days later I was told on arrival at the office that the Cabinet Meeting that morning had been cancelled, and that no reason had been given. A few minutes later my secretary came in and told me, almost in a whisper, that the King was dead. It was a terrible shock. His Majesty had been in such good spirits a few days earlier that one had dared to hope that his long spell of illness was over and that his fortitude had enabled him to recover his health. The streets of London were strangely silent all that day. The man for whom they mourned had been not only their King, but their trusted and much loved friend. For those who had been privileged to serve him at close quarters during the war, the loss was particularly grievous.

My departure for Lisbon coincided with the wedding of my youngest daughter Mary, and I had to drive straight from the Grosvenor Chapel to London airport, discarding my wedding garments en route. Mr Eden was already on the spot; but it was several hours before our chartered plane could be induced to start, and we did not reach Lisbon until the early hours of 20 February. Fortunately the only official engagement that day was a largely-attended ceremony at which Greece and Turkey formally acceded to the North Atlantic Alliance. It was ironical that their accession was particularly warmly welcomed by those who had castigated Churchill for having saved Greece from the clutches of the Communists in 1944. Once again he was entitled to say: 'I told you so.' But that was not his custom.

On the following morning I had my first experience of a meeting of the North Atlantic Council. It was an eye opener. The communiqué issued at the end of the Conference announced, with apparent satisfaction, that thirty-five ministers of fourteen countries had taken part in the discussions, but omitted to mention that about ten times that number of advisers had been in attendance, and that the vast hall had generally been so congested that there was not even standing room. In my ignorance of the technique of diplomacy, I thought it unlikely that any useful results would be achieved in a milling mob of this kind; but I was soon to learn that many knotty problems had already been settled by informal exchanges behind the scenes, and that all that the Council had to do was to place on record the views of the member Governments as expressed by their Foreign Ministers, and to give their formal approval to a variety of agreements which had already been reached.

As it turned out, the decisions taken at Lisbon were to prove a landmark in the history of the Alliance; but for the purposes of my narrative it will suffice to mention the special measures which were taken to centralise and simplify the Organisation. Perhaps the most important of these was the decision that in future the North Atlantic Council should have a permanent Headquarters in Paris, and be able to function in permanent session. Since Foreign Ministers themselves would obviously have to spend most of their time in their own capitals, it was agreed that each Government should appoint a Permanent Representative to represent it at all meetings of the Council at which a Minister could not be present. The Permanent Representatives, who could be of Ministerial rank or very senior officials, were to have the status of Ambassador, and to have the assistance of such national experts as were deemed necessary. Another important decision which, all unknown to me at the time, was to exercise a profound effect on my own future, was that there should be a Secretary-General who would be responsible for organising the work of the Council, and directing the work of the International staff, which was to be drawn from all the member countries. It was further agreed that the Council itself should assume the functions, hitherto performed by civilian agencies, such as the Council of Deputies, the Defence Production Board, and the Financial and Economic Board. There can be no doubt that all this streamlining and simplification were a vast improvement. Henceforward the Council, assisted by their own national delegations, and an international staff of experts, would be in a position to give a firm direction to, and exercise constant supervision over, all the multifarious activities of the Alliance. In addition they would be able to be called together at a moment's notice in the event of emergency.

I learned afterwards that the British element connected with NATO had been disappointed that Paris had been preferred to London as a site for NATO Headquarters. This seemed odd. It was difficult to understand what benefit an already over-crowded, under-housed London would derive from an influx of thirteen new ambassadorial establishments, and a vast international staff all demanding full diplomatic privileges. It was even more surprising to learn that there was a good deal of satisfaction in British circles at the decision that the first Secretary-General should be British. It seemed to me that this arrangement was likely to prove a disadvantage, because any Briton appointed to the post would be so anxious not to appear to favour his own countrymen that he would never give them the benefit of the doubt. When the time came, my anticipation proved correct.

But while these interesting organisational problems were being discussed by the Council, I myself and the other Ministers of Defence concerned were banished to a smaller room, to settle a problem of 'Common Infrastructure.' Here was one of those strange expressions which every new organisation seems to find it necessary to coin. The word infrastructure comes from France, where it has long been used to denote all the work that is necessary before a railway track can be laid, such as embankments, bridges and tunnels; and it was adopted by NATO in its early days as a generic term to define all the fixed installations which are necessary for the operation of modern armed forces — airfields, fuel supply dumps and pipe lines, navigational aid stations, radar warning, and so forth. To take the definition a stage further, such installations as were required for the use of international NATO forces were called 'Common Infrastructure,' and paid for collectively by member countries. The particular problem remitted to Defence Ministers at Lisbon was to find the sum of £150 million for the next stage of the Common Infrastructure programme. The American Secretary of Defence, Mr Robert A. Lovett, said that his country was prepared to pay the lion's share provided that the other members were willing to contribute to the best of their ability. Needless to say, there was scarcely a country whose estimate of what it could afford bore any relation to the sum which the other partners thought reasonable: and it was found that to induce a country to increase its contribution was as difficult as getting blood out of a stone. Eventually, however, after a wrangle that extended over sixteen hours in all, the target was reached, and we dispersed as fast as we could lest anyone should have second thoughts. I had felt like a fish out of water, and General Gruenther reminded me in later years that my last words to him at Lisbon were: 'This is the first that I have seen of NATO, and thank heaven it's the last.'

As I flew back to England after yet another new experience, I reflected on all the unexpected things that had happened to me since my retirement from the public service. First there had been the mission to India as Chief of Staff to the last Viceroy: secondly there had been a period of comparative leisure as Chairman of the Council of the Festival of Britain in 1951: and thirdly there had been the bombshell of my appointment as Secretary of State for Commonwealth Relations. I was rather tired of being a rolling stone, and comforted myself with the thought that, when my present job came to an end, it was absolutely certain that I would not be required to roll any more. But certainties do not always come off in real life any more than they do on the race course. In less than a fortnight after my return from Lisbon, Eden, who was ill in bed, asked me to go and see him as a matter of great urgency, and told me point-blank that it was the wish of all the NATO countries that I should be the first Secretary-General. My reaction was an immediate and emphatic negative, and I kept on saying 'No' as loudly as was permissible in a sick-room. Seeing that I was obdurate, he telephoned to the Prime Minister and asked him to join us. I felt rather like a defiant little boy who has been told that the headmaster was coming to deal with him, but I was too indignant to be apprehensive. Had I been in my senses, I would have known that I would gladly do anything in the world which my revered Chief asked or even advised. Churchill joined us almost at once and proceeded to pull out all the stops. He said that he was sure that I would accept the appointment when I understood the position. NATO provided the best, if not the only, hope of peace in our time, but it must be more effectively organised and managed. The immediate appointment of a first-class Secretary-General was long overdue. The member Governments had unanimously agreed that I had the experience and qualifications which were required for the job and had asked him (Churchill) to persuade me to accept it. I had always 'played up' in the past, and he would be disappointed if I were to shrink from this challenge. It need not involve a long absence: two years would be ample to get the organisation on the right lines and give it a good start. I wriggled as hard as I could. I protested that too much of my life had been spent out of England and that it was unfair to expect me to spend the evening of my days abroad. I had no experience of diplomacy and was too tired to provide the initiative and original thought which were called for. Why not give this 'plum' to someone who not only was fitted for it but also wanted it very much, instead of pressing it on a man who was neither suitable nor willing? If the Prime Minister now thought it had been a mistake to include me in his Cabinet, why not discard me altogether instead of transplanting me? If it were true that I had hitherto always 'played up,' there was all the less excuse for making further demands on my sense of duty. My arguments were demolished one by one, and there was nothing for it but to surrender. Was the Prime Minister prepared, I asked, to state categorically that it was my duty to accept? 'It is your duty to accept, Pug,' was the immediate reply. That settled it.

Things now moved very fast. My appointment as Secretary-General of NATO and Vice-Chairman of the North Atlantic Council was made public on 12 March 1952. On the 24th I surrendered to the Queen the Seals of Office which I had received from the hands of His Majesty, her father, less than six months earlier. A week later I made my last speech for several years in the House of Lords, on the case of Seretse Khama. On 4 April there was an inaugural ceremony at NATO's temporary headquarters in Belgrave Square, at which I formally took over my new appointment. On 14 April I left for Paris. I thought that my tour of duty would be two years at most, but it was over five years before I laid down my charge. To tell the story of those years in full would overload these memoirs: to tell them in part would be misleading. In these circumstances, I cannot do better than quote from a speech which I made at the last Ministerial Conference which I attended as Secretary-General. It was held at Bonn in May 1959. 'As I look back upon the five years during which I have had the honour of serving the countries which are bound together by the North Atlantic Alliance, I am conscious that NATO may have left undone much that it ought to have done. Nevertheless it has outstanding achievements to its credit. In the first place, the primary purpose of the North Atlantic Treaty has been fulfilled. Peace in Europe has been preserved. Soviet expansion westward has been halted. Not a square inch of territory in Europe has fallen under Communist domination since the Treaty was signed. Secondly, in the knowledge that the foreign policies of the partners must be in harmony if the Alliance is to prosper, there has been an ever-increasing measure of political co-operation between all the NATO Governments. This has been largely due to their foresight in establishing the Permanent Council in Paris as a forum for continuous consultation. Over one hundred private meetings of this council have been devoted to political affairs in the last five years. It would be idle to pretend that there have not been cases of failure to consult, but it may be hoped that these will be more and more rare as time goes on. Thirdly, a defensive shield has been built up which, though not yet as strong as might be wished, is an essential feature of the deterrent to aggression. Who would have believed that sovereign States would entrust their precious armed forces to the command of nationals other than their own in time of peace? But this is what has come to pass. The fact that all these different national components — land, sea and air — are trained together in time of peace, and would, in the event of war, operate under unified command in accordance with unified plans, adds immeasurably to the strength of the deterrent. Finally, a remarkable degree of unity has been built up between the partners of the Treaty at all levels, and in all spheres. For myself, I believe that this unity is our most precious and powerful asset.

'It must surely be the best way of preserving the peace for any aggressor to understand two things beyond any shadow of doubt. The first is that the North Atlantic Alliance is purely defensive, and that there is no possible question of their attacking anyone. And the second is that in the event of aggression against one of the partners, all the rest would spring to arms in defence of their territory, their freedom and their way of life, and that they would all fight in loyal comradeship to the last ounce of their strength.

'Let us, therefore, go on as we have begun. Let us more and more acquire the habit of looking at problems from the international rather than the strictly national point of view. And, if at times we find the burden heavy, let us remember that the North Atlantic Alliance is not only an obligation which sovereign States have undertaken of their own free will, but an insurance against the unspeakable horrors of a war which would destroy civilisation.

'I have always been convinced that the North Atlantic Alliance is the best, if not the only, hope of peace. After five years at the centre of NATO affairs, I am more than ever convinced that this is the truth. But there is no room for wishful thinking. There is no easy path that will lead us to our goal. We must be vigilant and resolute. We must have hope in each other's future, faith in each other's purpose, and tolerance towards each other's shortcomings. Above everything else, we must be united. And then all will be well.'

Towards the end, I found myself longing to get home. But when the time came, my wife and I were utterly miserable. The Council had been like a large family, and the international staff had seemed like our children. It had been hard enough to say good-bye to the Foreign Secretaries and their advisers at the Bonn Conference the previous month. But when it came to leaving Paris, we could hide our feelings no longer. As I passed slowly down the ranks of the French Guard of Honour at the airport, I felt that the *poilus* must have been astonished to see a British General with tears pouring down his face. Nevertheless, it was a wonderful feeling to arrive in England again, this time for good, and I had no regrets as I inspected the last Guard of Honour that would ever be mounted for me. That night we dined with Sir Winston and Lady Churchill, and his first words were: 'Have you forgiven me for sending you to NATO?' I could only reply: 'Sir, you were right, as always.'

INDEX

INDEX

[In order to avoid difficulty and delay in reference induced by several pages of sub-headings under the main heading 'Ismay, Lord', the author's activities have all been indexed under the persons, places, institutions, etc., to which they relate, his name, wherever appropriate, being indicated by *I*.]

467